THE IRWIN SERIES IN ECONOMICS

CONSULTING EDITOR

LLOYD G. REYNOLDS
YALE UNIVERSITY

BOOKS IN THE ERWIN SERIES IN ECONOMICS

INTERNATIONAL TRADE
Theory and Economic Policy

INTERNATIONAL TRADE

Theory and Economic Policy

by JAROSLAV VANEK

Associate Professor of Economics
Cornell University

1962

RICHARD D. IRWIN, INC.

HOMEWOOD, ILLINOIS

To My Parents

PREFACE

This study is an extended version of a set of lecture notes prepared for two courses given at Harvard University, one in theory, the other in policy of international trade. I received excellent cooperation from the students in the class, both in criticizing the manuscript as a whole and in pointing out—or letting me feel—that some passages were either too difficult or not sufficiently clear. A number of the chapters would not have been written were it not for my promise to the class to do so. For all this I express my sincere thanks to the Harvard graduate and undergraduate students who were in the course. My special thanks are extended to Messrs. John Brandl and Lawrence Officer, both of the Department of Economics, who took an active part in editing, checking on the mathematics, and preparing the bibliography. Mrs. Seiler of the Littauer Statistics Laboratory indefatigably typed the drafts and prepared them for class distribution.

With Professor Gottfried Haberler I discussed many of the arguments of the study over a cup of coffee, before ever they were put on paper. From this, and also from his later readings of the different chapters, I have received invaluable counsel.

If I have chosen to present the balance of payments as a consolidated statement of sectoral income statements and balance sheets, and used this approach in showing the relation between the national and foreign trade accounts, it is not so much my own idea as that of my friend Stephen Valavanis, now departed. Some years ago, he and I used this approach in presenting the national income accounts and definitions in an elementary course in economics.

Professor Murray Kemp, visiting at the Massachusetts Institute of Technology, often extended to me his helping hand and mind. Professors Lloyd Reynolds and Bela Balassa, both of Yale University, also provided me with useful suggestions and criticisms. I gladly acknowledge their contribution.

Finally, I would like to express my sincere thanks to all those who have contributed so much to my work without ever having seen the manuscript. The teaching staff of the Department of Economics at MIT, as well as my fellow students there, ought to be mentioned; but especially Professors Charles Kindleberger and Paul Samuelson. Also, I cannot but express my gratitude to Professor James Meade, without reference to whom hardly any study in international economics can nowadays be written.

JAROSLAV VANEK

Geneva, Switzerland
October, 1961

TABLE OF CONTENTS

PART I

Definition and Some Fundamental Notions. Anatomy of Balance-of-Payments Accounts. Problems of Valuation. Balance-of-Payments Data Recording and Performance of Transactions. The Significance of Equilibria and Disequilibria of the Balance of Payments. The Balance of Indebtedness.

Definitions in National-Income Accounting. Further Definitions and Simplification of Accounts. Reconciliation of National-Income and Foreign-Trade Accounts of Different Countries.

PART II

Some Definitions. The Forward Market. Stability of the Foreign-Exchange Market and the Balance of Payments: Fixed, Adjustable, and Freely Fluctuating Exchange Rates. Goods Markets and the Foreign-Exchange Market. Stability in the Foreign-Exchange Market Defined by the Export and Import Elasticities. The Balance of Autonomous Payments on Current Account and the Rate of Exchange. The Exchange Rate, the Terms of Trade, and the Balance-of-Payments Adjustment. Autonomous Transfer and the Foreign-Exchange Market. The Theory of Purchasing-Power Parity.

The Classical Model. The Keynesian Model.

Income Effects and Multiplier Effects. The Assumptions of the Multiplier Analysis. The Foreign-Trade Multiplier. The Balance of Payments and the Foreign-Trade Multiplier. Transfer under Keynesian Assumptions. Transfer under Classical Assumptions. The Rate of Interest, National Income, and the Trade Balance.

PART I

Chapter 1 INTRODUCTION

International economics, like any other scientific discipline, advances through a process of original contributions on the frontier of its various branches, coupled with a subsequent effort of consolidation. Notions in the field of international trade that appear commonplace today were considered advanced theory, say, twenty years ago and had resulted from original research, still another twenty years before that time. The efficiency of the learning process on the part of those who have a special interest in international economics is greatly enhanced if the "common knowledge" of any particular period is presented in a systematic fashion. The faster the "common knowledge" of a particular field is acquired, the sooner is the student able to come to his own original work, or the sooner is he able to apply it to concrete problems of policy or prediction. These considerations were the fundamental motivation of the present study. Original contributions or alternative approaches to known problems are not absent; however, the principal task of this text is to consolidate a field where the frontier has moved too far ahead with respect to the base camp.

Any such attempt can be rewarded with only partial success, and the present study is no exception in this respect. It will always be the mind and the opinion of the writer that will act as a filter, assigning weights of importance in selecting and giving emphasis to the different topics. A number of criteria, or auxiliary constraints, are used in selecting the material and in choosing the tools of analysis. I have attempted to conform with the general consensus of economists in the field. However, I am aware that many might not agree or might prefer to choose alternative avenues of approach.

Although the study is one primarily in the theory of international trade, a good deal of consideration has been given to questions

3

of economic policy. Actually, the method of analysis is shaped entirely in such a way as to fit the treatment of problems of policy. From the point of view of theory proper, it would have been preferable to state the entire argument in terms of a general equilibrium model, using unlimited numbers of parameters, structural relations, and unknowns. For practical considerations, however, such a theory would be hardly manageable and virtually nonoperational. Thus, following the approach of the large majority of international economists, I have sought to present each argument in as simple a way as possible, consistent with the nature of each particular problem.

It is true that such simplified representations often do not do justice to the complexities of reality and may lead to inaccurate results or omit important aspects of a problem. However, starting from the simplest point, it is frequently possible to rework a given analysis into one of greater generality. Also—and this may be even more important—the law of large numbers or the law of central tendency usually extends its helping hand when we treat large aggregates as single variables. We no longer have a perfect certainty about the validity of results obtained, but we can be sure that in ninety-nine cases out of a hundred our predictions are more or less correct.

Closely related to the problem of aggregation and simplification of economic models is the problem of the practical applicability of economic theory. It is fair to say that the gap between economic theory, on the one hand, and practical policy making and empirical analysis, on the other, has been wide and certainly has not been narrowed in recent years. Many of those belonging to the practical world still consider economic theory as something utterly irrelevant, and those dealing with theory often care very little about the real world. Also, it may well be true that it would take twice a man's resources both to master the theoretical side of his discipline and at the same time to acquire the correct sense for the very difficult art of economic policy. The argument, explicit or implied, usually is that the oversimplifications of theory make it unsuited to application, and hence the policy makers have to rely entirely on their qualitative judgment. In reality, it is most frequently the lack of full understanding of theory that prevents its fruitful application.

As an antithesis it ought always to be kept in mind that theory in itself cannot yield all the solutions that may be desired. It is only one important step in the whole of economics. Correct observation and data collection, formulation of hypotheses, the choice of assumptions, and testing are equally important tasks.

In many respects the abstract theory presented in the later chapters of our study is a good deal broader than the concrete analysis and applications that have been derived from it. One reason for this fact is quite practical. It would have taken considerably more space to exploit and interpret fully all the theoretical results obtained. Moreover, such analysis might have been quite unwarranted, in view of the fact that it would not have had bearing on reality. On the other hand, the many open ends of our theoretical analysis may provide the reader with a fruitful ground for further applications to specific problems of his own or may simply be used for the purpose of exercise or, finally, may lead to a constructive critique of our own work.

The study is organized in four distinct parts, in conformity with the traditional organization of the field of international economics. In the remaining two chapters of Part I, we complete the conceptual and methodological groundwork begun in this chapter. The principal purpose of Chapters 2 and 3 is to derive a set of foreign-trade accounts from different sectoral accounts of an economy and to relate such a foreign-trade account to the customary national-income accounts. In the process of this exposition, we also give a number of important definitions pertaining to balance-of-payments accounting and discuss problems of timing, valuation, and data collection. Finally, the foreign-trade and national-income components are presented and made consistent in a simplified fashion with regard to the later theoretical analysis based thereon.

In Part II we present what is often called the "monetary theory" of international trade or, more descriptively, the theory of the balance-of-payments adjustment mechanism. Partially following the historical development of the subject, partially led by considerations of efficiency of exposition, we present the material, starting with the simplest analysis of the foreign-exchange market and going as far as the combination of price, income, and interest-rate effects. We also show some simple applications of dynamic analysis to problems of balance-of-payments adjustment and discuss in greater detail the function and impact of speculation on the foreign-exchange market.

Part III has for its principal theme the pure, nonmonetary, or barter theory of international trade, in virtually all instances based on the classical assumptions of full employment and price and wage flexibility. As we have already pointed out, this theory is mostly presented in a simplified general equilibrium fashion. For completeness, however, we also state the usual multivariable case of general equilibrium applied to international trade and, wherever possible, seek an extension of the simple situations to theorems of greater generality.

Finally, Part IV is devoted to the theory of foreign-trade policy. While Chapter 16 examines in an abstract fashion the impact of tariffs and more generally of direct trade policy on the important variables of international general equilibrium, Chapter 17 deals with problems of over-all economic policies aimed at the attainment óf external and internal balance and price stability. The last chapter of the study is concerned with the very timely subject of customs unions and economic integration. In actuality, its purpose is twofold: not only does it deal with the specific problem of integration, but also it extends the usual foreign-trade analysis to a case where more than two trading partners engage in international exchange.

The Appendix is devoted to a simple exposition and explanation of the essential tools of analysis employed in the study. It may be completely disregarded by those acquainted with the elements of mathematical and geometrical analysis in economics. However, it may be most useful to those who do not have such a background, not only because it makes easily accessible all that is shown or proved in this book but also because it shows in a most elementary fashion a set of analytical tools having general applicability to all fields of economics.

Chapter 2

THE BALANCE OF PAYMENTS

2.1 Definition and Some Fundamental Notions

The commercial and financial transactions of any person, firm, group of people, country, or region with any other such unit over a defined period of time may be recorded in a pair of flow accounts: one account showing the flow of all in-payments or *credits*, the other showing the flow of all out-payments or *debits*. The *balance of payments* is such an account summarizing the transactions of a country with the rest of the world. Partial balances of payments may be constructed concerning transactions of a country with one or a group of countries or any other trading or financial unit, such as international monetary institutions.

The essential and almost tautologic characteristic of a balance-of-payments account is that it must always be in balance; i.e., total credits must equal total debits. In the case of pure bilateral trade, all partial balances with different countries also must balance. If trade is multilateral, however, only the over-all account must be in balance; there is no necessity that the regional subtotals in the credit account must equal the corresponding subtotals in the debit account.

Similarly, if a detailed listing of entries on the credit and debit sides of the balance of payments is shown corresponding to the different types of transactions (such as current and capital flows), no equality between any two such entries is necessary. As we are going to see later in this chapter, it is this type of *partial* imbalance that allows us to speak about states of *equilibria* or *disequilibria* of the balance of payments.

It is customary, but by no means necessary, to break down the credit and debit sides of the balance of payments into separate entries showing whether flows of funds were created by current or capital transactions, whether the transactions involved the private

7

or public sector, and whether capital flows were of a long- or short-run nature; finally, for current transactions a distinction is made between *visible* and *invisible* trade (i.e., between trade in *goods* and trade in *services*). Moreover, net movements of monetary gold are customarily entered separately, as are private and public donations (pure transfers) and loans and currency transactions with international monetary institutions. Thus, in simplest form, a balance of payments may be summarized as follows:

	Credits		Debits
Current account........................"	$\geqq \atop \leqq$		"
Goods..........................."	"	"	"
Services........................"	"	"	"
Transfers (donations)..................."	"	"	"
Capital account......................."	"	"	"
Private........................."	"	"	"
Long term....................."	"	"	"
Short term....................."	"	"	"
Public (official)..................."	"	"	"
Long term....................."	"	"	"
Short term....................."	"	"	"
International institutions................."	"	"	"
Monetary gold......................."	"	"	"
Total........................"	=		"

Greater detail and further discussion of the different entries of the balance-of-payments account will emerge from later sections of this chapter.

At this point we should reconsider the fundamental requirement of equality between total credits (or in-payments) and total debits (or out-payments). We may think of a simple case wherein two transacting units engage only in visible trade and total purchases of goods are not equal to total sales of goods, so that the trade and current accounts show a difference of, say, $100. Such a discrepancy, however, can *never* occur between total credits and debits. Either it was paid in monetary gold, extended as a credit to one of the traders, or given as a donation; in this way the totals of the two sides of the account are equated.

2.2 Anatomy of Balance-of-Payments Accounts

2.2.1 *Note on Elementary Accounting Concepts and Operations.* As with the balance-of-payments accounts, we define an *income state-*

ment of a commercial unit as a listing of all current credits or debits from and to all other accounts resulting from its current commercial or financial operations during a given period of time. The other accounts with which these transactions are performed may be the income statement (*IS*) of any other trader, the balance sheet (*BS*) of another trader, or the balance sheet of the same commercial unit.

The *balance sheet* is a complete listing of assets and liabilities of a commercial unit, including its ownership (i.e., liability to itself, or net worth) as of a given date. Flows from an income statement to a balance sheet will be recorded as a change in the balance sheet between the beginning and ending dates of the income statement. Thus, as an example, we may consider the income statement of a hypothetical corporation for a given year and the corresponding change in the balance sheet (ΔBS) :

IS		ΔBS	
Debits	Credits	Assets	Liabilities
Corporate saving........100	Total sales....500	Distributed among some or all asset entries.......+100	Net worth...+100
All other current outlays.....400			
500	500	+100	+100

It is possible to think of the balance sheet and the income statement as $n \times 2$ matrices *IS* and *BS;* that is, a matrix with n rows and 2 columns of numbers, one column representing credits and the other debits in an income statement, or assets and liabilities in a balance sheet. The only required property of the two matrices is that sums of the elements of the two column vectors be equal. Recording of changes in a balance sheet, such as ΔBS above, may also be represented by such a matrix. The n rows express any desired classification of credits and debits, assets and liabilities, or changes in assets and liabilities. In particular, classification by "source" and "destination" of the transactions recorded in the two flow accounts— i.e., the income statement and changes in the balance sheet—will be important for our present analysis.

Balance sheets, income statements, and changes in balance sheets may be added according to the usual rules of addition of matrices;

i.e., $(IS_{a+b}) = (IS_a + IS_b)$. In words, corresponding elements in the two columns are added together. For example, if we write the income statement of the ith economic unit (firm, individual, or group) as

$$IS_i = [i\text{'s credits from } j; i\text{'s debits to } j] \quad j = 1, 2, \ldots, n$$

where the n rows express current transactions with n flow accounts (IS or ΔBS), including the ith account,[1] then

$$C_m = \sum_{i=1}^{m} IS_i = \left[\sum_{i=1}^{m} (i\text{'s credits from } j); \sum_{i=1}^{m} (i\text{'s debits to } j) \right]$$
$$j = 1, 2, \ldots, n)$$

is the sum income statement of m of the n economic units.

If there is any trading among the m units, this matrix has very little economic meaning. What we actually want to obtain is the *consolidated* income statement of the m units or firms—i.e., a statement reflecting flows of the first m firms with the remaining $n - m$ firms, and not transactions within the m firms. Thus we may define as a *consolidated income statement* of the m firms the matrix C'_m, obtained from C_m by deleting the first m rows from that matrix. We may write it as the expression for C_m above, but with $j = m + 1$, $m + 2, \ldots, n$, rather than $j = 1, 2, \ldots, n$. Clearly, the remainder of the elements of the columns will again add up to an equal sum because the sums of the omitted elements in the two columns must be equal. The reader will be able to work out a simple example, say, with three or four firms, two of whom are consolidating, that will show these conclusions. Corresponding to this consolidating addition we may now designate an additive sign $\oplus$ for simple additions of two terms, and Σ^2 for addition of several accounting statements. Now it should be observed that a perfectly analogous operation of consolidation may be performed on a set of balance sheets, reflecting assets and liabilities. If assets of some accounting units are carried as liabilities of others and consolidation of these units is performed, such entries will again be deleted. Similarly, changes in balance sheets, representing flows per time as much as income statements do, may be consolidated among themselves or with other flow accounts.

The above definition of consolidation required only a classifica-

---

[1] It will be observed that entries such as "i's credits from i" or "i's debits to i" will be zero.

[2] All summation signs used henceforth in this chapter refer to consolidation.

tion by origin and destination. Later in our discussion, however, it will be useful to distinguish, under any single element of the accounting statements, between different subtotals, according to the type of payment, asset, or liability. Moreover, it should be recalled that flows in income statements may be directed toward another income statement or toward a balance sheet. In the following, it is assumed that inventory accumulations appear in the income statements as credits, similar to sales, debited to the balance sheet of the same economic unit. Thus, according to the usual terminology, we are considering the production statement, rather than the income statement, of each transacting unit.

2.2.2 *The Accounts of the Productive Sector of the Economy.* The economic activity of all the producers in the economy may be represented by a set of income statements and changes in the balance sheets of each producer. If we designate all the producers, whether corporations or individual (unincorporated) enterprises, by x_j, $j = 1, 2, \ldots, n$, the consolidated production statement of the economy will be found as

$$PS_p = \sum_j IS_{x_j}$$

In its conventional form, using hypothetical numbers to demonstrate the consistency of all accounts, it may be represented as follows:

PS_p, PRODUCTION STATEMENT OF THE ECONOMY

Credits		Debits	
Sales to consumers		*Wages and salaries*	
On current account	1,000	Domestic	800
Sales to government		Foreign	20
On current account	50	*Income of unincorporated enterprises*	200
On capital account	50	Interest {Domestic	30
Sales to producers on capital account and		Interest {Foreign	10
accumulation of fixed assets (gross)	300	Rent {Domestic	30
Inventory accumulation	50	Rent {Foreign	10
Sales abroad (goods and services)	150	*Gross corporate profits*	200
Goods	100	Corporation taxes	100
Transportation	10	Dividends {Domestic	45
Interest	10	Dividends {Foreign	5
Dividends	30	Surplus	50
		Purchases from abroad	100
		Depreciation allowances	100
		Indirect business taxes minus subsidies	100
Total	1,600	Total	1,600

The current productive activity recorded in the above statement will have a definite impact on the balance sheets of each enterprise. Thus the surplus will be added to the net worth of the productive sector as an increased liability. Similarly, increases in fixed assets and inventories, as well as depreciation, will be recorded as changes in the assets of the companies. Moreover, as many other changes in the producers' balance sheets may occur as there are entries in these accounts. Positive (negative) changes in assets may always be recorded as debits (credits); positive (negative) changes in liabilities are credits (debits). Again, the change in the balance sheet of the productive sector (including private banks) will be obtained as a consolidated statement of all the producers, i.e.,

$$\Delta BS_p = \sum_i \Delta BS_{x_i}$$

and in its conventional form:

ΔBS_p, CHANGES IN THE BALANCE SHEET OF THE PRODUCTIVE SECTOR

Changes in Liabilities		Changes in Assets	
Long-term debt		*Cash*	
Domestic	10	Foreign exchange	10
Foreign	10	*Demand & time deposits with*	
Short-term debt		*foreign banks*	20
Domestic	50	*Government securities*	
Foreign	20	Domestic	50
Demand deposits		Foreign	10
Private	50	*Private loans*	
Government	10	Domestic	100
Foreign	10	Foreign	20
Net worth		*Fixed assets*	
Common & preferred stock	300	Buildings & equipment	300
Surplus	50	*Depreciation*	−100
		Inventories	50
		Foreign equity	50
Total	510	Total	510

2.2.3 *The Government Accounts.* Consolidation of income statements (current budgets) and of the changes in balance sheets of federal, state, and local governments, and other public institutions, including the central bank, will yield the total government income statement and total government change in the balance sheet. Again, if we designate all the different independent governmental institutions by g_j, we may write

$$IS_g = \sum_j IS_{g_j} \quad \text{and} \quad \Delta BS_g = \sum_j \Delta BS_{g_j}$$

and state the principal credit and debit entries of these accounts as follows:

IS_g, INCOME STATEMENT OF THE GOVERNMENT

Credits		Debits	
Corporate taxes	100	Purchases	
Personal income taxes	100	On current account	50
Indirect taxes	100	Interest on govt. debt	
Property, real estate and other taxes	50	To nationals	100
		To foreigners	20
		Wages and Salaries	
		To nationals	100
		To foreigners	10
		Foreign aid	10
		Surplus	60
Total	350	Total	350

ΔBS_g, CHANGE IN THE BALANCE SHEET OF THE GOVERNMENT

Changes in Liabilities		Changes in Assets	
Surplus	60	Purchases on capital account	50
New govt. debt	60	Long-term loans to foreign countries	100
		Farm surplus sales to foreign countries	−30
		Sale of gold abroad	−10
		Domestic demand deposits	10
Total	120	Total	120

2.2.4 *The Consumers' (or Private) Accounts.* In the same manner as above, we now construct the income statements of the consuming public and the change in its balance sheet. Except for its transactions with foreign countries, this sector's accounts are fully derivable from the preceding two sets of accounts. We have

$$IS_c = \sum_j IS_{c_j}$$

IS_c, Income Statement of the Private Sector

Credits		Debits	
Wages and salaries		Property and real estate tax.....	50
Domestic..................	900	Personal income tax............	100
Foreign...................	20	Personal consumption..........1,000	
Dividends		Donations to foreigners.........	20
Domestic..................	45	Surplus.....................	315
Foreign...................	70		
Interest			
On government debt........	100		
On domestic private bonds....	30		
From abroad...............	70		
Rent			
Domestic..................	30		
From abroad...............	20		
Income of unincorporated enter-			
prises..................	200		
Total....................1,485		Total....................1,485	

For the change in the balance sheet of the private sector, we have, through consolidation and using a numerical illustration consistent with the preceding accounts,

Change in the Balance Sheet of the Private Sector

$$\Delta BS_c = \sum_j BS_{c_j}$$

Changes in Liabilities		Changes in Assets	
Borrowing from domestic private		Net purchase of government securi-	
institutions...............100		ties.....................	10
Surplus.......................315		Demand deposits...............	50
		Loans to the productive sector	
		Long term..................	10
		Short term..................	50
		Common and preferred stock......300	
		Sale of foreign equity............−5	
Total.....................415		Total.....................415	

2.2.5 *Consolidation of Sectoral Accounts into a Balance-of-Payments Account.* Consolidation of the three sectoral income statements—IS_c, IS_g, and PS_p—will yield a new account composed of two distinct parts. On the one hand, it shows all the current transactions of the economy, taken as a whole, with foreign countries and, on the other, all the transactions of the economy with its own stock account, i.e., the national balance sheet. Thus we may write

$$IS = IS_g \oplus IS_c \oplus PS_p = (IS_f + IS_{ka})^3$$

where IS_f stands for the current account of the balance of payments and IS_{ka} for an account of all the flows between the current account of the economy and its balance sheet.

A similar procedure will yield the change in the consolidated balance sheet—or stock account—of the economy:

$$\Delta BS = \Delta BS_p \oplus \Delta BS_g \oplus \Delta BS_c$$

As all the intersectoral flows are eliminated in ΔBS, this account will reflect the flows with two other accounts. On the one hand, it will contain a complete recording of all changes in national assets and liabilities brought about by the productive sector of the economy —we may designate this portion of the account as ΔBS_{dp}—and, on the other hand, ΔBS will contain all the changes generated by capital transactions with foreign countries, i.e., ΔBS_f. Thus we may write

$$\Delta BS = (\Delta BS_f + \Delta BS_{dp})$$

At this point we should recall that IS, the consolidated income statement of the economy, is a two-column matrix where one column represents credits and the other debits; in ΔBS we have recorded, also in two columns, changes in liabilities and changes in assets, respectively. But it is perfectly legitimate and feasible to transform such a statement of changes in assets and liabilities into one organized into credit and debit entries. Such a transformation of, say, ΔBS into bs will be simply effected if all increases in assets and decreases in liabilities in ΔBS are recorded as debits $(-)$ in bs and all decreases in assets and increases in liabilities are recorded as credits $(+)$.

Thus, for example, the decline in the stock of gold by 10 accounting units that we have recorded as a reduced asset in the balance sheet of the government will appear as a credit in bs. Another way of understanding this transformation is to consider a situation wherein an account of changing stock is thought of as representing the current operations of an enterprise. All positive changes in assets and all negative changes in liabilities may be taken as purchases (debits);

---

[3] Parentheses are used here to indicate a single account. Observe that IS_f and IS_{ka} do not have to be individually in balance; only the sum total of credits and debits of both accounts have to be equal.

all negative changes in assets and positive changes in liabilities may be understood as sales (credits).

Thus we may reorganize in this fashion the three changes in balance sheets in the above relation and write

$$bs = (bs_f + bs_{d_p})$$

Now bs_{d_p} and IS_{ka} contain identical entries on opposite sides because they reflect the same transactions, one from the point of view of the income account, the other from the point of view of the capital account. The two will cancel out through consolidation of the income statement of the economy and the transformed balance sheet bs; the only remaining entries of the consolidated sum will be those with foreign countries, i.e., the balance of payments BP. Thus

$$IS \oplus bs = BP = (IS_f + bs_f)$$

where bs_f shows all the stock changes brought about by foreign transactions of the economy; bs_f will also be the combined capital and gold account of the balance of payments, provided that the productive sector of the economy is the only sector engaging in international trading. If, for example, the government engaged in direct sales of farm surpluses from its inventories to foreign countries, without passing through a commercial agency, such a transaction would also be recorded in bs_f. By definition, however, such a sale should be recorded as a current transaction in the balance of payments. Actually, in our hypothetical balance sheet of the government we have assumed that such a sale did take place. If, however, it were sold to a domestic exporter, who in turn had exported it, the domestic transaction would have been netted out by the consolidation of the national balance sheet BS and the income statement IS of the economy; only the actual current sale by the exporter would have been recorded as "merchandise sales abroad."

With this reservation in mind, we may actually take the IS_f statement equal to the current account of the balance of payments and the bs_f statement as the combined capital and gold account; i.e.,

$$IS_f = BP_{ca} \quad \text{and} \quad bs_f = BP_{kg}$$

The hypothetical balance-of-payments account resulting from the consolidation of the three sets of accounts of the preceding sections is reproduced below.

THE BALANCE-OF-PAYMENTS ACCOUNT

Credits	Debits
Current account	
Merchandise exports 130	Merchandise imports 100
Rent 20	Rent 10
Interest 80	Interest 30
Dividends 100	Dividends 5
Wages and salaries 20	Wages and salaries 30
Transportation 10	
Total goods and services 360	175
	Donations to foreign countries
	Private 20
	Government aid 10
Capital account	
A. *Private*	
Sale of foreign equity 5	Purchase of foreign equity 50
Producers' long-term debt 10	Loans to foreign producers 20
Producers' short-term debt . . . 20	Purchase of foreign government se-
Foreign demand deposits with	curities 10
local banks 10	Demand deposits with foreign banks 20
	Acquisition of foreign exchange by
	local banks 10
B. *Government*	
	Long-term loans to foreign coun-
	tries 100
Total capital account 45	210
Gold 10	
Total credits 415	Total debits 415

2.3 Problems of Valuation

In our preceding discussion we have abstracted from the problems of valuation; i.e., we have implicitly assumed that the dividing line between what is domestic and what is foreign, both in time and in space, is well defined. In the real world, however, this is by no means so, and this accounts for a number of problems in balance-of-payments accounting.

Any commodity, from the time it starts being produced until it is finally consumed, generally passes through a number of stages. Also, there is not any single point at which a commodity passes from the sphere of "domestic" into that of "foreign." If, for example, $100 worth of sugar, entirely produced in country A, is shipped to country B, which provides transportation and insurance worth $10, by the time it arrives at the port of B it is worth $110. Should the statistician recording the trade balance of country B use $100 or $110 as the value of the merchandise? One possible solution is to use the value of the commodity as of the date when it legally changed hands between the exporter and the importer. A score of different ways of valuation will come to mind, none entirely satisfactory.

In choosing a criterion for valuation, the first postulate is consistency in valuation; i.e., the rule of valuation should be, so far as possible, identical for every commodity, service, or capital transaction. The rules of valuation of visible trade presently employed by all countries are based on a geographical criterion. The value assigned to merchandise entering international trade is its total worth when it crosses a given geographical line, usually the border of the importing or the exporting country.

Three different methods of valuation may be distinguished, corresponding to three internationally accepted abbreviations: f.o.b., c.i.f., and f.a.s. The first, "free on board," indicates the value of merchandise, including all costs, up to the border of the exporting country, including loading charges (if any) at the border. The second valuation, "cost insurance freight," includes the f.o.b. value plus the cost of insurance and transportation to the border of the importing country. Finally, f.a.s., meaning "free alongside ship," is merely a slight variant of the f.o.b. valuation, from which it differs only by the cost of loading.

Clearly, provided that sufficiently detailed information is available, a balance-of-payments recording expressed in one type of valuation may be converted to another; the resulting totals of the current-account balance will, however, be somewhat different. The problem of converting a balance of payments from f.o.b. to f.a.s. or to c.i.f. often arises in practice because some countries use as a unique demarcation line their own border and hence value their exports f.o.b. and imports c.i.f., while some other countries, including the United States, use either the f.o.b. or the f.a.s. values for both exports and imports. For example, construction of a regional balance will call for expressing all trade data in terms of the same valuation.

How such a recalculation may be performed will be seen from the following example. Below we show two balanced current-account recordings, one with f.o.b. exports and c.i.f. imports, and the other with f.o.b. exports and f.o.b. imports; both reflect identical transactions.

BALANCE OF PAYMENTS ON CURRENT ACCOUNT

	Case 1			*Case 2*	
Credits		Debits	Credits		Debits
Commodities		Commodities	Commodities		Commodities
Exports f.o.b..450		Imports c.i.f..500	Exports f.o.b..450		Imports f.o.b..400
Services		Services	Services		Services
Ship. & ins... 50					Ship. & ins... 50
Total......500		500	Total......450		450

We assume that one half of transportation and insurance is provided by the exporting country and one half by the importing country. Thus, in the first account, if imports are inclusive of insurance and transportation, worth $100, services valued at one half of this sum have to be understood as exported from the country considered for shipment to its ports. In the second case this transfer is considered as purely domestic (as it actually is), while only the other half of transportation and insurance, provided by foreigners, is recorded as a debit in the invisible (or service) trade balance.

It seems that the second method (f.o.b.), actually used by the United States, is preferable, because it reflects the real character of the transfer of funds. In fact, the $50 paid to domestic shipping companies never had to be cleared through the foreign-exchange market. But there seems to be another, more important, advantage of the f.o.b. valuation of both exports and imports. Suppose that only two countries engage in international trading. Then the balance of payments of one country will be, except for possible errors of recording or differences in timing, a mirror image of the balance of payments of the other country. Actually, to obtain one account from the other it is necessary only to interchange the labels *debits* and *credits*. This clearly would not be possible if either country or both used the definitions f.o.b. for exports and c.i.f. for imports. However, if both countries used the c.i.f. definition for both exports and imports, the international accounts of the countries would again be consistent with each other; nevertheless, the objection that the method involves recording domestic payments as international would still be valid.

By the same token, if one definition is used for imports and another for exports—and internal flows within a region are recorded —exports to the region will not be equal to imports from the region. Moreover, as we are going to see in the following chapter, under such conditions it will be difficult to reconcile national-income and foreign-trade accounts between different countries.

2.4 Balance-of-Payments Data Recording and Performance of Transactions

Actual balance-of-payments data recording raises innumerable problems. It is beyond the scope of our discussion to come near exhausting the subject; let us, however, at least survey the most important problems. Some are of a purely practical nature and are as numerous as international transactions; others are again, as in the previous section, problems of definition or accounting convention.

The first and most important question is that of timing. A balance of payments is a statement, or recording, of flows; it shows in terms of a currency how much merchandise, services, and financial transfers have flowed from one country to others within a given period of time. A particular transaction will or will not be recorded, depending on whether its actual reckoning falls within the given accounting period. Now if different methods of recording are possible, each registering a given transaction at a different point in time, the balance-of-payments accounts may differ, depending on whether one method or another is used.

To clarify this point let us refer to the schematic representation of an international transaction reproduced below. In terms of changes in balance sheets, we consider an export of $100 worth of sugar from B to A. The balance sheets affected in country A will be found on the left side, the balance sheets affected in country B on the right side. A's currency we may call "dollars" and B's currency "pounds"; however, let us assume for the sake of simplicity that the rate of exchange equals 1.

The diagram may assist us in distinguishing the various possibilities of recording balance-of-payments data. With Professor Meade (*The Balance of Payments*, chap. ii), we may conceive of three such accounting conventions or bases of recording. The first, marked (1) in the diagram, may be referred to as the *transactions basis* and consists in reckoning a transaction at the moment when the contract of sale is made. The second way (2), described by Professor Meade as the *movements basis,* consists in recording every transaction at the moment when a commodity or security crosses the border or a service is performed. Finally, according to the *payments basis* (3), international transactions are recorded at the moment of their actual payment. This method corresponds to the quite intricate part of the transaction described in the different balance sheets of financial institutions in the lower part of the diagram. It will be discussed below in greater detail.

Here let us point out some of the important implications of the three methods. It is clear that the value and timing of each particular transaction will vary, depending on which recording conven-

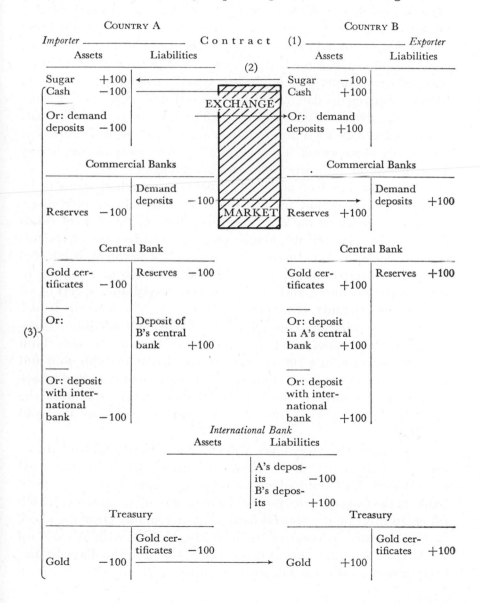

tion is followed. There may be delays between the times a contract of sale is made, the physical transfer is effected, and the commodities, services, or securities are actually paid for. Thus a transaction will be recorded in one accounting period or another, depending on the convention followed.

The time path of international transactions will determine the extent of the differences of data obtained under the various bases. If, for example, there were a perfectly steady flow of transactions, day by day, or if seasonal fluctuations of these flows were about the same every year, the annual balance of payments would be about the same, regardless of the basis used. If, however, there were a trend in international transactions or if important cyclical variations were present, balance-of-payments data could vary a good deal, depending on the way of recording. Another difficulty may arise if, as is often the case, contracts are made for a period longer than the accounting period of the balance of payments, if payments are effected only in part in any given period or if future deliveries are prepaid.

The most involved and most problematic method seems to be the third. We may now turn to the accounting scheme of a single transaction shown in the diagram. First, it shows the flow of funds through all the conceivable stages, without the direct use of the foreign-exchange market. In this case, finally, the payment is effected through a corresponding flow of gold from the importing country to the exporting country, and, in that process, the balance sheets of all parties—the treasury, the central bank, the commercial banks, and the traders in both countries—are affected. All possible secondary or tertiary monetary effects are neglected, assuming that both countries operate on a 100 per cent reserve basis, for both gold and commercial bank reserves. Observe that the settlement would have to assume this form if the transaction here considered were the only one of the period and the countries operated on the gold standard.

An alternative way of payment is conceivable through a bank of international settlements, a payments union, or an international central bank. Still another way of payment is conceivable, if central banks of the two countries hold short-term deposit accounts with each other. In this case the central bank of B may simply clear the check of the importer in country A, depositing dollars with A's central bank. More generally, any of the accounts shown in the diagram may carry part of its assets as a deposit (liability) with any other account.

Thus, at any stage of the transfer, the payment may be completed if the exporter or any financial institution or person of the exporting country is willing to extend a corresponding credit to the importer or any institution in country A. This will simply increase the current deposits of a bank or an individual of country B with a bank or individual of country A and create a short-term capital flow from B to A. It should be observed that, unless the exporter himself holds a dollar deposit with a bank in country A, anybody who cashed the check in country B in pounds and holds the corresponding amount in dollars on deposit in A actually performs the function, or is part, of the foreign-exchange market. Finally, any bank or individual in possession of the importer's dollar check or currency may use the foreign-exchange market and effect the payment directly in terms of foreign currency. In this case it has to be assumed that another transaction, also amounting to $100, was cleared through the foreign-exchange market, thus providing the necessary foreign currency. We have shown some of these alternative paths of settlement in the diagram. Any particular form of settlement may easily be traced through this or a similar diagram.

Apart from the international bank illustrated in the diagram, an international monetary fund may be used in effecting international settlements between countries. In this case a payment in pounds to the exporter will be effected with that currency purchased from the monetary fund for dollars. While in the case of an international bank, deposits of country A were depleted and those of country B increased, in the fund the currency of A will be accumulated and holdings of the surplus country's currency depleted.

This multiplicity of alternative modes of payment makes it extremely difficult to use the third method of recording in constructing the current account of the balance of payments. Actually, at any stage, when transfers are effected between two different accounts, a recording of the transfers could be made—at least in theory. This, however, would require extremely rigorous and cumbersome controls. Moreover, checks, cash, or letters of credit often do not specify the exact purpose of the transaction.

This discussion should not lead to the conclusion that banking records are useless in establishing the balance-of-payments accounts. But the information that may be derived from such records pertains to the capital rather than to the current account of the balance of payments. First of all, by comparing the foreign balances of our individuals and banks and foreign deposits in our banks, at the beginning and at the end of each accounting period, it is possible to obtain the gross and net flows of official and private short-term capital. Also, banks' and dealers' reports on transactions in securities with foreigners provide the necessary information on private and official movements of long- and intermediate-term capital. Similarly, treasury reports concerning the stock of gold at the beginning and end of the accounting period, together with data on domestic production and government purchases, make it possible to calculate the international gold movements.

It appears that the second method (the *movements basis*) is most accurate and practical for the major part of international transactions, those entering the current account in particular. It is this method that predominates in actual use. Thus every physical movement of a commodity is recorded when passing through a determined point—usually from customs documents—and is valued according to the conventions discussed above; every service—to the extent that this is feasible—is recorded in the period when it is rendered and is valued at cost.

Records of official loans and donations are easily obtainable from government accounts and bank reports. Private short-term capital movements data may be obtained from bank statements and securities dealers' reports, as discussed above. Information concerning international private equity movements may, again, be obtained from dealers' disclosures or company balance sheets. Private unrequited transfers (donations) often are difficult to estimate because of the difficulty of distinguishing between donations and other types of financial transfers undertaken by private individuals.

A special mention should be made here of unrepatriated retained earnings from domestic companies' operations abroad. These, although obtainable from the income statements and balance sheets of the companies, traditionally are not recorded in the balance-of-payments accounts, the reason being that they do not give rise to any international transfer of either securities or funds. It should also be noted that in some countries these unrecorded transfers and factor payments may be quite important. In particular, this was the case with British foreign investments in the nineteenth century. The reinvested earnings of American companies abroad have also been very important; in some years of the 1950's they have equalled total (other) direct investment abroad. Clearly, the equilibrium of balance-of-payments account will not be affected by this omission, but the net balance on capital account and that on current account will. If, for example, $1 billion was reinvested abroad and this were to be recorded in the balance of payments, the current-account credits and the capital-account debits would have to be augmented by $1 billion. This may raise problems when it comes to national-income accounting.

Using the methods, definitions, and rules of valuation that we have just examined, the balance of payments may be constructed. As an exercise, we may consider the different types of foreign-trade balance that would be brought about by the importation of $100 worth of sugar under various types of settlement. This representation would obtain equally for any other autonomous transaction—such as a donation or a loan—giving rise to a debit entry of $100, as does the importation of sugar here considered.

FOREIGN-TRADE BALANCE OF COUNTRY A

Credits	Debits
Current Account	
Visible trade	100
Balance on current account	100
Capital and Gold	
Gold 100	
Or: short-term foreign liabilities 100	
This credit entry results either from increased holdings of dollar balances by foreign individuals, banks, or central authorities with A's individuals, banks, or authorities, or, conversely, balances of A with individuals and institutions of B may have been reduced.	
Or: international institutions 100	
This means that payment was effected through the reduction of A's deposits with the international bank, while deposits of B were increased by the same amount. This entry may also represent a purchase of foreign currency from the International Monetary Fund, used in compensating the foreign exporter of sugar.	
Total balance on capital and gold account 100	
Total balance 100	100

Under ideal conditions the movement of goods and services, donations, capital transactions, and financial settlements on the credit side of the balance-of-payments account would be observed independently of similar entries on the debit side. By definition, under ideal conditions, the total credits and total debits of the balance have to be equal. This provides a valuable check on the precision of actual data recording. In practice, an equality of the two recordings is only rarely encountered; there is a great likelihood that some transfers will not be recorded at all or that an arithmetical error will be made in handling very large numbers of transactions. Possibly the most important source of such imperfections are changes in foreign bank deposits (i.e., short-term capital flows), not declared or not accounted for as foreign deposits. To reflect such statistical discrepancies, most balance-of-payments accounts explicitly include an entry of *errors and omissions,* equal to the difference between total recorded credits and recorded debits.

2.5 The Significance of Equilibria and Disequilibria of the Balance of Payments

Considering its relevance for the remainder of this study, the most important point of the present chapter remains to be made. What do we actually mean by saying that a balance of payments is in, or out of, equilibrium? Throughout this chapter we have stressed the fact that the total balance of payments must—by definition—be in balance. This apparent paradox is resolved by realizing two things: (1) that any particular portion of the balance, such as current account, capital account, gold, or other, is not required to be in balance and (2) that the balance of payments that concerns us in economic analysis is not the total accounting balance as we have known it so far, but only a portion of it.

The total balance of payments has to be reclassified into two parts, according to a motivational criterion. We have to ask ourselves, in examining every particular transaction or financial operation, whether it was brought about independently from the over-all balance-of-payments situation or not. If it was, we may refer to such a transaction or to such a payment as *autonomous;* if it was not, we may term the transaction *accommodating* or *induced.*

Corresponding to these two types of payments, we may distinguish between two parts of every balance of payments: the balance of autonomous payments and the balance of accommodating or induced payments. It is now possible to define an equilibrium of the balance of payments as a state wherein autonomous debits are equal to autonomous credits, while a disequilibrium is a state wherein autonomous payments (or debits) exceed or fall short of autonomous receipts (or credits).

The rationale of this important distinction is quite straightforward: most international transactions are effected for what we may call "economic" reasons (i.e., the prices of comparable goods or services are lower in one country than in another, or the interest rate varies among countries, etc.). Some other transactions, such as donations, are made on grounds of affection, family obligations, national security, etc. But both these groups are entirely unrelated to the state of the balance of payments. These transfers and/or transactions correspond to autonomous payments. On the other hand, we shall observe in the total balance of payments such payments as would not have occurred in the absence of the autonomous payments: these are the accommodating payments. Important examples of the latter type are movements of gold, accumulation or decumulation of balances with international payments institutions, accumulation or decumulation of foreign-exchange holdings, etc. Also, under special circumstances, accommodating official transfers (donations or loans) may take place if the government of a surplus country decides to finance the gap between autonomous credits and debits. Actually, most of the different ways of settlement described under (3) in the hypothetical example of the preceding section provide an illustration of accommodating or induced payments.

In the final analysis, it will depend on the judgment of the economist, in each particular case, whether a payment is entered as autonomous or accommodating. Sometimes a balance of payments of A with B may appear to be in balance from the point of view of A and out of balance from B's standpoint. One such case may arise if a gold-producing country sells gold in the international market; for that country this will represent an autonomous sale, while for the receiving country it may represent an accommodating payment. A similar situation may arise if a large country, such as the United States or the United Kingdom, assumes the function of an international banker; an autonomous increase in the international demand for liquidity may then be regarded by the large banking countries as induced by a deficit in their respective autonomous payments.

2.6 The Balance of Indebtedness

In concluding this chapter, let us define and construct the foreign *balance of indebtedness* of an economy. Using the accounting statements of Section 2 of this chapter, we may first define the national balance sheet (BS) as a consolidated balance sheet of the economy, i.e.,

$$BS = BS_p \oplus BS_g \oplus BS_c$$

This consolidated statement will be composed of two parts, one reflecting the domestic, the other the foreign, position of assets, liabilities, and net worth at a given point in time. Wherever corresponding entries are found in the domestic sectoral accounts on the asset and liability sides, these will be eliminated by consolidation; thus, for example, equity of domestic corporations held by nationals, or bonds, will not appear in BS. However, real domestic assets, such as buildings, equipment, etc., as well as accumulated surplus of corporations or individuals will be found in the national balance sheet. We may state the important entries and components of BS as follows:

NATIONAL BALANCE SHEET

Assets	Liabilities and Net Worth
BI_f	
Foreign assets	Foreign liabilities
BS_d	
Buildings, equipment, and other real domestic tangible and intangible assets	*Net worth* Accumulated surplus
Total	= Total

Again, only the totals of the right and left sides of the account have to be equal. The balance of indebtedness, BI_f, may be either in surplus or in deficit, i.e., the country may either be a net creditor or a net debtor vis-à-vis the rest of the world. However, whatever the position of foreign net indebtedness, it must be equal to the excess of domestic real assets over accumulated surplus of the economy.

Thus we have defined in abstract terms the foreign balance of indebtedness and related it to the total domestic asset and net-worth position. The practical evaluation of the net creditor or debtor position of a country presents innumerable difficulties; most are of the accounting variety, primarily problems of valuation and the existence or availability of accounts. Valuation of assets accumulated many years before is very difficult, if not impossible. Also, in order to construct the national balance sheet as we have shown it above, it would be necessary to be in possession of the balance sheets not only of all producers but also of every other physical or legal person in the country. Many of us have never even asked ourselves what our net-worth or asset position actually is.

The actual presentation of a balance of indebtedness usually employs the same classification as the capital account in the balance of payments, or one very similar. It should be stressed again, however, that, while the balance of indebtedness shows the position as of a given date, the balance of payments shows the flows per unit of time. Thus, as shown in the account below, a balance of foreign indebtedness includes assets such as private and official short- and long-term loans and equity, as well as direct investment, and similar entries on the liability side showing the different forms of debt to foreign countries. Where the net indebtedness (net creditor or debtor position) appears is arbitrary, provided that the correct sign is used. In the account below it is listed (similarly to the net worth in a balance sheet) together with liabilities to foreigners.

BALANCE OF INDEBTEDNESS
OR
INTERNATIONAL INVESTMENT POSITION

Assets	*Liabilities and net balance*
Private investment abroad	
Long term	*Long term*
Direct *	Direct *
Equity	Equity
Loans	Loans
Short term	*Short term*
Bank deposits	Bank deposits
Loans	Loans
Government	
Long term	*Long term*
Short term	*Short term*
	Net creditor $(+)$ *or debtor* $(-)$ *position*
Total	= Total

* By *direct investment* we usually mean direct ownership of real assets abroad. In practice, however, wherever corporate ownership is involved, direct investment is defined as 50 per cent ownership or more.

It is also possible, and sometimes important for economic analysis, to state the net short- and long-term positions separately. The United States, for example, has, ever since the First World War, been a net long-term creditor and a net short-term debtor, while its over-all balance has always been positive in this period.

Finally, let us recall the important fact, deriving from our preceding discussion, that the balance of indebtedness also will be found as the sum of all past changes in such a balance, derivable from all the past credits and debits in the capital account of the balance of payments. Of course, here again we have to assume ideal conditions, where no problems of valuation are present, and where all capital flows across the national border are recorded, irrespective of whether or not they are accompanied by security movements.

Chapter 3

THE BALANCE-OF-PAYMENTS AND THE NATIONAL-INCOME ACCOUNTS

3.1 Definitions in National-Income Accounting

Because exports of a country are produced by the country's economy and because its imports are paid for by a portion of national income, there must be a definite, purely accounting, relation between the balance-of-payments and the national-income accounts. In this section we shall briefly examine this relation. From the outset, we should realize that the national-income accounting concepts are arbitrary to some degree, and their definitions depend on accountants' convention. Thus differences of definition may arise among countries and between periods. For example, at present the Eastern Communist countries include in their national-income definition some entries excluded by Western nations, and vice-versa. Among the Western countries national-income definitions are fairly uniform. In what follows we shall usually employ the United States accounts as the basis for discussion.

In the preceding chapter we derived the balance-of-payments account as a consolidated statement of different sectoral accounts. Two of these statements—namely, the production statement of the economy (PS_p) and the income statement of the government sector (IS_g)—provide us with most of the information required to derive the gross national product (GNP), the net national product (NNP), and the national income (Y). Clearly, the most important portion of national product is generated by the productive sector of the economy; the government also—according to the accepted definitions—generates part of the national product.

Let us first consider the production statement of the productive sector and show its contribution to the gross national product. We refer the reader to the production statement, (PS_p), in Section 2.2 of Chapter 2. We may restate it here:

31

PRODUCTION STATEMENT OF THE ECONOMY

Debits (Outlays)		*Credits* (Sales and Stock Accumulation)	
To domestic sectors 1,455		*From domestic sectors* 1,450	
Wages and salaries	800	Sales to consumers on current	
Income of unincorporated		account 1,000	
enterprises	200	Sales to government	100
Interest	30	Gross private domestic capital	
Rent	30	formation	350
Gross corporate profits	195	Producers' buildings and	
Corporate taxes 100		equipment 300	
Dividends 45		Inventory accumulation 50	
Retained earnings (surplus) . 50			
Depreciation allowances	100		
Indirect business taxes	100		
To abroad	145	*From abroad*	150
Wages and salaries	20	Wages and salaries	0
Interest	10	Interest	10
Rent	10	Rent	0
Dividends	5	Dividends	30
Goods and other services	100	Goods and other services	110
Total 1,600		Total 1,600	

We assume that the productive sector comprises all productive activity. This means that no other sector transforms primary productive factors into finished goods or services sold in the market to the extent that such services or goods are at all represented in the accounts. Often, within a family, for example, services are performed and products produced that do not pass through any market and are not entered into any of the accounts; if this is the case, they do not concern us here. On the other hand, if households produce and consume some goods and services that are included in the national-income or product accounts, these activities are here to be considered as belonging to the productive sector. The important cases that come to mind here are the (imputed) income from owner-occupied houses and farms, as well as direct consumption of farm produce on farms. Such incomes (usually estimated) appear in the production statement of the economy (i) as sales to the consumers (credit in PS_p), and (ii) as income of unincorporated enterprises or proprietors' income (debit in PS_p). Fixed assets (buildings and equipment) yielding such income are also carried on the balance sheet of the productive sector.

Not all of the total of 1,600 of the above production statement enters the gross national product. Part of it was not produced by the economy but was imported from abroad. Thus, to obtain the productive sector's contribution to the *GNP,* or what we may term the "national value added," by the productive sector, we have to deduct the outlays on foreign goods and services, namely, 145 accounting units. The resulting total of 1,455, however, is not yet the gross national product. We have not yet accounted for the government's contribution to the *GNP.* Part of the impact of the government on the nation's use of resources has already been taken into account. Some resources were used by the productive sector and transformed into finished goods and services that were purchased by the government. In addition to these resources (equaling 100 in our example), the government also purchased some of the primary factors of production directly, without the intermediary of the productive sector. The important purchase (the only one considered in our accounts) is that of direct-labor services from its nationals. But the government could, and actually does, also rent land and buildings from outside the productive sector. Current interest on government debt, on the other hand, is not considered in current national-income accountants' practice as a component of the *GNP.*

Thus we may summarize the operations we have explained thus far and arrive at a sum very close, or equal, to the *GNP:*

Total receipts and stock accumulation of the productive sector...... 1,600
− current purchases from abroad of the productive sector......... −145
+ wages paid by the government to nationals................... +100

Total *GNP*.. 1,555

This sum is equal to the *GNP,* provided that neither the government nor the consumers' sector sells any services of *primary* factors of production to foreign countries. If it does, the above figure of 1,555 has to be augmented by the value of these factors to obtain the gross national product. Consequently, if an individual is employed by a foreign firm or in any other way earns wages or salary paid to him from abroad, this is counted as a portion of the national product. The same is true of interest and dividends from foreign securities owned by households. On the other hand, if households resell abroad commodities that they have purchased from the productive sector, the inclusion of such sales in the *GNP* would involve a double counting. However, such activities, by definition, are classified into the productive sector, and their purchase is netted out against the sale; hence no double counting occurs.

There is, however, a case somewhat similar to that just discussed wherein double counting could arise. Government sales abroad of commodities (such as farm surpluses) it holds in stock will, of course, be recorded in the balance of payments as a merchandise export. In our hypothetical accounts such a sale actually took place, totaling 30 accounting units. But such a sale does not increase the *GNP*. Whether it was produced in the current period or not, it was at one point already recorded as sale to the government by the productive sector. Similarly, gold exports or imports neither add nor subtract from the national product. It should be observed, however, that if changes of government inventories or of gold reserves were included in national inventory accumulation or decumulation, direct exports of such inventories by the government would have to be counted as a component of national product. All these accounting difficulties may be avoided if all institutions, public or private, who engage in commercial activities are always classified with the productive sector of the economy.

Let us now turn our attention to imports. It is clear that the productive sector's purchases from abroad (equal to 145 in the example) do not comprise all the imports of the economy. Other imports, mostly of services, were realized by other sectors; the household sector may have expended part of its income on foreign travel, transportation, or direct purchases of goods; the government may have done likewise. We have already indicated that such imports should not be subtracted from the national product. Now we may see clearly the reason: such imports have not contributed or served as factors of production in the output of the economy.

This causes an apparent complication of the *GNP* computation: while we add to the purchases of domestic sectors all exports on the current account (including those supplied by other than the productive sector) , we subtract from the total only the purchases of goods and services effected by the productive sector. This prevents us from simply including the net balance on current account as one of the main entries of the *GNP* account. However, there is a simple device, currently used in national-income accounts, to circumvent this difficulty.

Let us recall that in the production statement shown at the beginning of this section, the entries on the credit side, such as sales to the consumers' sector, to the government, etc., comprise only the produce of the productive sector sold to these domestic sectors. The sum total of the statement (1,600) will not be affected if any purchase of the nonproductive sectors from abroad is added to the corresponding sector and, at the same time, subtracted from exports. Similarly, the *GNP* will not be affected by such an operation. Thus we modify the *GNP* statement as expressed so far by listing, instead of "sales of the productive sector to the government," or "to the consumers," the somewhat different entries, "total purchases of goods and services by the government" and "total purchases of the consumers' sector." Furthermore, we subtract from the total not only purchases of the productive sector from abroad but also all other current purchases by other domestic sectors from foreign countries (i.e., total imports on current account); the above defined and calculated gross national product will then remain unchanged. It is important to keep in mind the fact that the listings of government purchases and of consumers' purchases include both those from abroad and those from the domestic productive sector. We may now summarize all the operations we have performed on the production statement of the economy in obtaining the *GNP* account. Again we are using the hypothetical data from the accounts in Chapter 2.

The Gross National Product Account

Wages and salaries			*Consumers' expenditures*	
From the productive sector	800		Domestic	1,000
From the government	100		Foreign	0
Income of unincorporated enterprises	200		*Government purchases of goods and*	
Interest	30		*services*	
Rent	30		Domestic	200
Gross corporate profits (excluding dividends to foreigners)			Foreign interest	20
Corporate taxes	100		*Gross private domestic investment*	
Dividends	45		Net fixed investment	200
Retained earnings	50		Inventory accumulation*	50
Depreciation (capital consumption) allowances	100		Depreciation (capital consumption allowances)	100
Indirect business taxes	100		*Exports of goods and services minus sales from government inventories*	330
Direct factor income of households from abroad			minus	
Interest	70		*Imports of goods and services*	−175
Rent	20			
Dividends	70			
Wages and salaries	20			
Direct factor income of government from abroad	0			
GNP	**1,735**			**1,735**

*Not including government inventories. If these were included, the corresponding figure would be 20, instead of 50, and 30 would not have to be subtracted from exports on current account. In either situation, *GNP* will be the same.

We have listed the income from abroad of households and of the government separately in the above account. However, these entries might be pooled—they actually are in the usual *GNP* accounts—and listed by type of income, such as wages, interest, rent, etc. In the foreign-trade portion of the right side of the account, we recognize the figure for exports of goods and services (360) diminished by the export of government-owned inventories (30) and the figure for imports of goods and services (175) as they were obtained in the detailed balance-of-payments account of the preceding chapter.

We have not included in the *GNP* accounts all the possible entries usually found in detailed *GNP* statistics. Thus, for example, business transfer payments, employers' contributions to social insurance, and current surplus of government enterprises are not shown in our accounts.[1] This should be attributed partly to our definitions and partly to the fact that our emphasis here is on the relation between the national-income, or product accounts, and the balance of international payments; the latter we have tried to discuss in greater detail. Nevertheless, we are confident that the reader will either be able to perform and understand such minor adjustments or find more specialized literature serving this purpose.

3.2 Further Definitions and Simplification of Accounts

The gross national product constructed in the preceding section reflects the total of new goods and services produced in the current year, expressed in terms of the prices at which such products were sold. However, any economy using capital goods in production will consume part of its capital stock in the course of the production period. Thus not all newly produced commodities add to the stock of capital or are used up in current consumption; some are used in substituting for that portion of the capital stock that has been used up. There is no unique way of evaluating this loss or usage of capital, but the accountants' concept of depreciation, or capital consumption allowances, is a satisfactory estimator of the portion of existing capital stock consumed as input in current production.

Thus, to obtain from the gross national product the net national product, we have to subtract from the former the sum of depreciation allowances. Thus

$$NNP = (Y) = GNP - \text{capital consumption allowances}$$

---

[1] Also, national-income accounts usually make an adjustment for possible changes in the value of inventories caused by price rather than quantity variations.

The concept and abbreviation *NNP* is found in American economic literature: English and Continental writers refer to it as the *national income at market prices.* This name is entirely legitimate because the net national product must be the (national) income that all the factors of production would have to earn in order to realize all purchases, private and collective, at market prices—that is, at prices used in valuing the aggregates on the right-hand side of the product account. The concept of net national product or net national income at market prices is most convenient and widely used in economic analysis; we may henceforth employ for it the simpler abbreviation *Y*.

The second interpretation, i.e., the national income at market prices, leads us to the third important concept of national-income accounting, namely, the *national income.* English and Continental writers refer to this concept as *national income at factor cost,* in order to differentiate it from the national income at market prices. The difference between the two statistics is made up predominantly by the indirect business tax and nontax liability minus business subsidies; net surplus of government enterprises, if any, also enters this difference. The net national product after these three adjustments yields the factor cost of total national output, i.e., national income (Y_f). Thus

$$Y_f = Y - \text{indirect tax and nontax liability}$$
$$+ \text{business subsidies}$$
$$- \text{net surplus of government enterprises}$$

Although the two sides of the national-income accounts, whether *GNP, Y,* or national income at factor cost, must always be in balance, the distinction between the right-hand side and the left-hand side offers different ways of looking at the same aggregate. While the left side shows the detail of the sources of national income by factors of production and by legal forms of producing units, the right side shows the allocation of the aggregate income to different purposes, such as consumption, investment expenditures, government expenditures, and foreign lending or transfers. It should be noted that *GNP* and *Y* are easily distinguishable both on the side of allocation and on that of sources; the factor income appears only on the side of sources.

Of paramount importance in the analysis of international trade is another distinction, namely, that between net national product

(Y) and net national expenditure (E), referred to by some economists as *absorption*. The two statistics will not be equal if exports on current account are not equal to imports on current account. Indeed, total national income (Y) is composed of total personal consumption expenditures on goods and services (C) plus net private domestic investment (I_d) plus government purchases of goods and services (G) plus exports minus imports $(X - M)$. Total national expenditure, however, includes only C, I_d, and G. Using these notations, we may now summarize all the definitions and identities obtained so far:

$$Y = GNP - \text{depreciation allowances}$$
$$= Y_f + \text{indirect taxes} + \text{surplus of government enter-}$$
$$\text{prises} - \text{government subsidies to business}$$
$$= (C + I_d + G) + (X - M)$$
$$= E + BP_{ca}$$

In the last two equalities we have used the aggregates C, I_d, and G as they are found in the national-income accounts. We have mentioned previously, and let us stress again, that consumption (C), government spending (G), and net domestic investment (I_d) are, or may be, composed of two parts, one attributable to foreign productive efforts, the other to domestic productive efforts.[2] Thus we may write

$$C = C_d + C_f$$
$$G = G_d + G_f$$
$$I_d = (I_d)_d + (I_d)_f$$

The second terms of the right sides of the equations are composed of direct imports by each particular sector or of imports of goods and services that have been used by the domestic sector in producing consumers' goods and services, goods and services supplied to the government, and capital goods. The other terms of the right-hand sides of the equations, on the other hand, represent the value added by the domestic factors of production. Thus, by definition,

$$C_f + G_f + (I_d)_f = M$$

and

$$C_d + G_d + (I_d)_d = E_d$$

where E_d represents domestic expenditure on domestically produced goods (or, to be precise, expenditure on the value added by domes-

---

[2] Observe that the same is generally true about exports of goods and services. This, however, complicates a good deal the national-income identities. We shall discuss this situation in greater detail in the next section of this chapter.

tic production). It is now possible to combine the identities established above and write

$$Y = E_d + X$$

and

$$E = E_d + M$$

The first relation states that national income at market prices (i.e., *NNP*) is equal to domestic expenditure on domestically produced goods and services plus exports (assumed to be derived entirely from domestic resources). The second relation shows the equality between total expenditure and domestic expenditure on domestically produced goods and services plus imports (assumed to be entirely consumed within the economy).

Although the definitions using total expenditures such as C, I_d, and G are convenient in the sense that they use concepts taken over from national-income accounting, they are of less value in the theoretical analysis of international trade. The second set of definitions, which distinguishes between domestically and foreign-produced goods, is preferable for this purpose.

In concluding this section let us recall the foreign-trade identities explained at an earlier stage. The balance of goods and services not only is equal to $X - M$, but also, following from the necessary balance of credits and debits in international payments, it may be explained as a sum of net government and private transfers (t) to (+) or from (−) abroad, net private and government foreign investment (I_f) (+) or disinvestment (−), gold (g) imports (+) or exports (−), and, in practice, errors and omissions. Thus we may complete the above identities and write

$$Y = E + t + I_f + g \ (\pm \text{ errors and omissions})$$

3.3 Reconciliation of National-Income and Foreign-Trade Accounts of Different Countries

So far we have focused our attention on a single country, its balance of payments and its national-income accounts. The first thing we would like to do in this section is to reconcile and show a possible way of recording of different national accounts. To do so, as we have done previously, we assume that all countries use the same foreign-trade valuation for exports and imports and that they all use the same definitions of national income. To avoid monetary complications, let us also assume that the international stock of gold is fixed. Assuming that there are n countries in the world, we may consider the matrix below. We use the notations from the preceding section, with subscripts representing the country of origin and superscripts the country of destination.

					Horizontal total
E_{d1}	X_1^2	X_1^3	....	X_1^n	Y_1
X_2^1	E_{d2}	X_2^3	....	X_2^n	Y_2
X_3^1	X_3^2	E_{d3}	....	X_3^n	Y_3
.	.	.			
.	.	.			
.	.	.			
.	.	.			
.	.	.			
X_n^1	X_n^2	X_n^3	....	E_{dn}	Y_n
Vertical total $\;E_1$	E_2	E_3		E_n	$E = Y$

In each row we find domestic expenditure on domestic goods and services (E_d) and exports on current account of one to all other countries. The same matrix, considered from the point of view of its columns, represents each country's domestic expenditure and imports from other countries. Thus the sum of the elements of the ith row represents the income (Y_i) of the ith country; a vertical sum of the jth column, on the other hand, will be equal to total expenditure (E_j). The sum of all national incomes has to be equal to the sum of all national expenditures and, in turn, to total world income and expenditure.

The balance of payments on current account between any two countries will be obtained as the difference between two terms symmetrical with respect to the northwest-southeast diagonal. Unless the trade is purely bilateral, however, this balance between any two countries does not have to be equal to the net flow of capital, gold, and unilateral transfers, as it has to for the total balance of payments. From the identities of the preceding section or by inspecting the matrix, we find the total balance on current account for each particular country (i) as the difference between its national income and expenditure (i.e., $Y_i - E_i$).

Using the above matrix, the consolidation of a number of countries' accounts into that of a single producing and trading unit is also simple. Let us suppose that countries 1 through 3 form a perfect economic union. What are their national income, national expenditure, and balance of payments with the rest of the world? Any export or import within the area of the three countries now becomes domestic expenditure, while all exports of the area to any other country are now added into a single export figure; the same is, of course, true for imports. Thus it is possible to add up the first three columns into one column and afterward the first three rows into one row. The nine terms expressing domestic expenditures and interarea trade will now add up to one term, namely, the domestic expenditure of the area $(E_{d1,2,3})$, while the remaining entries in the newly formed first row will show the exports of the area to all other countries, and the remaining entries of the newly formed column the imports of the area from all other countries. The horizontal sum of the new row will represent the national income of the union $(Y_{1,2,3})$, and the sum of the new column will be equal to the total national expenditure of the union $(E_{1,2,3})$. The balance on current account will again be found as the difference between these two statistics, i.e., $Y_{1,2,3} - E_{1,2,3}$. But, because

$$Y_{1,2,3} - E_{1,2,3} = Y_1 + Y_2 + Y_3 - E_1 - E_2 - E_3$$

we may also write

$$BP_{ca1,2,3} = Y_{1,2,3} - E_{1,2,3} = BP_{ca1} + BP_{ca2} + BP_{ca3}$$

In words, it is possible to obtain easily the balance on current account of the region with the rest of the world by summing up the respective total balances of the three economies entering the union.

A similar representation in a square matrix would be possible in expressing the flows of capital transfers, unilateral transfers, and gold. We shall not undertake a detailed discussion of this topic; however, let us point out some of the important relations between such a representation and the above matrix description of world output and trade. To simplify the matter, let us assume that all adjustments in a current-account balance of payments are performed through short-term capital movements; these, however, may move between any two countries in both directions. In a hypothetical matrix showing the short-term capital flows, all diagonal terms (where in the former matrix we found the E_d's) will be equal to zero. In its rows we would find all capital inflows and in the columns short-term capital outflows, as they were realized among the respective countries. The column sums thus represent total capital outflows, or debits of the capital account (k_i), and the row sums total capital inflows, or credits on capital account (c_i), of each particular country (i). The difference between the total capital outflow and total capital inflow of a country must be equal to the difference between exports and imports or national income and expenditure. Thus

$$Y_i - E_i = X_i - M_i = k_i - c_i = \text{net foreign investment}$$

However, unless there is pure bilateral trading, the current-account balance of a country with another country does not have to be equal to the net balance on capital account between the two countries. Total world capital outflow must be equal to total world capital inflow, in the same way as total world income is equal to total world expenditure.[3]

Our consideration of international flows of capital brings us to an important qualitative distinction between domestic and foreign investment. We often speak of domestic and foreign investment as of two very similar things. We should always be aware of the fact that in some respects there are important differences between these apparently similar operations. From the point of view of the nationals of a country, the two are comparable, and both contribute to, or are portions of, that part of national income that is not expended on current consumption but rather saved and invested. From the point of view of the physical form into which the corresponding funds are transformed, this is not, or not necessarily, so. While we may be sure that the entry in national-income accounts representing net domestic private investment has a very concrete physical counterpart in producers' equipment, construction, etc., the net foreign investment need not have any such counterpart. Funds that we have lent abroad might equally well have been consumed by the capital-importing country, although this may not have been the wisest policy on the part of the borrower.

[3] A simple three-country matrix may illustrate this discussion. The numbers in parentheses represent capital flows, numbers without parentheses represent exports or domestic expenditure, as in the trade matrix above. Figures in columns may be interpreted as *debits,* while those in rows as *credits.*

1 (0)	1 (5)	1 (7)	3 (12)
1 (3)	1 (0)	0 (5)	2 (8)
0 (10)	1 (2)	1 (0)	2 (12)
2 (13)	3 (7)	2 (12)	7 (32)

We have pointed out in the preceding section that, as domestic purchases of goods and services may be separated into purchases of domestic produce, on the one hand, and foreign produce, on the other, so the exports of a country will also be composed of portions produced from domestic primary resources and from foreign resources, either directly employed or embodied in foreign products. However, to simplify the analysis in this and the preceding sections, we have assumed that exports are entirely attributable to domestic resources and imports entirely consumed within the economy. Let us now relax this assumption. We may write

$$X = X_d + X_f$$

and

$$M = m + X_f$$

where m represents the portion of imports domestically consumed and X_f represents imports re-exported either directly or in the form of manufactures partially produced from foreign goods or services. With these relations in mind, it is now possible to write

$$Y = E_d + X_d$$

and

$$E = E_d + m$$

where E_d again represents domestic expenditure on domestically produced goods and services—that is, to be more precise, on the value added by domestic primary factors of production. To make the international accounts consistent, however, E_d, a country's domestic expenditure on domestic products, now has to be redefined to include also the re-exports of other countries of its own products toward itself. Let us use a two-country example and construct an income-expenditure matrix similar to that of the preceding section.

			Horizontal sum
	E_d^1	X_d^1	Y^1
	X_d^2	E_d^2	Y^2
Vertical sum	E^1	E^2	$E = Y$

For example, E_d^1 now includes also the import content of exports of country 2. In other words, domestic expenditure on domestic products is now understood to comprise both the purchases effected directly within country 1 and the purchases made indirectly through exports to, and re-exports from, country 2. Thus we may write

$$E_d^1 = e_d^1 + X_f^2$$

and

$$E_d^2 = e_d^2 + X_f^1$$

where the e_d's represent direct domestic expenditure on domestic products, while the X_f's represent the import content of exports of the country indicated by the superscript. Using these qualifications and the rationale of this adjustment, it is possible to construct a similar matrix for any number of countries, resembling that of the two-country situation just explained. The only additional complication that arises in this situation is that only the import content of exports of the "rest of the world" toward a country must be equal to the exports of that country returning to it through re-exports. Any other particular balance between any two countries, or between a country and a subgroup of countries, may not fulfill this condition.

PART II

Chapter 4

THE BALANCE-OF-PAYMENTS

Chapter

ADJUSTMENT MECHANISM:

4

OUTLINE AND PLAN OF

ANALYSIS

More than any other topic in the field of economics, the theory of balance-of-payments adjustment calls for a thorough work of organization and unification. There is a vast amount of literature dealing with this subject and, not surprisingly, a good deal of overlapping among different writings; arguments are restated, rediscovered, and arrived at through alternative roads over and over again. It is neither our task nor our desire here to criticize or try to explain this fact.

What we aim to do is to explain and analyze the adjustment process as fully and as efficiently as possible. We believe that important economies of scale can be realized through a unified exposition of the field. A full analysis of the adjustment process requires a good deal of close attention to be given to the many particular aspects of the problem. These will be examined one by one in the following chapters of Part II of this study. But, in order to acquire a coherent view of the problem of adjustment as a whole, the present chapter will be devoted to a general survey of the field.

Our first task is to explain what is understood by the balance-of-payments adjustment mechanism. It includes a host of theorems and causal relations, all having one thing in common, namely, the explanation of balance-of-payments fluctuations. Some of the adjustment theories, but not all, also explore the automatic equilibrating forces operating on the balance of payments. It is clear that no one single variable will explain all changes in the balance of payments. Going to one extreme of the spectrum of possible "adjustment theories," we might approach the problem as one in economic general equilibrium. Distinguished writers, such as Professors Samuelson[1]

[1] P. A. Samuelson, "Prices of Factors and Goods in General Equilibrium," *Review of Economic Studies,* Vol. XXI (1953–54) , pp. 1–20.

and Mosak,[2] have produced complete static models, in which international movements of goods and services are found explicitly as variables. The principal merit of this approach resides in its suitability in studying the existence, consistency, stability conditions, and uniqueness of solution of the system. It also comes as close as possible to the description of the real world, in the sense that it considers all goods and factors of production and corresponding prices as separate variables. Indeed, through the interdependence of all agents in the economy, the behavior of each particular firm should have its impact on the balance of payments.

Nevertheless, a general equilibrium approach to the adjustment problem has not proved the most fruitful. As in most fields of economics where answers to practical problems are sought, some generality had to be forgone in order to construct manageable theories and derive results simple enough to be applicable to questions of the real world. Thus the number of variables having an important role in the discussions of balance-of-payments adjustment is quite limited: domestic and foreign price levels, the exchange rate, the interest rate, real and money wages, income, employment, income distribution, productivity, and a number of institutional factors, such as monetary, fiscal, and commercial policy, are the most important. Time may also be explicitly introduced into the explanatory model of balance-of-payments adjustment.

The variables used in analyzing the balance-of-payments adjustment mechanism have depended on the concrete practice of international exchange in different periods and on the degree of the economists' understanding or scientific sophistication. Perhaps the oldest coherent theory is that of the *price-specie-flow mechanism* expounded as early as the eighteenth century by Hume and later elaborated by others. Like most of the classical doctrine, it stresses the importance of price changes in bringing about and maintaining the balance-of-payments equilibrium. The logical link between the state of the balance of payments and the price levels, with fixed exchange rates, is provided by the quantity theory of money, which was generally accepted in the classical period.

Variation in the velocity of circulation complicates the mechanism somewhat, but this possibility did not greatly trouble the classical writers. However, later in the nineteenth century, with the

---

[2] L. Mosak, *General Equilibrium Theory in International Trade* (Bloomington, Ind.: Principia Press, 1944) .

increasing use of short-term credit and fractional reserves, it became apparent that the price-specie-flow mechanism was not as simple and clear cut as was originally thought. Central banks under pressure from an extensive outflow of gold were able to resort to tight-money policies in their rediscount operations. Such tightening of credit would cause discrepancies between short-term rates in different countries, stimulating flows of short-term funds often sufficient to close the gap in the current balance of payments or even reverse the direction of gold movement. The Bank of England, then the financial center of the commercial world, operated on this principle in the nineteenth century and has not fully discontinued the practice to this day, though it is perhaps now applied with altered intensity and greater sophistication.

It is clear that the efficacy of the price-specie-flow mechanism would depend on the elasticities of demand for imports as much as the efficacy of exchange depreciation does. Moreover, adjustments of savings and investment are always a crucial factor in bringing about external balance in a fully employed economy. These considerations, again, hardly bothered the classical writers. Their confidence in automatic price adjustment and in the stability of all markets was complete. The smoothness of functioning of the foreign exchange markets and of the price mechanism in their period only reinforced their elasticity optimism.

With a virtually perfect stability of the price of gold throughout most of the 100 years preceding the First World War, there was very little concern or, for that matter, necessity to study the next important variable of the adjustment mechanism—the exchange rate. The theorists of international trade focused their attention on this variable only in this century and especially after the First World War, when many nations abandoned their gold parity and their time-honored exchange rates because of real and monetary maladjustments.

The discussion was and still is conducted mostly on the partial-analysis level. As we are going to see in the third part of this study, this analysis has its extension into the general equilibrium framework where stability of markets is also examined. In addition, exchange-rate fluctuations are not without relevance for the level of employment. Nevertheless, the main body of the exchange-rate theory of adjustment, largely influenced by Marshall, Lerner, and others, follows the partial-analysis approach.

The theory follows the classical line in the sense that it either (1) assumes a full-employment model, where all adjustments take place through price variations, or (2) leaves the analysis quite unrelated to the over-all conditions of the economy engaging in trade, by taking for its point of departure the supply and demand for imports and exports. Thus its principal concern is the foreign-exchange market, as defined by the demand and supply of foreign exchange and the market's equilibrium solution—the exchange rate. One of the most important considerations here is the stability of this market as expressed by the elasticities of supply and demand; as we shall see, these elasticities will determine the effectiveness of exchange depreciation as a tool of balance-of-payments adjustment. They will also determine how difficult or how costly it will be for the government to peg the exchange rate at a given level and, finally, will indicate the amplitude of fluctuations to be expected in a free market.

Because it is most difficult to make any a priori evaluations of the crucial elasticities involved directly in the foreign-exchange markets, most economists dealing with the subject have attempted, with greater or less sophistication, to express the stability criteria in terms of the underlying elasticities of demand and supply of exports and imports. This, of course, requires a study of the relation between the commodity supply and demand curves, on the one hand, and the foreign-exchange supply and demand, on the other.

The terms of trade, i.e., the ratio between the domestic and foreign prices, which played such an important role in the price-specie-flow mechanism, is also relevant in the discussion of exchange-rate adjustment. The importance of the terms of trade is further increased by the fact that traditionally, following from the earliest welfare propositions concerning international exchange, the terms of trade were used as a rough indicator of the gains from international trade. It is clear that if the exchange rate is altered by a country, unless foreign demand for imports and supply of exports are both infinitely elastic, the terms of trade will be affected in one way or another. Thus a problem subsidiary to that of exchange-rate alteration is the problem of how, exactly, the terms of trade will be affected by such a policy or by such an autonomous change in the foreign-exchange market.

Another topic that has to be dealt with in relation to the study of foreign-exchange markets is the transfer problem. Actually, it arises in the context both of price and of income analysis—and it is only fair to say that writers on the subject paid greater attention to the problem in the latter context; we shall return to the income adjustment of transfer presently. However, there is a good deal of interest in explaining how the foreign-exchange market and the terms of trade will be affected by autonomous capital or other transfers. Two solutions now have to be sought, one under conditions of freely fluctuating exchange rates, the other with rigid rates and an international gold standard. Also, in one sense at least, the classical assumption of constant real income will have to be abandoned in this case. Actually, a transfer must affect the incomes of the two countries, and consequently income as well as price parameters have to be used in the analysis.

Although the classical writers only rarely attempted to make a rigorous connection between the problems of external balance and the over-all internal equilibrium, an attempt will be made later in this part of the study to establish such a relation. It will be useful to us in showing the logical transition from the classical system predominantly based on the price mechanism to the post-Keynesian model, where the relation between external balance and the over-all level of income plays an all-important role. If in this way we conceive of the foreign-trade balance in the classical model as being only a component part of the total system, other variables will enter the balance-of-payments adjustment mechanism. Thus we often find flexibility of wages mentioned as one of the factors or conditions of adjustment. This concern about the conditions in the labor market is only subsidiary to the price flexibility, i.e., to the conditions of the goods markets. More important, however, the rates of interest, savings and investment, price expectations, and a score of other factors will now have to be introduced into the analysis. As we have already noted, this presentation of the classical adjustment mechanism in the context of the complete classical system offers perhaps the most convenient transition to the later, Keynesian, approach to our specific problem. It is variable national income and employment, savings, investment, and consumption as well as the money markets and the general price level that determine the levels of exports and imports in the Keynesian and post-Keynesian theory.

In its simplest, or what we may term its extreme formulation, the income approach is just the opposite of the classical approach. While in the former, prices and wages are assumed to be rigid, in the latter all depends on price adjustment. Also, the crucial assumption of the classical model, namely, the full employment of productive resources based on Say's law, is rejected in the Keynesian model, and its rejection actually constitutes the essential building block of the theory. Of course, this drastic reshuffling of assumptions, however realistic or unrealistic, throws light on a number of new elements not most welcome for those concerned with economic policy. While in the classical world all markets, including the foreign-exchange market, had their automatic stabilizing forces, this is no longer so in the present-day income approach, with fixed exchange rates. With exports and imports depending primarily on the levels of economic activity abroad and at home, respectively, there is no longer any reason why autonomous exports should be equal to autonomous imports. The gap between the two, i.e., the autonomous balance on current account, may or may not be filled by autonomous capital movements. Because there is no simple internal mechanism that will produce such an equality, the imbalance has to be settled either through gold transfers or through induced short-term capital movements. In either case, the balance of autonomous payments will be out of equilibrium.

Clearly, the system of freely fluctuating exchange rates is not incompatible with the Keynesian analysis. Our previous discussion of the fluctuating exchange rates pertains here also. Provided that the important condition of stability in the foreign-exchange market prevails, this market will again be sufficient to guarantee the external equilibrium. Strictly speaking, however, this equilibrium will be brought about through both price and income effects. The analysis of this case, as much as that of exchange-rate alteration, now becomes a good deal more complicated. It is no longer possible to assume the terms of trade constant throughout because, in terms of domestic prices of either trading country, relative prices of imports will vary with exchange-rate fluctuations. Thus it is necessary to move from a pure income analysis to one of both prices and incomes. We shall return presently to the interaction of price and income effects in adjustment.

In some recent writings an attempt has been made to circumvent the difficulty of dealing rigorously with price and real-income variations by introducing the concept of absorption, familiar to us from the preceding chapter. In defining the money deficit or surplus in the balance of payments as the difference between money income and (money) absorption, it may be possible to analyze more

conveniently the case of adjustment under full employment. Whatever happens to prices, the balance-of-payments deficit or surplus cannot be eliminated unless income and absorption are brought to
equality. In my opinion, the absorption approach does not contribute
anything essential to the income analysis of the adjustment process,
except perhaps as an analytical convenience to those who have become used to thinking in its terms. All the propositions resulting
from the absorption analysis may be derived from the more traditional income analysis, often with greater rigor and detail.

While the assumptions of the simplest Keynesian approach
to the balance-of-payments determination may have been adequate
for the depressed conditions of the period when the model was designed, it does not offer a satisfactory approximation of reality when
the economy always remains reasonably near full employment. In
such a situation, price and income changes will interact in determining the autonomous balance of payments. Actually, prices in all markets, not only in the commodity market, will become relevant. In
particular, wages and the interest rate play an important role in
the Keynesian model. Keynes himself did not introduce foreign
trade into his general theory in a systematic fashion. This enabled
him to assign to prices a secondary importance, simply assuming
that these were determined for the entire economy through the rules
of marginal productivity, the level of output, and a given money
wage.

Only later did writers attempt to translate the Keynesian assumptions rigorously into the situation of an open economy. As we
have already noted, this does not present any difficulty in the "depressed" case where all prices may be assumed rigid. However,
when prices, interest rates, and wages fluctuate at different rates in
different countries, the simple analysis no longer applies. One simple, but rather unsatisfactory, way of disposing of the explicit treatment of prices and real variables is to deal with incomes, exports,
and imports expressed in terms of money—as Keynes himself often
liked to do. This approach, however, which also is used in the absorption analysis, has the disadvantage of blurring the important relationships and behavioral functions on which the Keynesian analysis
is based. Thus, for example, an import function (or what we often
call the "propensity to import schedule") if expressed entirely in
terms of money rather than real income and real imports, will be
different, depending on how much movement from one point to an-

other of that function is accomplished through money and how much through real changes in income and imports.

It appears to the present writer that there is no simple way around the difficulties arising from the simultaneous consideration of price and income changes in the balance-of-payments adjustment process. Significant advances in this field of analysis have been made in recent years. By no means is it possible to say, however, that this treatment of the adjustment mechanism is complete or definitive. A good deal of work is needed in this field, both in order to supply the policy maker with the answers he needs to face present-day problems of international payments and in order to satisfy our scientific curiosity.

Another significant aspect of the present *status questionis* of the adjustment process is the introduction of dynamic analysis. Actually, this analysis pertains to and may be applied to all the explanatory models of the balance of payments that we have discussed so far. While time in the static and comparative static theories is only implied (in the sense that such theories mostly operate with variables expressing flows over an identical unit of time), the dynamic analysis introduces time explicitly as a variable. This enables us to study the transition of a given system from one equilibrium state to another and to establish its dynamic stability conditions. So far, the benefit from dynamic analysis of the adjustment mechanism has been theoretical. Application of the dynamic approach to concrete problems has been hindered by the extreme difficulty of establishing empirically all the data that would fit the abstract models. Thus, broadly speaking, the static and comparative static approach still remains the tool of the applied economist or the policy maker. This is not to say, however, that concrete application of dynamics could not prove fruitful in the future or that it would not be a useful field of scientific endeavor. In the next to the last chapter of this part of the book, we shall discuss briefly the dynamics of the adjustment process, in such a way as to familiarize the reader with the general nature and scope of the problem.

Short-term capital movements play an important and varied role in the balance-of-payments adjustment mechanism. These are of several types: some are autonomous and mostly profit motivated. They may be associated with the problems of monetary policy and with the theory of forward markets. Some are induced and to that extent may be treated like gold movements. Finally, such movements may be speculative in nature, arriving at a profit either from a controlled exchange-rate alteration or from fluctuations of a free exchange rate. In the latter case, short-term capital movements are of paramount importance for the stability of the foreign-exchange market and may play an important role in choosing between one exchange market arrangement and another. Because the theory of speculation is a subject quite apart from the rest of the adjustment theory, it requires special treatment of its own. The last chapter of Part II is devoted to that subject.

Chapter 5 | THE FOREIGN-EXCHANGE MARKET

5.1 Some Definitions

We may define the foreign-exchange market as all places where foreign exchange is traded. The reason why we are able to describe the foreign-exchange market thus is that the commodity traded is, under normal conditions, almost perfectly and speedily transferable and also is perfectly homogeneous in quality. If, for one reason or another, mobility from one trading place to another is impeded, it is preferable to speak of a number of markets of foreign exchange. The high degree of mobility, perfectly homogeneous product, and a large number of well-informed buyers and sellers make the foreign-exchange market one of the most perfect markets in existence.

Two sets of classification of the foreign-exchange market are useful. In the first place, there is not one but a large number of foreign currencies. Second, the total supply and demand of foreign currency is derived from different types of transactions, which provide a convenient classification for the study of the market for exchange.

The foreign-exchange market may be described through a set of supply and demand relations, expressing quantities of foreign exchange as functions of the rates of exchange. If we define the rate of exchange, r_i, as the number of dollars needed to purchase one unit of the ith currency and if there are n foreign currencies traded in the market, then we may write a set of demand relations

$$D_i = D_i(r_1, \ldots, r_n) \qquad i = 1, 2, \ldots, n \qquad (1.1)$$

and a set of supply relations

$$S_i = S_i(r_1, \ldots, r_n) \qquad i = 1, 2, \ldots, n \qquad (1.2)$$

The nature of each such function will depend on a number of factors; as we shall see later, the supply and demand for exports and imports in different countries, as well as incomes, are perhaps the most important.

Thus there are n rates of exchange to be determined. n equilibrium conditions

$$S_i = D_i \qquad i = 1, \ldots, n \qquad (1.3)$$

provide us with n equations that are necessary to find the n exchange rates. As we shall see later, there may be one or more or an infinity of sets of such solutions.

For each individual currency, we may distinguish a number of components of the total demand and supply of foreign exchanges. The different purposes for which foreign exchange is offered or demanded may make different portions of supply or demand react to exchange-rate fluctuations in different ways. Thus the amount of pounds needed for imports from England may vary a good deal, depending on the rate of exchange, because such imports will accordingly be more or less expensive in the United States. Demand for pounds for investment in the London short-term money market, on the other hand, may depend primarily on the rate of interest there and, possibly, on the rate of change of the exchange rate over time.

The classification of transactions explained in Chapter 2, distinguishing between goods, services, donations, short- and long-term capital movements, and gold movements, provides one functional way of analyzing the total supply and demand of foreign exchange. Above all, however, we should retain from Chapter 2 the dichotomy between autonomous and accommodating supply and demand for foreign exchange. Henceforth, whenever we speak of supply and demand for foreign exchange, we shall mean the *autonomous supply* or *autonomous demand,* unless otherwise specified.

We may now proceed to define some other concepts that are useful in analyzing the foreign-exchange market. One such concept is the *excess demand* for foreign exchange; it is the difference between demand and supply of a given foreign exchange, at a given set of rates of exchange of the n different foreign currencies. A complete schedule of excess demand for the ith currency is defined as

$$ED_i = f_i(r_1, \ldots, r_n) = D_i - S_i \qquad (1.4)$$

Further, we define the supply and demand elasticity for the ith foreign exchange with respect to the jth exchange rate as the relative change in supply or demand of the ith currency divided by the relative change in the rate of exchange, r_j: i.e.,

$$E_s^{i/j} = S_{i,r_j} \frac{r_j}{S_i} \quad \text{and} \quad E_d^{i/j} = D_{i,r_j} \frac{r_j}{D_i}$$

where the subscript r_j following S_i or D_i represents the partial derivative of the function with respect to r_j.

5.2 The Forward Market

Any commodity, service, or currency to be delivered at a given future date and paid for either at present or at any future date may have a special market of its own, provided that there is a sufficient number of buyers and sellers. Markets settling such future purchases exist in a number of primary commodities and also in foreign exchange. In all cases, their function is to avoid possible loss that could result to buyers from a price increase and to sellers from a price drop. If a forward market in foreign exchange is established, all uncertainty as to future transactions may be eliminated for those trading in the forward market. This method of averting risk is often referred to as "hedging."

In the particular case of foreign exchange, any firm may carry on its balance sheet a number of claims in foreign currency (A) and a number of liabilities in foreign currency (B), both due at some future date, say, in 3 months. If A is larger than B in value, the firm is in a *long position,* and, after the 3 months have elapsed, it will hold a net amount $(A - B)$ in foreign exchange. If B exceeds A, the firm is said to be in a *short position,* and in 3 months it will need $(B - A)$ of foreign currency to settle its net debt. In the first case, such a firm may proceed to sell foreign exchange forward; in the second it will buy forward.

If both at home and in the foreign country investment in the short-term capital markets by foreigners is absolutely prevented by exchange authorities, there will be no tie between the spot and the forward exchange markets. Price in the former will be determined by the situation of supply and demand resulting from present autonomous transactions, and in the latter, by autonomous clearing of short and long positions of those who desire to avoid exchange risk as well as by speculative transactions. Thus the spot and forward rates may be very different.

If, however, it is possible for a foreigner to lend or borrow in at least one of the two countries, the two rates of exchange must be in a definite relation to each other, depending on the short-term rates of interest in the two countries. This may easily be shown in the following way. The horizontal distance represents the period of 3 months separating the spot from the future market; r and r_f are the spot and the forward rates of exchange (prices of B's currency in terms of A's currency), respectively, while i_a and i_b represent the short-term rates of interest in A and in B.

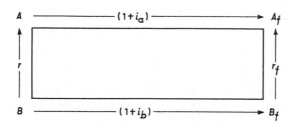

The four important positions in our diagram are the four corners of the rectangle. Transfer from one such position of any amount of currency may be effected, if in the direction of the arrows, by multiplying by the appropriate factor; if against the arrow, by dividing by the same factor. Thus, for example, $1\pounds$ at position B_f, i.e., 1 pound in England (country B) in 3 months, may be transferred to the present in B into $(1\pounds)/(1+i_b)$ and to the present in A, into $(1\pounds) r/(1+i_b)$, and finally, from the present in A it may be transferred to the future in A into $[(1\pounds)/(1+i_b)] r(1+i_a)$. But this amount, if proceeding in the other direction "around the lake," may also be obtained through the forward market as $(1\pounds) r_f$. It is clear that if both directions of transfer are open, the two expressions must be equal. If they were not, competitive forces would have to bring them into equality. Thus we may write $[(1\pounds)/(1+i_b)] r(1+i_a) = (1\pounds) r_f$, and, consequently,

$$r_f = r \frac{1+i_a}{1+i_b} \tag{2.1}$$

In words, the important result to retain is that if the two rates of interest in the two countries are equal, the present and the forward rate of exchange should be equal. If the domestic rate is greater (smaller) than the foreign rate of short-term interest, the forward rate will be greater (smaller) than the spot rate.

If, for example, with equal interest rates the forward exchange rate were 1 per cent below the spot rate, it would be worthwhile for traders in A having a long position to hedge by borrowing at present the corresponding amount in the foreign money market, buying domestic currency spot, and investing in the domestic money market. But this would lower the supply of forward foreign currency and increase the spot supply. Thus the forward rate of exchange would have to go up and the spot rate down, until traders became indifferent between one way of hedging and the other; this would happen at $r = r_f$, as defined in (2.1).

Empirical observation of spot and forward rates generally does not bear out exactly the theoretical relation 2.1. Small differences between actual forward rates and those predicted by relation 2.1 may arise for a number of reasons. Transaction costs, imperfect knowledge, partial controls of short-term capital movements, liquidity considerations, and imperfectly competitive behavior on the part of bankers and dealers provide an ample explanation of such discrepancies.

5.3 Stability of the Foreign-Exchange Market and the Balance of Payments: Fixed, Adjustable, and Freely Fluctuating Exchange Rates

In the remaining sections of this chapter we shall restrict ourselves to the discussion of a simple case where only one type of foreign exchange is traded. We may refer to such an exchange as *pounds* and to the domestic currency as *dollars*. Many of the results obtained for this simple case may be generalized for a larger number of currencies. These generalizations are sometimes quite straightforward, and the reader may use the analysis here presented as a starting point in deriving such results. The literature dealing with the subject is almost exclusively restricted to the two-currency case. In practical applications of the theory to concrete problems it is often possible (and quite legitimate in view of the crudeness of the data) to consider all foreign currencies as a single currency; in particular, such a simplification is possible if all exchange rates may be assumed to fluctuate in about the same way.

Let us now have a closer look at the foreign-exchange market where only pounds are traded. A typical supply curve S and demand curve D for foreign exchange are shown here in Figure 5.3.1 a. Next to it, in Figure 5.3.1 b, we have derived the excess demand curve ED. In a later section of this chapter we shall derive rigorously these functions for the case wherein they are generated by international current

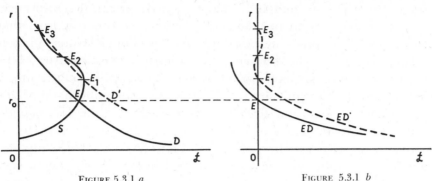

FIGURE 5.3.1 *a*   FIGURE 5.3.1 *b*

transactions. At present, however, we may think of the supply and demand curves as two relations between the rate of exchange and the quantity of foreign exchange (either supplied or demanded) that would be obtained from a controlled experiment wherein the exchange rate would be varied and corresponding quantities recorded. While such an experimental construction of the schedules may be performed, we assume that all prices, including the rate of interest and factor earnings, and quantities of all goods and services and productive factors are permitted to adjust to their equilibrium level. Moreover, the total supply of money in both countries is assumed constant.

Keeping in mind that the supply of foreign exchange is primarily generated by foreign importers and our exporters and the demand for it by our importers and foreign exporters, we may now point out some of the important properties of the two functions. Most likely there will be some positive exchange rate small enough to make our goods so expensive to foreign buyers that no pounds would be offered at all. As the rate of exchange increases above this level, the supply of foreign exchange will be increasing as more and more commodities are now exported. At some quite high rate, foreign importers will be obtaining increasing amounts of dollars, sufficient to purchase more commodities with a rising exchange rate, without increasing their own supply of pounds. This is the point of maximum supply of pounds; also, at this point, the elasticity of supply drops down to zero. Beyond this point, it is negative, as is the slope of the supply curve. At very high rates of exchange the supply curve will approach asymptotically the vertical axis. On the limit, at an infinite rate of exchange, it would take any finite small fraction of a pound to purchase any number of dollars. However theoretically interesting this case may be, it has very little practical significance.

Turning now to the demand relation, we observe, first, that there should be some rate of exchange high enough to make prices of all foreign goods and services prohibitive to domestic buyers. This exchange rate corresponds to the zero-demand point, or the upper intercept of the demand curve. Elasticity in the neighborhood of this point is very large and negative. As pounds become increasingly less expensive in terms of dollars, larger and larger amounts of foreign exchange will be purchased. Thus the elasticity of the demand curve throughout may be assumed negative; whether it will have a lower intercept or approach the foreign-exchange axis asymptotically will depend on whether domestic buyers ever reach a satiation point. Again, this question has very little real significance whenever any degree of discipline can be assumed on the part of monetary authorities.

If the rate of exchange is allowed to fluctuate freely, its equilibrium level will be determined by the equality of autonomous supply and demand. Such a "normal" equilibrium is found in our diagram at r_0. As in any other market, this equilibrium is stable because the elasticity of supply exceeds in algebraic value the elasticity of demand. The excess demand curve at this level of r is downward-sloping, and the excess demand is equal to zero.

Another, rather unusual, situation arises if the demand curve assumes a position such as D' and consequently the excess demand curve a position such as ED'. In this case three different rates of exchange fulfill the equilibrium conditions. However, the stability conditions,

$$E_s > E_d$$

are found only at E_3 and E_1. The above inequality is not fulfilled at E_2; also at this point the excess demand curve is upward- rather than downward-sloping. This means that if the market equilibrium rate were moved slightly upward from E_2, more foreign exchange would be demanded than supplied, and this, through competitive bidding, would keep driving the rate of exchange upward until E_3 is reached. The same argument holds for any small displacement downward from E_2. The important fact is that we can always be sure, if one or more unstable equilibria are present, that there will be a highest and a lowest equilibrium (such as E_3 and E_1 in our example) that will be stable and that would prevent the rate of exchange from "running away" to either zero or infinity. The shapes of the two functions, as discussed above, guarantee this proposition under the static assumptions made here. Of course, if the monetary authorities of one of the two countries were willing to expand the money supply to infinity, this might happen—not, however, because of an unstable static equilibrium in the foreign-exchange market but because of the infinite expansion of money causing one of the market schedules to move to an absurd position.

Every market, whether of foreign exchange or not, where one commodity is traded and the other commodity used as *numeraire,* may be transformed into another market, its mirror image, where the *numeraire* is considered as the commodity traded and the commodity traded as *numeraire.* The equilibrium price in one market will be the reciprocal of the price in the other market. Although such transformation is of little use in most markets, the analysis of the foreign-exchange market, wherein both the commodity traded and the means of payment are currencies, may often be simplified, thanks to this symmetry. A demand curve for dollars can easily be derived from a supply curve of pounds by plotting, for every given rate of exchange r, the quantity of pounds supplied times r, against the reciprocal of r (i.e., $1/r = R$), where R is the price of dollars expressed in terms of pounds. The reader may verify that it is only the general shape of the two curves in Figure 5.3.1 a that yields supply and demand curves of similar shapes in the transformed market. It is often useful to realize that every proposition that we may make concerning the situation above an equilibrium in the dollar market we also make concerning the situation below the corresponding equilibrium in the market of pounds.

Let us now use the simple representation of the foreign-exchange market in interpreting balance-of-payments equilibria and disequilibria. Whether under freely fluctuating, fixed, or adjustable fixed exchange rates, it is possible to assume the existence of an autonomous supply function and an autonomous demand function of foreign exchange. As we have indicated in Chapter 3, these two relations do not depend on the balance of payments itself or on the foreign-exchange market, but rather it is these functions that define the market of foreign currency.

Now in what way the equilibrium will be attained depends on the particular institutional circumstances. If the authorities of both countries do not interfere in any way with the operation of the foreign-exchange market, no lasting payments problem can arise, and the foreign-exchange market will find its equilibrium solution. From the preceding discussion it follows that it is most unlikely that such an equilibrium would persist if unstable—at least in the real world where there are always some disturbances present that are sufficient to move the market away from an unstable solution.

If the authorities of both countries define the prices of their respective currencies in terms of gold or in terms of the foreign currency and are willing and able to buy or sell unlimited amounts of their own currency in terms of gold or in terms of the foreign currency, then the rate of exchange, by definition, will be equal to the parity thus established. In this situation, however, autonomous supply and demand of foreign exchange, i.e., autonomous receipts and expenditures of a country, no longer have to be equal to each other. This will happen whenever the legal exchange rate differs from the competitive equilibrium rate. Such a situation is depicted in Figure 5.3.2, where r_0 is the official rate and r_e the autonomous equilibrium rate.

Since r_e here is above r_0, the government of the dollar country is forced to supply OA' worth of foreign currency to the market in order to keep the rate at r_0. This it may do either by depleting its reserves of pounds, or by buying pounds for gold or dollars from the authorities of the foreign country. Thus, assuming that the excess demand curve pertains to the accounting period of the balance of

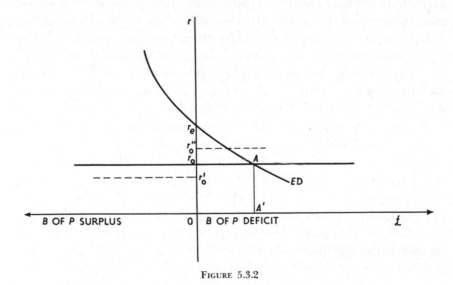

FIGURE 5.3.2

payments, OA' represents the deficit in the balance of autonomous payments of the dollar country expressed in foreign currency, and the rectangle defined by the two axes, O and A, represents the deficit in terms of the home currency. A minor modification is needed if the transfer of gold from one country to the other, or transfer of foreign currency, is not perfectly costless. If, for example, it cost $r_0'' - r_0$ dollars to transport 1 pound worth of gold from the United States to England in order to purchase pounds in the latter country, then pounds supplied in the foreign-exchange market through this accommodating operation can be sold only at the price r_0'' rather than r_0. Here r_0'' is the so-called "gold-export point."

A situation symmetrical in all respects arises if r_e falls short of r_0. The surplus of the balance of autonomous payments will now be measured to the left of the vertical axis, as an abscissa if in terms of pounds; as a rectangle defined by the abscissa and the ordinate, if in terms of dollars. Similarly, if gold has to be shipped from the United Kingdom to the United States in order to purchase pounds in excess supply for dollars, the pounds may be bought only at a rate r_0', smaller than r_0, that is, at the rate corresponding to the gold-import point.

If the governments of the two countries commit themselves to buy and sell gold at the given parities of their respective currencies, without performing any other stabilizing activity, the rate of exchange will be permitted to fluctuate freely between the gold import and export points. That is, whenever the equilibrium rate r_e falls within that margin, it will determine the actual rate of exchange. Whenever it falls outside the gold limits, the latter will determine the actual rate, and, of course, accommodating movements of gold will take place at the rate called for by the level of excess demand, at the relevant gold point.

5.4 Goods Markets and the Foreign-Exchange Market

The vast majority of the literature dealing with problems of balance-of-payments stability and with the effects of exchange-rate alteration on the autonomous balance of payments makes the attempt to relate the conditions of the foreign-exchange market to the conditions in the export and import market. Although this approach is of less generality than the direct discussion of conditions in the foreign-exchange market, it is very advantageous whenever we try to apply economic theory to concrete problems of policy. Even those who are actively concerned with the problems of external balance will have very little, if any, intuitive or experimental knowledge of the supply and demand elasticities in the foreign-exchange market. Often, however, we hear economists assert that the elasticity of demand for imports or exports of such and such country is high or low. The nature of the products being traded may offer such insights. Thus it may be advantageous to relate the conditions in the exchange market, crucial in discussing balance-of-payments problems, to conditions in the export and import markets.

By doing this, we actually restrict our definition of the foreign-exchange market to include only such supply and demand for foreign exchange as derives from current transactions. This often restricts the generality of analysis only very little. A greater complication arises from the fact that it is quite difficult to design conditions in the two economies considered that will leave the demand and supply curves for exports and imports unaltered when conditions in the exchange market are changing. One such set of conditions is to assume that the volume of trade in comparison to total product or income of the two countries is very small. In this case, income effects, monetary effects, and structural price adjustment within the economy resulting from changing export and import prices may be assumed negligible. Also, to avoid other complications, the assumption is often made that exports and imports each consist of only one homogeneous commodity.

If exports and imports represent an appreciable fraction of national income and expenditure, relating commodity markets to the foreign-exchange market causes some difficulty. This difficulty stems from the fact that the export supply schedules can generally no longer be considered independently of import prices, or import demand schedules independently of export prices. Hence, it is illegitimate to discuss the conditions in the export market in isolation from conditions in the import market, and vice-versa. Of course, it would be possible to introduce such additional assumptions into a theoretical model. But this would make the analysis virtually unmanageable. Also, it might be unwarranted because the nonmonetary general equilibrium analysis of the export and import markets takes all such interdependencies into account. This approach will be presented in Part III of this book.

Some writers, in an attempt to simplify the analysis, make the assumption of an infinite elasticity of supply of exports. But this is legitimate, if at all, only in a situation of less than full employment.

Yet the study of pure price effects and exchange-rate adjustment is usually conducted in a classical full-employment setting. To circumvent this difficulty, some international economists substitute for the assumption of infinite supply elasticity the assumption of constancy of export prices, in terms of domestic currency, guaranteed by an appropriate monetary policy. Even under such conditions, however, the demand for imports will depend not only on the import price but also on the conditions in the export market, reflected by the monetary policy stabilizing the price of exports.

With these observations in mind, we may proceed to show the relation between the supply of foreign exchange for current-account transactions and the export market that generates such supply. It will be left to the reader to establish such a relation for the demand function of foreign exchange. Later in this section we shall show rigorously the relations between the elasticities in the import and export markets, on the one hand, and the elasticities of supply and of demand for foreign exchange, on the other.

Pounds will be supplied in the foreign-exchange market, in order to purchase for dollars in the United States commodities demanded by the British consumer. In terms of pound prices, the demand curve for United States exports is fixed; in the somewhat cumbersome, but very useful, construction of Figure 5.4.1 it is depicted as D_x. The vertical axis passing through O measures prices of United States exports in British currency and the horizontal axis the physical

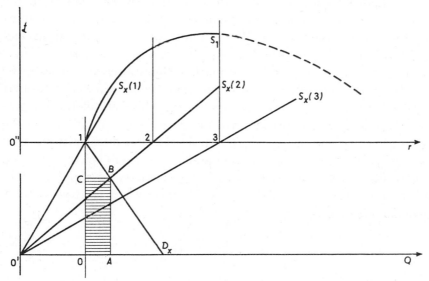

FIGURE 5.4.1

quantity of such exports. The supply curve of United States exports will be steeper or flatter in the British market, depending on whether the rate of exchange (i.e., price of pounds in terms of dollars) is low or high. Supply curves for three rates of exchange, $S_x(1)$, $S_x(2)$, and $S_x(3)$, corresponding to rates of exchange $r = 1$, $r = 2$, and $r = 3$, are shown in the diagram. They determine three equilibrium levels of exports and three equilibrium pound prices. All that has to be done in order to obtain the supply schedule of foreign exchange is to relate the three rates of exchange to corresponding products of the pound prices and quantities of exports as obtained by the construction.

This may easily be done in the diagram itself if we observe that all the rotating supply curves have to pass through one point on the horizontal axis, O', and that their intersections along any horizontal ray (not identical with the horizontal axis passing through O' and O) must show proportions of the different rates of exchange. Thus the three supply curves intersect a new horizontal axis passing through O'' at points 1, 2, and 3 units of distance to the right of O''. Using this axis for measuring the rate of exchange and plotting on the coordinate the areas of the rectangles, such as $OABC$ (the number of pounds supplied), we obtain the complete supply curve of foreign exchange, $S_\pounds$. We notice that at the rate of exchange $r = 3$ the supply of pounds is maximum—the elasticity of D_x being unity—and declines for higher rates of exchange.

When we want to study the relation between changes in the foreign-exchange market and changes in the export and import markets, it is often unnecessary to know the complete supply and demand schedules in the export and import markets and their relation to the foreign-exchange market. Sometimes it suffices to be able to relate elasticities of supply and demand in a particular foreign-trade market to the corresponding elasticity of the foreign-exchange supply or demand schedule. As we are going to see in the remaining part of this section, a simple relation does exist between the elasticities in the trade markets and the foreign-exchange market.

Using E_s and E_d to represent the elasticity of supply and of demand for foreign exchange, respectively, we may express these two magnitudes as

$$E_s = E_s(s_x, d_x) \tag{4.1}$$

and

$$E_d = E_d(s_m, d_m) \tag{4.2}$$

where s and d represent the elasticities of supply and demand, respectively, and the subscripts x and m are used to indicate exports and imports.

The derivation of these functions in explicit form is quite straightforward. We may write the supply curve of foreign exchange (pounds) as

$$S = S(r) \tag{4.3}$$

and the supply and demand functions of exports, generating this supply, as

$$S_x = S_x(P_\$) \tag{4.4}$$

and

$$D_x = D_x(P_\pounds) \tag{4.5}$$

where $P_\$$ and $P_\pounds$ represent dollar and pound prices, respectively. In order to be able to establish equilibrium in the export market and thus derive the supply of pounds, it is necessary to express the dollar price in terms of the pound price and the rate of exchange, i.e.,

$$P_\$ = P_\pounds \cdot r \tag{4.6}$$

Substituting relation 4.6 in 4.4, we obtain

$$S_x = S_x(P_\pounds \cdot r) \tag{4.7}$$

We know that the elasticity of supply of foreign exchange E_s is actually

$$E_s = S'(r) \frac{r}{S} \tag{4.8}$$

where S' is used to express a derivative of S, and S is equal to the product of pound price and the quantity of exports, i.e., using relation 4.5,

$$S = P_\pounds \cdot D_x(P_\pounds) \tag{4.9}$$

Thus we may write $S'(r)$ as

$$S'(r) = \frac{dS}{dr} = \frac{dP_\pounds}{dr} \cdot (P_\pounds \cdot D'_x + D_x) \tag{4.10}$$

From the equilibrium conditions of the export market, i.e.,

$$S_x = D_x \tag{4.11}$$

after differentiating with respect to r and rearranging, we obtain

$$\frac{dP_\pounds}{dr} = \frac{P_\pounds \cdot S'_x}{D'_x - S'_x \cdot r} \tag{4.12}$$

where "primes" again are used to indicate derivatives.

Substituting 4.12 in 4.10 and noticing that $r = P_\$/P_\pounds$, after a little reorganization of the terms in the fraction, using the fact that S_x and D_x in equilibrium are equal to exports, and using relation 4.9, we finally obtain

$$S'(r) = \frac{S}{r} \cdot \frac{1}{(D'_x/rS'_x) - 1} \left(1 + D'_x \frac{P_\pounds}{D_x}\right) \tag{4.13}$$

Thence, using the definitions of the elasticity of demand for exports, d_x, and of the elasticity of supply of exports, s_x, we may write the important result

$$E_s = \frac{d_x + 1}{(d_x/s_x) - 1} \tag{4.14}$$

A perfectly analogous computation (omitted here) leads to a similar expression for the elasticity of demand for foreign exchange:

$$E_d = \frac{s_m + 1}{(s_m/d_m) - 1} \tag{4.15}$$

where the subscript m represents imports.

Relations 4.14 and 4.15 are very important because they permit the derivation of a large number of important theorems concerning the balance-of-payments adjustment mechanism. Such derivations are quite simple, much simpler than those usually found in the literature dealing with the subject. We shall refer to these relations on a number of occasions in the later sections of this chapter.

In concluding this section we should again bring to mind the symmetry between the dollar and pound markets. Relations 4.14 and 4.15 show the elasticities of supply and demand for pounds. The elasticities of supply and demand for dollars in terms of pound prices will be obtained simply by replacing in the right-hand side of relation 4.14 the subscript x by m and in relation 4.15 m by x.

5.5 Stability in the Foreign-Exchange Market Defined by the Export and Import Elasticities

We have indicated in the preceding sections of this chapter how important a role the elasticities in the foreign-exchange market play in any concrete consideration of an exchange-rate alteration. For example, in Figure 5.3.2 we observed that if the rate of exchange were moved from its equilibrium level r_e downward, an autonomous deficit in the balance of payments would result for the dollar country. This deterioration in the balance of payments is closely linked to the fact that the equilibrium at r_e is stable; if it were unstable, i.e., if the *ED* curve at r_0 were upward-sloping, a depreciation of the foreign currency (appreciation of domestic currency) would improve, rather than worsen, the balance-of-payments position of the dollar country.

Thus, for small movements in the neighborhood of the equilibrium rate r_0, the conditions for stability and instability of the foreign-exchange market are perfectly identical with the conditions for the balance of autonomous payments to improve or deteriorate from the depreciation of the home currency. The earlier writers fully accepted this identity of conditions for all cases and discussed problems of appreciation and devaluation in terms of the stability conditions. As we shall see in the next section, this correspondence is somewhat modified if in the initial situation the balance of payments were out of balance; actually, it is this case that is more pertinent to the problems of exchange-rate alteration, because, in practice, there would be very little reason to depreciate or to appreciate if the balance of autonomous payments were in balance.

Nevertheless, it will be useful to consider at first the case of stability and instability as determined by the elasticities of the export and import markets and thus establish the relation between changes in the exchange rate and the balance of payments. The stability conditions require that the elasticity of supply in the exchange market be larger in algebraic value than the elasticity of demand. Assuming that only transactions on current account depend on the rate of exchange and using relations 4.14 and 4.15, this yields

$$\frac{d_x + 1}{(d_x/s_x) - 1} > \frac{s_m + 1}{(s_m/d_m) - 1} \tag{5.1}$$

and, after regrouping and elimination of the fractions,

$$s_x \cdot s_m \cdot (1 + d_x + d_m) - d_x \cdot d_m \cdot (1 + s_x + s_m) < 0 \tag{5.2}$$

or

$$1 + d_x + d_m < \frac{d_x \cdot d_m}{s_x \cdot s_m} (1 + s_x + s_m) \tag{5.3}$$

We notice that the right side of the latter inequality must always be positive, except, of course, if either the export or the import commodity were an inferior good, subject to "Giffen's paradox." Thus the market could be unstable only if the left side of the last inequality were positive, i.e., if the sum of the demand elasticities were larger than -1. But even under such conditions stability could be found, provided only that the right side were large enough. Thus the positive sign of the left-hand side is only a necessary, but not a sufficient, condition of instability or of balance-of-payments deterioration after devaluation of currency. To state the same proposition in reverse, the negative sign of the left-hand side is a sufficient, but not a necessary, condition of stability in the foreign-exchange market.

It is only in the special case where the elasticities of supply of exports and imports are infinite that the above-stated conditions are both necessary and sufficient. In this case, the right side of the inequality becomes zero, and thus the market must be stable whenever the left-hand side is negative. It is the latter case that is usually referred to—rightly or wrongly—as the Marshall-Lerner conditions for devaluation or stability. Again from the symmetry of markets it follows that whatever proposition we have made so far about the dollar market we have also made concerning the pound market. Actually, the numerical value of the left-hand side of inequality 5.2 will be the same, regardless of which exchange market we consider.

5.6 The Balance of Autonomous Payments on Current Account and the Rate of Exchange

In the preceding section we have roughly established the direction of change in the balance of payments that will result from an alteration in the exchange rate. It may be more interesting, however, for practical policy considerations to evaluate exactly the change in the balance of payments that may be expected from a given alteration in the rate of exchange. In the preceding section we have only dealt with the case in which the autonomous payments and receipts on current account are initially in equilibrium; we shall relax this assumption here and assume, more realistically, that the balance of payments on current account is out of equilibrium prior to devaluation or appreciation.

The change in the pound value of exports of the dollar country resulting from a small relative change in the rate of exchange will be equal to the initial value of exports times the elasticity of supply of foreign exchange times the assumed relative change in the exchange rate. Mathematically,

$$dX_\pounds = E_s \cdot X_\pounds \cdot \frac{dr}{r} \tag{6.1}$$

Similarly, if we let $M_\pounds$ represent the pound value of imports, the change in this value resulting from exchange-rate alteration is

$$dM_\pounds = E_d \cdot M_\pounds \cdot \frac{dr}{r} \tag{6.2}$$

Consequently, the change in the balance of payments, expressed in terms of foreign currency $(\pounds)$ will be

$$dBP_\pounds = dX_\pounds - dM_\pounds = \frac{dr}{r} \cdot (X_\pounds \cdot E_s - M_\pounds \cdot E_d) \tag{6.3}$$

It is now apparent that if exports are equal to imports, all the conclusions relative to stability and balance of payments obtain. If, however, current exports and imports are not equal in the initial situation, these conditions may be altered. Thus, for example, even with the elasticity of supply of foreign exchange larger in algebraic value than the demand elasticity, a surplus balance of payments (i.e., $X > M$) may improve from appreciation of currency; or a deficit balance may improve, even though the elasticity of demand for foreign exchange exceeds in algebraic value the elasticity of supply. It is clear that such situations may arise because the initial values of exports and imports may give different weights to the elasticities of supply and demand for foreign exchange in relation 6.3. The reader may use the method of calculation used in the preceding section to establish for himself a new relation, in terms of the elasticities of supply and demand for exports and imports, expressing the condition of balance-of-payments improvement as a result of devaluation; it becomes

$$s_x \cdot s_m \cdot \frac{X_\pounds}{M_\pounds} \cdot \left(1 + d_x + d_m \cdot \frac{M_\pounds}{X_\pounds}\right) - d_x \cdot d_m \cdot \left(1 + \frac{X_\pounds}{M_\pounds} \cdot s_x + s_m\right) + \left(1 - \frac{X_\pounds}{M_\pounds}\right) d_m s_x < 0 \tag{6.4}$$

Often a country will be concerned not so much about what will happen to its balance of payments as a result of exchange-rate changes, in terms of foreign currency, as in terms of its domestic currency. Also, it may be concerned with the amplitude of exchange-rate fluctuations in a free market resulting from given autonomous shifts in the supply and demand of domestic, rather than foreign, currency. In this case it will be preferable to express the relation between the exchange-rate changes and the balance of payments in domestic currency rather than in foreign currency, as we have done so far. A simple inspection of the graphical representation of the foreign-exchange market, such as that illustrated by Figure 5.3.2, will convince the reader that the change in the balance of payments expressed in one currency will not be proportional to the change in the balance expressed in the other currency. This is immediately apparent from the fact that the deficit (or surplus) in terms of foreign exchange is measured on the abscissa of the diagram, while the deficit (or surplus) in terms of the domestic currency is measured as the area of the rectangle formed by the abscissa (foreign exchange) and the coordinate (the rate of exchange). Actually, for a small change in the exchange rate, the balance might improve in terms of foreign exchange and deteriorate in terms of domestic currency. Such a situation is the more likely, the greater the initial deficit and the smaller the algebraic difference between the elasticities of supply and demand of foreign exchange.

Thus let us write the balance of payments in terms of domestic currency ($) as

$$BP_\$ = r \cdot BP_\pounds \qquad (6.5)$$

and differentiating

$$dBP_\$ = dr \cdot BP_\pounds + r \cdot dBP_\pounds \qquad (6.6)$$

But, substituting relation 6.3 in 6.6, we obtain, after a slight rearrangement,

$$dBP_\$ = \frac{dr}{r} \cdot r \cdot (X_\pounds - M_\pounds) + \frac{dr}{r} \cdot r \cdot (X_\pounds \cdot E_s - M_\pounds \cdot E_d) \qquad (6.7)$$

i.e.,

$$dBP_\$ = \frac{dr}{r} \cdot [X_\$ \cdot (1 + E_s) - M_\$ \cdot (1 + E_d)] \qquad (6.8)$$

because the pound values in 6.7 multiplied by r are equal to corresponding dollar values of exports and imports. Again it may be preferable to rewrite relation 6.8, using the elasticities of the exports and import markets rather than those of the foreign-exchange market. Using relations 4.14 and 4.15, this is extremely simple and is left to the reader.

It will be noticed that if, initially, the balance of payments is in equilibrium, i.e., $X_\$ = M_\$$, then relation 6.8 will be simplified to a relation resembling relation 6.3, except for the fact that the value of trade is expressed in domestic rather than foreign currency. For any small displacement from equilibrium, the change in the balance of payments will be exactly the same, whether expressed in terms of domestic or of foreign currency, provided, of course, that one is converted into the other at the original rate of exchange.

As a question of policy, it is often argued that devaluation of a currency as a tool for restoring external balance is undesirable on grounds of the low elasticities of demand for imports. From relations 4.14 and 4.15, it is immediately apparent that, if this is so, for any "normal" values of the elasticities of supply both the elasticities of supply and demand for foreign exchange are likely to be low and negative. Even if this does not lead to instability in the autonomous foreign-exchange market, the slope of the excess demand curve for foreign exchange is likely to be quite high in absolute value. Under such conditions, equilibration of the accounts might require an appreciable alteration of the rate of exchange. We shall observe later, in Chapter 8, that if income effects are also introduced into the adjustment mechanism, such difficulties in restoring the external balance through devaluation may become even more serious.

If the elasticities of demand for imports are so low as to render the foreign-exchange market unstable, then appreciation of currency rather than devaluation can be used in restoring the external balance.

If the elasticities of demand for imports are low, it also follows from the analysis of the present section that a free exchange rate will fluctuate rather widely as a result of relatively small autonomous shifts in the supply of and/or demand for foreign exchange. It may be argued, however—and on quite solid grounds—that exchange speculation and interest arbitrage might provide a sufficient stabilizer.

Also, the question still remains to be answered whether the

elasticities are in actuality so low. We will return to some of these problems with greater thoroughness later in this chapter.

5.7 The Exchange Rate, the Terms of Trade, and the Balance-of-Payments Adjustment

In Part III of our study we shall turn in greater detail to the discussion of the terms of trade, i.e., to the ratio between export and import prices. Let us simply observe here that the *terms of trade* is an important index expressing the purchasing power of exports in paying for imports. If a country's terms of trade improve, less of its real product exported will be needed to purchase one unit of real product of the rest of the world and vice-versa. It is clear from our preceding discussion in this chapter that, unless some special conditions are fulfilled (to be stated presently), the terms of trade will move in one direction or another whenever the rate of exchange changes either as a matter of deliberate policy or, in free adjustment, in response to changing conditions in the exchange market. Thus the balance of payments, if the rate of exchange is pegged at a given rate, will be related to the terms of trade and the terms of trade to the balance of payments. Also an autonomous transfer from one country to the other will affect the export and import prices of the trading partners. While we shall concentrate in greater detail on the transfer problem in the next section, our present task is to relate the terms of trade to the key concepts and variables of the foreign-exchange and the export and import markets.

To illustrate the problem in a simple example, consider a case in which both trading countries, for one reason or another, are able to supply their exports at a fixed price in terms of their domestic currencies. It is easy enough to see that in this situation the terms of trade $(TT = P_x/P_m)$ of either country will vary in inverse proportion with the changes in the exchange rate, defined as the price of foreign currency in terms of domestic currency. This will hold true whether the exchange-rate fluctuation is a result of official exchange-rate adjustment or free rate fluctuation. Thus, if under our assumptions the dollar were devalued by 1 per cent, the terms of trade, whether expressed in domestic or foreign prices, would deteriorate by 1 per cent.

Similarly, if the elasticities of demand for imports in both countries were infinite, the terms of trade of each country would always move in proportion with the exchange rate. If, for example, the dollar were devalued by 10 per cent, export prices in terms of dollars would increase by the corresponding amount, while dollar import prices would remain unchanged. Thus the terms of trade would improve by 10 per cent. It is evident that the same result would be obtained for the terms of trade if pound prices were considered; however, in this case the export prices would remain unchanged, while those of imports would go down by 10 per cent.

In the "normal" case, where neither both supply nor both demand elasticities are infinite, the result is no longer so clear cut or self-evident. However, it may easily be derived. Suppose that the rate of exchange of the dollar country is changed by dr This may happen either because of official exchange-rate adjustment or because an autonomous capital transfer takes place that does not affect the supply and demand functions of exports and imports. The pound value of imports $M_£$ may be written as the product of the pound price and quantity of imports supplied S_m; i.e.,

$$M_£ = P_£ \cdot S_m \tag{7.1}$$

The change in this value resulting from a small change in the exchange rate may be expressed as

$$dM_£ = dP_£ \cdot S_m + P_£ \cdot S'_m \cdot dP_£ \tag{7.2}$$

where S'_m represents the derivative of the supply of imports function with respect to the pound price of imports. But the change in value of imports also, as we saw in the preceding sections, must be equal to the product of the elasticity of demand for foreign exchange (pounds) times the value of imports times the per cent change of the exchange rate. Thus, using relation 7.2, we may write

$$dP_£ \cdot S_m + P_£ \cdot S'_m \cdot dP_£ = E_d \cdot P_£ \cdot S_m \cdot \frac{dr}{r} \tag{7.3}$$

Rearranging a little and dividing both sides of the equation by $P_£ \cdot S_m$, we obtain

$$\frac{dP_£}{P_£} \left(1 + \frac{S'_m}{S_m} \cdot P_£\right) = E_d \cdot \frac{dr}{r} \tag{7.4}$$

But we notice that the second term in the parentheses is actually the elasticity of supply of imports s_m. Using our fundamental relation 4.15 and expressing the demand elasticity for foreign exchange in terms of the import elasticities and solving relation 7.4 for the relative change in the import price, we finally obtain the desired result

$$\frac{dP_{\pounds,m}}{P_{\pounds,m}} = \frac{dr}{r} \cdot \frac{1}{(s_m/d_m) - 1} \tag{7.5}$$

the second subscripts m being used here to indicate prices of imports. In words, the relative change in the import price in terms of foreign currency should be equal to the relative change in the rate of exchange (that has caused this change of price) times the elasticity of demand for foreign exchange divided by 1 plus the supply elasticity of imports. Again we leave it up to the reader to derive a similar result for the relative change in the pound export price resulting from a given relative change in the exchange rate. As we may expect, this relation is symmetrical with that for imports and may be written as

$$\frac{dP_{\pounds,x}}{P_{\pounds,x}} = \frac{dr}{r} \cdot \frac{1}{(d_x/s_x) - 1} \tag{7.6}$$

From an easily verifiable relation between the changes in dollar and pound prices resulting from exchange-rate alteration, namely,

$$\frac{dP_s}{P_s} = \frac{dr}{r} + \frac{dP_{\pounds}}{P_{\pounds}} \tag{7.7}$$

we derive the relative change in import and export dollar prices

$$\frac{dP_{s,m}}{P_{s,m}} = \frac{dr}{r} \cdot \left[1 + \frac{1}{(s_m/d_m) - 1} \right] \tag{7.8}$$

$$\frac{dP_{s,x}}{P_{s,x}} = \frac{dr}{r} \cdot \left[1 + \frac{1}{(d_x/s_x) - 1} \right] \tag{7.9}$$

These results are perfectly sufficient to analyze the impact of exchange alteration on dollar and pound export and import prices and consequently on the terms of trade. Sometimes it may be preferable to express the change in the terms of trade directly as a function of the relative change in the rate and of the export and import elasticities. This will be easily done if we observe that, for sufficiently small changes of the value of the currency, the relative change in the terms of trade is simply the difference between the relative change in the export and import prices. Obviously, it is no longer important whether we consider the dollar or the pound prices, because the terms-of-trade index (as well as its alteration) is identical whether measured in terms of one set of prices or the other. Thus

$$\frac{dTT}{TT} = \frac{dr}{r} \cdot \left[\frac{1}{(d_x/s_x) - 1} - \frac{1}{(s_m/d_m) - 1} \right] \quad (7.10)$$

This relation enables us to state a very simple condition for the terms of trade (TT) to (i) move in the same direction with r, (ii) to remain unchanged, and (iii) to move in the opposite direction from r, namely,

i) If
ii) If $\quad s_x \cdot s_m \; \begin{array}{c} < \\ = \\ > \end{array} \; d_x \cdot d_m \quad$ or $\quad \dfrac{d_x \cdot d_m}{s_x \cdot s_m} \; \begin{array}{c} > \\ = 1 \\ < \end{array} \quad (7.11)$
iii) If

Thus, if the elasticities of supply are large in proportion to the elasticities of demand for exports and imports, a depreciation of a country's currency will worsen its terms of trade, and appreciation will improve its terms of trade. The extreme case of infinite supply elasticities discussed in the beginning of this section now provides us with a check: we know that in this case the terms of trade will fall in proportion to devaluation, i.e. the terms of trade move with the rate of exchange r (domestic currency per unit of foreign currency) in inverse proportion; effectively, condition iii obtains.

Before concluding this section, we may establish an interesting relation between the stability and balance-of-payments adjustment conditions studied in Section 5 and the present result concerning the terms of trade. In relation 5.3 the fraction on the right-hand side of the inequality is exactly the fraction found in the conditions expressed in relations 7.11 above. Because the elasticities of demand must be negative and the elasticities of supply positive, the equilibrium of the foreign-exchange market can be unstable only if $(d_x \cdot d_m) / (s_x \cdot s_m)$ is smaller than 1, i.e., only if condition iii above holds. In words, whenever we know that the balance of payments deteriorates as a result of domestic currency devaluation, i.e., whenever we know that the foreign-exchange market is unstable in the neighborhood of equilibrium, we also know that devaluation will worsen the terms of trade. Thus market instability is a sufficient— but not necessary—condition for the terms of trade moving in the opposite direction from r, defined as the price of foreign currency in terms of domestic currency.

5.8 Autonomous Transfer and the Foreign-Exchange Market

In Chapter 2 we made the distinction between current and capital transactions in the balance of payments. It is a fair approximation to say that it is only the former type of payments, i.e., the current transactions, that are exchange-rate and price elastic in a static market. Therefore, we have analyzed the foreign-exchange market by assuming that it is based only on the current transactions.

This is not to say that capital transfers or donations would not have to be cleared through the foreign-exchange market; however, these transactions, not being very responsive to the rate of exchange, may be considered and introduced separately into the analysis. This also permits us to study the effect of transfer on the foreign-exchange market. An objection may be raised that a financial transfer will affect the real and money incomes in the two countries and consequently also the supplies and demands for exports and imports; this, of course, would also modify the supply of and demand for foreign exchange for current transactions. No doubt, such income effects of transfer generally will occur; and actually they represent the more interesting aspect of the transfer mechanism. However, we shall discuss them only later, when we have better mastered the necessary analytical framework. At present, we confine ourselves strictly to a brief exposition of what we may term the pure price and exchange-rate effects of transfer.

We define as transfer (tr) the portion of foreign exchange that is supplied or demanded for autonomous transactions in the foreign-exchange market over and above the supply and demand generated by autonomous current transactions.

The situation is quite trivial if the rate of exchange is fixed. In this case, obviously, the rate of exchange will not be affected. The supply and demand for exports and consequently the foreign-exchange market serving current-account transactions will not be affected by transfer. The full amount of transfer will be settled through flow of accommodating payments in the same direction. To give an example, in this situation a transfer of, say, $1 billion from the United States to the United Kingdom will be fully effected through an accommodating outflow of gold or inflow of short-term capital: in terms of our previous diagrammatic representation of the foreign-exchange market, the demand for foreign exchange will move to the right by $1/r \cdot \$1$ billion in the market of pounds, and the supply curve of dollars by $1 billion to the right in the market of dollars, while the exchange rate will remain unchanged.

The more interesting case arises if the rate of exchange is permitted to adjust freely to the transfer. Considering, now, the market of pounds with outward transfer of dollars (tr), we may write the supply of foreign exchange as

$$S_{\pounds} = S(r) \tag{8.1}$$

and demand as

$$D_{\pounds} = D_{cu}(r) + \frac{1}{r} \cdot tr_{\$} \tag{8.2}$$

While the elasticity of supply of foreign exchange remains unchanged, the elasticity of demand for foreign exchange now becomes

$$E_d = E_{d,ca} \cdot \left(1 - \frac{tr_{\$}}{r \cdot D_{\pounds}}\right) - \frac{tr_{\$}}{rD_{\pounds}} \tag{8.3}$$

where $E_{d,ca}$ represents the elasticity of demand for foreign exchange for current-account transactions, as defined by relation 4.15 in terms of elasticities of demand and supply of imports. The elasticity of demand for foreign exchange now is no longer a function only of the import elasticities but also of the percentage of transfer in total supply of dollars, or, what is the same thing, a function of the total demand for pounds, the rate of exchange, and the dollar transfer. An inward transfer could be considered as an outward transfer either in the dollar market, and the analysis would proceed along exactly the same lines as above, or in the pound market, where the supply of foreign exchange would be shifted to the right exactly by the pound value of transfer.

Stating the market equilibrium conditions in terms of supply and demand of foreign exchange as defined by relations 8.1 and 8.2, assuming that initially there was no transfer, and differentiating with respect to tr, we obtain the change in the exchange rate resulting from a small change in transfer, $d(tr_{\$})$, from the initial zero level

$$\frac{dr}{d(tr_{\$})} = \frac{1}{S(E_s - E_{d,ca})} \tag{8.4}$$

where S represents the equilibrium number of pounds initially traded and E_s and $E_{d,ca}$ the two elasticities defined by relations

4.14 and 4.15. Perhaps, more conveniently, relation 8.4 may be stated to relate the relative change in the rate of exchange dr/r, and the relative size of transfer $d\,(tr_s)\,/S_s$, as

$$\frac{dr}{r} = \frac{d(tr_s)}{S_s} \cdot \frac{1}{E_s - E_{d,ca}} \tag{8.5}$$

Using the results of the preceding section, it is now possible to evaluate the effect of "pure" monetary transfer not only on the rate of exchange but also on the export and import prices, as well as on the terms of trade. The reader may derive such formulas for himself; as an example, combining relations 8.5 and 7.10, we may write the relative change in the terms of trade resulting from a small transfer, $d\,(tr_s)$, positive or negative, from the initial zero level as

$$\frac{dTT}{TT} = \frac{d(tr_s)}{S_s(E_s - E_{d,ca})} \cdot \left(\frac{s_x}{d_x - s_x} - \frac{d_m}{s_m - d_m}\right) \tag{8.6}$$

where S_s is the initial dollar value of exports or imports on current account.

The direction of change in the rate of exchange and in the terms of trade resulting from an autonomous financial transfer is very easy to evaluate. The change in the rate of exchange dr will have the same sign as the transfer (outward +, inward --) if the foreign-exchange market is stable.

If the foreign-exchange market is unstable, according to relation 8.5, the opposite results should be obtained. However, it is most unlikely that the unstable equilibrium would be preserved after the transfer. Rather, the rate of exchange would settle at a stable equilibrium in the vicinity of the original unstable situation. This, of course, would reverse the direction of change of the exchange rate. Consequently, the rate of exchange would move in the same direction, whether the foreign-exchange market initially were in a stable or an unstable equilibrium. The sign of the change in the terms of trade for a given change in the rate of exchange is given in relations 7.11.

5.9 The Theory of Purchasing-Power Parity

At different times in the past and until quite recently, international economists have attempted to explain the rate of exchange and its variations through the price levels in different countries. Thus the rate of exchange r could be written as

$$r = \frac{\Sigma_i P_a^i Q_0^i}{\Sigma_i P_b^i Q_0^i} \tag{9.1}$$

where r expresses the price of country B's currency in terms of country A's currency, the P's the prices in domestic currency, and the Q's corresponding weights. The choice of commodities and prices entering such an index will depend on the purpose of the computation or on the definition chosen. Most often the prices in the two sums refer to a representative bundle of commodities with assigned weights Q_0. Thus they will most often represent the cross-section of all commodities or, possibly, the export prices of the two countries or regions considered.

For practical considerations, where changes in, rather than absolute levels of, the rate of exchange are sought, an alternative index is generally used, comparing the rates of inflation in different countries. This may be expressed as

$$I = \frac{r}{r_0} = \frac{I_a}{I_b} \tag{9.2}$$

where I_a and I_b are price indexes in country A and country B, respectively, comparing the change of prices between the base and the current periods; r/r_0 then expresses the predicted change of the exchange rate. If there is a systematic bias in the value of a currency with respect to the "static" purchasing power index (9.1), not changing significantly over time, the index of 9.2 may still explain satisfactorily the changes in the equilibrium rate of exchange, whether relation 9.1 is fulfilled or not.

The common sense of such definitions of the rate of exchange is that the same amount of money should purchase the same representative sample of commodities in both countries (whence the term *purchasing-power parity*) or that the purchasing power of money, if expressed in terms of one currency, should change *pari passu* in different countries. The theory may serve as a crude approximation but does not offer a satisfactory explanation of the exchange rate. There are at least two broad sets of objections that may be raised, the first purely statistical, the second deriving from the theory of foreign-exchange markets.

The first type of criticism does not have to detain us very long. It pertains to the entire spectrum of index-number difficulties, well known to us from other fields of economics. Unless all prices in each country are in constant proportion to each other, i.e., unless $P_a^i/P_b^i = $ constant, for all i, the choice of weights Q_0 will influence the value of r. The discrepancies between results obtained from different sets of weights may be quite large.

A definition of the rate of exchange, as given in relation 9.1 or 9.2, is based on some intuitive notion that such a rate of exchange should yield an approximate balance of the trade accounts, whatever happens to prices. Such an intuition seems to deny the validity of the monetary theory of international trade—except for one situation that has some importance.

The rate of exchange as here defined will provide a perfect basis for predicting changes in the rate of exchange from changes in comparative price levels, if perfectly static and, in addition, classical assumptions are made about the operation of both economies. Under full employment in both countries, with no structural changes, money expansion or contraction in one country will be translated into a proportional upward or downward shift in all domestic demand and supply curves (in that country), including those of exports and imports. If, under such conditions, the price of foreign currency also moves in proportion with all other prices, as required by relation 9.1, the import supply and export demand schedules expressed in domestic currency will move upward in proportion to the general price level. Nothing will happen to the volume of exports or of imports. The value of trade in terms of foreign currency will remain unchanged.

Under other and often more interesting conditions—when a structural change takes place in either economy or if Keynesian assumptions are made about income and foreign-trade determination —the purchasing-power-parity approach has very little meaning. It would require an undue amount of space to enumerate and explain all such instances. However, let us give at least one example.

Suppose that an autonomous (or structural) downward shift in the supply curve of exports of country A takes place as a result of improved technology. Suppose, moreover, that the export supply elasticity is infinite. Assuming unit elasticity of demand for A's exports, the supply of foreign exchange generated by the export market will remain unchanged at the current rate of exchange. Thus the equilibrium rate of exchange will remain unchanged. According to the parity formula, it would have had to drop by the full amount of the decline in export prices, if those were considered, or by some fraction of it, if all commodities, domestic as well as exported, were included in the purchasing-power-parity index.

Chapter 6

INCOME DETERMINATION AND THE BALANCE OF PAYMENTS

6.1 The Classical Model

At this point we should pause a little. Before discussing the role of income in the balance-of-payments adjustment process, let us survey briefly the static models of income determination in an open economy, i.e., in an economy engaging in external trade. We shall limit ourselves to the two important approaches, the classical and the Keynesian. In both cases we shall show the important variables and the solutions of the two systems as they derive from domestic and external conditions.

It should be clear that there is no single classical model of income determination and no single Keynesian model. Different writers may differ in emphasis, in detail, and even sometimes in the substance of analysis. However, it is possible to abstract from such minor discrepancies and formulate the two major types of thought in such a way as to preserve what is essential. We shall restrict ourselves to the simplest possible representation compatible with the degree of detail we want to attain in analyzing the balance of payments.

In the case where no foreign trade takes place, the classicists were able to separate entirely the determination of real income, consumption, investment, and savings from the monetary factors. The monetary variables, on the other hand, were determined through a single money equation, relating the money supply, prices, and real output. Assuming that at every given period there is a given stock of reproducible productive resources, i.e., capital (K_0), resulting from past accumulation of such resources, assuming that there is a given labor force (N_0) and a given state of technology, total real output of the period (X_0) is also known. Thus we may write as our first relation the aggregate production function of the economy

$$X = X(N_0, K_0) \qquad (1.1)$$

Say's law and/or perfect price flexibility in all markets provided the classicists with a sufficient guarantee of full employment of all productive resources.

Once real product and income of the economy are determined, all that remains to be shown, in the absence of foreign trade, is the distribution of this *given* magnitude between consumption (C), on the one hand, and savings (S) and investment (I), on the other. Using the accounting identities established in Chapter 3, we may write

$$X = C + I = C + S \tag{1.2}$$

It would be possible to think of a number of factors explaining this distribution. The classicists, however, attributed primary importance to a single market—that of savings and investment—and to a single variable of adjustment—the rate of interest. Once equilibrium savings and investment are determined at a given rate of interest, consumption will also be found as a residual. This is not to say that the three important aggregates would be all independent of income. However, as shown by relation 1.1, the latter is to be considered as a given constant. As in the Keynesian theory, it is possible to express the propensities to consume, invest, and save as functions of the rate of interest and real income, remembering that the latter variable is fixed at the level X_0. Thus we may write the propensity to save as

$$S = S(X_0, i) \tag{1.3}$$

and the propensity to invest as

$$I = I(X_0, i) \tag{1.4}$$

where i represents the rate of interest. The equilibrium condition of the investment market

$$S = I \tag{1.5}$$

then suffices to determine equilibrium levels not only of the rate of interest, savings, and investment but also of consumption. Formally, relations 1.1 through 1.5 represent a system of six equations in five variables, namely, X, C, I, S, and i. The system is not overdetermined, however, because one of the relations is not independent of the others. Observe, for example, that relation 1.5 combined with one of the relations in 1.2 implies the other relation of 1.2. The five independent relations are consistent with the equilibrium values of all five variables.

The form and position of the savings function (1.3) will generally depend on consumers' preferences, on relative prices of consumers' and investment goods, and possibly on the rate of change of the general price level. The investment schedule, on the other hand, will depend on the marginal productivity of capital, as determined by technology, the existing stock of capital, and the labor force. Expectations, considerations of uncertainty, and relative prices will also play a role in its determination.

All the key real variables being determined, only the money equation remains to be added to establish the level of prices; namely,

$$M_0 \cdot V = P \cdot X_0 \qquad (1.6)$$

where X_0 is derived from relation 1.1; M_0, representing total supply of money, is an exogenous variable given either by the stock of gold or by the monetary policy of the central bank; V represents the average velocity of circulation of money and may be assumed either constant or exogenously determined. P, the general level of prices, is thus the only variable and may be determined from relation 1.6.

The classical model of a closed economy, as shown so far, pertains to a short-run equilibrium, where capital stock and the labor force are assumed constant. Only a minor alteration is needed to trace the path of the economy and of all its key variables through time. Assuming, now, that all variables used previously pertain to a given period t, a dynamic model may be constructed if we observe that

$$K_t = \sum_{j=0}^{t} I_j \qquad (1.7)$$

and

$$N_t = f(t) \qquad (1.8)$$

The first relation simply states that the total stock of capital is the sum total of all past accumulated net investments, while the second expresses the labor force as an autonomous function of time. Ricardian, Malthusian, or Marxian assumptions about population behavior might easily be included; the $f(t)$ function could be adjusted to that effect. If technology were changing over time, relation 1.1 would have to be modified into

$$X_t = X(K_t, N_t, t) \qquad (1.9)$$

The case interesting us most in this chapter pertains to an open economy. In other words, How will all the important variables be determined if the country engages in international trade? To discuss this problem, let us first generalize the concept of the equilibrium solution of the system by making the distinction between two types of equilibria. Let the first type be characterized by a situation wherein the foreign-exchange market is not in equilibrium, while in the second case all markets, including that for foreign exchange, are balanced. In the first situation accommodating payments will take place; in the second, autonomous payments and receipts will be equalized. We assume in our simple model that autonomous transactions pertain solely to the current account and that the rate of exchange is fixed throughout, equal to unity.

To make the analysis simple, let us first assume that the foreign price level, p_2, is constant, and so is the foreign rate of interest. Exports will now depend only on the terms of trade, T, permitted to vary only with the domestic price level, p_1. The volume of imports, on the other hand, will now depend on the terms of trade and on the rate of interest, and so will domestic savings and investment. Both the rate of interest and the terms of trade now have to be introduced as explanatory variables into the propensities to save, invest, and import to allow for possible substitutions among these aggregates resulting from changes in the two variables. To allow for changes in the terms of trade, imports now have to be entered into the expenditure equation (comparable to relation 1.2 above) multiplied by p_2/p_1, that is, by $1/T$. With these observations in mind, we are in a position to state the equilibrium condition of the classical system where foreign trade is permitted, namely,

$$I(X_0, i, T) + x(T) - S(X_0, i, T) - \frac{1}{T} m(X_0, i, T) = 0 \quad (1.10)$$

where x and m stand for quantities of exports and imports, respectively. The rate of interest and prices being assumed fixed in the foreign country, exports depend only on the terms of trade. This is a somewhat strenuous assumption; it will be relaxed presently when the equilibrium of both countries is considered simultaneously. At present, this simplifying assumption is made only to facilitate exposition of the system.

Relation 1.10 contains two unknown variables, T and i. The equality of savings and investment, on the one hand, and of exports and imports, on the other, is not required, but the difference between exports and imports has to equal the difference between savings and investment. With a higher level of terms of trade, the rate of interest may rise, remain the same, or decline.

Higher domestic prices relative to foreign prices will tend to produce a deficit in the balance of payments,[1] that is, excess of domestic expenditure (absorption) over domestic income, and excess of investment over saving. Although a given relation between the rate of interest and the terms of trade is formally implicit in the statement of classical theory, the economics of such a relationship is not quite self-evident. Actually, the classicists often fail to explain it in their writings, contenting themselves with the direct consideration of the foreign-exchange market and neglecting the internal adjustment. Suppose that the terms of trade of a country improve. Why should there be a surplus of investment over savings matching the deterioration in the balance of payments? While the real income produced remains unchanged, by assumption, the real consumable resources available to the economy are now increased because of the favorable terms-of-trade effect. If this does not have any effect on real savings and real investment, i.e., if S and I are perfectly terms-of-trade inelastic, the rate of interest has to decline, to produce the desired excess of investment over savings. On the other side of the spectrum of possible alternatives, the investment may increase because of improved expectations with higher prices, or savings decline at any rate of interest, some of the disposable income thus liberated being spent on cheaper imports. In this case, no change in the rate of interest has to take place. A relation between the rate of interest and the terms of trade emerging from relation 1.10 may be illustrated by the line *aa* in Figure 6.1.1. However, as we have indicated, it is not a necessary one; the line *aa* might be horizontal or upward-sloping, depending on the price and interest-rate elasticities of the functions appearing in relation 1.10.

Now we should recall that in the short run the level of domestic prices is determined through relation 1.6. Assuming the money supply as given, say at the level M_0, the domestic price level and hence

---

[1] This is the postulate usually made by the classicists, implying that the sum of elasticities of demand for imports is greater than unity. If it were otherwise, the opposite results would be obtained; in particular, an excess of savings over investment would have to accompany an improvement in the terms of trade. It should be observed, however, that such a situation, under conditions of perfect price flexibility, would be unstable and could not last for any extended period of time.

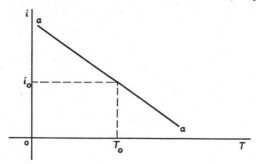

FIGURE 6.1.1

the terms of trade are determined, say, at T_0. But, as shown in the diagram, corresponding to T_0 there is also a known level of rate of interest. These two variables, together with the functions entering relation 1.10, determine the equilibrium level of exports, imports, savings, and investment. We should recall at this point that the equilibrium solutions thus obtained pertain to the first type of solution of the classical system, where external balance is not required.

Monetary reserves will now flow from one country to the other by the amount of current surplus or deficit in the balance of payments. Thus, for any given period, t, we may write that the change in monetary reserves will be equal to the balance of autonomous payments,

$$\Delta M = M_t - M_{t-1} = T_t x - m = F(T_t) \qquad (1.11)^2$$

But this change in monetary reserves will, in turn, affect the terms of trade T. Accommodating somewhat the money equation (relation 1.6) and assuming with the classicists that monetary reserves and total money supply are identical, we obtain

$$M_t = p_2 \cdot T_t \cdot X_0 \cdot \frac{1}{V} \qquad (1.12)$$

Remembering that the foreign price level is assumed to be fixed, we may substitute M_t and M_{t-1} from relation 1.12 in 1.11 and obtain a first-order difference equation in T,

$$\frac{1}{V} \cdot p_2 \cdot X_0 (T_t - T_{t-1}) = F(T_t) \qquad (1.13)$$

---

[2] For simplicity, we assume here that $p_2 = 1$. Observe that $F(T_t)$ will be obtained from relation 1.10, by solving that equation for i in terms of T and substituting such values of i into x and m.

This relation permits us to study the path toward the second type of equilibrium from any initial state of equilibrium of the first type. It contains the simple dynamics of the price-specie-flow mechanism. Clearly, the stationary state (i.e., what we have called the "second equilibrium") will be reached when $T_t = T_{t-1} = T_0$. In this situation the balance of autonomous payments is in equilibrium, and savings are equal to investment. There will generally be one equilibrium level of the terms of trade, T_0, and, corresponding to it, equilibrium levels of all the other key variables.

If money supply is divorced from the balance of payments, i.e., if relation 1.11 is not fulfilled, relation 1.13 has to be modified into

$$\frac{1}{V} \cdot p_2 \cdot X_0 \cdot (T_t - T_{t-1}) = F(T_t) + A \qquad (1.14)$$

where A is an autonomous factor controlled by the monetary authorities or, possibly, affected by current production of gold. In this situation, as indicated by relation 1.14, stable terms of trade are inconsistent with a balance in autonomous payments. Note that the balance-of-payments equilibrium condition is expressed by $F(T_t) = 0$. With a positive A—that is, with positive *autonomous* increments in money supply—stable terms of trade are compatible only with a balance-of-payments deficit equal to A. A balance-of-payments equilibrium, on the other hand, is impossible because if money supply is rising, terms of trade have to improve. But, as we have indicated above, there will generally be only one level of the terms of trade that corresponds to the equilibrium of the second kind. Actually, even the case of stable terms of trade is unrealistic, because it would presuppose gold sterilization on the part of the other trading partner. In actuality, gold outflow would tend to raise prices in country 2, and this would again affect the balance of payments in the other direction.

Let us now turn to, and state briefly, the general case where equilibria of both countries, under classical assumptions, are determined simultaneously. Using superscripts 1 and 2 for the two countries and remembering that real incomes produced in both countries are fixed in the short run at X_0^1 and X_0^2, the two equilibrium income-expenditure relations may now be written as

$$I^1(i^1, T) + x^1(i^2, T) - S^1(i^1, T) - \frac{1}{T} m^1(i^1, T) = 0 \qquad (1.15)$$

and

$$I^2(i^2, T) + m^1(i^1, T) - S^2(i^2, T) - Tx^1(i^2, T) = 0 \qquad (1.16)$$

Dividing the two money equations of the two countries and assuming given supplies of money, we obtain

$$\frac{M_0^1}{M_0^2} = T \cdot \frac{V^2}{V^1} \cdot \frac{X_0^1}{X_0^2} \tag{1.17}$$

The three relations 1.15, 1.16, and 1.17 determine the three unknowns—the rate of interest in country 1, i^1; that in country 2, i^2; and the terms of trade. This permits derivation of all key aggregates in the two countries; the equilibrium is of the first kind.

One additional relation will determine the distribution of monetary reserves between the two countries corresponding to the state of equilibrium of the second kind, where both economies are in external balance. Assuming that the total reserves of the two countries are fixed, say, at M_0,

$$M^1 + M^2 = M_0$$

we observe that

$$\Delta M^1 = -\Delta M^2 = p_1 x^1 - p_2 m^1 \tag{1.18}$$

From relation 1.17 we obtain, by differentiating it with respect to T and using relation 1.18,

$$\Delta M^1 = \Delta T \cdot K \tag{1.19}$$

where K is a constant. A stable value of the terms of trade T over time (i.e., $\Delta T = 0$) will be obtained only if the money supply in each country is stable. As may be seen from relation 1.18, this is possible only if the balance of payments is in equilibrium. The value of T, say T_0, fulfilling this condition is the equilibrium level of the terms of trade of the second type. It also determines all the other equilibrium values of the second kind, including the distribution of monetary reserves.

The reader may find it interesting to modify the analysis and examine the case in which total monetary reserves are not fixed but are influenced by monetary policy. In this case relation 1.18 will be altered, the terms of trade may fluctuate, and the balance of payments generally will not be in balance. Also, it may be interesting to study the case in which short-term capital movements take place, equalizing interest rates in the two countries. A continuous transfer of funds from one country to the other would alter the supply functions of loanable funds to such an extent as to bring about equality of rates of interest. At the same time, the terms of trade would have to change to the point where the surplus or deficit in the balance of payments on current account would exactly match the imbalance of the capital account. Only under such conditions could the equilibrium of the second kind, characterized by stable prices, be attained.

Before concluding this section, an important set of observations has to be made concerning the case—neglected so far—in which the rate of exchange is permitted to vary and adjust to its equilibrium level in the foreign-exchange market. Our previous distinction between the equilibrium of the first and second kinds is now no longer necessary. By definition, external equilibrium between the two countries engaging in trade will always be maintained. Consequently, no international flows of monetary reserves will take place. Assuming the gold standard and no gold production in either country, monetary reserves and internal price levels of domestically produced goods and services will be constant. Under such conditions, T, the terms of trade of country 1, must always be proportional to r, where r is defined as the price of currency of country 1, expressed in terms of the currency of country 2; that is, $T = ar$, where a is a constant proportionality factor equal to the ratio of the constant price levels of the two countries. Substituting this expression in relations 1.15 and 1.16 and replacing relation 1.17 by a relation stating the equality of exports and imports valued in terms of one currency, we again obtain a set of three relations in three unknowns, r, i^1, and i^2. These three relations are perfectly identical with the three relations defining the equilibrium of the second kind under the international gold standard and fixed exchange rate, with the single exception that we have now written ar instead of T. Consequently, all the static solutions will also be identical under either set of assumptions; in particular, $T_0 = ar_0$, where r_0 is the equilibrium rate of exchange.

While there is a perfect correspondence between the *static* solutions of the two systems, the *dynamic* process of convergence toward equilibrium may be different under fixed and free exchange rates. The speed and form of adjustment in the two situations will depend on the rate of flow of international reserves, mobility of resources, elasticity of expectations, and a number of other factors.

6.2 The Keynesian Model

The important innovations that Keynes and his followers introduced into economic macro-analysis are (i) that national income is no longer considered as constant, even in the short run, and (ii) that money is used not only for domestic and foreign transactions but also in liquid form as an asset. By no means does the Keynesian approach supplant the classical model of income determination. It may be shown that in most respects the Keynesian model differs from the classical only in the forms assigned to certain behavioral functions and that, unless such special assumptions are made, results identical with those of the classical model will be obtained. The only important change introduced by Keynes in the structure of the model is in the money equation.

Let us first summarize the Keynesian model for a closed economy. Using the same notations as in the preceding section, the equilibrium income-expenditure relation may again be expressed as equality of savings and investment. Contrary to relation 1.5, however, real income, X, now has to be assumed as one of the variables to be determined within the system. Thus we may write

$$S(X, i) - I(X, i) = 0 \qquad (2.1)$$

where S and I are the savings and investment functions, respectively. In the short run the stock of capital is assumed fixed at K_0 as it was in the classical system; the labor supply, N, however, is now permitted to assume different values smaller than, or equal to, N_0, the total available labor force. The production function relating output X to variable employment N may now be stated as

$$X = X(N) \qquad (2.2)$$

Once the technique of production is known, the demand function for labor is also known, under competitive conditions, of course; but this is always assumed by Keynes on the demand side of the labor market. It may be stated as

$$\frac{dX(N)}{dN} = \frac{W}{P} \qquad (2.3)$$

where W represents the money-wage rate. The condition expressed here is that the real wage should be equal to the marginal physical product of labor.

Finally, the Keynesian money equation may be derived by adding to the demand for transaction money, known from the classical model, the demand for liquidity, or asset money. While the former demand depends, as before, on money income, i.e., the product of real income and the price level, the other type of demand is a function of the rate of interest, i. Combining these two sources of money demand, we may express them in a single behavioral function

$$M = M(p \cdot X, i) \tag{2.4}$$

As before, M is an exogenously determined variable, determined and controlled by the monetary authorities, foreign transactions, and gold production. For any given price level, relations 2.1 and 2.4—with X no longer fixed—are sufficient to determine the level of real income, the rate of interest, the level of real savings, of investment, and hence of consumption.

But, if we know the level of real output, we also know employment and the corresponding real wage. Thus, for any assumed level of prices, we also know the money wage, and, vice-versa, for any assumed level of money wages we also know the price level. Consequently, if the money-wage rate is given by custom, collective bargaining, or government decree, the entire system is determined. Of course, if there were a competitive supply function of labor and the quantity theory of money did hold, as was customarily assumed by the classical economists, there would be only one possible real wage, one possible level of output, one possible level of prices and money wages, etc.

It may be useful to represent this solution of the Keynesian system graphically. Consider Figure 6.2.1. In the lower right-hand quadrant we find the LL curve, expressing graphically relation 2.4, corresponding to a level of prices p_1. In the same quadrant IS_1 and IS_2 express the relation between real income and the rate of interest, permissible by two alternative relations 2.1. As will be seen from the numbers in the brackets indicating the corresponding relation, the other two quadrants show the production function and the conditions of the labor market, respectively. In situation 1 we find the "quasi"-classical case of perfect labor market with full employment determining output and the required position of the LL curve generating such level of output, with price level p_1. In the second situation, owing to depressed effective demand, the rate of interest falls into the famous Keynesian liquidity trap. No price adjustment is now capable of restoring full employment; employment declines to N_2. According to the Keynesian theory, real wages should now rise to W_p. If money wages are exogenously determined, the price level is also known. Conversely, if prices are fixed at the assumed level p_1,

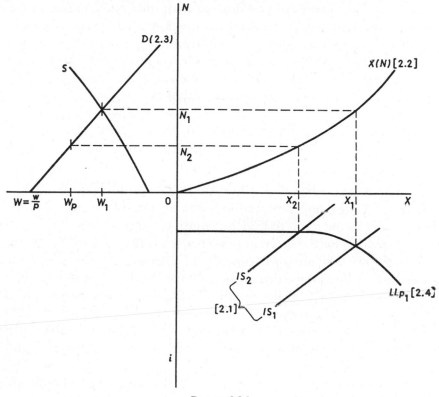

FIGURE 6.2.1

money wages must have increased from where they were in the first full-employment equilibrium.

These last statements reproduce the orthodox line of argument of the Keynesian school. It is beyond the scope of this chapter to argue their validity. The reader, however, may think of a score of reasons why the labor-market situation in a depressed economy could be different, all leading to different levels of real wages, money wages, and price levels. We leave this exercise and also its extension to the foreign-trade situation to the reader.

At present, let us turn to the general problem of income determination in an open economy. Two important alterations have to be made. First, we have to introduce into the income-expenditure relation the export and import functions. Second, the relative price levels, i.e., the terms of trade T, now have to be considered explicitly as a factor of demand not only for exports and imports but also for consumption of domestic products, investment, and savings.

To avoid the difficulty of dealing with only one country in the case of international trade, let us state immediately the complete equilibrium conditions of the two trading partners. We assume that the rate of exchange is fixed at $r = 1$. Using superscripts 1 and 2 for country 1 and country 2, respectively, the income-expenditure equilibrium conditions may now be stated as

$$I^1(X^1, i^1 T) + x^1(X^2, i^2, T) - S^1(X^1, i^1, T) - \frac{1}{T}x^2(X^1, i^1, T) = 0$$

and $\hspace{10cm}$ (2.5)

$$I^2(X^2, i^2, T) + x^2(X^1, i^1, T) - S^2(X^2, i^2, T) - Tx^1(X^2, i^2, T) = 0$$

where I, S, and x represent real investment, real saving, and real exports and T is the terms of trade of country 1, i.e., p^1/p^2.

Assuming for the moment price levels in both countries as given, the terms of trade are also known, and relations 2.5 determine for each country a relation such as the *IS* curve in the diagram once the rate of interest and real income in the other is known; we may now term it the *ISXM* curve. Also, because prices are assumed to be given in both countries, there will be a known *LL* function for each country and, corresponding to its position, a given level of real output.

The simultaneous solution for both countries can be better understood by means of the so-called *reaction functions*. Assume a given level of real income in country 2, X^2. To it corresponds, determined by the *LL* function in that country, a given level of rate of interest, i^2. These two values carried into the *ISXM* function of country 1 will, together with the money equation of country 1, determine uniquely the rate of interest i^1 and the real income X^1 in country 1. In this somewhat roundabout way we have obtained from a prescribed level of income in country 2 the corresponding income in country 1. Such a reaction function may now be written as

$$X^1 = X^1(X^2)$$ (2.6)

An analogous construction yields the reaction function of X^2 on X^1, that is

$$X^2 = X^2(X^1)$$ (2.7)

The two reaction functions in two unknowns then determine the two equilibrium real incomes in the two countries, and these then lead to the complete solution of the system. It is apparent that only such values of X^1 or X^2 will fulfill the two above relations as are simultaneously the value "reacted to" and that "reacting," that is, values given by the intersection of the two reaction curves.

In terms of the equations shown for the case of a closed economy, the money equations (1.4) in both countries remain un-affected. Adding to these the two effective demand relations, the two production functions, and two demand curves for labor, we have, altogether, eight equations, to determine eight unknowns—namely, the two price levels, the two rates of interest, the two levels of real output (or income), and the two levels of employment. Of course, as for the case of a closed economy, we have to assume that money wages are determined outside the system or that a competitive supply curve of labor is given.

We may now observe that if a perfectly inelastic supply of labor were given at

$$N = N_0 \qquad\qquad (2.8)$$

where N_0 is the level of full employment or the total labor force, with perfectly flexible prices and wages, the Keynesian solution comes very close to the classical macro-economic model. Unless the rate of interest drops as low as the liquidity trap, there will be full employment, and the rate of interest and prices will affect only the allocation of national product among investment, savings, exports, imports, and consumption. The same holds for any "real" supply curve of labor.

If, however, prices are inflexible in the downward direction, with a given supply of money, the LL function in Figure 6.2.1 can-not move to the right and upward. Thus, any movement of IS_1 to the left, that is, decline in effective demand, necessarily will depress real income below the assumed full-employment level X_1. Similarly, in the typical Keynesian case where money wages are inflexible, a left-ward movement of IS_1 will be accompanied by a decline in the price level, because the real wage now has to rise, and this will move the LL curve to the right; finally, an equilibrium level will be attained, again, at less than full employment.

So far we have assumed that the total money supplies in the two countries are exogenously determined. This is the assumption usually made in the context of Keynesian analysis. However, there would be no technical or conceptual difficulty in handling the case wherein the foreign-trade balance was the only factor affecting monetary reserves. The analysis presented in the preceding sec-tion dealing with this case could easily be applied here; the price-specie-flow mechanism is usually associated with the classical conditions but is by no means restricted to such a situation.

Throughout this chapter we have assumed a rigid exchange rate —for simplicity, equal to 1—and consequently dealt with the case where autonomous payments may be out of balance. The conditions under freely fluctuating rates emerge from the analysis in the preceding chapter and will be discussed further in the following chapters of Part II. Even at present, however, we may observe that there would be no difficulty in introducing the free-rate assumption into the analysis of this chapter. Under classical conditions, it is easily seen that, with given quantities of paper money in both countries, exactly the same solution for the terms of trade and all other variables would be reached as in the equilibrium of the second kind reached through the price-specie-flow mechanism.

Because in the Keynesian world money may have a direct impact on the level of economic activity, the case is somewhat more complicated here, but not too much. There is one additional variable— the rate of exchange, r—expressing the price of foreign currency in terms of domestic currency, and one additional equation, stating the balance-of-payments equilibrium. Thus, for example, we may write

$$p^1 \cdot x^1 - p^2 \cdot x^2 \cdot r = 0 \tag{2.9}$$

or

$$T \cdot x^1 - x^2 = 0 \tag{2.10}$$

where x^1 and x^2 represent the volume of exports of country 1 and country 2, respectively, both functions of the terms of trade, real incomes, and rates of interest in the two countries. Because the terms of trade now are defined in terms of the currency of the first country as

$$T = \frac{p^1}{p^2 \cdot r} \tag{2.11}$$

this expression now has to be substituted for T in relations 2.5. Relation 2.9 and the eight equilibrium equations shown above are now sufficient to determine the nine variables, i.e., the rate of exchange, two prices, two outputs, two interest rates, and two levels of employment once money wages are given. For the case where prices can be assumed rigid and known, the reader will find it easy to trace through the different relations the solution of the system under flexible exchange rates. We will examine this situation more closely in Chapters 8 and 17.

Chapter 7

NATIONAL INCOME, THE BALANCE OF PAYMENTS, AND THE FOREIGN-TRADE MULTIPLIER

7.1 Income Effects and Multiplier Effects

To associate Keynes with income changes and the classical writers with price changes does not mean that the former entirely neglected price adjustment and the latter, income adjustment. Nevertheless, it is fair to say that the emphasis was primarily given to the one aspect by the Keynesians and to the other by the classicists. This difference in emphasis, as we have observed in the preceding chapter, was not a sheer a priori preference for one explanation over the other. Each school found sufficient grounds for its approach both in the conditions prevailing in its respective times and in the general state of economic theory.

Income changes, in the pre-Keynesian period, were recognized as a factor determining demand. This, of course, was primarily the concern of micro-demand analysis rather than that concerning the functioning of the whole economy: on the level of macro-analysis, Say's law was still a powerful enough argument to explain the total level of income through the supply of resources and technology only. Total effective demand as an independent factor had very little importance. Also, the important fact remained that national income or personal income, if used as a factor of demand, still was an independent variable as much as were prices themselves. The circular effect of income on demand and of demand on income was unnecessary in the Marshallian partial equilibrium analysis and irrelevant in the classical model of national-income determination. As one of its main contributions, the Keynesian analysis introduced income and employment as variables determined by the conditions of both supply and demand for real product. Effective demand, in turn, is determined by the level of real income. This reciprocity, or circularity, results in the important multiplier effect in the Keynesian system.

Actually, in the classical model it is only in the case of an *open economy* that the income fluctuations may play a certain, though limited, role. As we saw in the preceding chapter, under classical assumptions, exports and imports and consequently national income and national expenditure are equal in equilibrium. The distribution of income among consumption, investment, savings, exports, and imports depends on the rate of interest and the terms of trade. If an autonomous international transfer of purchasing power now takes place, income earned or the disposable income of the two trading partners will be affected, even though the real product of each country remains unchanged. To what extent the transfer will be effected in real terms and to what degree through an adjustment in the terms of trade will depend precisely on what we may call the "pure" income and price effects in the balance of payments. We shall analyze this situation rigorously later in this chapter, Sections 7.5 and 7.6, and also in Chapter 14. At this point, let us simply use this discussion to distinguish between what we have called the "pure" income effect and the Keynesian multiplier effect. While the first simply introduces real or money income as a variable into the demand for imports, in the same way as we often do in demand analysis, the second presupposes not only an adjustment of imports (or exports) to income but, in turn, of income and employment themselves, through the multiplier effect.

These two types of income effects, just explained, may further be distinguished from the "real-income effect" known from demand theory. The latter is the effect on demand caused by a change in real income resulting from a change in price of the commodity demanded. This type of impact on demand, known to us from the Slutsky formulation of demand theory, is perhaps too subtle for the purpose of balance-of-payments adjustment analysis. It may, however, be of great interest in the pure theory of international trade, but that portion of our discussion is reserved for Part III of the study.

7.2 The Assumptions of the Multiplier Analysis

The multiplier analysis essentially is one in the field of comparative statics. It attempts to show the change in national income or any other related variable resulting from an autonomous change in any of the underlying functions or parameters of the system. Most often the multiplier is associated with changes in investment; however, equally interesting may be multiplier coefficients relating income to autonomous changes in exports, imports, savings, consumption, technology, or the liquidity preference. The concept of multiplication stems from the fact that, by the time all variables adjust to any autonomous disturbance in the income-determining system, the change from their original value will be some multiple of the autonomous change.

In the context of our particular problem of balance-of-payments adjustment, the multiplier analysis aims at showing the changes in the balance of payments resulting from a spontaneous disturbance in the income-determining model of an open economy. In most cases, students of the subject have restricted themselves to an extremely simple model, in which the only variable is national income in one or both of the trading countries. Levels of investment, saving, exports, and imports are thus made functions of national income alone. We shall follow the same procedure part of the way in this chapter; in later sections, however, and especially in the next two chapters, we shall introduce other variables into the income-determining model.

Referring to the static Keynesian model discussed in the preceding chapter, we may now formulate precisely the assumptions required by the foreign-trade multiplier analysis. The first concept that should be made clear is that of the national income. Often it is not clearly specified whether the income variable used refers to money or real income. Clearly, it will make a difference (unless some very special assumptions are made) whether one or the other measure of national income is used; a propensity to consume will be different, depending on whether real income is changing or only prices are going up with unchanged real income. Along with our exposition of the Keynesian system in Chapter 6, we prefer always to speak of the propensity to consume, save, invest, or import in real terms rather than in money terms. This permits us to separate the effects of price fluctuations from real-income changes.

Of course, a multiplier model that considers only real-income changes will not make sense unless other key variables of the Keynesian system have a neutral effect. Thus, in order to eliminate the possible effects of the interest rate, price level, and money wages on the process of adjustment, it is necessary to make some appropriate assumptions about these variables. The most important is to neutralize the rate of interest. One way of doing this is to assume that the economy we are considering in our multiplier model is in an extremely depressed state and consequently the interest rate is perfectly income-inelastic. In other words, the equilibria before and after the autonomous change fall into the horizontal stretch of the *LL* curve (see Fig. 6.2.1). This condition will also be fulfilled if we assume that the monetary authorities supply the economy with, or withdraw from it, a sufficient amount of money to keep the rate of interest stable at a given level. If either of these two conditions is satisfied, real savings and investment will depend on real income only, and thus the simple assumptions of the multiplier model are fulfilled. The level of real income in a closed economy will now depend only on the propensities to save and to invest. Another assumption that would fulfill this requirement—although quite unrealistic —is to consider both savings and investment perfectly interest-inelastic.

Another question that may be raised is how employment and marginal productivity affect the multiplier analysis. First, we should observe that real income cannot move above the level of full employment. Strictly speaking, as soon as real income reaches the level of full employment, the multiplier process in real terms will be arrested, and all further adjustment to an autonomous change should assume the form of price, wage, and interest-rate adjustment. But even before real income attains its maximum level, additional employment may produce diminishing marginal increments of real output. Can such a process be neglected in the simple multiplier analysis, where only real income is considered as the explanatory variable? Assume that an autonomous upward shift (dC) of the consumption function takes place. To produce additional consumer goods, the industry will hire additional workers; if the marginal productivity of labor is constant, real wages will remain unchanged, and income generated through the autonomous change will increase by the same amount (dC). Of course, further repercussions of the multiplier variety will take place later. Now, if the marginal productivity of labor diminishes with additional employment, assuming with Keynes that money wages are fixed in the short run, real wages will drop and the price level go up. This, in turn, could affect the rate of interest through the Keynesian money equation; not necessarily, however. Either the rate of interest may be so low as to be independent of real income, or the monetary authorities may neutralize the effect through money expansion and keep the interest rate unchanged. Money income would increase faster than real income.

The employment effect would be strong, relatively larger than the increase in real product—of course, only up to the point of full employment. In an open economy, some of the autonomous increase in effective demand would now be offset by an adverse terms-of-trade effect on exports and imports.

Once full employment is attained, an autonomous increase in consumption or any of the propensities will necessarily create an inflationary gap. This can be closed only through monetary discipline, resulting in higher interest rates, or through higher, but stable, prices. In the case of an open economy, an additional check on the inflationary gap would come from the terms-of-trade effect on the balance of payments—usually at the cost of a balance-of-payments deficit.

The important conclusion that we want to draw from our discussion is that stability of prices and marginal productivity of labor are equally as necessary for the simple multiplier analysis as is the assumption of a constant rate of interest, if the economy engages in international trading. The same holds for a closed economy, if total money supply is kept constant. If the monetary authorities stabilize the rate of interest in a closed economy, whatever happens to the price level, the simple multiplier analysis conducted in terms of real variables will still yield correct results. Of course, we are assuming throughout that money illusion is absent and that full employment is never attained before an equilibrium is reached. If the latter condition is not fulfilled, prices and/or the rate of interest have to complete the adjustment, real income remaining unchanged.

Actually the precise relation between the changes in all the variables may be shown only through a differential analysis of the entire Keynesian model; we shall try to approximate such solutions later in this chapter and in the following one. At present, let us simply keep in mind the important assumptions that underlie the simplified system, where real income is the only explanatory variable.

7.3 The Foreign-Trade Multiplier

We are coming now to the central problem of the present chapter—namely, How is the balance of payments affected by autonomous changes in either the domestic or the foreign economy through the income-adjustment mechanism? Using the assumptions explained in the preceding sections and the formal presentation of the Keynesian model in Chapter 6, we may state the equilibrium conditions of two economies (*a* and *b*) engaging in mutual trading as

$$Y_a = C_a(Y_a) + I_a(Y_a) + X_a(Y_b) + k \cdot A \qquad (3.1)$$

and

$$Y_b = C_b(Y_b) + I_b(Y_b) + X_b(Y_a) + f \cdot A \qquad (3.2)$$

where Y, C, I, and X stand for real income, real domestic consumption, real domestic investment, and real exports, respectively, while the parentheses following any such variable should be read as "function of."

Actually, each equation summarizes the expenditure side of the national-income accounts discussed in Chapter 3. The equations state the equality between factor income, on the one hand, and the sum of the different propensities or uses that have absorbed the product of the different productive factors. While in Chapter 3 we were concerned mainly with the accounting identity implied by these relations, here we have made a simple behavioral assumption, namely, that the different aggregates of expenditure depend on the level of income. Here k and f are two parameters whose meaning we shall explain later, and A is a shift parameter, whose initial value we assume to be zero and whose change, dA, may reflect an autonomous shift of any of the functions on the right-hand side of equations 3.1 and 3.2.

The two equations fully describe the operation of the two economies. Generally there will be one set of solutions, Y_a^0 and Y_b^0, satisfying relations 3.1 and 3.2; these are the equilibrium levels of real income of the economies. Consumption, investment, exports, and imports are readily obtainable as $C(Y^0)$, etc. The stability conditions of the system will be fully spelled out later (Chap. 9) as a proposition of dynamic analysis. However, in an intuitive way, we may postulate, even at the present stage of our analysis, that the system will be stable, provided that in both economies the marginal propensity to save exceeds in algebraic value the marginal propensity to invest (i.e., $S' > I'$). The economic rationale of this proposition is simply that if income moves above its equilibrium position Y^0 in either country, the desired investment increases less than desired saving. This, of course, must reduce demand for domestically produced goods below the output of such goods; inventories accumulate, and producers contract output back to the equilibrium level Y^0.

Of course, if the equilibrium level of real income in either country exceeds the full-employment level, relations 3.1 and 3.2 can no longer hold. Real income in such a case will settle at the full-employment level, and the rest of the adjustment takes place through price, wage, and interest-rate alterations. Such a case, however, does not concern us at present. It will be discussed later in this chapter and in the following chapter.

Strictly speaking, the foregoing model does not necessarily presuppose fixed exchange rates. If imports of both countries were perfectly price-inelastic and dependent only on real income, the system would settle at its equilibrium values Y_a^0 and Y_b^0, irrespective of the rate of exchange. Only the monetary balance of payments would be affected by the exchange rate. However, this situation is extremely unrealistic; consequently, we shall henceforth assume that the rate of exchange is fixed and that imports depend on income only, because prices in both countries are assumed to be fixed.

The rationale and the derivation of the foreign-trade multiplier proceed along customary lines. If desired consumption, investment, or exports increase or fall by a given number, say dA, at any level of income, i.e., if either of these propensities shifts upward by dA, income will at first increase by the same amount; however, as income increases, expenditure will also increase, and this will further increase income. Such a circular process of increased spending and income will continue until a new equilibrium is reached, consistent with the set of relations 3.1 and 3.2 and the autonomous increase in spending, dA. The only way in which the present analysis differs from the usual multiplier analysis is that income changes in one country also affect income in the other country. This happens because imports of the first country generate income in the second country and vice-versa.

The exact impact on real income in the two countries of a change of $k \cdot dA$ in spending in country a and of $f \cdot dA$ in spending in country b may be precisely calculated by differentiating relations 3.1 and 3.2 with respect to A and solving for dY_a/dA and dY_b/dA. Using primes to express first derivatives (marginal propensities), the two relations, after differentiation, become

$$(1 - C_a' - I_a') \cdot \frac{dY_a}{dA} - X_a' \cdot \frac{dY_b}{dA} = k \tag{3.3}$$

and

$$(I - C_b' - I_b') \cdot \frac{dY_b}{dA} - X_b' \cdot \frac{dY_a}{dA} = f \tag{3.4}$$

Solving the two equations in two unknowns, we obtain

$$\frac{dY_a}{dA} = \frac{1}{D} \cdot [k \cdot (1 - C_b' - I_b') + f \cdot X_a'] \tag{3.5}$$

and

$$\frac{dY_b}{dA} = \frac{1}{D} \cdot [f \cdot (1 - C_a' - I_a') + k \cdot X_b'] \tag{3.6}$$

where

$$D = (1 - C_a' - I_a') \cdot (1 - C_b' - I_b') - X_a' \cdot X_b' \tag{3.7}$$

Relations 3.5 and 3.6 are the most general statements of the foreign-trade multiplier with foreign repercussions. Special, or more limited, multipliers may be derived from these expressions, depending on the different assumptions we may want to make. We may recall at this point that the derivatives C_a', I_a', and X_a' are the marginal propensity to consume in a, the marginal propensity to invest in a, and the marginal propensity to import in b, respectively.

To take an example, consider a case where, say, consumption in country a increases autonomously by \$1, i.e., $dA = 1$; the marginal propensities to consume domestic products in both countries are equal to 0.7, to invest 0 (i.e., zero), and to import 0.1. Since there is no autonomous change in country b, f is equal to zero, and k is equal to $+1$. The change in the real income of country a will be

$$\$\frac{dY_a}{dA} = \$\frac{1 \cdot (1 - 0.7)}{(1 - 0.7) \cdot (1 - 0.7) - (0.1) \cdot (0.1)} = \$3.75$$

and that of country b

$$\$\frac{dY_b}{dA} = \$\frac{1 \cdot (0.1)}{(1 - 0.7) \cdot (1 - 0.7) - (0.1) \cdot (0.1)} = \$1.25$$

A simple multiplier of country a without foreign repercussion may be obtained from relation 3.5, assuming that all the marginal propensities of country b are zero and so is f. In this case the other country will not respond at all to any changes in a's income, and the foreign-trade multiplier becomes

$$\frac{dY_a}{dA} = \frac{1 \cdot k}{1 - C_a' - I_a'} \tag{3.8}$$

With the assumptions of the above example, the change in a's income resulting from an increased expenditure of \$1 would be \$3.33, i.e., somewhat less than if the foreign economy reacted to income changes in country *a*.

The reader should be reminded that $1 - C'$, i.e., one minus the marginal propensity to consume domestically produced goods, is equal to the marginal propensity to import plus the marginal propensity to save. Using this relation, the multipliers in relations 3.5, 3.6, and 3.8 could be rewritten. Often in the literature the latter formulation is used.

The changes in the different functions, or propensities, appearing on the right-hand side of relations 3.1 and 3.2 are now easily obtainable if we recall that

$$\frac{dF(Y)}{dA} = F' \cdot \frac{dY}{dA} \tag{3.9}$$

where Y is a function of A and the "prime" is used to represent a derivative. Thus, for example, the change in consumption in country *a* will be equal to the marginal propensity to consume in country *a* times the change in income in *a*, i.e., dY_a/dA, as given by relation 3.5. Of course, if we want to evaluate the total change in the propensity that caused the original increase in expenditure by $k \cdot dA$, we have to add the autonomous change itself to the change computed as in relation 3.9. Thus, for example, if the change were caused by increased consumer spending on domestically produced goods, the total change in this propensity would be

$$\frac{dC}{dA} = C' \cdot \frac{dY_a}{dA} + k \tag{3.10}$$

The first term of the right-hand side of this relation expresses the increase in consumption induced by increased income, while the second term reflects the autonomous shift in the propensity schedule.

7.4   The Balance of Payments and the Foreign-Trade Multiplier

Once we are able to evaluate the impact of autonomous changes in spending on national income, only a minor step remains to be made to calculate the impact of such a change on the balance of payments. As we have assumed, the rate of exchange and prices in both countries are fixed at a given level. For the sake of simplicity, let us assume that prices in both countries and the rate of exchange are equal to one.[1] The balance of payments on current account will al-

---

[1] Observe that the physical units of measurement and the currencies in the two countries may always be defined in such a way as to fulfill this condition.

ways be equal to the difference between autonomous exports and autonomous imports. Also the change in the balance of payments, *BP*, resulting from an autonomous shift in domestic spending by country *a* of $k \cdot dA$ and by country *b* by $f \cdot dA$ may be written as

$$\frac{dBP_a}{dA} = X'_a \frac{dY_b}{dA} - X'_b \frac{dY_a}{dA} \tag{4.1}$$

Using relations 3.5 and 3.6, i.e., the foreign-trade income multipliers, we have

$$\frac{dBP_a}{dA} =$$

$$\frac{f \cdot X'_a \cdot (1 - C'_a - I'_a - X'_b) - k \cdot X'_b \cdot (1 - C'_b - I'_b - X'_a)}{D} \tag{4.2}$$

D being defined in relation 3.7. If the initial change in spending took place in the exports either of country *a* or of country *b*, a corresponding term, either *k* or *f*, should either be added to or subtracted from the right-hand side of relation 4.2.

Using the data of our example in the preceding section, assuming that an increase of $1 took place in the domestic expenditure of country *a*, the change in *a*'s balance of current payments will be equal to

$$\$ \frac{dBP_a}{dA} = \$ \frac{1}{0.08} [-1 \cdot (0.1) \cdot (1 - 0.7 - 0.1)] = -\$0.25$$

i.e., the balance of payments has deteriorated by 25 cents. Note that in our example *k* is equal to 1 and *f* to zero because the autonomous change took place in country *a* and no such change in spending took place in country *b*. The change in spending was realized on domestic consumption or investment in country *a*. If exports of that country were increased, our above result would have to be augmented by the amount of this increase, i.e., $1. Thus the balance of payments of country *a* would have improved by 75 cents rather than worsened.

Our last remark raises an interesting problem. Can an autonomous increase in exports, uncompensated for by reduced domestic spending in the importing country, ever worsen the balance of payments of the country that realized the initial increase in exports? Using relation 4.2, this condition may be expressed as

$$1 - \frac{1}{D} \cdot X'_b(1 - C'_b - I'_b - X'_a) < 0 \tag{4.3}$$

Recalling that $1 - C'_a$ is equal to $S'_a + X'_b$, and stating *D* explicitly as given in relation 3.7, this inequality may be reworked into the condition

$$\frac{(S'_a - I'_a)(S'_b + X'_a - I'_b)}{(S'_b - I'_b)X'_b} < 0 \tag{4.4}$$

If the marginal propensity to save in country a were exactly equal to the marginal propensity to invest in that country, the left-hand side of the inequality would be equal to zero. Whenever the stability conditions in isolation are fulfilled in both countries, i.e., $S' > I'$, the left-hand side must be greater than zero; consequently, the balance of payments of a country whose exports undergo an autonomous increase, uncompensated for by reduced domestic consumption in the foreign country, must improve. A similar consideration of relation 4.2 leads us to the conclusion that the balance of payments of a country whose income increases from an autonomous rise in domestic spending can never improve, provided that the income-determining model (i.e., relations 3.1 and 3.2) yields a stable solution.

The assumption of uncompensated increase of one of the propensities is actually another way of saying that the increased spending comes from reduced savings. Alternatively, one propensity to spend might increase at the expense of another. If such a substitution takes place between two domestic expenditures, no change in the total income of either country will occur. If, however, expenditure on domestic products is reduced and that on imports increased by the corresponding amount, the income of both countries and the balance of payments will be affected. If, for example, there is an autonomous \$1 increase in demand for exports of country a, matched by reduced spending on domestic products in country b, k becomes equal to $+1$ and f to -1 in the above results. Moreover, the right-hand side of relation 4.2 now has to be augmented by $+1$, to reflect the original increase in exports of country a. In our example the balance of payments of country a would now increase by 0.5. The improvement in the balance of payments of country a will be smaller than with uncompensated increased imports by country b. However, the balance of payments of country a must still improve, provided that in both countries the marginal propensity to save is greater than the marginal propensity to invest.

7.5 Transfer under Keynesian Assumptions

We have already discussed and given an accounting definition for transfer in Chapter 2. In this section, we want to discuss the monetary and real aspects of the transfer mechanism. If one country donates or lends a certain sum, say dA, to the other country every year, such a transfer of purchasing power will generally affect disposable incomes of both the transfer-providing and the transfer-receiving country. If both economies operate under conditions of less than full employment and in all other respects fulfill the assumptions underlying the income-determination model defined by relations 3.1 and 3.2, the economies of both countries will be affected. The income of the paying country will diminish and undergo further reduction through the effect of the foreign-trade multiplier, and the income of the receiving country will increase through the same mechanism. The balance of payments of the two countries will change. However, unless the balance of payments of the transfer-receiving country deteriorates by exactly as much as the value of the transfer dA, we have what many international economists call *the transfer problem*. Either the real adjustment to the transfer did produce a balance-of-payments deterioration exceeding dA, and in this case the autonomous transfer will be accompanied by an accommodating flow of gold or foreign exchange in the opposite direction; or the balance of payments did not deteriorate sufficiently to effect the transfer of purchasing power. In the latter situation, some accommodating payments to the transfer-receiving country will have to be made to make up for the insufficient adjustment of the balance on current account.

In this section we shall show the impact of transfer on the balance of payments and establish rigorously the conditions for transfer being exactly effected, undereffected, or overeffected. Of course, we proceed with the assumptions and the income-determining model derived in the preceding sections.

The effect of a financial transfer of dA from country a to b on the incomes and expenditures of the two countries will depend on the particular way in which such funds are raised and spent. A number of possible assumptions, corresponding to each concrete case and policy, could be stated. If the governments of the two countries effect the transfer, for example, we could assume that government expenditure in country a is reduced autonomously by dA and in country b increased by the same amount. The government of country a could also transfer money to the government of b, without reducing its own spending at home, through deficit spending.

For the purpose of our analysis, the important consideration is what portion of the funds transferred affects expenditure on domestic products in the two countries, on the one hand, and on foreign products, on the other. Let us first assume that autonomous spending in the country providing transfer (country a) is reduced by dA; a fraction p of dA is the initial reduction of country a's imports, while a fraction $1 - p$ represents the initial reduction of domestic spending. In the receiving country b, on the other hand, a fraction q of dA is the autonomous increase in spending on imports, while $1 - q$ is directed toward domestic products of country b. It is not necessary that a transfer dA affect the expenditure of the two countries by exactly the same amount. A number of situations could be thought of where this would not be so. However, this simple situation may be interpreted as the "normal" case. A typical case in the real world compatible with this assumption arises when one government makes a grant to another, with a balanced budget and unchanged tax rates in both countries.

More generally, a transfer causing the expenditure *of* country a to increase by $k \cdot dA$ (decrease if k is negative) and that of country b to increase by $f \cdot dA$ will increase spending *on* goods produced in country a by $dA\,[(1 - p) \cdot k + q \cdot f]$ and that on goods produced in b by $dA\,[(1 - q) \cdot f + p \cdot k]$. We should recall at this point the distinction between the expenditure of a country and the expenditure on products of a country. It is the former that we have called expenditure (E) in Chapter 3 and the latter that we have called income (Y).

With these observations we may now derive the balance-of-payments multiplier expressing the change in the balance of payments of country a resulting from an autonomous transfer of dA to country b. For this purpose we may use relation 4.2, remembering that the original changes in exports and imports of country a, i.e., $(q \cdot f)$ and $(p \cdot k)$, have to be included in the expression and also that the coefficients k and f in relation 4.2 now become more complicated and assume the forms shown in the preceding paragraph. Thus

$$\frac{dBP_a}{dA} =$$

$$\frac{[(1 - q) \cdot f + p \cdot k] \cdot X_a' \cdot (1 - C_a' - I_a' - X_b') - [(1 - p) \cdot k + q \cdot f] \cdot X_b' \cdot (1 - C_b' - I_b' - X_a')}{D}$$

$$+ q \cdot f - p \cdot k \quad (5.1)$$

where D is defined by relation 3.7. Coefficients k and f express the impact of transfer dA on autonomous changes in expenditure (E) in country a and country b. The sign of these coefficients expresses the direction of such changes ($+$ increase, $-$ decrease). Of course, in the usual case where autonomous changes of expenditure are equal to the transfer itself, k will be -1 and f $+1$.

To illustrate this result we may compute a hypothetical solution, based, as before, on the assumptions $C' = 0.7$, $I' = 0$, and $X' = 0.1$ in both countries. The transfer is fully reflected in expenditures, i.e., $k = -1$ and $f = +1$. Moreover, we assume that q and p, i.e., the proportions of transferred funds expended on and withheld from exports of country a and country b, respectively, are equal to the marginal propensities to import, 0.1. Thus we obtain the change in the balance of payments of country a, per dollar of transfer, that is, the balance-of-payments multiplier

$$\frac{dBP_a}{dA} = \frac{0.8}{0.08} \cdot [(0.1) \cdot (1 - 0.7 - 0.1) + (0.1) \cdot (1 - 0.7 - 0.1)]$$
$$= 0.6 \qquad\qquad\qquad\qquad + 0.1 + 0.1$$

Thus, within the assumed model of income determination and with the assumed values of the parameters, we may conclude that the balance of payments on current account of country a would improve only by $0.6. Consequently, only this amount of the transfer would assume a real form; the remaining $0.4 would have to be transferred through accommodating outflow of gold or foreign exchange.[2] We may denote such a situation as *undertransfer*. The opposite case, where the change in balance on current account is larger than the financial transfer, may usefully be called *overtransfer*. The three conditions—under-, over-, and exactly effected transfer—can be analyzed by putting the right-hand side of relation 5.1 respectively smaller than, greater than, or equal to 1. We leave it to the reader to study the restrictions on the different parameters imposed by such inequalities. The number of situations that relation 5.1 could describe as special cases is much too large to lend itself to any exhaustive treatment; the reader may find the relation useful in dealing with any particular case.

Nevertheless, we may at least outline briefly the scope of possible applications of relation 5.1. In the first place, we should observe that the values of k and f by no means have to be equal to -1 and

---

[2] The different effects of the transaction on the balance of payments of the receiving country may be summarized as follows:

CHANGES IN THE BALANCE OF PAYMENTS OF COUNTRY b

	Credits	Debits
Goods and services........................		60
Transfers................................	100	...
Gold and foreign exchange................		40
Total	100	100

1, respectively. For example, k will be zero if the lender or donor in country a does not reduce his current expenditure in order to finance the transfer. Such a situation of deficit spending either on the part of the government or on the part of a private person may be quite plausible if the economy operates at less than full employment. On the other hand, the receiving country may increase its expenditure by more than dA, i.e., $f > 1$, if the original borrowing or grant was intended to finance some investment project that cost more than the value of the transfer itself.

The parameters p and q are valuable in establishing the effect of the distribution between domestic and foreign spending of transferred funds on the balance of payments. For example, a tied loan or grant to country b by country a may be expressed as a situation in which $q = 1$. In such a case, it may be observed from relation 5.1 that the transfer may again be either more or less than the adjustment of the balance of payments. Of course, the likelihood of fully performing the transfer without running into payments difficulties is now increased.

A new problem arises if the government in the lending country raises funds for transfer through taxation, while the receiving country reduces taxation by the amount of the transfer. The result in relation 5.1 may easily be adjusted to handle this situation. Assuming that investors and the government spend money only on domestic products, a transfer of dA, if financed through taxation, initially reduces expenditure in country a not by dA, but by $(C'_a + X'_b) \cdot dA$. Similarly, a reduction in taxes in country b by dA produces an autonomous increase in b's expenditure of $(C'_b + X'_a) \cdot dA$. Consequently, it is possible to obtain the "tax-multiplier" from relation 5.1 by substituting, for k and f, $-(C'_a + X'_b)$ and $+(C'_b + X'_a)$, respectively. In the more realistic case where funds are raised through taxation in country a and used for additional spending in country b, k will be equal to $-(C'_a + X'_b)$, while f will remain equal to $+1$.

We should observe that the entire analysis of this section pertains to a situation in which transfer is considered as a flow and not as a stock. In other words, we were considering a permanent change in the balance of payments resulting from continuous lending of dA, indefinitely. If a grant or loan of dA once and for all were considered, the present analysis would apply; but a few further qualifications would have to be made. If this transfer once and for all of dA dollars were made, say at the beginning of the balance-of-payments accounting period, and we were able to assume that the different propensities in the two countries would adjust immediately for the duration of the accounting period, all our conclusions concerning continuous transfer would also hold in this particular case. In the context of purely static, or comparative static, analysis, after the accounting period had elapsed, all variables would again settle at their original pretransfer level. Of course, the stock of gold or foreign exchange of the two countries would be modified to the extent that the transfer was over- or undereffected in real terms.

It is true that all the assumptions underlying the analysis of transfer offered in this section are quite unrealistic, except, perhaps, in the case where both economies operate well below full employment. Nevertheless, it would not be correct to conclude that the analysis is therefore useless in considering any concrete situation of transfer. If prices or exchange rates are flexible, the portion of financial transfer that is over- or undereffected in real terms will be corrected through these variables. We are not in a position yet to say how much of such price adjustment will be necessary; however, from the sign of the difference between real and financial transfer, we may draw conclusions at least with respect to the direction of such adjustment. Actually, the analysis of the price and exchange-rate mechanism of Chapter 5 may then, as a first approximation, be superimposed on the present income analysis, and a crude opinion may be formed as to the direction and degree of necessary price and/or exchange-rate adjustment. In Chapter 8 we shall make an attempt to formalize with greater precision the interaction between the multiplier and price effects in the process of adjustment.

In this section we have focused our attention on the balance-of-payments effects of transfer. The question as to what will be the impact of transfer on the levels of income in the two countries is much easier to answer. Relations 3.5 and 3.6 provide the solutions; but k and f in these relations now have to be replaced by the more complicated expressions $[(1 - p) k + qf]$ and $[(1 - q) f + pk]$, explained earlier in this section.

7.6 Transfer under Classical Assumptions

We have already indicated the importance that Say's law and the assumption of continuous full employment of resources played in the classical analysis. If, in the short run, $Y = Y_0$, where Y_0 is full-employment income and output, solely determined by the stock of productive resources and technology of the period, it is possible to write

$$D_m = D_m(P_m, Y_0^1) = D_m(P_m) \qquad (6.1)$$

and

$$D_x = D_x(P_x, Y_0^2) = D_x(P_x) \qquad (6.2)$$

In words, the aggregate demands for imports and exports are functions only of corresponding prices and not of income, because the latter may be assumed fixed in the short run. Actually, the analysis of Chapter 5, where we studied the conditions of the foreign-exchange and export and import markets, is founded on these assumptions. In the context of the complete classical model, the rate of interest should also be included as a variable. However, to keep the problem within manageable dimensions, we follow here the customary analysis.

The important exception where income effects have to be considered in the classical model even in a short-run analysis is the case of transfer. If a country transfers an amount dA of its real purchasing power to another country, the full-employment incomes or products Y_0 of the two countries will not be affected, by definition, but the disposable incomes of the two trading communities, say Y_d, will change by the amount of the transfer. It is disposable income, rather than national product, that enters the demand functions 6.1 and 6.2. Consequently, under classical assumptions, the transfer process will be accomplished through an interaction of price and *pure* income effects. The multiplier effect cannot enter because the products of both countries remain unchanged. The reader may reconstruct for himself, however, an asymmetrical situation wherein one country behaves as if in the classical world, while the other leaves full employment and its real income declines through an income multiplier process. A combination of the analysis of the preceding and the present sections may be used in this case. We shall expand the analysis in this direction in the next chapter.

Before dealing with the price-income adjustment to transfer under classical assumptions, let us point out the simple situation in which prices, for one reason or another, do not change and where also the exchange rate is fixed. In this case, the demands for exports and imports become

$$D_m = D_m(Y_d^a) \qquad (6.3)$$

and

$$D_z = D_z(Y_d^b) \tag{6.4}$$

The disposable income of country a which exports capital A is

$$Y_d^a = Y_0^a - A \tag{6.5}$$

and that of the receiving country is

$$Y_d^b = Y_0^b + A \tag{6.6}$$

Thus the balance of payments, using these four relations and assuming that all prices and the rate of exchange are one, may be expressed as

$$BP_a = D_z(Y_0^b + A) - D_m(Y_0^a - A) \tag{6.7}$$

Differentiating with respect to A, we obtain the change in the balance of payments caused by a small increment of transfer dA, namely,

$$\frac{dBP_a}{dA} = D_z' + D_m' \tag{6.8}$$

In words, the change in the balance of payments of country a resulting from \$1 of transfer of real purchasing power to country b will be equal to the marginal propensity to import of b plus the marginal propensity to import of a (note that D' is precisely the marginal propensity to import) . The transfer will be exactly effected if the sum of the marginal propensities is exactly equal to 1; over-effected (in real terms) if the sum is larger; and undereffected if it is smaller than 1. In the first case, our assumption of fixed prices is justified. In the other two cases, prices and/or the exchange rate will have to adjust. The terms of trade will move against country a if the critical sum of propensities is larger than 1, and in its favor if the sum is smaller than 1.

It is possible to show the price, income, and exchange-rate adjustment simultaneously if the exchange rates fluctuate freely. No accommodating monetary flows will have to take place in this case. For simplicity, let us assume that prices in the two countries are constant. We may write the two demand functions for exports and imports of the transferring country (a) as

$$D_m = D_m(P_z^b \cdot r, \ Y_0^a - A) \tag{6.9}$$

and

$$D_z = D_z\left(P_z^a \cdot \frac{1}{r}, \ Y_0^b + A\right) \tag{6.10}$$

where r is the value of foreign currency in terms of domestic currency, A, in the same way as Y is defined in terms of real purchasing power, and its initial value is zero. Assuming $P_x^a = P_x^b = 1$, the balance of autonomous payments of country a in terms of foreign currency now becomes

$$BP_a = \frac{1}{r} \cdot D_x - A - D_m \qquad (6.11)$$

Differentiating relation 6.11 with respect to A, we obtain the change in the trade balance per unit of transfer A

$$\frac{dBP_a}{dA} = \frac{dr}{dA} \left[-\frac{dD_x}{d(1/r)} \cdot \left(\frac{1}{r}\right)^3 - \frac{dD_m}{dr} \right] + \frac{1}{r}\frac{dD_x}{dA} + \frac{dD_m}{dA} -$$
$$\left(\frac{1}{r}\right)^2 \cdot D_x \frac{dr}{dA} - 1 \quad (6.12)[3]$$

To comprehend better relations 6.11 and 6.12, some qualifications are in order. Suppose that the government of country a levies a tax amounting to dA, say \$1, and transfers it to country b, using the foreign-exchange market. This will in turn increase the disposable money income of country b by \$1 times whatever the new equilibrium rate of exchange may be. In order for relations 6.9 and 6.10 to hold rigorously, it has to be assumed that the real value of that transfer to the community of country a and country b is exactly dA. It has to be realized that such an assumption is somewhat unrealistic because, as the rate of exchange and consequently the terms of trade change, real income in the two countries, if it can be defined at all, will be affected differently. As a consequence, our results should be regarded only as approximations. Another limitation of the present approach, although not a complete hindrance, is the fact that the rate of interest is not included as a variable. Actually, it should be, in the context of a classical full-employment theory.

With these observations in mind, let us now recall that, under conditions of free exchange, the balance of payments must always be in equilibrium. Thus both sides of equation 6.12 must be equal to zero. Recalling that the elasticity of demand for imports is

$$e_m = \frac{dD_m}{dr} \cdot \frac{r}{D_m}$$

[3] We use here the symbol d for partial derivation; from the context of the problem it should be apparent, however, where partial and where total derivatives are used.

and the elasticity of demand for exports is

$$e_x = \frac{dD_x}{d(1/r)} \cdot \frac{(1/r)}{D_x}$$

and that the two partial derivatives with respect to A are actually the marginal propensities to import, we obtain from relation 6.12 the required result, for the case where the initial value of r is 1,

$$(dr =) \frac{dr}{r} = -\frac{dA}{D_m} \cdot \frac{1 - MPM^a - MPM^b}{1 + e_m + e_x} \qquad (6.13)$$

On the left-hand side of the equation we find the percentage change in the rate of exchange, while the first fraction on the right-hand side expresses the amount of the transfer as a proportion of the initial volume of imports. Alternatively, we might say that it is the proportion of the value of transfer to the initial value of imports or exports in either currency.

Examining relation 6.13, we observe that it contains both the "pure" income conditions for transfer derived earlier in this section and the stability condition of the foreign-exchange market, i.e., the simple Marshall-Lerner condition. If the two propensities to import add up exactly to 1, the rate of exchange will not change at all. If the foreign-exchange market is stable and the sum of the propensities is smaller than 1, the rate of exchange r will have to go up; i.e., the domestic currency will be devalued. If, with stability, the propensities together exceed unity, the rate will drop; that is, the domestic currency will appreciate. With an unstable foreign-exchange market, strictly speaking, the opposite should hold. However, it is very likely that if the exchange market were left perfectly free, the disturbance caused by the transfer would make the equilibrium settle at a stable solution. This might reverse the direction of change of the exchange rate. If the sum of the elasticities is -1, the problem remains undetermined; all we are able to say is that the change in the exchange rate will be quite large.

Finally, we should observe that, under our present assumptions, the rate of exchange r also expresses the terms of trade of the receiving country (b) and $1/r$ the terms of trade of the transferring country (a). Thus, whatever conclusions we may derive from relation 6.13 as to the rate of exchange r we have also derived for the terms of trade of country b, and similarly for country a.

It would be possible to deal with the present problem by relaxing the assumption of constant prices, assuming the rate of exchange fixed and the two economies operating under the gold standard. As we have shown in Chapter 6, except for possible dynamic complications, the results would be exactly the same. The adjustment to an over- or undereffected transfer would now be accomplished through price, rather than exchange-rate, alterations. Instead of r in relation 6.13, we would now have to write T, the terms of trade of the receiving country.

7.7 The Rate of Interest, National Income, and the Trade Balance

Throughout this chapter, whenever we have used the Keynesian model in explaining the relation between the trade balance and the level of national income, in an under-full-employment economy, we have made three crucial assumptions: (i) all prices are fixed, (ii) the rate of interest does not change, and (iii) the rate of exchange is fixed. In the following chapter we shall examine the more complete and more realistic situation in which both prices and the rate of exchange are permitted to adjust to changing conditions of the balance of payments and income. Without introducing flexible prices and exchange rate, it is possible to generalize the foreign-trade multiplier analysis by letting the rate of interest and the money supply vary. This will be our task in the present section.

The assumption of fixed interest rate does not require any additional restriction on the model we are using; to be able to assume that prices remain unchanged, we have to assume that money wages are fixed and the marginal physical productivity of labor is constant in the neighborhood of the equilibrium considered. If it were otherwise, as we have indicated earlier in this chapter, changes in real expenditure would produce changes in real wages, and, with rigid money wages, the price level also would have to change.

Assuming that prices and the rate of exchange are set at unity, we may now derive the simple foreign-trade multiplier without foreign repercussion relating the level of income to changes in total money supply. As we have noted in several instances, the total supply of money is the one variable controlled by the central authorities. Through its variation, the central bank may affect the rate of interest and all other variables in the economy, such as investment, saving, real income, and imports. With the same notation as before, and letting m be total supply of money, we may describe our hypothetical economy, using the Keynesian money equation and the income-expenditure equation. Exports, as in the case of the simple foreign-trade multiplier without foreign repercussion, are assumed to be fixed, and imports a function of income only:

$$m = f(i, Y) \tag{7.1}$$

$$0 = I(i, Y) + X - M(Y) - S(i, Y) \tag{7.2}$$

Differentiating with respect to m, we obtain

$$1 = f_i \frac{di}{dm} + f_Y \frac{dY}{dm}$$

and

$$0 = (Y_i - S_i) \cdot \frac{di}{dm} + (I_Y - S_Y - M_Y) \cdot \frac{dY}{dm}$$

where subscripts represent partial differentiation with respect to the particular variable. Solving for the two total derivatives, we obtain

$$\frac{dY}{dm} = \frac{1}{D} \cdot (I_i - S_i) \tag{7.3}$$

and

$$\frac{di}{dm} = -\frac{1}{D} \cdot (I_Y - S_Y - M_Y) \tag{7.4}$$

where

$$D = f_Y \cdot (I_i - S_i) - f_i(I_Y - S_Y - M_Y) \tag{7.5}$$

Relation 7.3 shows the change in real national income resulting from a dollar change in total money supply. Relation 7.4 shows a change in the rate of interest attributable to the same cause. Noticing that f_Y is positive and f_i negative, the denominator D in both expressions must be negative, provided that the savings investment market is stable and that the pure income-determination model is stable.

Although the policy variable here considered is total money supply and not the rate of interest, we often prefer to speak of the impact of the rate of interest on the level of income, exports, imports, and investment. A result may be derived, showing the impact of interest rate on income; of course, we have to specify that such a change in income is caused by a corresponding alteration in the money supply. All we have to do is divide relation 7.3 by relation 7.4; we obtain

$$\frac{dY}{di} = \frac{S_i - I_i}{I_Y - S_Y - M_Y} \tag{7.6}$$

The change in imports resulting from a given alteration of the rate of interest through appropriate manipulation of the money supply by the government may then be obtained as

$$\frac{dM}{di} = M_Y \frac{dY}{di} = M_Y \cdot \frac{S_i - I_i}{I_Y - S_Y - M_Y} \tag{7.7}$$

Functions of price (i.e., interest rate) and income both appear in the relation. Therefore, to make the relation more directly applicable to concrete problems, it may be preferable to rewrite it in terms of elasticities. Using d_I and s_S for the interest elasticity of demand and supply of investment funds, respectively, and e_I, e_S, and e_M for the income elasticities of investment, saving, and imports, relation 7.7 may be reformulated as

$$\frac{dM}{M} \bigg/ \frac{di}{i} = e_M \cdot \frac{d_I - s_S}{e_S + (M/I)e_M - e_I} \tag{7.8}$$

The left-hand side of the equation shows the percentage change in imports per 1 per cent change in the rate of interest, or what we may call the interest elasticity of imports. If we notice that under our assumptions the change in the balance of payments is the change in imports with a minus sign, we may also write

$$dBP = -\frac{di}{i} \cdot M \cdot K \tag{7.9}$$

where K represents the expression on the right-hand side of relation 7.8.

Chapter 8

PRICE AND INCOME EFFECTS COMBINED IN THE BALANCE-OF-PAYMENTS ADJUSTMENT PROCESS

8.1 Terms of Trade, the Exchange Rate, and Income in the Adjustment Process

Beginning with Chapter 4, we have been progressing in the direction of a more complicated, but also more comprehensive, theory reflecting with greater precision the balance-of-payments adjustment mechanism in the real world. The present chapter is designed to further this process and combine the principal elements of analysis that we have discussed so far. The relationships among the important variables of adjustment, income, interest rate, terms of trade, and exchange rate are known to us already from Chapter 6. There we explained the principles of income determination in an open economy under two alternative sets of assumptions —that of the classical full-employment economy and that of a Keynesian less-than-full-employment economy. The logic of the adjustment processes corresponding to these two analytical frameworks is contained in Chapter 6. However, the theory presented there is nonoperational, in the sense that it does not permit us to study concrete cases of balance-of-payments adjustment from given or assumed parameters, such as the different marginal propensities and elasticities of supply and demand.

To obtain such a workable theory, let us start by examining the interaction of price and income effects in determining the balance of payments, exports and imports, as well as the level of income, consumption, investment, and savings. Departing from the simple Keynesian approach, where only level of income is used as an independent variable, let us construct another functional representation of a two-country equilibrium with both income and relative prices used as adjustment variables. Clearly, such a theory is better suited to describe the conditions of the real world. For example, an increase in demand for a country's exports will affect the terms of trade and/or the exchange rate, in addition to increasing effective demand. Alternatively, a devaluation will have an impact on both the terms of trade and the level of income in an economy that does not operate at full employment.

To make the theory manageable, let us first assume that two economies operate at less than full employment and that elasticities of supply are infinite at the level of marginal and average costs (and consequently, under competition, at the level of prices). Prices in both countries will be assumed equal to unity—if they are not in reality, units of output could always be redefined in such a way as to make them fulfill this requirement. In the initial equilibrium that we are trying to determine, the rate of exchange, r_0, is also assumed to be equal to 1, established at this level either through a gold parity or through pegging by central banks.

Each of the propensities or demand functions for the different aggregates, such as imports, consumption, investment, savings, etc., may now be expressed as depending on two factors: real income,[1] as in our previous discussions, and relative prices. Because prices of output in each economy are, by assumption, rigidly set at the level of 1, differences in prices may be brought about only by an alteration in the exchange rate. For example, demand for imports (in real terms) from country 1 to country 2, m_{12}, will now be a function of real income of country 2 and of the rate of exchange. Defining the exchange rate, r, as the number of units of country 1's currency paid for one unit of country 2's currency, we observe that the price entering the demand for imports of country 2 (with fixed prices in the two countries in terms of domestic currency) will be equal to $1/r$. The relevant price in the import function of country 1, on the other hand, will be r. Thus we may write

$$m_{12} = m_{12}\left(Y_2, \frac{1}{r}\right) \tag{1.1}$$

and

$$m_{21} = m_{21}(Y_1, r) \tag{1.2}$$

---

[1] To be precise, we understand here by real income the physical volume of national product. With unchanged domestic prices, this will also represent national money income. If the terms of trade change, with unchanged employment, the volume of national product will remain unchanged, but the satisfaction of the community derived from consumption (or what may be termed "enjoyment income") will be altered.

For the remaining discussion of this chapter we may always keep in mind that the first subscript pertains to the supplying country, where income is generated, while the second subscript refers to the demanding country, on whose income, in the sense of Keynesian propensity, the variable m depends. With these observations, we may now define symmetrically two other variables, m_{11} and m_{22}, reflecting the demand of each country for its own products; in other words, they are magnitudes that both generate income and depend on income of one country. Then m_{11} and m_{22} represent the sums of domestically produced consumption, domestically produced investment goods, and government demand for domestic products. Because prices in both countries are fixed in terms of domestic currency, these aggregates cannot depend on such prices. However, they will depend on import prices, i.e., on the rate of exchange. When import prices change, substitution between domestic and foreign products will take place whenever the cross-elasticity of demand is different from zero, which is, virtually without exception, the case. Thus we may write m_{ii} also as a function of country i's real income and of the exchange rate; with the same observations as for relations 1.1 and 1.2, we have

$$m_{11} = m_{11}(Y_1, r) \tag{1.3}$$

and

$$m_{22} = m_{22}\left(Y_2, \frac{1}{r}\right) \tag{1.4}$$

For any given prescribed level of the rate of exchange, such as the $r_0 = 1$ assumed here, it is now possible to state the two usual income equations, which, together with relations 1.1 through 1.4, determine the levels of all total propensities, as well as the level of income in both countries, namely,

$$Y_1 = m_{11} + m_{12} \tag{1.5}$$

and

$$Y_2 = m_{21} + m_{22} \tag{1.6}$$

Note that it would be possible to state a third relation, claiming equality of exports and imports in terms of one or the other currency. This, together with relations 1.1 through 1.6, would be sufficient to determine all three independent variables, Y_1, Y_2, and r. We shall discuss this case of free exchange rate in Sections 4 and 5 of this chapter. Note also that we have omitted from relations 1.5 and 1.6 domestic prices, all being equal to 1. All variables are expressed in real terms.

Having determined the static equilibrium conditions of the two economies, we may now ask how income, exports, imports, and the balance of payments will react to an alteration in the rate of exchange. The answer is of paramount importance for practical making of policy. In Chapter 5, with special qualifications, we provided the answer for an economy operating under full employment. Here we want to examine the effects of devaluation (or appreciation) on incomes and on the balance of payments, under the assumption that both incomes and relative prices change when the rate of exchange changes.

Differentiating equations 1.5 and 1.6 with respect to r, we obtain in matrix form

$$\begin{vmatrix} (1 - m'_{11}) & -m'_{12} \\ -m'_{21} & (1 - m'_{22}) \end{vmatrix} \begin{vmatrix} \dfrac{dY_1}{dr} \\ \dfrac{dY_2}{dr} \end{vmatrix} = \begin{vmatrix} \dfrac{1}{r} A_1 \\ \dfrac{1}{r} A_2 \end{vmatrix} \qquad (1.7)$$

where

$$A_1 = d^+_{11} m_{11} - d_{12} m_{12} \qquad (1.8)$$

and

$$A_2 = d_{21} m_{21} - d^+_{22} m_{22} \qquad (1.9)$$

The primes, such as in m'_{11}, indicate partial derivatives with respect to income, i.e., the marginal propensities; and d_{ij} represents the elasticity of demand[2] for products from country i by country j, with respect to the rate of exchange, i.e., with respect to the relative prices of exports and imports, or the terms of trade. The cross superscript is used to indicate a cross price elasticity; such elasticities generally, but not necessarily, will be positive. If they are, this indicates that higher relative prices of imports will produce substitution of domestic products for foreign goods. The (own) elasticities of demand will generally be negative, indicating falling demand for imports with higher import prices, assuming, of course, that income remains unchanged.

[2] I.e., $\dfrac{\partial m}{\partial r} \cdot \dfrac{r}{m}$, or $\dfrac{\partial m}{\partial (1/r)} \cdot \dfrac{(1/r)}{m}$.

Solving relation 1.7 for the changes in incomes, we obtain

$$dY_1 = \frac{dr}{r} \cdot \frac{1}{D} \cdot [A_1 \cdot (1 - m_{22}') + A_2 \cdot m_{12}'] \qquad (1.10)$$

and

$$dY_2 = \frac{dr}{r} \cdot \frac{1}{D} \cdot [A_2 \cdot (1 - m_{11}') + A_1 \cdot m_{21}'] \qquad (1.11)$$

where D is the value of the coefficient determinant, the same as that used in our discussion of pure income multiplier effects in the preceding chapter; i.e.,

$$D = (1 - m_{11}') \cdot (1 - m_{22}') - m_{12}' \cdot m_{21}' \qquad (1.12)$$

D will be always positive, provided that in both countries the marginal propensity to save is greater than the marginal propensity to invest. In addition to relations 1.10 and 1.11, we are now in a position also to state the impact of an exchange-rate change on the balance of payments. First, we note that the trade balance of country 1, BP_1, in terms of the currency of country 1, may be written as

$$BP_1 = m_{12} - m_{21} \cdot r \qquad (1.13)$$

The change in the balance of payments resulting from a given relative change in the exchange rate dr/r is, using relations 1.10 and 1.11 and remembering the assumed initial condition $r = 1$,

$$dBP_1 = \frac{dr}{r} \left\{ \frac{1}{D} \cdot [A_1(m_{12}'m_{21}' - m_{21}'[1 - m_{22}']) + A_2(m_{12}'[1 - m_{11}'] - m_{12}'m_{21}')] - A_3 \right\} \qquad (1.14)$$

where A_3 is an expression containing price elasticities, similar to A_1 and A_2, namely,

$$A_3 = m_{21} + d_{12}m_{12} + d_{21}m_{21} \qquad (1.15)$$

Actually, we recognize in $dr/r \cdot (-A_3)$ the "pure" price effect of exchange-rate variation on the balance of payments.

Let us stress again that relations 1.10, 1.11, and 1.14 are the important results showing the effect of changes in the rate of exchange on the real incomes of two trading countries and on their balance of payments, allowing for effects of both relative prices and incomes. Relation 1.14 may be thought of as a "generalized" Marshall-Lerner condition. It should be used in its complete form in establishing in each particular case whether devaluation will improve or worsen the balance of payments.

It is impossible to express the conditions for balance of payments to deteriorate or improve in terms of simple inequalities. Nevertheless, we may point out some of the implications of relation 1.14. The most important seems to be that the Marshall-Lerner condition (contained in A_3) is no longer sufficient for a balance-of-payments improvement. Income effects will tend to offset price effects of devaluation, and consequently the balance of payments may improve, deteriorate, or remain unchanged, even if the Marshall-Lerner condition obtains, i.e., even if A_3 is negative.

Considering relations 1.8 and 1.9, we observe that A_1 will generally be positive and A_2 negative, the own elasticities being negative and the cross-elasticities generally positive. In relation 1.14, on the other hand, the term multiplied by A_1 must be negative and that multiplied by A_2 must be positive. Consequently, if A_3 is zero, i.e., the foreign-exchange market is just on the brink between stability and instability on the Marshall-Lerner criterion, the balance of payments, of necessity, will deteriorate. As all the price elasticities become larger, the first term in the brackets on the right-hand side of 1.14 (multiplied by $1/D$), with unchanged marginal propensities, will grow, always remaining negative. On the other hand, $(-A_3)$ will assume increasing positive values, growing faster in absolute value than the negative term. Consequently, for some sufficiently large value of the price elasticities, the price effects will just about offset the income effects, and the balance of payments will start improving. Additional insight into these relationships will be obtained in the next section, where we apply our analysis to a hypothetical concrete case.

We may now turn to the effects of devaluation on real income and, consequently, on employment. If the two symmetrical terms A_1 and A_2 have comparable absolute values, the income of country 1 will increase, while that of country 2 will deteriorate. This may be termed the "normal" outcome. If, on the other hand, say A_1 were much smaller than A_2, incomes of both countries could deteriorate, that of country 2 always declining more than that of country 1.

Our analysis presented in this section so far has assumed the rate of exchange as the changing parameter. However, as we have already indicated and as the reader may have observed, the discussion and the results pertain equally to the situation in which the rate of exchange is rigidly set, and general price levels in each country change autonomously in different proportions as a result of domestic inflation or deflation. The only adjustment we make now is to write everywhere $1/T$, the inverse of the terms of trade of country 1, instead of r. For example, a 10 per cent proportional price inflation of domestically produced commodities in country 1 will have exactly the same effect on the real income of the two countries and on their balance of payments as a 10 per cent currency appreciation.

One very important conclusion follows from the discussion of this section. Because the price effects tend to be operating in the opposite direction from the income effects, it may well happen that foreign trade will have a depressing effect on the economy of a country, this not being at all observable from the state of the trade balance. For example, with demand elasticities for imports adding up to well above 1—say 2—relative inflation of prices in one country, while improving its terms of trade, may leave the balance of payments of the country unaffected but produce a sizable decline in its real *GNP* and employment.

As a corollary of this conclusion we may argue that in a less than fully employed world where elasticities of demand for imports are fairly large, domestic price inflation will generally be translated into a deterioration in the balance of payments; yet such a gap in the balance of payments will generally underestimate the deficiency of effective demand caused by the foreign-trade sector.

Another corollary of our proposition is that a country operating below full employment may expect to garner from currency devaluation more important gains in its over-all level of activity and employment than those it will realize in its external balance; the latter may not be affected at all or may even deteriorate.

8.2 A Concrete Case

The discussion of the preceding section may appear somewhat cumbersome because of the large number of parameters entering the solutions. For this reason it was difficult to analyze in detail the impact of each particular propensity or elasticity on the results in the same way as is customary when dealing with the simpler case of pure income or pure price effects. Consequently, it appears desirable to apply the results of the preceding section to a concrete situation, using some at least roughly realistic values for the parameters. An additional benefit we should like to derive from our example is to illustrate at least the order of magnitude of the impact of a terms-of-trade or exchange-rate adjustment on the income and the balance of payments of the United States.

Let us discuss briefly the assumptions of the case; since we are concerned only with a rough approximation, the magnitudes of the parameters do not have to be very precise, nor do the results. There are two economies—the United States and the rest of the free world. The national product of each is equal to $500 billion. Although the product of the rest of the free world is, in actuality, somewhat larger, this does not have to distort our results significantly. As we shall see later, our assumption of cross-elasticity of demand for domestic products will tend to offset such a possible bias. In all other respects the two world economies are assumed comparable, i.e., the marginal and average propensities, elasticities, and cross-elasticities have the same values in both economies.

The average propensity to import goods and services in the United States is somewhere near 4 per cent. In view of the fact that many of our imports are quite highly income-elastic, we consider it a conservative estimate to take the marginal propensity to import (m'_{ij}) equal to 5 per cent, i.e., 0.05. An assumption of 0.1 for the marginal propensity to save, also somewhat above the average propensity, seems reasonable, and consequently we may take the marginal propensity to consume equal to 0.85. Assuming that investment and government spending are independent of current income, this yields $0.85 = m'_{ii}$. Lacking any precise knowledge of the cross-elasticity of demand for domestic products with respect to the terms of trade, let us take a value $d^+_{ii} = 0.05$. This expresses the condition that with, say, a 20 per cent fall in import prices, there will be approximately a 1 per cent change in domestic expenditure. This, of course, with a roughly $480 billion expenditure on domestic products, would correspond to an elasticity of demand for imports near -1, if all the reduction of domestic spending took the form of substitution with imports. Also, let us take the closest realistic rounded figure for imports and exports of the two regions, namely, $m_{ij} = 20$.

Together with these assumptions, let us try two different sets of values for the elasticities of demand for imports, (i) $d_{ij} = -1$, and (ii) $d_{ij} = -2$. Rough estimates of the effect of a 10 per cent currency devaluation, or of a 10 per cent proportional price deflation in the United States (country 1), consistent with these assumptions is shown on page 132.

Change in	Y_1	Y_2	BP_1
$d_{ij} = -1$	+20	−20	0
$d_{ij} = -2$	+30	−30	+3

Of course, the equality of the effect on the real incomes of the two countries is a consequence of our symmetry assumptions. Our conclusion from the last section concerning the insufficiency of the traditional Marshall-Lerner condition is borne out by our example. With the sum of demand elasticities equaling 2, rather than 1, the balance of payments of the United States did not improve at all. Actually, it would be only for values of the sum larger than 2 that the balance of payments would have improved. Nevertheless, the income effect of devaluation was substantial. On the alternative set of assumptions, with the sum of elasticities equal to 4, the balance of payments has improved by $3 billion, and, of course, the effect on real income was even stronger.

If it does not exactly answer questions about the actual size of elasticities, our example, combined with empirical evidence, at least raises a number of problems. On the one hand, it would appear that the case of elasticity optimism is weakened, because it seems that in our case substantially larger limits on the sum of elasticities have to be imposed than those suggested by Marshall, Lerner, and others. On the other hand, using our common sense in examining the real world, we wonder whether, after all, the belief of the classicists as to the size of the elasticities and the ease of price adjustment is not justified. The situation of the United States in the second half of the 1950's is not incompatible with our assumptions. Between 1953 and 1960, the United States terms of trade, with a rigid exchange rate, improved by about 10 per cent. In this period export prices got out of line with European export prices by about the same amount and in the same direction. Our balance of autonomous payments deteriorated, neglecting short-run cyclical effects, by about $3 billion in the period considered. Moreover, our economy was operating mostly at less than full employment of capacity and of labor resources in the period 1958–60, precisely when the deterioration took place. It appears that the gap between potential and actual output was widening and that the rate of growth of the economy had declined. In 1960, quoting the President of the United States (Message to the Congress, February 2, 1961), we could have produced in the United States $35 billion more product if our existing capacity and labor resources had been fully utilized (not to speak about the capacity and output that could have been generated if more satisfactory conditions prevailed in this country through the seven-year period). The outlook for 1961, according to experts, was no brighter.

Our assumption of fairly high demand elasticities for imports yields results compatible with the situation of our economy in the later 1950's. The more than flourishing state of some other industrial countries, their overfull employment, 7 per cent real rates of growth, and accumulation of international reserves beyond reasonable limits may provide the other side of the story. Of course, the theory presented here, however complicated mathematically, is far too great an oversimplification of the real world; consequently, the results should be considered with the utmost reserve and due regard for the other facets of the problem. We may proceed now to discuss some of these special qualifications.

8.3 Further Discussion of Assumptions; Money, Interest Rates, Full Employment

In the preceding two sections we have not introduced money and the rate of interest explicitly into the discussion. These two factors also play a role in the determination of national income and the external balance. This was shown in Chapter 6 and also in the preceding chapter. Also, we have assumed that full employment is never reached and that an inflationary gap never arises. If we have assimilated the case of devaluation to that of a price deflation in one of the two countries, this has been done on the assumption that such price changes are autonomous, while the rate of interest is constant, for one reason or another.

It is now time to relax such assumptions and move in the direction of a more adequate representation of the real world. As full employment is approached or attained, the rate of interest and the price level may change. Consequently, the effects of an exchange rate alteration on income and the balance of payments will generally be different from those obtained in the preceding sections.

In Figure 8.3.1, we show the familiar LL_1 function (see Chap. 6, Sec. 2) and three different positions of the $ISXM$ function of a depreciating country. $ISXM_1$ represents the initial situation, while $ISXM_2$ and $ISXM_3$ represent two shifts in effective demand, the first corresponding to a 5 per cent, the second to a 10 per cent, devaluation. The corresponding levels of real output, Y_2 and Y_4, measured from Y_1 show the total income effect of devaluation, as computed through relation 1.14. Let us now further assume that Y_2 also represents full-employment output, consistent with the technology and the capacity of the economy. Consequently, the level of output Y_3 is not attainable. We recall from our discussion of Chapter 6 that LL_1 corresponds to a given price level; in the particular case discussed in Section 1 of this chapter this price is equal to 1. Pressure on resources brought about by a level of effective demand consistent with $ISXM_3$ will produce an increase in the general price level. This, in turn, will increase demand for transaction money and shift the LL curve to the left and upward. Price inflation, on the other hand, will have exactly the same effect on the $ISXM$ curve as currency appreciation by the same proportion. Consequently, as the LL curve moves to the left and upward, $ISXM$ will move to the left. The intersection point E of $ISXM_3$ and LL_1 may be imagined as traveling to the left until it settles at an equilibrium point E' on LL_2 and $ISXM_3'$ consistent with the productive capacity of the economy. When the solution E' is reached, the rate of interest will be above its minimum level i_0, and prices will have moved up from the initial level $p = 1$. This increase, however, must be lower than 5 per cent, because, if it were as high as 5 per cent, $ISXM_3$ would have moved all the way to the position $ISXM_2$, corresponding to a 5 per cent currency depreciation. Also, the LL curve would have moved above the LL_2 position, and there could not have been any full-employment equilibrium.

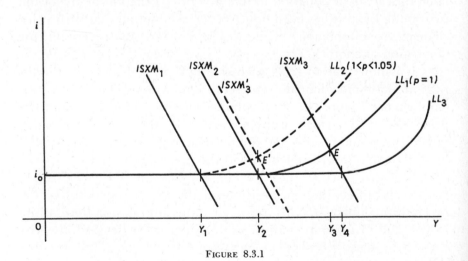

FIGURE 8.3.1

Nevertheless, there is a possibility that the entire adjustment would be carried out through price inflation without any increase in the rate of interest. If the initial position of the *LL* function were such as LL_3, yielding a real income equal to Y_4 if sufficient labor force and capacity were available, prices could increase by the full amount of 5 per cent before the *LL* curve moved to the left of LL_1. In this case the balance-of-payments and real-income effect of a 10 per cent devaluation would have come out exactly the same as those of a 5 per cent devaluation. Prices, however, would be inflated by 5 per cent, thus offsetting one half of the total loss of value of domestic currency.

In the other case, to be considered as the normal outcome, an equilibrium such as E' is established. The income effect of a 10 per cent currency depreciation would be exactly the same as that of a 5 per cent depreciation; however, the balance-of-payments effect is no longer precisely calculable from relation 1.14. As domestic prices rise, while the E' solution is being approached, the rate of interest also changes. But such changes in the interest rate may, and most likely will, affect the structure underlying relation 1.14. Only as a rough approximation, we may suggest that the balance-of-payments effect will not be much different from one caused by a currency depreciation of X per cent, where X is the effective drop in the value of domestic currency diminished by the percentage increase in domestic prices causing the upward shift of the *LL* function to E'.

The situation of the other country, i.e., the country that appreciates, is the reverse of the situation of country 1 just discussed. If it was initially at, or below, full employment and its rate of interest was at its minimum level, the analysis of Section 1 of this chapter obtains. In all other cases, before moving to a less than full-employment income in the process of adjustment to appreciation, it could have remained at full employment for some time, with declining prices and interest rates. However, once the rate of interest had fallen to i_0 and price deflation had been arrested, further income and balance-of-payments effects would have followed the paths shown in Section 1.

Of course, prices and wages may be inflexible in the downward direction; in this case, reduction of real income in the country whose currency has relatively appreciated will get under way immediately. The rate of interest, even with rigid prices and wages, will decline because of declining demand for transaction money. Observe that the *ISXM* curve now shifts leftward, from a point such as *E'*, while the *LL* curve remains unaffected.

Another assumption that should concern us in this section is that of a timeless world. All we have done so far was to examine the relation between one static equilibrium and another, corresponding to two different assumed values of a parameter—in our particular case, of the rate of exchange or of the terms of trade. In the real world the different factors of adjustment, such as income and prices, will act with a certain delay, or time lag. Moreover, the time lags of different factors may be different. Although after a sufficiently long period we may be quite confident that the new equilibrium determined by the comparative static analysis will be attained, the path toward such an equilibrium will depend not only on the parameters of the static model but also on the time lags involved. In brief, this is a matter of economic dynamics; we shall discuss such problems in greater detail in the next chapter. Nevertheless, it seems appropriate to point out, at least briefly and without any use of mathematics, the important implications that the time element may have for an income and balance-of-payments adjustment, if the rate of exchange is altered.

Time lags will always exist in the real world, in all possible types of adjustment to changes of structural or institutional parameters. What seems to be a special feature in the case presently considered is that the time lags, or speed of adjustment of different factors, may be different. The important forces introduced here are incomes and relative prices. There is good reason to believe that adjustment through the latter will be faster than through the former. As one country devalues, the terms of trade are affected immediately, and, with the excess capacity that we have assumed, the balance of payments may improve considerably within a fairly short period of time. However, it is possible to expect that it will take a while before, say, three fourths of the multiplier effect will work itself out. Thus the offsetting income effect on the balance of payments and the adjustment of income itself may last for some time. Consequently, it seems reasonable to expect that the balance of payments will at first undergo a stronger improvement (or less deterioration) than that indicated by our comparative static analysis. Later it may deteriorate somewhat as a result of delayed income effects. Of course, the long-run demand curves may be more highly elastic than the short-run demand curves. In this case the detrimental income effects in the later stage of the adjustment may be fully or partially offset by a gradual increase in the elasticities and cross-elasticities of demand.

The differences in speed of adjustment may play an important and beneficial role in the case where an overvalued currency, instead of being devalued, is freed to find its competitive value in the foreign-exchange market. In this situation, if the negative income effects operated at an equal speed with the price effects, this might precipitate an almost immediate sharp decline in the value of the currency, which could be further accelerated through foreign-exchange speculation. This might, at least for a time, lead to panic and disorder. With a delay in income adjustment, on the other hand, a substantial "first-round" improvement in the nonspeculative demand for domestic currency might provide a powerful cushion for speculative purchases of foreign exchange.

8.4 Income Adjustment under Freely Fluctuating Exchange Rates

One important topic remains to be discussed in this chapter. It is the relation between the levels and changes in effective demand in different countries and the levels and changes in income under conditions of freely fluctuating exchange rates. In other words, we want to examine the foreign-trade multiplier mechanism in a world where the foreign-exchange market is always permitted to adjust to its equilibrium level. The latter condition may also be explained by saying that in such a market no accommodating sales or purchases of currency are ever effected.

We shall not examine fully all the possible cases of shifts in effective demand, such as those of investment, government spending, consumption, and exports. Only the impact of the last of these factors on income and the exchange rate will be considered here in greater detail. Nevertheless, it will be easy for the reader to use the analysis presented here in studying any other type of structural change. Later in this section we shall discuss briefly some of these alternative applications. If we limit ourselves to the case of an autonomous increase in exports, caused by an autonomous increase in demand for import products by the foreign country, we may easily (i) define the equilibrium of the system and (ii) study its comparative static properties. Using the definitions of propensities m_{ii} and m_{ij} explained in Section 1 of this chapter, we have only to add to the two income equations 1.5 and 1.6 an additional condition expressing the equality of exports and imports in terms of one currency or the other; we have

$$Y_1 = m_{11} + m_{12} + a \qquad (4.1)$$
$$Y_2 = m_{21} + m_{22} \qquad (4.2)$$
$$0 = m_{21} \cdot r - m_{12} - a \qquad (4.3)$$

The parameter a is zero in the initial equilibrium, while da represents the autonomous shift in exports of country 1. Prices and average costs again are assumed to be constant in both countries, equal to unity. Also observe that increased spending by country 2 is not compensated for by a reduction in other expenditures. With these assumptions, relations 4.1 through 4.3 determine the three equilibrium values, namely, Y_1, Y_2, and r. Once r is found, physical units of measurement and prices in one country or the other may be redefined in such a way as to yield $r = 1$. Thus in the rest of our analysis we may assume that initially both the rate of exchange and all prices are equal to 1.

An example may illustrate this assumption. Suppose that under present conditions the equilibrium rate of exchange in a free exchange market is 3 dollars to 1 pound, all foreign countries using pounds as currency. Physical units of measurement are chosen in such a way both in the United States and in the rest of the world that every product or service costs one unit of local currency. It is now possible to redefine the foreign currency as dollars and divide every physical unit into three, so that one third of the original unit will now represent one new unit. All prices and the rate of exchange will now equal 1.

Suppose, now, that physical demand for exports of country 1 increases autonomously by da. The effect of this change on the simplified world economy may be traced out by means of differential analysis. Differentiating equations 4.1, 4.2, and 4.3 with respect to a, with a little algebra, we obtain

$$\begin{vmatrix} (1 - m'_{11}) & -m'_{12} & -A_1 \\ -m'_{21} & (1 - m'_{22}) & -A_2 \\ -m'_{21} & +m'_{12} & -A_3 \end{vmatrix} \begin{vmatrix} \dfrac{dY_1}{da} \\ \dfrac{dY_2}{da} \\ \dfrac{dr}{da} \end{vmatrix} = \begin{vmatrix} +1 \\ 0 \\ -1 \end{vmatrix} \qquad (4.4)$$

where all terms are defined as in Section 1 of this chapter, including A_1, A_2, and A_3, terms containing the elasticities and cross-elasticities of demand, whose explicit form will be found in relations 1.8, 1.9, and 1.15, respectively. The solutions of this system of linear equations in the three derivatives with respect to a will be found through the usual Cramer method, namely,

$$\frac{dY_1}{da} = \frac{1}{E} [(1 - m'_{22})(-A_1 - A_3)] \tag{4.5}$$

$$\frac{dY_2}{da} = \frac{1}{E} [m'_{21}(-A_1 - A_3) - A_2(1 - m'_{11} - m'_{21})] \tag{4.6}$$

and

$$\frac{dr}{da} = \frac{-1}{E} [(1 - m'_{22})(1 - m'_{21} - m'_{11})] \tag{4.7}$$

where E is the value of the coefficient determinant; it may be expressed in different ways, but, for the purpose of our analysis, it is preferable to write it as

$$E = A_1[m'_{12}m'_{21} - m'_{21}(1 - m'_{22})] - A_2[m'_{12}m'_{21} - m'_{12}(1 - m'_{11})] - \\ A_3[(1 - m'_{11})(1 - m'_{22}) - m'_{12}m'_{21}] \tag{4.8}$$

These equations determine the change in the real incomes of the two countries and the change in the freely fluctuating exchange rate resulting from a small increase in demand for exports of country 1. Although it is only the precise knowledge of the parameters—elasticities of demand and marginal propensities—that may yield the exact solution of each particular case, it may be interesting to examine the general properties of the solutions.

Our first task is to examine the sign of the determinant E. Recalling the definitions of A_1 and A_2, we observe that the first term on the right-hand side of relation 4.8 will be negative and the second (including its sign), also negative. The third term (including its sign) will be negative or positive, depending on whether A_3 is positive or negative. E thus can be negative or positive. It must be negative if A_3 is positive, that is, if the conventional Marshall-Lerner condition is not fulfilled. Because negative value of E_3 implies instability in the foreign exchange market in the case where incomes are permitted to adjust, nonfulfillment of the conventional Marshall-Lerner condition becomes a sufficient, but not a necessary, condition of instability in the case considered here. Indeed, as we will see in the following section, the sum of the absolute values of elasticities of demand for exports may be well over unity, and the foreign-exchange market (with income adjustment) still will be unstable. The case against floating rates thus will be strengthened when the economies involved operate below full employment and when the elasticities of demand for imports are low.

Of course, the situation cannot be excluded where E is equal or very close to zero; in this case all solutions of the problem would be indeterminate. Such a situation is comparable to a case in which the demand for foreign exchange has the same elasticity as the supply of foreign exchange at a given market rate of exchange; any autonomous shift of one schedule would make the rate of exchange go to infinity or to zero. It would be necessary to know in this case the elasticities at all points of the schedules; to know the elasticities in the neighborhood of equilibrium is not sufficient.

We may eliminate from consideration this rather unlikely case and retain the fact that if E happens to be very small, the changes in incomes and the rate of exchange resulting from an autonomous shift in effective demand may be quite large; in such a case it is safer to learn a little more about the nature of the different functions before a conclusion is drawn. Also, for the rest of this section, let us examine only what we may describe as the normal case, based on the assumption of stability in the foreign-exchange market. In other words, we assume that E is positive, meanwhile remembering that this is at most a likely and by no means a necessary outcome.

In this situation, the simplest solution appears to be that pertaining to the change in the rate of exchange. As indicated by relation 4.7, if the market of foreign exchanges is stable, the assumed autonomous shift of demand for country 1's exports will lower the price of foreign currency in terms of the currency of country 1. In other words, the result that would be obtained through a simple analysis of the foreign-exchange market, without income effects, will generally (but not necessarily) be preserved under the conditions presently assumed. Let us recall that if no income repercussions were present, an increased demand for exports of country 1 would increase demand for its currency, and thus, if stability in the exchange market were fulfilled, the price of foreign currency in terms of the first country's currency would drop.

The direction of change of real income of country 1 is less unequivocal, contrary to views sometimes found in the literature. As the right-hand side of relation 4.5 indicates, the income of country 1 may either increase or deteriorate. It is useful to expand the term $(-A_1 -A_3)$ in terms of the elasticities of demand. This yields

$$-A_1 - A_3 = -m_{11}d_{11}^+ - m_{21}(1 + d_{21}) \qquad (4.9)$$

If, for example, the cross-elasticity is quite low and the elasticity of demand for imports in country 1 high in absolute value, the income of country 1 may increase, even though its currency has appreciated. But if foreign trade is only a minor portion of national product and the cross-elasticity is not negligible, increase in the demand for exports will lower real income; this is the outcome sometimes considered necessary. Actually, it may be considered as the normal or most likely outcome for the following reason. If the change in the rate of exchange and the terms of trade causes a substitution between imports and domestic products and there is no net gain or loss of effective demand, i.e., $m_{11}d_{11}^+ + m_{21}d_{21} = 0$, then $-A_1 -A_3$ must be negative, and the income of country 1 will decline. With the expansion of the term $-A_1 -A_3$ given in relation 4.9, it is easy to examine the direction of change of income in country 2. The first term in the brackets on the right-hand side of relation 4.6 will be positive or negative, depending on whether the income of country 1 increases or decreases. Because, for all practical considerations, A_2 must be negative, the second term in the brackets (including its sign) must be positive, if the marginal propensity to save of country 1 is greater than that to invest. Thus we may conclude that if the income of country 1 increases, that of country 2 must increase; if the income of country 1 declines only a little, there still is a good likelihood that the income of country 2 will rise. But if the parameters of the system are such that there is a strong decline in income of country 1, the income of country 2 may also decline.

Let us recall at this point that the foregoing analysis was based on the assumption that an autonomous increase in demand for exports of country 1 takes place, uncompensated for by a corresponding decline in other propensities of country 2. Consequently, the implicit assumption is made here that such a change in expenditure is taken from the savings of country 2. On the other hand, if domestic expenditure in country 2 declines by the same amount as imports have increased, in the column vector on the right-hand side of relation 4.4 the middle term (zero) would have to be changed to -1. The rest of the analysis is quite straightforward and may be carried out by the reader. Similarly, any combination of substitution of imports for savings and for other expenditures may be analyzed by assigning appropriate weights, or coefficients, to the terms on the right-hand side of relation 4.4.

Also, the effects of a transfer on incomes in the two countries and on the exchange rate and the terms of trade may easily be studied by assigning appropriate values to the terms on the right-hand side of relation 4.4. As an example, we observe that the top term of the column vector will be equal to -1, the second term to $+1$, and the third to zero, if a transfer of purchasing power is effected from country 1 to country 2 and if only spending on domestic products is altered in the two countries by the amount of the transfer.

Finally, it is possible to conceive of a situation wherein an autonomous increase in the domestic expenditure of country 1 takes place. As there is no shift in the propensities to import here, the bottom term (-1) on the right-hand side of relation 4.4 now becomes zero, and the solutions become quite simple, namely,

$$\frac{dY_1}{da} = \frac{1}{E}\left[A_2 m'_{12} - A_3(1 - m'_{22})\right] \tag{4.10}$$

$$\frac{dY_2}{da} = \frac{1}{E} m'_{21}(A_2 - A_3) \tag{4.11}$$

and

$$\frac{dr}{da} = \frac{1}{E} m'_{21}(1 - m'_{22} - m'_{12}) \tag{4.12}$$

The interpretation and analysis of these results is again left to the reader. A general observation is in order, however. The incomes of both countries may or may not improve, the likelihood of this being greater in country 1. The rate of exchange and the terms of trade will always turn against country 1.

One brief remark should be made before we conclude this section. The entire analysis was conducted here on the assumption of flexible exchange rates. As in Section 1, it is again possible to assume rigid exchange rates and perfectly flexible terms of trade, while writing terms of trade of country 2, say T_2, instead of r. Also, we have to recall the assumption of a constant rate of interest underlying the entire discussion of this section and assume a quantity theory of value. The latter assumption is not quite compatible with the assumption of under-full employment; consequently, the case of terms-of-trade adjustment should not be taken as very realistic. Nevertheless, the theoretical proposition may still be retained. The case of a flexible exchange rate has far greater practical relevance. Also, it should at least be pointed out that the time paths of adjustment (i) under flexible exchange rates and (ii) with price flexibility and rigid rate of exchange would be quite different; the latter process would be quite a bit slower, owing to the roundabout way of adjustment through the price-specie-flow mechanism.

8.5 The Foreign-Trade Multiplier under Flexible and Fixed Exchange Rates Compared; Further Concrete Examples

We may recall the simple foreign-trade multiplier discussed in Chapter 7. In that chapter we assumed the rate of exchange to be fixed. An autonomous increase in demand for exports of country 1 would necessarily have increased the real income of both countries and turned the balance of payments in favor of country 1.

When flexible exchange rates are assumed, a similar autonomous shift in demand may or may not increase the income of both countries. The normal expectation is that country 1 will actually realize a decline in its real income. Such a decline may be caused by the appreciation of the first country's currency and the ensuing negative price effects on income and output. As for the second country, whose demand for imports has increased, its real income will generally rise. The total gain in both countries' incomes will always fall short of the aggregate increase in income under conditions of stable exchange rates. Under normal conditions, where elasticities of demand for imports are fairly high, the general conclusion may be drawn that the income of the second country, whose demand for imports has risen, will usually increase from such an autonomous change. Its rate of exchange and the terms of trade will deteriorate somewhat; the other country, on the other hand, will normally be very little affected by the autonomous change. Its terms of trade, as well as the rate of exchange, will improve as a general rule. The smaller such an improvement, the more likely it is that country 1's income and employment will also improve.

On the whole, it is possible to compare the two exchange-rate arrangements by saying that free exchange rates will tend better to isolate and protect a country from autonomous shifts in effective demand abroad. By the same token, free exchange rates will tend to make an economy more sensitive to fluctuations in domestic expenditure. In particular, an increase in demand for imports will usually be translated in an increase of domestic, rather than foreign, employment.

In the table below, we have used the numerical assumptions made in Section 2 of this chapter describing crudely the foreign-trade situation of the United States and of the rest of the world, and computed some numerical results. Three alternative sets of assumptions were made as to the size of the elasticities of demand for imports here and abroad. Changes in income and the rate of exchange are compared for these three sets of assumptions; also we have shown the pure foreign-trade multiplier effects on the two incomes, calculated from relations 3.5 and 3.6 of the preceding chapter.

EFFECTS OF A UNIT INCREASE IN AUTONOMOUS DEMAND FOR EXPORTS
OF COUNTRY 1 ON REAL INCOME AND THE RATE OF EXCHANGE;
ASSUMING $m_{ij} = 0.05$, $m'_{ii} = 0.85$, $d^+_{ii} = 0.05$, $m_{ij} = 20$, $m_{ii} = 480$

Change in	r_1	r_2	dr/r
Assuming:			
foreign trade multiplier only........	+7.5	+2.5	0
$d_{ij} = -1$	(+90)	(−80)	(+0.0375)
$d_{ij} = -2$	−1.36	+11.07	−0.034
$d_{ij} = -3$	+2.08	+7.93	−0.013

The results in brackets correspond to a situation of instability in the foreign-exchange market and are very large because the determinant E is very small. In actuality they could never be attained under flexible rates; rather, the market being unstable, the autonomous change in demand would lead to an explosive change in all three variables in a direction opposite to that indicated by the signs in brackets.

For the two normal (stable) outcomes, corresponding to elasticities of −2 and −3 respectively, we observe that, as the magnitude of the demand elasticities is increasing, the appreciation of the currency of country 1 becomes smaller and smaller. The increase in income of country 2 is reduced with higher elasticities. The loss in income of country 1, on the other hand, is gradually reduced, and eventually, for some value of the demand elasticities between −2 and −3, the first country's income also increases.

Chapter
9

ELEMENTARY DYNAMICS IN THE BALANCE-OF-PAYMENTS ADJUSTMENT MECHANISM

9.1 Introduction

Economic dynamics and its various applications to international economics are much too vast a subject to be treated exhaustively in the present study. The subject matter is one of the most recently developed fields of economics. It may be that, at its birth, greater achievement was expected from it than it has subsequently yielded. Nevertheless, it ought not to be underestimated. There are important insights to be derived from the dynamic approach that otherwise would be less apparent or could not be discerned at all.

Actually, all the analysis of Part II of the present study could be rewritten—with greater or less difficulty—in terms of dynamics. What we have discussed so far may be viewed as the timeless essence of a more involved theory that introduces time explicitly as a variable and permits of differently dated variables. If the static stability criteria, such as the restrictions imposed on the elasticities of supply and demand for foreign exchange, were always sufficient in determining whether a given equilibrium were stable or unstable, if we could always be sure that every equilibrium were stable, on other grounds, and if it were easy to ascertain the time needed for a system to move from one equilibrium to the other, economic dynamics would have very little practical significance. Now it seems that all such conditions are not fulfilled. The static stability conditions only usually, but not always, are sufficient in determining whether any particular real situation is stable or unstable. Consequently, dynamic analysis may yield additional, but never perfect, insight into whether any such situation is effectively stable or not. The advancement of economists' knowledge will always depend on the degree of conformity between a dynamic model and the real conditions.

Some more empirically minded economists might argue that neither static nor dynamic conditions are necessary in evaluating whether the real economic equilibrium is stable or unstable. It may be sufficient for them to observe that different real markets explode only rarely and that this still may usually be imputed to an explosive movement of one of the structural relations underlying each particular situation rather than to a lack of fulfillment of stability conditions. It is true that market instability may sometimes explain minor movements in price or any other economic variable without leading to a cataclysm. But it is usually impossible to find out whether such a movement was due to instability or to other causes; and, because the other causes usually play a far more important role in the operation of an economy, the case of instability may, for all purposes of empirical analysis, be neglected.

Finally, if it is at all possible to evaluate the length and distribution of time lags between causes and effects in the working of a real economy, the difference-equation analysis provides us with an extremely useful accounting device in establishing the duration of any given adjustment. Simple examples of this will be found later in Section 3 of the present chapter. Moreover, it gives us the possibility of studying whether given conditions will lead to a cyclical or a noncyclical adjustment. The usefulness of the latter, however, may be disputed by some because the exact values of economic parameters and the nature of the particular model determine whether any given adjustment will be cyclical or not. Such exact values and correct representation of the real world most often cannot be known, and, consequently, the only practical benefit derivable from the dynamic approach in this context may be reduced to the assertion that cyclical or noncyclical dynamic movements of an economy are consistent with dynamic economic doctrine.

It would be unjust toward economic dynamics not to point out, in concluding, its purely intellectual value. There are few other fields of theoretical economics that offer equal possibilities for advanced applied mathematics and philosophical cogitation.

9.2 Simple Dynamics of the Foreign-Exchange Market

As a first useful application of the dynamic approach to the questions treated in this text, we may consider the foreign-exchange market and study the movement of the exchange rate in the neighborhood of its equilibrium value. Let us first deal with the simple case wherein only autonomous purchases of currencies serving current transactions are effected in the market.

Let us assume, as we did in Chapter 5, that the supply and demand schedules of foreign exchange are defined and derivable from conditions of supply and demand for exports and imports on current account. No other transactions—so far—are cleared through the foreign-exchange market. Consequently, the excess demand is also defined, namely,

$$ED = f(r) \tag{2.1}$$

where r is the rate of exchange in terms of domestic currency. To study the time path of the exchange rate from any position of disequilibrium, we have to relate the rate of change of the exchange rate to the excess demand. The traditional static theory postulates that if demand exceeds supply, prices will tend to rise through competitive bidding of buyers and sellers, and vice-versa in the opposite case. Thus we may say that the rate of change in the rate of exchange will depend in some way on $f(r)$. The simplest assumption that can be made is that it will be directly proportional to $f(r)$, with a constant proportionality factor k, i.e.,

$$\frac{dr}{dt} = k \cdot f(r) \tag{2.2}$$

where t stands for time and k is a positive constant, its magnitude expressing the speed of time adjustment; large values of k indicate substantial rates of change in the exchange rate over time, all other things being equal. For relatively small displacements from equilibrium, this equation has a simple solution, namely,[1]

$$r(t) = A \cdot e^{k \cdot f'(r_0) \cdot t} + r_0 \tag{2.3}$$

[1] By Taylor's expansion,

$$f(r) = f(r_0) + (r - r_0)f'(r_0) + 1/2(r - r_0)^2 f''(r_0) + \ldots$$

Observing that, by definition, $f(r_0) = 0$, writing $R = r - r_0$, and dropping all but the first-order term in the expansion, for small R, we have, from relation 2.3,

$$\frac{dR}{R} = k \cdot f'(r_0) \cdot dt$$

whence

$$\text{Log } R = k \cdot f'(r_0) \cdot t + a$$

with a a constant. This immediately yields solution 2.3 above.

where A is a constant to be determined from the original position of the rate of exchange rate and r_0 is the (static) equilibrium rate of exchange.

Suppose, now, that the equilibrium rate of exchange is $r_0 = 3$ and the initial value of the rate of exchange $r(0) = 3.5$. This yields the value for A, namely, $A = 0.5$. The rate of exchange $r(t)$ will now travel a time path indicated by relation 2.3. With k positive, it can approach the equilibrium value only if $f'(r_0)$ is negative; in this case, for large values of t, the first term of the right-hand side of relation 2.3 will become very small, and $r(t)$ will asymptotically approach r_0. If $f'(r_0)$ were positive, the market situation would be unstable, and the rate of exchange would move away from r_0. Thus the stability condition of the particular market here considered can be simply expressed as

$$f'(r_0) < 0 \qquad (2.4)$$

But, remembering that $f(r) = D(r) - S(r)$, where the latter two functions represent demand and supply for foreign exchange, respectively, we immediately observe that this condition is equivalent to the traditional static condition,

$$d - s < 0 \qquad (2.5)$$

where d and s represent the elasticities of demand and supply in the neighborhood of equilibrium. This simply confirms the intuitively obvious conclusion that the foreign-exchange market will be stable, under the assumptions made, in the vicinity of an equilibrium solution, if the supply curve intersects the demand curve from below. The dynamic approach, although more realistic, does not change the conditions of stability of the market.

The dynamic analysis appears more fruitful in examining the conditions of a speculative foreign-exchange market. Suppose that, in addition to the demand for foreign exchange for foreign transactions, there is also a speculative demand for currency. A number of behavioral assumptions may be made. Perhaps the simplest is to assume that net speculators' demand for (or supply of) foreign exchange depends directly on the rate of change of the price, i.e., on the rate of change of the exchange rate. Thus we may write the excess demand for speculative purposes, ED_s, as

$$ED_s = q \cdot \frac{dr}{dt} \qquad (2.6)$$

where q expresses the nature of the elasticity of expectations. With positive q, we may say that the expectations are positively elastic. Speculators expect that the present trend will continue, and therefore they buy when prices are rising. Negative values of q indicate the expectation of a future decline in the exchange rate, inducing speculators to sell when prices are rising. The absolute magnitude of q expresses the importance of the speculative market, as well as the magnitude of the elasticity of expectation. The intermediate situation in which $q = 0$ indicates that speculators at all times expect prices to remain the same, and consequently all speculative transactions are deemed unprofitable. The solution for $q \neq 0$ is only a slight modification of the preceding situation and may be written as

$$r(t) = A \cdot e^{[k/(1-q)]f'(r_0)t} + r_0 \tag{2.7}$$

It will be observed that here the traditional stability conditions, i.e., $f'(r_0)$ negative, may no longer be sufficient. With a high positive value of q, the rate of exchange may no longer converge to the equilibrium value r_0.

Perhaps a more realistic assumption would be that, in a world of autonomous cyclical fluctuation, speculators buy foreign exchange whenever they feel that the rate is above some "normal" level and sell whenever the rate is below it. One way of studying such a situation would be to assume that speculators' demand is a function of the second time derivative of the exchange rate. We shall discuss this and other cases in a somewhat less rigorous, but more comprehensive, way in the next chapter. Nevertheless, the reader interested in dynamic analysis may enjoy studying these and other situations, using the elements presented here as a point of departure.

9.3 *Dynamics of the Foreign-Trade Multiplier*

Another important application of dynamic analyis, perhaps more fruitful than that of the preceding section, is the study of the dynamic adjustment of income and of the balance of payments to an autonomous change in effective demand. The comparative statics of such a situation was studied in detail under different assumptions in the preceding two chapters. The timeless changes in income and the different propensities were related to the magnitude of the autonomous shift in demand through the customary multiplier coefficient. Very little mention was made, however, of the path through which the systems would move from one equilibrium to the other. Moreover, it was usually only tacitly assumed, or stated without any further explanation, that the system would effectively attain the new equilibrium, i.e., that both equilibria are actually stable. These problems may now be examined with greater ease by using dynamics.

As in the preceding section, it will be impossible to reiterate all the comparative static analysis of the preceding chapters and rewrite it in terms of dynamics. Actually, we shall be able to study only one typical situation in detail and point out some of its extensions and applications. Nevertheless, at least some of the conclusions here obtained are quite interesting and throw additional light on the properties of the static equilibria studied in the preceding and some subsequent chapters. The two important points that we want to stress here are the stability conditions of the income-determining models and the timing of balance-of-payments and income adjustment.

The use of differential equations, as in the preceding section, and the use of difference equations are well suited to the problem at hand. The latter approach in essence does the same thing as the former, with the exception that it uses discrete time intervals rather than continuous time. The advantage of the difference-equations approach is that it permits us to introduce time lags, reflecting cause-effect relationships in the mechanism of income determination and hence appears to be better suited to describe the real world. Moreover, the difference-equations approach circumvents entirely the problem of infinitesimal differentiation of time—present in the analysis of the preceding section—and is simple to explain without any use of mathematics.

Let us consider the foreign-trade multiplier with foreign repercussion, studied in Chapter 7. The only two explanatory variables are the real incomes of two trading partners, prices and the exchange rate being invariant. The implicit assumption made previously was that the permanent state of the economy is one of equilibrium, where variables expressing flows per unit of time remain unchanged; an adjustment to a structural change takes place in a timeless or instantaneous "jump" from one equilibrium level to another. It is more realistic to assume that such changes take a certain amount of time. The logic of this contention is that it generally will take a certain amount of time before the behavioral agents, such as consumers or producers, react to changed conditions in the markets determining their behavior. Consumers' conservatism and producers' lack of immediate information on changes in their own and national markets are perhaps the most important causes of such delayed reactions.

It is clear that if such time lags exist in the operation of an economy, a virtually infinite number of possible theories of dynamic income determination may be constructed, each reflecting given assumptions about the distribution and magnitude of the time lags. No such model could ever describe reality perfectly. There are approximations, ranging from good to poor: The one we want to use here in illustrating the problem at hand is one of the most simple ones. We assume what may be called a consumption lag. Specifically, consumers and investors are assumed to react to changes in income with a delay of one unit of time; in other words, expenditure on domestic products or expenditure on imports in a given period will no longer depend on income of that period but rather on income of the preceding period—say, three months ago. If we now date our variables and assume given constant marginal propensities to spend on domestic products (c) and to import (m) in the two countries, we may write

$$x_t = c_2 \cdot x_{t-1} + m_1 y_{t-1} + b \tag{3.1}$$
and
$$y_t = c_1 \cdot y_{t-1} + m_2 x_{t-1} + a \tag{3.2}$$

where x and y represent real income in country 1 and country 2, respectively, while the subscripts of these two variables indicate the period of reference. Both equations merely state that income produced (and earned) in each period will be equal to output for domestic consumption plus output for exports, these two depending on the incomes of the respective groups of consumers of the preceding period.

The system of equations 3.1 and 3.2 permits of a fairly straightforward mathematical solution. This will be shown and studied in the later part of this section. At present, it may be interesting to undertake a simple numerical exercise, assuming certain values for the different parameters and for the initial conditions of the adjustment process, and work out the path of the two economies and of the balance of payments for a number of periods. Let us assume that the marginal propensities to import and to spend on domestic produce are 0.1 and 0.8, respectively. Note that these parameters are fairly comparable to the propensities assumed in the examples of

Chapter 8. Moreover, we assume that incomes in both countries initially are 1,000 each, while total consumption in each country is 800 and total imports 200. These conditions will be found in the first line (for $t = 0$) of Table 9.3.1. At each period of time (t), the consumption of a country, say, country 2, may be calculated as the product of the marginal propensity to consume and the income of the preceding period, i.e.,

$$\text{Consumption}_t = (0.8) \cdot y_{t-1} \tag{3.3}$$

and similarly for country 2. Imports of country 1 (i.e., exports of country 2), on the other hand, are assumed to be equal to the product of the marginal propensity to import and income of the importing country in the preceding period, plus a constant term, a or b in relations 3.1 and 3.2, indicating the level of imports with zero income; in the example $a = b = 100$. Thus, using superscripts 1 and 2 to indicate the particular country, we have

$$\text{Imports}_t^1 = (0.1)x_{t-1} + 100 \tag{3.4}$$

and

$$\text{Imports}_t^2 = (0.1)y_{t-1} + 100 \tag{3.5}$$

As in our static analysis, we assume that the structural disturbance that sets the dynamic system in motion is translated as an autonomous increase in imports by country 2, i.e., exports of country 1, by 100. That is, in period 1 the constant term on the right-hand side of relation 3.4 changes from 100 to 200 and remains at that level for all subsequent periods. With these assumptions, it is possible to derive the values of the variables for each succeeding period from the variables of the current period. For example, we observe that the only change that took place in period 1 is that income and exports of country 1 have increased by 100 and the balance of payments has improved by the same amount. In period 2, the incomes of both countries have increased. Exports of country 1 have remained at their previous level of 300 because the income of country 2 in the preceding period has not moved. However, exports of country 2 now have gone up by 10 because of an increase in income of 100 of country 1 in the preceding period. The reader will find it easy to use the preceding discussion, or the expressions heading the table, in deriving successively the tth stage of the dynamic multiplier process from the preceding $(t - 1)$ st stage. We have carried out the calculations —not with absolute precision—through the first 13 periods.

It will be observed that the incomes of the two countries grow

TABLE 9.3.1

Period t	$x_t = (0.8)x_{t-1} + (0.1)y_{t-1}$ $+100$ or $+200$			$y_t = (0.8)y_{t-1} + (0.1)x_{t-1}$ $+100$			Balance of Payments of Country 1
0...	1000	800	200	1000	800	200	0
1...	1100	800	300	1000	800	200	100
2...	1180	880	300	1010	800	210	90
3...	1244	943	301	1026	808	218	83
4...	1298	995	303	1047	823	224	79
5...	1345	1040	305	1068	838	230	75
6...	1389	1082	307	1092	857	235	72
7...	1426	1117	309	1111	872	239	70
8...	1454	1143	311	1132	889	243	68
9...	1474	1161	313	1149	903	245	67
10...	1495	1180	315	1168	920	248	67
11...	1515	1198	317	1187	937	250	67
12 ..	1531	1212	319	1205	953	252	67
13...	1544	1222	320	1215	962	253	67
..							
..							
..							
..							
∞ ...	1667	1334	333	1333	1066	267	67

continuously at a decelerated rate, from their original levels, approaching asymptotically the new static equilibrium level. This level cannot be reached in a finite number of periods, although it can be approached with any desired degree of proximity. The income, export, domestic expenditure, and balance-of-payments figures found at the bottom of the table for t = infinity are precisely those that would be obtained through the comparative static analysis of Chapter 7.

In the example used here, it may be calculated that after 12 periods, about 80 per cent of the adjustment in the income of country 1 will take place. Over the same period, only a little over 60 per cent of the path of the income of country 2 toward the new equilibrium level will be accomplished. It is extremely difficult to estimate the length of the unit of measurement of time used here—i.e., to estimate the average length of the time lag in consumption. A plausible guess might be that such a unit period is that of 3 months. Under this assumption, the above-quoted percentages of adjustment would pertain to periods of 3 years (12 periods). However crude such an estimate may be, it is possible to conclude that if the simplified model underlying our example is at all realistic, the time required for the multiplier adjustment to changing conditions is quite substantial. This is one conclusion that was not perfectly clear from the comparative static analysis.

Moreover, it may be found either through other numerical examples or through direct mathematical analysis that the length of the period of adjustment is not very sensitive to changes in the parameters, i.e., in the marginal propensities. Actually, higher propensities to import and lower propensities to consume domestic products are even likely to lengthen the period of adjustment. For example, with a marginal propensity to import of 0.4 and to spend on domestic products of 0.5, only about 67 and 57 per cent of the increase in incomes of country 1 and country 2, respectively, would have taken place after 12 periods. The balance of payments, on the other hand, will generally approach its new equilibrium level quite fast. In our example, for instance, in the seventh period it is within 3 per cent of its equilibrium value of 67; this is due primarily to the fact that it is a difference between two variables, both approaching a given equilibrium level at comparable speeds.

We may now focus our attention on the stability properties of the dynamic income-determining system here examined. The first thing to observe is that the particular numerical case at hand is stable. The original disturbance, i.e., an autonomous increase in exports of country 1, only made all the variables move to new finite levels, the rate of change over time being a diminishing function of time, asymptotically approaching zero. To make any more general statements about the stability properties of the model, we have to use the customary mathematical approach.

Relations 3.1 and 3.2 constitute a simple system of linear first-order difference equations. Although they are not homogeneous (since they contain constant terms), we may easily transform them into homogeneous relations by taking the first differences. Using capital letters for these first differences, such as

$$X_t = x_{t+1} - x_t \qquad (3.6)$$

the difference between two equations of the form of 3.1 at two consecutive periods immediately yields

$$X_t = c_1 X_{t-1} + m_2 Y_{t-1} \qquad (3.7)$$

and, similarly,

$$Y_t = c_2 Y_{t-1} + m_1 X_{t-1} \qquad (3.8)$$

Equations such as 3.7 and 3.8 permit of solutions of the form

$$X_t = A \cdot q_1^t + B \cdot q_2^t \tag{3.9}$$

and

$$Y_t = C \cdot q_1^t + D \cdot q_2^t \tag{3.10}$$

where A, B, C, and D are constants to be determined from the initial conditions, to be shown presently, and q_1 and q_2 are given functions of the four marginal propensities appearing on the right-hand side of relations 3.7 and 3.8. They are the so-called *latent roots* of the coefficient matrix

$$\begin{bmatrix} c_1 & m_2 \\ m_1 & c_2 \end{bmatrix}$$

It is beyond the scope of this discussion to provide proofs of these propositions; let us simply define q_1 and q_2 as roots of a quadratic equation

$$\begin{vmatrix} (c_1 - q) & m_2 \\ m_1 & (c_2 - q) \end{vmatrix} = (c_1 - q)(c_2 - q) - m_1 m_2 = 0 \tag{3.11}$$

This, using elementary algebra, yields

$$q_{1,2} = \frac{1}{2} [c_1 + c_2 \pm \sqrt{(c_1 + c_2)^2 - 4(c_1 c_2 - m_1 m_2)}] \tag{3.12}$$

It is immediately apparent from relations 3.9 and 3.10 that an equilibrium consistent with 3.7 and 3.8 can be stable only if q_1 and q_2 are smaller than 1. In this case, any initial conditions will either produce a stationery state at $X_t = Y_t = 0$ or an asymptotic convergence toward such a state. Assuming that the marginal propensities c_1 and c_2 are positive, we simply may require that the larger of the two roots be smaller than 1, i.e.,

$$c_1 + c_2 + \sqrt{(c_1 + c_2) - 4(c_1 c_2 - m_1 m_2)} < 2 \tag{3.13}$$

A little algebra leads from here to the equivalent condition,

$$D = (1 - c_1)(1 - c_2) - m_1 m_2 > 0 \tag{3.14}$$

where D is the determinant of the coefficient matrix appearing in the denominator of many of the multiplier coefficients studied in Chapters 7 and 8. This conclusion derived from dynamic analysis only supports our intuitive notion of the comparative static analysis. Observe that, for $D = 0$, the value of the static multipliers would be infinite. For values of D less than zero, the multiplier would again assume a finite value, but the induced changes in income, exports, balance of payments, etc., would have the opposite sign from what could be expected on grounds of economic common sense. Moreover, it is clear that under such conditions an autonomous increase in effective demand would produce a lower static equilibrium of income. At the same time, however, deficiency of output at any level of income above such an equilibrium and consequently inventory decumulation would give rise to a continuous movement of income away from equilibrium.

As an application we may now derive the complete solutions of the concrete dynamic case studied earlier, using the above mathematical results. Introducing the values assumed, $c = 0.8$ and $m = 0.1$, into relation 3.12, we obtain $q_1 = 0.9$ and $q_2 = 0.7$. Both values being smaller than 1, the system is stable. We may now observe the initial conditions, given by the income data in the three top rows of Table 9.3.1, namely, $X_0 = 100$, $X_1 = 80$, $Y_0 = 0$, and $Y_1 = 10$. These values, together with the calculated q_1 and q_2, lead to four equations of the type 3.9 and 3.10 in four unknowns, A, B, C, and D. The solutions are

$$A = B = 50$$

and

$$C = -D = 50$$

Introducing these values into relations 3.9 and 3.10, we finally obtain

$$X_t = 50(0.9)^t + 50(0.7)^t \tag{3.15}$$

and

$$Y_t = 50(0.9)^t - 50(0.7)^t \tag{3.16}$$

Recalling the definitions of the variables X and Y, i.e.,

$$X_t = x_{t+1} - x_t \tag{3.17}$$

and

$$Y_t = y_{t+1} - y_t \tag{3.18}$$

and the fact that x_0 and y_0, the initial values of incomes in the two countries, are 1,000, we may now derive the actual solutions of the system as sums of converging geometric progressions, i.e.,

$$x_t = 1{,}000 + 50 \left(\frac{1 - (0.9)^t}{0.1} + \frac{1 - (0.7)^t}{0.3} \right) \qquad (3.19)$$

and

$$y_t = 1{,}000 + 50 \left(\frac{1 - (0.9)^t}{0.1} - \frac{1 - (0.7)^t}{0.3} \right) \qquad (3.20)$$

for values of $t \geqq 0$. It will be observed that, as time tends toward infinity, the exponential terms of the right-hand sides of the two equations tend toward zero, and the entire expressions approach a finite limit, i.e., the equilibrium levels of income corresponding to the assumptions made, namely,

$$x_m = 1667, \qquad \text{and} \qquad y_\infty = 1{,}333$$

Observe that in the simple case discussed here, for any admissible values of the marginal propensities, the key solutions q_1 and q_2 cannot be complex numbers, the value of the expression under the square-root sign in relation 3.12 being necessarily positive. However, at least in theory, if this expression were negative, q_1 and q_2 would be a pair of complex conjugate numbers. Without going into any detail of such solutions, let us simply observe that if this were the case, an original disturbance of the equilibrium would tend to produce a sinusoidal oscillatory movement.

Other more complicated representations of dynamic income adjustment may yield such complex conjugate roots. In that case the adjustment through time will assume the form of a cyclical path that may be dampened, i.e., converging toward a finite equilibrium value, or accelerated, i.e., fluctuating around the new static equilibrium value in a cycle of increasing amplitude. As an example of a situation where this is likely to happen, we may mention dynamic income models of two countries in which more than one time lag appears. Alternatively, dampened or accelerated oscillation will be found with the familiar cobweb model of market adjustment. Students who desire to acquire a greater familiarity with such more complicated situations and with their mathematical treatment are referred to the literature on the subject.[2]

[2] R. G. D. Allen, *Mathematical Economics* (London: Macmillan & Co., Ltd., 1959) ; William J. Bamol, *Economic Dynamics* (New York: Macmillan Co., 1951) ; and P. A. Samuelson, *Foundations of Economic Analysis* (Cambridge: Harvard University Press, 1958) .

Chapter 10

SPECULATION AND STABILITY IN THE FOREIGN-EXCHANGE MARKET

10.1 Introduction

The subject matter of speculation, whether in foreign exchanges or any other commodity, is interesting from both the purely theoretical and the practical point of view. It throws light on and answers questions concerning the stability of the foreign-exchange market that could not be obtained from a strictly static analysis. It is not easy to define speculative purchases or sales in theory, nor is it easy to identify speculative currency movements in practice. For the purpose of our analysis we may define a speculative transaction as one whose sole motive is profit from another transaction in the same commodity *at a later date*. The time element here is the essential part of the definition; it differentiates speculation from all other commercial transactions. Observe that by transaction we here understand both contract and physical exchange.

The element of uncertainty, that is mostly associated with speculation in practice, we prefer to exclude from our definition. Some readers may prefer to think of the case corresponding to our definition as of exchange-rate arbitrage over time. In fact, a good deal of the theory of speculative transactions may be carried out on the assumption of certainty about things present past and future. At a later stage in our discussion we shall examine the realistic case, in which market conditions in the future are known with different degrees of confidence, but never exactly.

Using our definition, it is possible to divide transactions in any market into two groups: speculative and nonspeculative. There are many markets wherein the speculative component is nonexistent either because of a lack of a sufficient number of buyers and sellers or because of the high costs of transferring commodities from one point in time to another or, finally, because of the prohibitive degree of uncertainty about future market conditions. Many other markets, such as the foreign-exchange, raw-materials, and grain markets, serve both nonspeculative and speculative purposes.

For completeness, on the other side of the spectrum, we might mention purely speculative markets, wherein the other component is entirely missing. But in such instances it is more fitting to speak about gambling than about speculation. On the whole, our discussion in this chapter pertains to the intermediate case in which both types of sales and purchases are made. Specifically, we shall deal with speculation in the market of foreign exchanges, where price is permitted to adjust freely to autonomous conditions of supply and demand, and study the impact of the speculative element on the operation of the whole market.

Most often, speculation in foreign exchanges is discussed in connection with cyclical, seasonal, or some other recurrent fluctuation in the price of the nonspeculative and autonomous component of the market. This, however intellectually stimulating or theoretically interesting it may be, does not answer all the practical problems raised by speculation. The case in which cyclical movements are superimposed on a trend or where only a long-run trend in price exists may be just as important. We shall study both situations.

10.2 Cyclical Speculation under Certainty; Discrete Market

To introduce the subject of speculation, let us start with a very simple case. Assume that time is divided into a number of discrete intervals, say of three months in duration. Purchases and sales of currency are effected only at the beginning of each interval, instantaneously. Thus we may visualize a situation comparable to the static market conditions discussed in Chapter 5, taking place every three months. Autonomous nonspeculative dealings in foreign exchanges establish a competitive equilibrium rate every three months. Assume that at every even interval the equilibrium rate is equal to three units of domestic currency and at every odd period equal to two. Thus the market operates indefinitely. Everybody is aware that this happens.

Under these conditions, let us consider two cases. In the first case there is a single speculator permitted to operate in the market; in the second, the speculative portion of the exchange market is perfectly competitive, i.e., everybody is perfectly well informed, and free entry into the market is guaranteed. Moreover, we assume in both cases, for the moment, that holding, borrowing, and lending currency are costless. Let us make the usual assumption that all speculators have an urge to maximize profits and behave accordingly.

The monopolistic speculator will maximize his profit by buying foreign exchange in the odd period and selling in the even period in such a way as to equalize marginal cost to marginal revenue. The complete solution of our simple speculative foreign-exchange market, where a single speculator is operating, is seen from Figure 10.2.1.

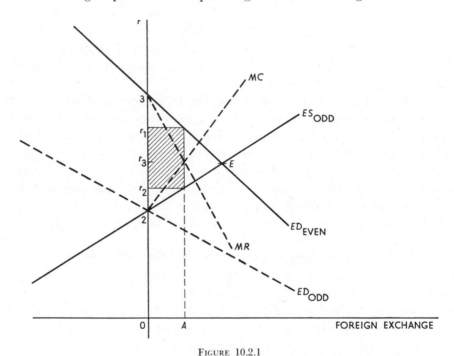

FIGURE 10.2.1

The line ED_{even} and ED_{odd} (*dotted*) are the excess demand curves for foreign exchange in the even and odd periods, respectively. They correspond to the two assumed equilibrium levels of the rate of exchange resulting from nonspeculative transactions. The excess supply curve, ES_{odd}, is derived from the excess demand curve in the odd period by symmetry with respect to the vertical axis. The marginal cost curve MC is derived from ES_{odd} and expresses the cost of the last unit of exchange purchased by the monopolistic speculator. Similarly, the marginal revenue curve MR is derived from the average revenue, or ED_{even}, and expresses the revenue from the sale of the last unit of foreign currency.[1] Maximum profit will be reached if OA of foreign exchange is transacted every period by the speculator, i.e., at the point A defined by the equality of marginal cost and marginal revenue. The profit of the monopolist is measured by the rectangle defined by A, ES_{odd}, and ED_{even} and is equal to OA $(r_1 - r_2)$, where r_1 and r_2 are the new rates of exchange in the even and odd periods, respectively.

Provided that the foreign-exchange market is stable, both rates must be within the range of the autonomous rates of exchange, i.e., in the range of 3 and 2 units of domestic currency. That the market in either period would be unstable is inconceivable, because, in such a case, any slightest speculative purchase or sale in such a market would make the equilibrium rate run to one or the other *stable* equilibrium bordering the unstable one (for greater detail of this proposition, see Chaps. 5 and 9). Thus we may conclude that if there is a single rational speculator operating in the foreign-exchange market, under perfect certainty and assuming the comparative static situation of our simple example, speculation will be stabilizing.

Only a minor step is necessary to show the effects of speculation, in our simple example, if the speculative portion of the market is competitive. Referring to the diagram, under the assumptions made, the equilibrium level of the rate of exchange will be established at r_3, in both periods. Speculative profits will be reduced to zero, and the volume of speculative transactions will be determined by the abscissa of point E, the competitive equilibrium.

In this situation, as may be seen, the rate of exchange will be perfectly stabilized. It may be interesting to observe that the equilibrium rate r_3 may be anywhere between the original noncompetitive equilibria 3 and 2 and not, as is sometimes implied in the analysis of speculation, exactly halfway between the two. The exact position will depend not only on the original exchange rates (without speculation) but also on the elasticities of nonspeculative supply of and demand for foreign exchange.

Before turning our attention to the more realistic case of continuous trading, let us examine briefly some of the other assumptions we have made so far. The first was costless borrowing and

---

[1] It may be useful to observe at this point that there exists a simple relation between any pair of average and marginal variables, functions of Q, of the form $M \ldots = A \ldots + Q \times$ slope of $A. \ldots$ In place of the dots, cost, revenue, product, or any other economic function may be introduced.

lending of currencies. Strictly speaking, this assumption is not required. If the rates of interest are equal in the home and foreign country and transactions are made within a very short time and without any brokers' or bankers' charges, proceeds from the sale of domestic currency in the foreign-exchange market may be lent in the foreign country at the same rate as their domestic counterpart was borrowed in the home country. The interest earnings from investments abroad may be employed in paying interest charges at home. Actually, a slight additional profit would be made by the monopolistic speculator in this case because he would be selling foreign exchange, including the interest returns, at a higher rate of exchange and thus obtaining more than was necessary to pay interest charges at home. The reader may construct a rigorous case taking this fact explicitly into account. Such effects are insignificant, however, and thus may be excluded from our analysis.

If there is an interest-rate differential between the two currencies, the above-obtained results will have to be modified somewhat. But let us wait with this analysis until after we have discussed the case of continuous trading.

10.3 Cyclical Speculation under Certainty; Continuous Trading

The comparative static conditions assumed in the preceding section may appear quite restrictive. In actuality, they are not. Most, if not all, of the conclusions obtained apply also to the continuous case under certainty and, as we shall see in the later sections of this chapter, even to situations of uncertainty about future market conditions. The new assumption we are introducing in this section is that the exchange rate established in the nonspeculative market fluctuates continuously, without trend, around some given level, r_0. The length of the cycle is constant, and so are the amplitude and the entire path of any given cycle. As an example, we may think of the autonomous nonspeculative path of the exchange rate as of a sine curve and express it in functional form as

$$r = r_0 + a \sin (t) = f(t) \tag{3.1}$$

If time is measured in periods of six months, the duration of one complete cycle would be 2π, i.e., a little over three years, and the maximum and minimum rates of exchange would be $r_0 + a$ and $r_0 - a$, respectively.

Speculators now are permitted to trade at any moment in time. The monopolistic speculator will again maximize his profits by buying when the rate of exchange is low and selling when the rate of exchange is high. Of course, he knows that, depending on the volume of his sales and purchases, the amplitude of the cycle will be reduced and his unit gain thereby reduced. There will be some optimum path, depending on $f(t)$ and, as shown in the preceding section, on the elasticities in the nonspeculative market, that will maximize his profit. The amplitude of the new path, in a sense to be defined presently, *must* be smaller than that of the original cycle. If the new path happens to be a sine curve, a', its amplitude coefficient must be smaller than a in relation 3.1.

To study exactly what happens to the amplitude of the new cycle, i.e., to find out whether and to what degree speculation in the present case is stabilizing or destabilizing, we would have to know in explicit form the time functions of autonomous supply and demand generating the nonspeculative path of the rate of exchange; but, even if we were given such information, the task might involve cumbersome or unmanageable calculation. Without mathematics, however, using the arguments of the preceding section it is possible to answer the question.

By destabilizing speculation we may understand such type of speculative sales and purchases as would bring the exchange rate further away from the average rate r_0 than a, the maximum amplitude. If at any point in time the speculator should cause the exchange rate to go beyond such a point, this would necessarily imply that he is buying at a higher rate than he can ever hope to regain by selling, or selling at as low a rate as he could ever recuperate by buying. In either case he would make a loss, and this is inconsistent with our assumption and definition of rational behavior. Thus we may again conclude that speculation in this case would be stabilizing.

Another question of stability arises if we want to find out whether the rate with speculation will ever be brought outside the nonspeculative cyclical path at all, not only at the extreme points. From our discussion of the preceding section it follows that, depending on the elasticities in the foreign-exchange market, the average rate of the speculative cycle, say, r_0', may not be equal exactly to r_0; such equality will be obtained only if special conditions of symmetry of elasticities are fulfilled. Thus it is possible that, at points near the intercepts of $f(t)$ with $r = r_0$, the speculator will buy or sell rather than not doing anything. Consequently, near such points it is possible that the speculative rate will be "on the outside" of the non-speculative cycle. This, of course, may hardly be called destabilization.

If r_0 is effectively equal to r_0', even our second type of stabilizing effect will be fulfilled, that is, the speculative rate will always remain within the original cycle of $f(t)$. The proposition is very simple. Consider a monopsonist who, observing the downswing (the half of the cycle below r_0) of price, wants to purchase a certain amount of foreign currency, knowing that if he waits for a while, he will be able to resell the same currency at a higher price than he has paid. It would be irrational on his part to sell in the downswing or buy in the upswing.

The case of competitive speculation with continuous selling and buying is quite simple. Whenever, under our assumptions, any fluctuation in the rate of exchange arose, somebody could make a profit. But this is incompatible with the assumption of perfect competition. Consequently, the rate would be perfectly stable, provided, of course, that nobody was willing to accumulate balances in foreign exchange indefinitely. This situation, however, seems to be eliminated by the fact that such a speculator would hardly be able to make any money from such accumulation, even if borrowing, lending, and transacting were costless. In the real world, of course, such costs would make indefinite accumulation impossible.

10.4 Speculation, Interest Arbitrage, and Exchange-Rate Stability

So far we have always assumed that the short-term borrowing and lending rates in the two countries are equal. In this way we have eliminated, by assumption, all possible impact of short-term money markets on the balance of payments and on the rate of exchange. This is unrealistic. Short-term rates in the real world differ from period to period, depending on the level of economic activity in different countries, and may also be different persistently because of different rates of growth, different monetary policies, or different states of technology, demand, and factor endowments.

International interest arbitrage cannot be separated entirely from exchange-rate speculation. Every speculator, if rates of interest are different in different countries, is at the same time an interest arbitrageur, and every interest arbitrageur is a speculator.[2] It is in-conceivable that a rational businessman would base his decisions exclusively on one factor or the other. Both the level of interest rates in the two countries and the rate of exchange will shape his decisions. Let us consider briefly this case. We do not yet have to relax the assumption of perfect certainty.

Two situations should be analyzed: one where rates of interest fluctuate cyclically, the other where there is a persistent tendency for interest rates in one country to be higher than in the other country. Clearly, in the first case it is the difference between or the ratio of the two rates of interest that is important. Let us use the latter measure and assume that i_1/i_2, where i_1 is the short-term rate in the first country and i_2 is the rate in the second country, fluctuates cyclically. Moreover, because similar forces act upon the rates of interest as on the rate of exchange, let us assume that the frequency of this fluctuation is equal to the frequency of the exchange-rate cycle.

If both cycles—that of the exchange-rate and that of the interest-rate ratio—are a result of over-all fluctuations in business activity in the two countries, the "normal" expectation is that the nonspeculative price of country 2's currency will be low when the in-terest rate ratio is low and vice-versa. Relatively depressed economic conditions at home will generally be connected with low interest rates and a low price of foreign exchange. In this case, of course, speculation and interest arbitrage will be mutually reinforcing in stabilizing the price in the foreign-exchange market. If the funds moving across national borders are large enough, the rates of inter-est, *ceteris paribus*, will also be stabilized. Both on account of lower rates of exchange in country 1 and on account of the possible gain from higher interest rates abroad, short-term funds will tend to flow abroad. Of course, such a co-operation of the two effects may operate only to the point where the rate of exchange is perfectly stabilized. If interest arbitrage were so strong as to reverse the cycle in the exchange rate, speculation would then tend to counteract such a cyclical movement. In either case, it is possible to conclude that, under "normal" conditions, cyclical speculation combined with

---

[2] Observe that we do not have to consider the forward market because the as-sumption of perfect certainty is still maintained.

cyclical interest arbitrage will co-operate in bringing about stability in the foreign-exchange market.

At this point, we may permit ourselves a small excursion from theory into the real world and refer to the state of United States balance of payments in the period 1958–60. With widely different conditions of prosperity in these three years and fixed exchange rates, fairly comparable total deficits were realized every year, while the structure of the deficits, i.e., distribution between the current and capital (primarily short-term) accounts, was changing substantially. This indicates that, had the rate of exchange been free, *ceteris paribus*, it would have been lower than at present, but quite stable. Only interest arbitrage and possibly some speculation on dollar devaluation were operative in this case. The additional effect of speculation under free exchange rates might have erased even the small fluctuations in the exchange rate that were not taken care of by short-term funds seeking higher returns.

So far, we have considered only the stabilization of the exchange rate through the monetary mechanism. The real repercussions of equilibrating short-term capital flows may be expected to provide further stability, not only of the exchange market, but also of the whole economy. The short-term capital outflow in depression —while contributing to exchange-rate stability—would generate a surplus in the nonspeculative balance of payments. This would increase effective demand, real output, and employment in the depressed economy and, in turn, act as a stabilizer on the exchange rate and the rate of interest.

If the ratio of short-term rates of interest fluctuates independently of the nonspeculative cycle of the exchange rate, the impact of speculation and interest arbitrage will at certain times co-operate in producing exchange-rate stability, at other times be offsetting. If we make the rather tenuous assumption of perfect certainty, the impact of this situation on the rate of exchange will be largely determined by the nature of the short-term capital markets in the two countries. Unless perfect stability of interest rates in the two countries is produced through profit maximizing, interest arbitrage, and speculation, the exchange rate cannot be entirely stable.

10.5 Cyclical Speculation under Uncertainty

Let us now turn to the realistic case of speculation under uncertainty. We assume here that present and past conditions in the foreign-exchange market are known exactly, while those in the future are known only with some degree of certainty, i.e., any actual or potential speculator has some subjective or objective way of ordering cardinally or ordinally the likelihoods of different outcomes in future markets. These ways may be anything from a "feeling" for an exchange rate three months hence to an elaborate econometric projection.

Although the discussion of the preceding sections does not, by its assumptions, conform to the conditions of the real world, one very important, generally valid, conclusion may be retained. If we say that, in a given free and autonomous market, speculation is or was destabilizing, i.e., if prices have fluctuated on the whole more widely than they would have without speculation, we are also saying, although sometimes we may not realize it, that the speculators as a group were losing money. Of course, this does not prove that speculation must be stabilizing. But it establishes a presumption that it will be stabilizing.[3] The distribution of gains and losses is important here. As in every business, some presumably small and uninformed speculators will always lose money. But that this group would be so important as to offset the gains of larger professional speculators is questionable. This presumption is even strengthened by the fact that, in the real world, entry into the speculative market for small operators is impeded by comparatively high borrowing and transaction costs, unit overhead, and so forth.

The statistics on the average lifetime of a business firm in the United States reveal that there is a large number of small firms in almost every field who enter and leave the market every year. A similar pattern may exist in small-scale speculation. However, it would seem difficult to claim that an industry as a whole, operating at a loss year after year, would survive for any long period of time.

The different profitability of small and large speculators, often indicated by empirical analyses of other markets, can hardly undermine the hypothesis that cyclical speculation in the foreign-exchange market should be stabilizing. However, if there is such a correlation between average unit profit and the volume of transactions of speculators, it may be concluded that the speculative market is oligopolistic rather than purely competitive. As in any other indus-

---

[3] For more discussion of this argument, see M. Friedman, *Essays in Positive Economics* (Chicago: University of Chicago Press, 1953) , and E. Sohmen, *Flexible Exchange Rates* (Chicago: University of Chicago Press, 1961) .

try, here also diminishing costs and capital availability create an important barrier to entry. An additional barrier, typical of the speculation business, is a superior ability to forecast on the part of large speculators.

Although there are good reasons to believe that speculation in a free foreign-exchange market would be stabilizing, the hypothesis can never be proved on a priori grounds. Only a close empirical investigation of a particular market might yield a better insight. Unfortunately, evidence of this type is extremely sparse and rather inconclusive. Perhaps one thing may be safely claimed: that speculative transactions in foreign exchanges, with internal monetary discipline, have never been strongly destabilizing. In the rest of this section and in the one following, we shall discuss the different behavioral and economic factors underlying speculation. While formulating hypotheses about the impact on the foreign-exchange market of each particular set of conditions, we should always be aware of the fact that such analysis only reflects the assumptions and can never be understood as a conclusive proof.

We may now turn to a more detailed discussion of cyclical speculation under uncertainty. We preserve the assumption of equal borrowing and lending rates in both countries and assume that in the long run the average nonspeculative rate remains constant. We also assume that all speculators are rational in the sense that they do not enter the market as gamblers but that they use some past experience of objective facts in deciding whether to buy, sell, or not do anything. Two sets of assumptions can be made about the behavior of the speculator. Because we have assumed only cyclical fluctuations without any trend in the nonspeculative rate of exchange, the speculator may be expected to have in his mind some idea of a "normal" or average price in the market, to buy when price is sufficiently below and sell when it is sufficiently above such average level. In this case all theory of speculation is reduced to determining what is the "sufficient" margin. In the other situation, the speculator takes what we may call a shorter view and speculates on the movement of price itself, without any notion of a "normal" rate. The second case is in no way different from a speculation on a trend in price; we relegate this discussion to the next section. It should also be recalled that a simple situation of this type was analyzed in Section 2 of the preceding chapter.

The width of the range within which the speculator will neither buy nor sell will depend on two things, the first deriving from the past experience of each speculator, the second from his preferences. On the one hand, the speculator, under uncertainty, cannot know exactly what the "normal" level of the exchange rate is. The precision of his judgment—that is, the confidence interval of the expected rate—will depend on the precision with which he is able to evaluate such a range. Given such a distribution of possible future outcomes, however, not all speculators will behave in the same way. This leads us to the second important factor. It is the speculator's preference with respect to risk taking, on the one hand, and with respect to profitability, on the other.

At this point it may be useful to distinguish between two types of speculators: one group less sophisticated, the other more. The first group will content itself with simply thinking that the rate of exchange has exceeded the margin and will sell, or that it has fallen below the margin and will buy. The volume of such transactions for each individual speculator will depend on his total liquid assets, availability of credit, his utility function, and a number of other factors. The total volume of purchases or sales, of course, will be controlled by the size of the exchange market itself.

The more sophisticated group of speculators, in addition to an experience of the past average or normal level, will also have registered the average amplitude of the past cycles. Also, they will be in a better position to evaluate the present amplitude from current economic conditions. Again the precision of such estimates will depend on the length of experience, on precision of observation, and possibly also on the dispersion of the amplitudes of past swings. Such speculators may postpone their sales or purchases in expectation of further increases or decreases in the rate of exchange.

It is possible to conclude that the evaluation of the average rate by the speculative group as a whole will be quite close to the "true" average rate. Under such conditions, there will be *net* selling for rates above the average rate and *net* buying below it. (This does not exclude the possibility that some, presumably small, speculators will misjudge the situations and behave in the opposite way.) But if this is so, the exchange-rate cycle will be dampened by speculation; that is, greater stability will be attained. However, the perfect stability of the exchange rate that would be attained under the ideal conditions assumed in the foregoing sections can never be reached. Market imperfections, imperfect foresight, transactions costs, and a score of other factors will prevent perfect stability of the exchange rate.

Before we leave this section, one final remark should be made on a point that is often neglected in the discussion of speculative markets. Let us define as *strength of the autonomous exchange market* the ratio of nonspeculative transactions per unit of time, say a year, to an average *net* rate of speculative selling or buying in the same market. In an a priori evaluation, the latter number should be understood only as an order of magnitude. Now it is often argued that speculation might reverse the market entirely and make it conform solely to its own vagaries. Such an argument will be the less valid, the greater the strength of the autonomous market. To take an example, the United States foreign-exchange market clears about $25 billion per annum on account of autonomous nonspeculative transactions. If the rate of exchange were free, we might ask ourselves the question, What would be the required order of magnitude of speculative transactions needed to make the movement of the nonspeculative rate irrelevant for speculators' decisions.

It seems that there are some natural limits to funds that may be used for speculative or arbitrage purposes in the foreign-exchange market. At present, with rigid exchange rates and perfect certainty with respect to covered funds, annual *net* short-term capital movements in search of higher interest rates hardly ever exceed $1–$2 billion. It is fair to say that under fluctuating rates the speculative margin of the foreign-exchange market could hardly be any wider than that of profit-oriented short-term capital movements at present. But, if this is so, the speculator can only assume a docile and inferior role next to the man dealing in goods and services and long-term investment.

Moreover, it should be realized that the $1–$2 billion would be just about all that the foreign-exchange market would require for perfect stabilization of any conceivable cycle in the nonspeculative rate of exchange. If that sum or any larger one were employed in such a way as further to destabilize the market, the losses on the part of the speculators would be disastrous.

10.6 Speculation and Long-Run Changes in the Exchange Rate

First of all, we should be a little more specific about what we understand by long-run changes in the exchange rate. Unwise and irresponsible monetary policies may lead an economy into a state of hyperinflation, where, along with other prices, the price of foreign exchange will also rise at a disastrous rate. There is no doubt that speculation in the foreign-exchange market could in this case only hasten the collapse of a currency. On the other hand, even a well-advised and highly responsible government may not be able, or willing, to prevent a slow long-run movement in its rate of exchange. Such changes may be 1, hardly 2, and, as a most unlikely extreme case, 3 per cent per annum. They may be caused by different rates of productivity growth in different countries, by different demand conditions, and by many institutional factors—entrepreneurial and union policies, government transfers, or commitment to preserve full employment.

It is the latter case that we want to discuss in this section. More specifically, we want to analyze and evaluate the function of speculation in the case of mild exchange-rate inflation or, for that matter, deflation.

Throughout this section we shall assume that the short-term rates of interest in both countries are identical in the long run. Under ideal conditions, funds may be borrowed in one country at a given rate and reinvested in the other at the same rate of interest. However, in order to earn this rate of interest, some minimum investment period must be assumed. To be realistic, let us say that the investor has to purchase securities of three months' maturity. The rates that he could obtain on time or demand deposits having a greater degree of liquidity may be thought of as prohibitively low in view of the possible exchange gain of 1–2 per cent per annum. Similarly, brokers' and other charges resulting from redemption before maturity are assumed prohibitive.

With these fairly realistic conditions, we may say that the speculator must make his decisions, under uncertainty, by envisaging the foreign-exchange market for periods of three, six, or nine months hence. Smaller speculators, whose unit transaction and overhead cost exceed the possible maximum gain of, say, $\frac{1}{2}$ per cent per trimester, are automatically eliminated from the market because they cannot help losing.

Thus only the largest and most experienced speculators may be able to enter the market. But even such speculators will be forced to spend some money on each transaction, and consequently their maximum expected gain may be well below the half per cent per trimester. At this point, even without introducing the argument of uncertainty, a plausible hypothesis can be made on purely static cost considerations: namely, that nobody will speculate on the long-run changes in the exchange rate if such changes do not exceed 2 or even 3 per cent per annum. There are two main reasons supporting such a hypothesis: (1) in the real world, there may be a small difference between the borrowing and lending rates; such a difference, added to the minimal unit costs of even the largest operators, may be sufficient to eliminate the type of speculation here considered, and (2) even if there remains a slight net profit margin after all unit transaction costs are deducted, say $\frac{1}{4}$ per cent, the speculator who does not have an unlimited supply of funds may have another investment opportunity that promises a better gain. Forward exchange arbitrage not involving any risk may provide one such important outlet for investment.

The most important factor affecting long-range exchange speculation remains to be discussed. It is uncertainty. Even if the speculator has observed a gradual slow increase in the exchange rate for a long period, he cannot predict exactly the rate in three months, half a year, or a year. Actually, his degree of uncertainty will be increasing more than in proportion with the distance of his contemplated horizon. Let us assume that he chooses to speculate on the rate of exchange in three months. In one way or another he has estimated a probability distribution of possible outcomes,

$$P(r) = f(r)dr \tag{6.1}$$

yielding an expected value of the exchange rate in three months, r_3, that is $\frac{1}{2}$ per cent above the present observed rate, r_0. After deducting all the possible costs to be incurred in a transaction, he comes out with a mean expected gain of 1 per cent, at annual rate, on capital used. And yet he may not undertake the investment while being perfectly rational because of the uncertainty factor.

Suppose that the speculator is contemplating investing a major part of his available funds in the purchase of foreign exchange, say a sum A. Then, designing the unit transaction cost by a, his profit will be equal to

$$pr = A(r - r_0 - a) \tag{6.2}$$

Assume further that he has a utility function, relating all possible gains and losses to a utility index,

$$U = U(pr) = U(pr[r]) \tag{6.3}$$

such that $U(0) = 0$. The normal hypothesis is that $U'' < 0$, i.e., that the satisfaction of every additional dollar gained, or of every additional dollar not lost, is smaller than that of the preceding dollar. The expected value of the speculator's satisfaction may now be expressed as

$$E(U) = \int_0^\infty U(pr) \cdot f(r) \cdot dr \qquad (6.4)$$

The value of $E(U)$ may be negative, even though the expected value of profit is positive. The likelihood that this will happen will be the greater, the faster the marginal utility of gain diminishes, and the greater the dispersion of the expected rate r, i.e., the greater the degree of uncertainty of the future exchange rate.

Of course, at least in theory, the reverse outcome should be mentioned, corresponding to what we may call gambler's mentality, where marginal utility of gain or income is increasing with the level of income. Here equation 6.4 may yield a positive result with a negative expected value of profit. Although this is unlikely, such a mentality, if shared by the majority, will tend to reduce the minimum expected increment of the rate of exchange consistent with speculation and thus be destabilizing.

If mild secular changes in the exchange rate produce speculative movements, in spite of all the possible obstacles just discussed, they are not likely to be important, and consequently they are not likely to be strongly destabilizing. On the whole, it may be expected that there are some natural and/or institutional limits to accelerated accumulation of foreign short-term balances. Observe that such accumulation is implied by a long-run alteration of the rate of change of the exchange rate. After such limits are reached, long-run speculation may continue with a constant level of operating balances in terms of foreign currency; however, the net impact of such a speculation on the foreign-exchange market will be nil. Only now and then some speculators will pay a little to some others in terms of real purchasing power. The rate of exchange will now follow its autonomous path. Moreover, as soon as the operating balances are reduced, the rate of exchange will fall behind its autonomous path, and the speculators will lose.

As we pointed out in the preceding section, speculation conditioned by the rate of change of price over time, so far discussed in relation to long-run trends, may also arise within the cycle. Some will argue that this case is more pertinent to the real world than cyclical speculation, wherein decisions are based on a notion of a "normal price."

If the cycle of the nonspeculative rate is fairly long, that is, if the frequency of oscillation is low, speculators' behavior of the type examined in the preceding section may be quite unlikely indeed, because of the rapidly increasing risk of holding speculative balances over extended periods of time. Under such conditions, the speculator may shorten his horizon and base his decisions on the movement— whether cyclical or long run—immediately preceding his transaction.

In the cycle the rates of change of the exchange rate may be a good deal higher than the 2 per cent tentatively assumed as a reasonable maximum for long-run changes. Consequently, our previous arguments for lack of speculation are no longer pertinent to the cyclical movement; here extensive speculative transactions may take place.

The customary analysis dealing with this situation is based on the concept of the elasticity of expectation. It simply makes the expected price a function of the present rate of change of price. We used the concept when discussing the dynamic stability of the foreign-exchange market in Section 2 of the preceding chapter.

If the elasticity of expectation is positive, that is, if a change in the rate makes the speculators expect further changes in the same direction, the speculators will buy on the upswing and sell on the downswing. This may both increase the amplitude of the cycle and put it out of phase. It still holds, however, that if the average amplitude of the cycle with speculation is greater than that without, speculators will lose money.

It seems that such a theory is not a good approximation of real conditions. It is hard to believe that net sales of speculative balances would take place only by the time the rate started declining. Rather, it seems that the early comers (near the trough of the cycle) will start selling well before the peak is reached. As the upswing goes on, an increasing volume of such sales may be expected, eventually producing net speculative sales well before the peak of the cycle is reached. This, of course, would produce a pattern comparable with that discussed in the preceding section, that is, greater stability of the exchange rate. Therefore, it would be possible to argue that speculative supply and demand are a function not only of the rate of change of price—as implied by the elasticity of expectations approach—but also of the rate of change of the rate of change (that is, the second derivative).

10.7   Leads and Lags or Nonspeculators' Speculation

Only a minor step remains to be made to complete our discussion of speculation. So far we have assumed that speculators and all other traders of foreign exchange are two distinct groups. In reality, exporters and importers, as well as long-term investors, may often assume the role of speculators. Depending on their expectations as to what will happen to the exchange rate in the future and also depending on the levels of short-term rates in the two money markets, they may either delay or expedite their foreign-exchange transactions. Of course, such leads and lags will have the same effects on the foreign-exchange market as transactions of professional speculators.

Most of the previous discussion of speculation pertains to this case, and most of the forces influencing the decisions of speculators will also act on the payments leads and lags of nonspeculative traders. However, there is one new factor to be considered in relation to the "nonspeculators' speculation." It is related to the dual function (i.e., to a joint product) of the trader using the practice of leads and lags.

Some, although not the present writer, may argue that it is more likely that an exporter or importer whose primary purpose is current transactions in goods and services may not be able to impute his profit correctly to (1) his trade function and (2) his speculative function. Thus, while realizing an over-all profit, he may lose as a speculator and gain as a trader. Of course, such a pattern of business behavior on a continuing basis might, as we have argued in the previous sections, destabilize the foreign-exchange market if the speculative losses of the nonspeculators offset the speculative gains of the professional speculators. Only a detailed empirical investigation could verify such a supposition. Even on a priori grounds, however, it is possible to argue that businessmen on the whole are able, at least approximately, to impute their gains from joint production to two different products. Actually, in our particular case, they have the same information about exchange market rate quotations as do the professional speculators. It would be only a matter of simple arithmetic for them to realize that they were continuously buying or selling with leads and lags under less advantageous conditions than they would have without such an arrangement, or with leads and lags in reverse order.

10.8   The Forward Exchange Market and Speculation

Speculation in foreign exchanges is usually discussed together with the forward market. The function and mechanics of the forward exchange market was discussed in Chapter 5. In this chapter we have deliberately excluded consideration of the forward market, first, in order to make the analysis as simple as possible and, second, because strictly speaking, it is unnecessary. This is not to say that the forward exchange rate does not play any role in exchange speculation.

Instead of buying foreign exchange spot and investing it abroad in expectation of a future rise of price of foreign exchange, the speculator might also purchase foreign currency forward, hoping to sell it at a future date with a profit. The effect on both exchange markets, however, will be very similar, if not identical. Suppose that the speculator wants to hold one million dollars in the form of foreign currency three months hence. If he buys spot, this will affect the spot market rate somewhat, and a short-term capital outflow will take place. Under competition and unchanged interest rates in both countries, the required relation between spot and forward rates (see Chap. 5, Sec. 2) will be attained through covered interest arbitrage, reducing the spot dollar price of foreign currency and raising the forward rate. If the speculator buys forward, under perfectly competitive conditions, the forward rate initially will go up, but again the required relation between spot and forward rates will be attained through interest arbitrage. In this case, however, the arbitrageurs' funds will move in the opposite direction, thus raising the spot rate and reducing the forward rate to the required levels. In either case, both the spot and the forward rates will increase, as compared with the initial situation, and one million dollars of uncovered funds will be available to the speculator in foreign currency three months hence. Some difference between the impact of one type of speculative transaction and the other may arise if the elasticities of demand, or of supply, are different in the spot and forward markets.

PART III

Chapter 11

PURE THEORY OF INTERNATIONAL TRADE AND TRADE POLICY; SURVEY OF THE FIELD

The organization of the two remaining parts of our study resembles that of Part II. The entire field of pure theory of international trade and its extension to economic policy is, again, much too extensive to allow a concise treatment that would at once reveal the logical structure of the subject, pose questions, and, at the same time, provide solutions. Consequently, we shall make an attempt in this chapter to survey the subject in its entirety, show its organization, and outline the principal questions it is designed to answer. The later chapters will show in greater detail the propositions and proofs of the theory.

Often we refer to the pure theory of international trade as nonmonetary or barter theory. Effectively, money plays an extremely unimportant role here, if any at all. Actually, our distinction between the monetary adjustment theory and the pure nonmonetary theory follows the approach of classical economics. The real magnitudes of the system are assumed to be determined entirely separately from the monetary phenomena. As we saw in the preceding part of the study, on grounds of theories that have followed the classical way of thinking, such a separation is not perfectly legitimate. Money, under some conditions at least, may affect the physical equilibrium of an economy.

This leads us to the first important assumption of the nonmonetary theory; it is that of continuous full employment of productive resources. In other words, almost without exception, we are in the "classical world," where Say's law and flexible prices guarantee full employment, where only relative prices and relative factor earnings are of interest and are determined independently of the supply of money.

The restrictiveness of these simplifying assumptions—not made

179

in the monetary adjustment theory—is outweighed by the fact that we are able to disaggregate variables that had to be treated globally in the adjustment theory. Moreover, it is now possible to approach international trade as a situation of general equilibrium rather than as a set of often unjustified partial equilibria.

We should observe at this point, however, that the separation between the pure theory and the monetary theory of international trade is by no means necessary. A theory that would include elements of both is conceivable, though no doubt it would be quite complicated and would probably reach unmanageable dimensions. The division of the two approaches is, to a large extent, a historical accident, only revealing the inertia of economic thinking. Also, to a degree, it derives from the fact that one approach is better suited for one type of problem, namely, the balance-of-payments adjustment process, and the other for another.

The field of pure theory may be subdivided into two broad sets of problems. The first set belongs to what we may call (somewhat loosely) positive economics, the second to the field of welfare economics. In the first group we study the impact of a given set of premises on a number of internally determined variables and also the relations among such variables. The task of welfare economics in international trade is primarily to study the effect of trade on real income, total satisfaction, or utility of countries, regions, or social groups. Often the demarcation line between the two areas is not clearly drawn. Conclusions obtained in the former are relevant for the latter and vice-versa. Nevertheless, the distinction between the two areas is useful; we employ it in organizing the following chapters.

Another important distinction pertaining to both these areas is that between theory proper and the theory of imperfect markets. While in the first case we make the assumption of perfect competition in all markets, except for international factor markets, in the second we consider a number of situations wherein markets are imperfect in one way or another. Consideration of commercial policy, tariffs, quantitative restrictions, transportation costs, taxation, imperfect mobility, and monopolistic tendencies belong to the latter group.

The positive theory of international trade provides answers to a number of concrete problems. One of the most important questions that economists have tried to answer ever since they became concerned with problems of trade is what determines the structure, direction, and volume of trade. In other words, what are the forces determining whether one type or another of produce will be exported or imported, and how much of each commodity will be traded? A number of theories have been offered. David Ricardo, one of the earliest writers dealing with the subject, provided an explanation based primarily on relative differences of labor productivity among different countries. The important contribution of Ricardo is his proof that not absolute but relative differences in cost or productivity are the necessary condition for trade.

In the period following Ricardo's early writings, the pure theory of international trade underwent changes and generalizations very much in line with the development of economic theory as a whole. Thus, alternatively, emphasis was given to technology, relative factor endowments, and differences in demand conditions. Finally, a merging of all factors took place in a general equilibrium model of international trade.

It is clear that none of the three important sets of factors— technology, factor endowments, and demand conditions—taken separately is capable of fully explaining international exchange. Thus only the general equilibrium approach may provide us with a satisfactory explanation of trade. Nevertheless, as a means of studying the subject, it is useful to separate the three sets of explanatory parameters and treat each individually while assuming the impact of the others as nil or, to be more precise, as neutral.

We shall show the factor proportions and productivity approaches in the following chapter. Along with this discussion we shall prove a number of important theorems that are directly related to and easily derivable from such analysis.

The factor proportions theory simply relates the direction and structure of international trade to the relative abundance of different productive resources in different countries. Thus it states—somewhat loosely—that countries relatively well endowed with a particular resource will tend to export primarily commodities which, in their productive processes, use a large proportion of the abundant resource. Clearly, this theory requires a more rigorous proof and also some special assumptions and qualifications. But we have to postpone such details until the next chapter. In a symmetrical way, even if countries are endowed with resources in comparable proportions, trade may result—as in the simple Ricardian case—from divergent technologies in different countries: countries relatively more efficient in one type of production than others will tend to export such products and to import commodities wherein the outside world is relatively more efficient. Even if both technology and factor endowments were exactly the same in two countries, mutual exchange would generally be possible and beneficial to the two trading partners, provided that demand conditions (or preferences) were not identical.

Precise conceptualization of demand and utility is quite difficult and requires a number of special assumptions where social groups rather than individuals are assumed to be the units engaging in exchange. Therefore, we shall devote Chapter 13 to this particular problem. The correspondence between individual and social preferences will be studied in this chapter in relation to the determination of international trade equilibria under different conditions.

The familiar dichotomy between problems of value and problems of volume is also present in the pure theory of international trade. If we have separated the problem of the physical nature of exchange in the preceding paragraphs, it was only to organize better and clarify the organization of the subject. In reality, no quantitative equilibrium can be determined independently of an equilibrium of value. Thus, together with our analysis of the impact of factor endowments, technologies, and demand conditions on physical exchange, we shall, at appropriate stages, show the relation of these factors to relative prices of commodities traded, marginal and average costs, relative factor prices, etc. In relation to such value indicators it is possible to analyze income distribution and the impact of trade on the absolute and relative levels of factor prices in different countries.

In addition to finding the relation between the basic parameters and equilibrium ratios of exchange, many economists have been at different times concerned with the more philosophical question: What actually is the cause of value in international exchange or in exchange in general? Ricardo founded his system on the labor theory of value, claiming that commodities will exchange in proportions determined by the quantities of labor required in producing them. A later refinement of this theory, deriving from the notion that the actual cost of producing depends on the pain or irksomeness of the labor expended, has led to the real-cost theory of value. This theory actually is an extension of the utility theory to the supply of factors of production.

The opportunity-cost theory, coined by Professor Haberler, has yielded the very useful opportunity-cost function. It asserts that international values in exchange will depend on the marginal or opportunity cost of one commodity in terms of the other. The difference between the opportunity-cost and the real-cost approach is only apparent and consists primarily in emphasis and depth. We shall show in the following chapter that the two approaches are consistent and that both lead, if properly interpreted, to the same results.

Although the next two chapters contain material essential for understanding the underlying mechanics of international exchange and its component parts, the most important step of our exposition is left for Chapter 14. There we shall synthesize all the building blocks into one simple general equilibrium model. In doing this, we cannot overemphasize our indebtedness to Professor Meade, on whose exposition we draw heavily.[1] In effect, our main task in Chapter 14 is to present in an efficient and concise way the analysis presented by Professor Meade. Perhaps in some respects our assumptions are more general and thus more applicable to real conditions, and perhaps we derive from this analysis some new insights. The great advantage of this general equilibrium approach is that it permits study of the relations of any set of factors or variables within the system. Moreover, it is possible to use it in showing the effects of commercial policy, transfer, or balance-of-payments disequilibria on the solutions of external trade. Many of the analytical tools and concepts used in the more traditional discussions of international trade may now be derived as special cases.

One such important concept is the Marshallian reciprocal demand, or offer curve, showing the relations between relative export and import prices and the willingness to trade. Closely connected with it is the concept of elasticity of demand and supply of exports and imports in barter exchange. These elasticities are closely related to the "money" elasticities used in Part II of the study. They are as important in the discussion of market stability as the "partial" elasticities used in discussing the adjustment process. Problems of market stability, the relation between barter and monetary equilibrium, problems of long-run structural change, and a score of applications of the pure theory to problems of commercial policy will occupy our attention in the remaining parts of Chapter 14 and in Chapter 16.

[1] James Meade, *A Geometry of International Trade* (London: George Allen & Unwin, 1952).

We have also introduced in our discussion in Chapter 14 the exposition of a general equilibrium theory where an arbitrary number of products is traded and many factors of production are used. Although such a model is generally nonoperational in dealing with concrete situations of trade, it is very useful in examining the consistency of the system and in conceptualizing the operation of a real economy.

In Chapter 15 we turn to the second important area of pure theory, namely, the welfare aspects of international exchange. In essence, in that chapter we extend the usual welfare economics to include situations of international exchange. Starting from Ricardo's early propositions concerning comparative advantage and the gains from international trade, it is possible to formulate the entire analysis in an up-to-date setting. This includes showing the impact of trade on the welfare of nations, of different groups, and of individuals. Similarly, restriction of trade or market imperfections may be related to the total gain or loss of social or individual welfare. Clearly, results obtained in the chapters preceding Chapter 15, such as the relation between trade and factor prices and income distribution, as well as the discussion of social utility presented in Chapter 13, have a good deal of relevance for the welfare argument.

The problem of customs unions is closely related to, and actually falls primarily within, the scope of welfare economics and of the theory of tariffs. It could be treated as a special situation of international trade, and thus the usual analysis of foreign trade could suffice. However, the fact that at least three countries or trading regions have to be considered in this case adds a good deal of new complexity to the problem. Moreover, it is often necessary to discuss the problem of customs unions within the framework of both pure theory and monetary theory. Finally, it is the timeliness of the problem nowadays that calls for a separate treatment of the customs-union issue. The last chapter of the study is devoted to this question. In addition to its immediate purpose, such discussion may be useful to the reader, in that it shows the possibility of extending the often oversimplified analysis of this study to cases dealing with larger numbers of countries.

In concluding this survey chapter, I should like to make two remarks concerning the application of pure theory to practical problems of international trade and trade policy. I am led to the first observation by a conversation with one of my graduate students. His question was: "Why do we discuss pure theory of trade at all? By now, all that counts is monetary equilibrium, the balance-of-payments adjustment process . . . , that's all that everybody talks about these days." I was forced to agree, on the whole, but I take the liberty of adding that this state of the art of international economics is deplorable. Actually, it will always be the elements of pure theory that create the setting and the conditions of any monetary state of balance-of-payments equilibrium. Only if we understand pure theory will we be able to apply correctly the monetary adjustment analysis. I further dare to say that a good deal of misunderstanding and mismanagement on the part of our policy makers stems from this neglect of pure theory.

My second remark concerns the practical application of pure theory itself. At first sight, most of the writings on the subject, including the present study, appear as extreme oversimplifications of reality that scarcely may serve more than to satisfy the intellectual appetite of the theorist. Actually, this is not so. If we deal most often with models including two countries and hardly more than two commodities traded or two factors of production used, this does not mean that the representation is utterly unsuited as a description of the real world. It is always possible, either through a precise reformulation or through a mere mental exercise, to adjust the simple theories to reality. Instead of thinking in terms of wine and cloth, as in the traditional Ricardian example, we may think in terms of manufactures and primary products, produced from two somewhat loosely defined factors—labor and capital. The results thus obtained may not be as accurate as if a theory including millions of commodities and millions of factors were used. The great advantage is, however, that the former are easily obtainable, while the latter's complexity surpasses any human ability of data collection, estimation, or computation. The orderliness of the universe, hand in hand with the law of large numbers, usually does not let us down completely.

Chapter 12

FACTOR ENDOWMENTS AND TECHNOLOGY IN INTERNATIONAL TRADE

12.1 Factor Endowments; Rigorous Theory

As we have argued in the preceding chapter, it is impossible to explain international trade by any single cause. A number of factors always simultaneously influence international exchange. Earlier authors sometimes either attempted to construct a theory on only one set of forces or at least gave a predominant role to a single factor. In particular, this was the case with factor endowments. We shall reiterate here the essentials of the factor-proportions theory; but we have to keep in mind that in the context of our analysis it is not the complete theory of trade but only a part of it.

In this section we shall demonstrate rigorously the factor-proportions approach in a simple case where only two countries are involved in trading, only two commodities are produced by each country, and only two factors of production—capital and labor—are used in production and are fully employed. Later we shall relax some of these assumptions in constructing a more general case. Also we assume that technologies in both countries are the same for identical products. Throughout most of this section we make a further assumption that is not strictly required but that makes our analysis more simple and more realistic, namely, that all technologies are subject to constant returns to scale. In other words, in producing any commodity the scale of production is irrelevant for average and marginal cost; these costs remain constant and equal to price, whatever the level of output, provided, of course, that factor prices do not change.

In terms of mathematics, this assumption presupposes that either of the two products x_1 and x_2 may be produced from capital C and labor L according to a production function

$$x = x(C, L) \tag{1.1}$$

that may also be written as

$$x = L \cdot X \left(\frac{C}{L}\right) \tag{1.2}$$

i.e., the production functions are homogeneous of the first order. A single equal product line, for any given level of output, defines the entire technology.

It may be useful to digress a little and find from the Appendix the economic significance of this assumption. It corresponds very closely to competitive conditions in the factor and goods markets. A technology of an industry operating under such conditions will have such a production function, even if identical technologies of individual firms are subject to decreasing costs up to a point and increasing costs thereafter. In the long run, each firm in the industry will operate at its minimum average cost, equal for each producer, and any expansion or contraction of output will be realized solely through an increase or decrease in the number of firms. The average and marginal costs, measured in terms of the output taken as a numéraire, will not change.

To construct the production possibilities of the two economies, endowed with L_a and L_b of labor and C_a and C_b of capital, respectively, we may use the so-called Edgeworth-Bowley box diagram. Let us consider, say, economy a and construct a rectangle whose two dimensions correspond to the factor endowments of country a, namely, L_a and C_a. This is shown in Figure 12.1.1. Inputs into commodity x_1 are measured from origin O_1 and inputs into commodity x_2 from origin O_2, in the opposite direction in such a way as to use up the total factor supplies defined by the box. Any point

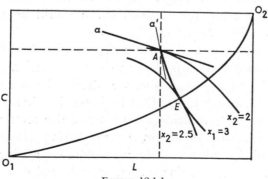

FIGURE 12.1.1

within the box, such as A, defines an allocation of available productive resources between the two commodities produced. The outputs corresponding to such an allocation of resources are given by the two equal product lines (isoquants) passing through A, i.e., $x_1 = 3$ and $x_2 = 2$.

It is immediately apparent that production at such a point as A could take place only if some imperfection existed in the factor market. Profit-maximizing producers could produce at A only if relative prices of capital and labor in the two industries were reflected by the slopes of lines a and a', tangent to the two isoquants passing through point A. If, however, competitive conditions exist in the capital and labor market, relative prices of capital and labor have to be equal in both industries. Now we may observe that such a situation will be attained at a point, such as E, where the two equal product lines are tangent to each other. Also, we notice that point E represents a more efficient allocation of productive resources between the two outputs, because, with the same total inputs and output of x_1 as at A, it is now possible to produce 2.5 units of commodity x_2. Of course, there will be an infinite number of such "most efficient" points of resource allocation, all defined by the fact that the equal product lines passing through them have the same slope and also by the fact that, at any such point, the output of one commodity (with given resources) cannot be increased unless the output of the other commodity is reduced.

The locus of all efficient points such as E will generally run from the origin O_1 to O_2. We have drawn such a locus, usually referred as a *contract curve* or efficiency locus, in the diagram. It will be convex downward or upward, depending on whether commodity x_1 is labor-intensive relative to commodity x_2 or not, in the relevant region where production takes place. On the limit, if both technologies were exactly the same, the contract curve would be a straight-line diagonal connecting O_1 and O_2.

It is very easy now to read from any point such as E the levels of output (such as 3 and 2.5) of the two commodities. Plotting such observations in an $x_1 - x_2$ plane, we obtain the *production possibility curve* of country a, P_a. This is shown in Figure 12.1.2. With the assumptions we have made, such a locus, also often referred to as the *opportunity cost curve* or *transformation function*, will be convex upward, its slope at different points expressing the increasing marginal rate of transformation, or marginal cost (opportunity

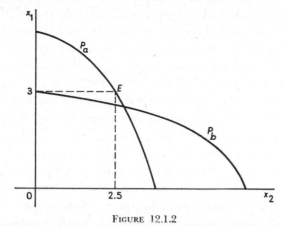

FIGURE 12.1.2

cost) of one commodity in terms of the other as the output of the former is increased. Only in the case of identical technologies, with unit homogeneous production functions, would the production possibility function be a straight line. We have also plotted on P_a point E, corresponding to E in the preceding diagram.

The construction of the production possibility curve of country b proceeds along exactly the same lines. The only thing that is different now are the availabilities of capital and labor, C_b and L_b. To simplify the derivation, let us assume that country b owns the same number of units of capital as country a owns of labor and vice-versa. In this case the box diagram will have the same dimensions but will stand on its shorter side.

If a country specializes entirely in one product, say x_1, it will produce at O_2; the output of x_1 at this point will be given by the isoquant of x_1 passing through O_2; similarly for product x_2 and the origin O_1. Now, if commodity x_1 is labor-intensive relative to commodity x_2 for any set of factor prices, country a will necessarily be able to produce, with complete specialization, a greater amount of commodity x_1 relative to commodity x_2 than country b. To state somewhat loosely the result that may be derived by the reader through a simple geometrical construction, country a has a comparative advantage in the labor-intensive commodity because its factor endowments are better suited to the output of that commodity. A perfectly symmetrical argument may be made for commodity x_2 from the point of view of country b.

Consequently, a new opportunity-cost curve may be constructed for country b—P_b in our diagram—expressing the productive capacity of that country. Considering the intercepts of the two loci with the two axes and their over-all shape, we observe that country a has a comparative advantage in specializing in producing commodity x_1 and country b in producing x_2. In an international equilibrium, where only one set of relative product prices can exist, it is most likely that both countries will produce both products, but country a will necessarily produce a larger proportion of x_1 than country b. Also, provided that the spending habits (preferences) of the two communities are comparable, country a will tend to export x_1 and import x_2, and vice-versa for country b. In later sections and in the following two chapters we shall substantiate rigorously these propositions, once some additional notions are proved.

Two important points remain to be made in this section. We have specified in the preceding discussion that one product's technology must be labor-intensive relative to the other for any set of factor prices. But this does not necessarily have to be so. For example, it might happen that, for high capital-labor ratios, one technology is relatively capital-intensive, and for low capital-labor ratios (i.e., high relative price of capital) the same technology is labor-intensive relative to the other. In our preceding construction, then, one contract curve might be convex downward, while the other, for different factor endowments of the second economy, convex upward. The important conclusion that follows in this case is that the comparative form of the two production possibility contours (as in Fig. 12.1.2) no longer has to reflect unambiguously the relative factor endowments of the two countries. Indeed, it is no longer possible to state that one country will have a comparative advantage in producing, say, the capital-intensive product, the latter being no longer uniquely identifiable.

Our second concluding observation pertains to the assumption of unit homogeneous production functions. It is not really required for our preceding discussion. At least in theory, both techniques could be subject to equally increasing or decreasing costs; that is, mathematically, both productions could be homogeneous of the same order, smaller or greater than unity. In this case the production possibility loci are still defined and may be convex downward if costs are rapidly falling. The important fact to be observed here is that under the assumed conditions, all production possibility curves corresponding to different levels of factor endowments, but to a fixed proportion of such endowments, would resemble each other, except for scale; that is, they would be in the same relation to each other as any two isoquants of a homogeneous function. Some difficulties, however, may arise if we want to study a market equilibrium based on such production possibility functions. A market solution may no longer be compatible with competitive conditions in the case of diminishing costs because the industry producing under such conditions may no longer be able to price at marginal cost.

Perhaps a more interesting case is that of increasing cost in one or both industries. Here competition is possible. The technology of an industry operating under such conditions may be described by a set of isoquants farther and farther away from each other, as output or factor inputs increase. A relevant example here is agricultural or any other natural-resource product. As inputs of capital and labor increase, output will not grow in proportion, owing to the diminishing quality of the third factor, land, that has to be utilized. Using the box-diagram technique, the reader will find it easy to establish that in this situation the production possibility curve will be more concave than it would have been, *ceteris paribus,* with a unit homogeneous technology. However, as we have pointed out already, with equal degrees of homogeneity in both industries, the propositions of the factor-proportions theory still must hold true, as derived for the case of constant costs. Specifically, the country relatively better supplied with capital will produce a relatively larger quantity of the capital-intensive product, and export it, provided that the necessary conditions of demand— noted above—prevail in the two countries. If the two production functions are not of the same degree of homogeneity, it will be observed, no simple factor-proportions theory can be designed.

12.2 Marginal Costs, Average Costs, and Prices

We have already pointed out that the slope of the opportunity-cost curve expresses the marginal rate of transformation of commodity x_1 into commodity x_2, or the marginal or opportunity cost of one commodity in terms of the other. This slope may also be explained by reference to concepts taken from cost and price theory.

Consider a slight movement along the contract curve in Figure 12.1.1, in the neighborhood of E, toward O_2. This means that output of commodity x_1 is slightly increased and that of x_2 slightly reduced. The rate of transformation is apparent from the slope of P_a in the neighborhood of E. For a small displacement, the transfer of resources from commodity x_2 to commodity x_1 is dC and dL, and the additional cost in producing x_1 is dc,

$$dc = P_C \cdot dC + P_L \cdot dL \tag{2.1}$$

Because prices of factors of production have to be equal in both activities along the contract curve, the additional cost in x_1 must be equal to the reduction of cost in x_2. Thus, considering the signs of these changes, we have

$$dc_1 = -dc_2 \tag{2.2}$$

Now the marginal costs of the two commodities are defined as

$$mc_1 = \frac{dc_1}{dx_1} \quad \text{and} \quad mc_2 = \frac{dc_2}{dx_2} \tag{2.3}$$

Introducing relations 2.3 into 2.2 and reorganizing somewhat, we obtain the important condition

$$\frac{mc_1}{mc_2} = -\frac{dx_2}{dx_1} \tag{2.4}$$

In words, the slope of the transformation curve (measured with respect to the x_1-axis) must be equal to the negative ratio of marginal cost of product x_1 to product x_2. This is a general proposition, independent of whether the production functions (or technologies) are subject to constant returns to scale or not. If they are, the left-hand side of relation 2.4 will also be equal to the ratio of average costs, because these are always, under such conditions, equal to marginal costs.

Another important result follows. Under competitive conditions in the product market, marginal costs will also be equal to prices, and, consequently, we may write in summary

$$\frac{mc_1}{mc_2} = \frac{P_1}{P_2} = -\frac{dx_2}{dx_1} \tag{2.5}$$

Thus, whether the country engages in international trading or not, whenever both commodities are produced and sold under competitive conditions, we may be sure that relative prices used in exchange are given by the slope of the transformation function. It may be easily shown also that this proposition has a general validity, whether two or more products are produced or whether two or more factors of production are used. We may rewrite the above relation to account for this fact as

$$\frac{mc_i}{mc_j} = \frac{P_i}{P_j} = -\frac{dx_j}{dx_i} = -MRT_{i/j} \qquad (2.5')$$

$$i, j = 1, 2, \ldots, n$$

where n is the number of commodities produced; MRT is the marginal rate of transformation of one commodity into the other; and dx_j/dx_i represents the slope of the production possibility surface observed in a plane defined by given values of all x's but x_j and x_i.

12.3   Generalization of the Factor-Proportions Theory

A number of the assumptions made in Section 1 in proving the proposition of the factor-proportions theory do not describe the conditions of the real world very closely. In this section we shall consider a somewhat more general case of the factor-proportions theory. We shall retain the assumptions made in the main part of Section 1 concerning demand conditions and technology but shall deal with the case in which a larger number of productive factors are used and where many commodities are traded. We shall not be able to provide as rigorous a proof of the theory as in the simple case of two commodities and two factors of production; however, the theory may be shown to be sufficiently valid for all practical purposes.

Our first task is to define factor intensiveness of trade in the case in which many commodities are traded and a number of factors of production are used. In the two-commodity, two-factor case, this was quite simple because only one commodity was exported and one commodity imported, each using different proportions of capital and labor. It is possible, in the many-commodity case, to break down any bill of goods exported or imported into its value components of productive contribution of different factors, say $v_1, v_2, \ldots, v_m$.

As a mathematical proposition, it may be shown (by Euler's theorem) that under competition and constant costs (unit homogeneous production function) the entire product of a commodity is distributed as payments or earnings of the different factors. Thus it is possible to write

$$x = MPP_1 \cdot v_1 + MPP_2 \cdot v_2 + \cdots + MPP_m \cdot v_m \qquad (3.1)$$

where MPP_i represents the marginal physical productivity of the ith factor of production, equal, as we know from competitive pricing theory, to the real wage (unit cost) of the ith factor. Thus, summing up over all commodities exported or imported, all the terms such as

$MPP_i \cdot v_i$, each multiplied by the price of the particular commodity, p^j, we obtain the value content of exports or imports of factor v_i, say V_i; i.e.,

$$V_i = MPP_i \cdot \sum_j v_i^j \cdot p^j \qquad (3.2)$$

where, of course,

$$\sum_i V_i = \text{total value of exports or imports.}$$

Now, if the number of commodities traded in each direction is larger than the number of factors of production, i.e., $n > m$, the relative factor prices in the two countries will be equalized (we shall discuss this proposition later in this chapter). Under such conditions, factor proportions in different products will be equal in both countries. By definition, prices of commodities in both countries are the same.

The relative factor endowments v^0 of the two trading countries, say, a and b, may be ordered according to relative abundance, starting, say, with $v_{1,a}^0$ being the relatively most abundant factor of country a; i.e.,

$$\frac{v_{1,a}^0}{v_{1,b}^0} > \frac{v_{2,a}^0}{v_{2,b}^0} > \cdots > \frac{v_{m,a}^0}{v_{m,b}^0} \qquad (3.3)$$

If, for any given set of factor prices, there is no correlation between any two or more factor-output ratios observed over all the different products, the following may be expected: The relative value contents of exports (x) and imports (m) will approximate the order of the relative factor endowments stated in relations 3.3. Thus, in our particular case,

$$\frac{V_1^x}{V_1^m} > \frac{V_2^x}{V_2^m} > \cdots > \frac{V_m^x}{V_m^m} \qquad (3.4)$$

We cannot prove this proposition rigorously, mostly because it is impossible to find a simple way of ordering relative factor intensiveness of productive processes where a large number of factors of production are used. However, the correlation between the relative factor contents of trade and the relative factor endowments is intuitively clear, provided, of course, that the independence of factor-output ratios holds. The reader will be able to prove for himself the postulates of relations 3.3 and 3.4 in the simple case where only 2 factors of production are used and many commodities are produced and traded.

Finally, we should observe that if the independence condition is not fulfilled, the above results may not hold. If, for example, a high land-output ratio usually requires a high capital-output ratio, as actually seems to be the case in the real world, the inequalities in 3.4 may show a different order from that in relation 3.3. A relative abundance of capital of a country may not be reflected exactly in its external trade, being disguised by a strong scarcity of natural resources.

12.4 Technology and External Trade

We do not have to detain ourselves very long with the problem of technology. The preceding sections of this chapter provide us with many of the analytical tools we need in showing the impact of different states of technology or technological progress on international trade. Nevertheless, some definitional groundwork is needed. We should make clear what we understand by "different technique" and how we are able to evaluate such a state from empirical data.

Often we associate the concept of technological advancement with the concept of productivity. This is not entirely correct. Differences in productivity may—but not necessarily do—imply different states of technology. Let us write a simple production function, such as those used in the preceding sections, relating inputs of capital C and labor L to the level of output; in addition, we use two multiplicative parameters, a and b, which provide us with a way of showing the state of technology:

$$x = x(a \cdot C, b \cdot L) \tag{4.1}$$

a and b may be thought of as technological parameters; their increase represents a technological advancement. If, for example, a and b increased from 1 to 2, only one half as much labor and capital would be needed in producing any given amount of output x as previously. Capital and labor productivity would increase by 100 per cent, and so would total productivity. While the isoquants or equal product lines would remain unchanged in the capital-labor plane, the scales of the capital and labor axes would have to be renumbered by dividing any ordinate or abscissa by 2. Alternatively, with unchanged scales of the two axes, each isoquant would now have to shift downward and to the left, thus expressing a lower input of productive factors for any given output. This type of transformation we may call "technological change"; on the other hand, those situations wherein two sets of a and b appear for an identical product we call "difference in technology." More generally, any shift of isoquants toward the origin represents an improvement in technology; any difference of the isoquant maps for the same product represents a difference in technologies.

Of course, a change in capital and labor productivity might have taken place simply because of the substitution of one factor for another or because of a change in scale of production. Both these situations are compatible with a single production function, i.e., in our example, with a single set of parameters a and b. In this case we should speak of a difference in individual factor productivities rather than in technologies.

Often it is impossible to establish empirically whether one type of difference or the other is present or whether both are realized simultaneously. This does not have to bother us in our theoretical analysis because all depends on the conditions assumed. In examining real-world conditions, however, a total productivity index, combining individual factor productivities with appropriate weights, may yield, at least in rough terms, the answer to the problem. Our confidence in such a result may be improved if we have some a priori notion about the over-all nature of the technology under consideration.

With these remarks we may now turn to the relation between technology and foreign trade. To eliminate the possible impact of factor endowments on trade, let us assume that the two trading partners are endowed with identical quantities of capital and labor. In terms of the analysis in the preceding sections, this means that the box diagrams of both countries have the same dimensions. Let us also assume that the technologies in the two countries are different. Both products' production functions may be written as

$$x_1 = D \cdot f_1(C, L) \tag{4.2}$$

$$x_2 = K \cdot f_2(C, L) \tag{4.3}$$

with, say, D equal to 1 in country a and equal to $\frac{1}{2}$ in country b, and the reverse for K. As before, we assume that the production of both products is subject to constant costs. Consequently, the allocation of productive resources between x_1 and x_2 may be obtained from the same box diagram, with the same contract curve (efficiency locus).

Only the numbering of different levels of output at different points of the contract curve will be different in the two countries, reflecting the differences in D and K.

The resulting transformation functions or production possibility curves will reflect these differences in total productivity and may be described by a pattern perfectly comparable with that found in Figure 12.1.2. All the rest of the analysis holds. With international competitive trading and with a neutral effect of demand conditions, country a will tend to specialize in producing commodity x_1, export the same, and import x_2; the reverse will be observed for country b.

As a matter of historical interest, we may mention here the classical case of Ricardian comparative advantage. Here the only factor of production used is labor L, and all production functions are linear; i.e.,

$$x = K \cdot L \qquad (4.4)$$

where K represents the inverse of the labor cost of a particular product. There will be four different values of the parameter K, for the two products in two different countries. The only condition for trade in the Ricardian system is that the K's be not proportional between the two countries. The absolute level of productivity in the two countries is not important for trade; only the relative productivity, or opportunity cost of one commodity in terms of the other, has to be different in the two countries for trade to take place. An absolute advantage of one country over the other in both products without a difference in opportunity costs will lead to no trade.

Of course, the same proposition may be made with respect to the two-factor case discussed above. Proportional differences in technology in both (or all) products between two countries may lead to no trade. If, for example, D as well as K assumed twice as large a value in one country as in the other, the resulting production possibilities, with identical factor endowments, would be perfectly proportional, although of different size. This, with comparable demand conditions, would tend to produce a situation of equal proportions of output of commodities in the two countries and no trade whatsoever.

Actually, in the real world, it is the latter, less interesting, case that often arises. A technically more advanced country is likely to demonstrate fairly similar degrees of skills and technical advancement in most fields of productive activity. It is primarily because of some other factor not accounted for explicitly in the production functions, such as natural resources, climatic conditions, or the organization of managerial skill, that the relative differences in technology conducive to trade will arise.

Some may argue that, if this is the case, it is still possible to assume that technologies are identical and that all may be explained through differences in factor endowments. This is probably true in many cases. However, introducing differences in such extraneous factors as weather conditions or humidity—or even natural resources—as a parameter rather than a variable of a production function is useful. It may both simplify the analysis and account for the fact that some of these factors are really uncontrollable by the business decision-making unit; and, what is more important, such factors may be assumed of different quality. Our previous example of increasing costs in a natural-resource industry with a virtually infinite number of different grades of land may illustrate the point. Here only capital and labor were counted as variable inputs, while land availability was directly reflected in the form of the production function.

12.5 Variable Factor Supplies and International Trade

So far we have assumed that different countries engaging in trade are endowed, in the short run at least, with fixed quantities of productive factors. There are two ways in which such an assumption may not be fulfilled. On the one hand, over longer periods of time, population and labor force, the stock of capital, and available natural resources may either expand or contract. If it is possible to ascertain such changes over long periods of time as influenced either by external or exogenous forces or by some internal mechanism such as capital accumulation or resource depletion, a new equilibrium model may be constructed for every period. There is no difficulty in such a procedure.

The second case deals with a situation in which all or some factors of production are not perfectly fixed in supply but vary with factor prices. This situation seems to be more realistic with respect to labor. Either total labor supply may depend on the real wage, or different types of labor may be supplied in different proportions, depending on relative real wages paid in different activities. Actually, both these assumptions seem to be realistic because they allow for the fact that labor supply, just as much as commodity demand, depends on some utility index and consequently will vary with relative price.

One way of dealing simply with such a situation is to consider leisure, I, as a commodity and construct a transformation function among two commodities x_1 and x_2 and leisure I, i.e.,

$$T(x_1, x_2, I) = 0 \qquad (5.1)$$

Instead of dealing with total labor supply as before, we may define the maximum expendable amount of labor L^0, and I as a difference between this amount and the quantity of labor L actually supplied, namely,

$$I - L^0 - L \qquad (5.2)$$

Assuming as before that the stocks of capital and of natural resources are given and fixed, it is now possible to construct for a given value of L^0 a box diagram as in Section 1. Doing this for all admissible positive values of I, we obtain a three-dimensional transformation function T, such as that shown in Figure 12.5.1. Given relative product prices p_1/p_2 and given real wage in terms of either of the two prices, i.e., either w/p_1 or w/p_2, the production point on T, as before (see Sec. 13.2) will be found where

$$MRT_{x_1/x_2} = -\frac{p_1}{p_2} \qquad (5.3)$$

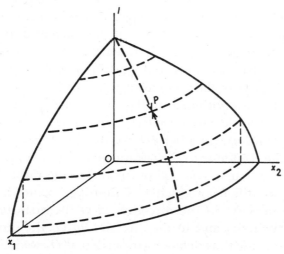

FIGURE 12.5.1

and

$$MRT_{x_1/I} = -\frac{p^1}{w} \tag{5.4}$$

Geometrically, such a point as P in the diagram will be obtained at the point of tangency of the T surface and a plane

$$Y = p_1x_1 + p_2x_2 + wI \tag{5.5}$$

where Y is a parameter determined by the position of such a plane and p_1, p_2, and w are given prices. Actually, Y is the value of national income augmented by the value to the community of unexpended leisure. The precise point of international trade will be derived in the next chapter, where demand conditions are explicitly considered.

There is another possible approach to the problem of variable factor supplies, very useful with a number of practical problems, such as imperfect labor mobility, noncompeting groups, preference for one type of activity over another, and a number of others. To take a concrete example, let us assume that a given labor force is not indifferent between two different types of work—say farm labor and mining activity. Such a preference may be summarized through a simple transformation between labor L_1 (farming) and L_2 (mining); the transformation may resemble one of the contours P in Figure 12.1.2, if different people have different preferences between the two activities; or it may be a straight line whose slope expresses the rate of preference and relative wages, if everybody has the same feelings about the two types of employment. As a special case, the slope would be equal to 45° if the usual assumption of perfect mobility and indifference between employments is made.

If such a relation is known, it is again possible to derive the opportunity cost curve of the economy and determine exactly the points of output and consumption, as well as the quantities of commodities traded. To do this, let us consider Figure 12.5.2. Starting from the origin O, we measure upward (OO_1) the given stock of capital K available to the economy; to the left the quantity of labor employable in x_1 (farming), namely, v_1 and down and to the right the quantity of labor employable in producing x_2 (mining), namely, v_2. Starting from O_1 we measure in the direction of O the quantity of capital used in producing x_2 and in the direction of O_2 the quantity of labor v_2. In the plane thus defined with origin at O_1 we may now draw the equal product lines of x_2, very much in the same way as we did

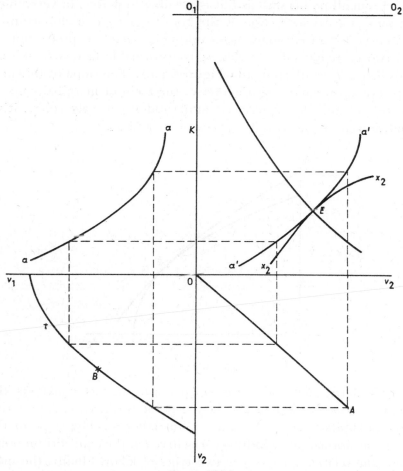

FIGURE 12.5.2

in Section 1. One such typical isoquant, x_2x_2, was drawn in the diagram. In this same plane it is now possible to draw a locus, comparable to the isoquant of x_1, showing for a given level of output of x_1 (corresponding to the aa isoquant in the second quadrant) all possible combinations of capital K and labor v_2 available for producing x_2 and consistent with the labor-transformation curve t in the third quadrant. Using the diagonal OA and the "labor indifference function" t, we have constructed one such locus $a'a'$. It is clear from the construction that the most efficient point of output, consistent with our assumptions, will be attained at point E. An infinity of such points may now be derived, for all admissible levels of output of x_1; this is the locus cc in the first quadrant of the diagram.

From all points such as E it is possible to derive, in very much the same way as in Section 1, the transformation or opportunity-cost curve for an economy using one fixed factor of production K and two mutually substitutable or transformable factors v_1 and v_2. This locus, T, is illustrated in Figure 12.5.3. The slope of this new transformation curve again expresses the ratio of marginal costs of the two commodities produced and, under perfectly competitive conditions, also the relative prices of x_1 and x_2.

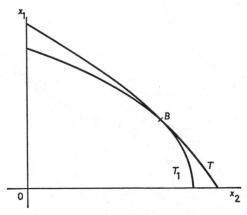

FIGURE 12.5.3

Similarly, under perfect competition in the factor markets, the common slope of $a'a'$ and x_2x_2 at the point E expresses the relative price of capital and the second type of labor v_2. The slope of the labor-transformation or indifference curve t at the equilibrium point shows the relative wage of the two types of labor. Finally, the marginal rate of substitution of v_1 and K (i.e., the slope of aa) at equilibrium will be equal to the relative prices of these two factors.

In addition to some purely theoretical conclusions that may be drawn from this situation, to be discussed in the next section, we may use this analysis in dealing with a number of concrete problems of international trade. The first thing we should observe is that if the t curve happens to be a 45° line, downward-sloping, the entire construction reduces itself to the usual box-diagram analysis known from the preceding sections. Actually, in this case labor is indifferent between employment in x_1 or x_2. The equal product map of x_2 is now simply translated from the second into the first quadrant, and the usual box-diagram and contract curve are obtained.

Any imperfection of mobility of one factor from one employment to the other may now be expressed through a special form assigned to the t function. On the limit, the existence of two perfectly noncompeting groups of labor v_1 and v_2 may now be expressed by a single point in the v_1v_2-plane whose coordinates are the fixed and untransferable quantities of v_1 and v_2. It may be easily shown that a transformation curve T_1 derived from such a situation will show a greater curvature than one where factors of production may move freely from one occupation into the other. Actually, the latter more general curve, T in Figure 12.5.3, will be an envelope of all such partial curves (without mobility of labor) as T_1. The only point of contact, where the ratios of marginal costs of the two commodities, i.e., the marginal rates of transformation, will be equal whether labor is mobile or not will be at point B, corresponding to B and E in the third and first quadrants of Figure 12.5.2, where relative prices of v_1 and v_2 are exactly the same whether labor mobility is permitted or not.

Another possible application may be found in the case where x_1 and x_2 use different raw materials, both of which are available in limited supplies. In this case the parallel with noncompeting labor groups is perfect. However, if such materials may be exchanged in a market at some prescribed set of relative prices, or through some technological transformation, reflected by the t function, the more general case applies. The country will now be able to produce anywhere along a locus such as T in Figure 12.5.3, rather than along T_1, to which it was constrained in the absence of transformation of one material into the other.

12.6 Real-Cost and Opportunity-Cost Approaches to the Theory of International Values

At times, mostly in the past, it has been a matter of great concern to the theorists of international trade to discover what it is that actually determines relative values or prices in international exchange. Marginal analysis in the general equilibrium setting provides the answer: the terms of trade are determined, like all other variables, by the conditions of demand, technology, and factor endowments in different parts of the world. The equations stated in Section 2 of this chapter show some of the required quantitative relationships. In the past, however, two major theories were proposed to answer the question, one relating international values to real costs, the other to opportunity costs. Often, unfortunately, ill feelings arose between the defenders of the two approaches.

The analysis of the preceding sections and in particular that of Section 5 make it possible not only to explain these two approaches but also to reconcile them. Actually, if properly stated, both theories lead to the same result.

The real theory of relative values, originated by Ricardo, claims that commodities will exchange in proportions given by the inverse of the relative inputs of labor in one unit of output. In the simple case where the production possibility locus becomes a linear function of all commodities produced, the theory obviously holds, provided that all products are produced. Moreover, it is not inconsistent with the opportunity-cost approach claiming that commodities will exchange in proportions given by the marginal rate of transformation of one product into the other.

The situation becomes somewhat more complicated when a more refined formulation of the real-cost theory is adopted. Some later writers have attempted to redefine the real-cost theory in relating relative values not to relative labor inputs but to the relative irksomeness or disutility of labor entering production. Clearly, such an approach brings the real-cost theory of value into the sphere of demand theory. This is perfectly legitimate, provided that marginal rather than average disutility or irksomeness of labor is used in constructing relative values.

To prove this, we may refer to the preceding section and in particular to the analysis presented in its latter part. Instead of saying that the t function (in the third quadrant) is the only locus reflecting the community's willingness to work, we may say that it is a social indifference curve, corresponding to a given index of disutility U^0. A number of other such loci could be constructed for other levels of utility. But let us return to the t locus as shown in Figure 12.5.2 and to the rest of the related analysis. The transformation curve T in Figure 12.5.3 is no longer the only production possibility but, rather, the production indifference curve corresponding to U^0.

Now let us assume that the community is producing at a point such as B. Corresponding to this point on T there is also a point B on the t indifference curve, reflecting the optimal allocation of labor between the two activities x_1 and x_2, say v_1^0 and v_2^0. Corresponding to this allocation of labor, now assumed fixed, it is possible to derive an opportunity-cost curve such as T_1 in the same fashion as we indicated in the preceding section for noncompeting groups. But we know that T_1 will have the same slope as T at the point of production B. We also know that the slope of T_1 at B (or any other point) reflects the ratio of marginal costs and consequently, under competitive conditions, the terms of trade or relative commodity prices also. Now the slope of T at point B, because T is an indifference curve, reflects the ratio of marginal disutilities of producing x_1 and x_2. Consequently, relative prices will reflect both the opportunity cost of one commodity in terms of the other and the relative (marginal) *real* cost of producing x_1 and x_2.

It will be clear to the reader that this conclusion is generally valid, whatever the number of commodities or factors of production that are variable in supply and subject to positive or negative utility. Of course, we always have to assume that all the functions used or derived are continuous and that any pair of commodities whose relative prices are examined is effectively produced by the economy in equilibrium.

12.7 Factor Prices, Income Distribution, and International Trade

The discussion of economic welfare and international trade will occupy our attention only in Chapter 15 and parts of subsequent chapters. The analysis of the present chapter, however, has some relevance for the theory of welfare because it allows us to study one important aspect of welfare economics, i.e., the distribution of income and relative prices of factors of production.

Our first task is to show the impact of trade on relative shares of income of different income groups, such as labor, capital owners, land owners, etc. In the case where all factors of production are assumed to be fixed in supply and competitive conditions prevail throughout the economy, the answer is quite simple. The only important considerations are relative factor prices. Suppose that international trade or any other cause, such as change in commercial policy, induces the economy to move from one point of production to another point. In terms of the box diagram, this corresponds to a movement along the contract curve, say, from A to B, as shown in Figure 12.7.1. A greater proportion of productive resources is now

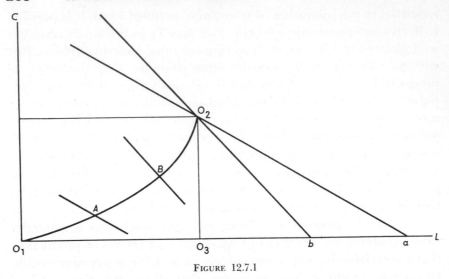

FIGURE 12.7.1

devoted to the production of x_1. Again we assume competitive conditions throughout; the technologies are subject to constant returns to scale.

The change in relative prices of capital and labor will be reflected by the difference in slopes of the common tangency of isoquants at points A and B. As shown in the diagram, capital is less expensive relative to labor at B than it was at A. For any given set of factor prices, total national income, expressed in terms of one factor or the other used as a numéraire, may be read in the plane O_1–C–L from a line passing through O_2 and having the slope equal to minus the price of labor divided by the price of capital. Two such lines, corresponding to the relative factor prices at A and at B, have been drawn through point O_2. Because any point on one such line expresses the same level of national income, valued at corresponding factor prices, the intercept of this constant income line with an axis does also. Thus national income expressed in terms of labor is measured by O_1a if the economy is producing at A, and by O_1b if it is producing at B. Naturally, the income of labor in terms of labor is the total labor supply itself, O_1O_3, while the income of capital in terms of labor is measured by the segments O_3a and O_3b for the corresponding two situations, respectively. To obtain the total money incomes of the two productive factors, we would have to multiply these measures by money wages. We are unable to derive income measured in terms of one product or the other at the present stage of the analysis. To do so, we would have to know the product prices in the two situations as well.

The important result is that whatever prices or wages, relative earnings of capital and labor have changed from

$$I_a = \frac{O_1 O_3}{O_3 a}$$

to

$$I_b = \frac{O_1 O_3}{O_3 b}$$

I_a being greater than I_b, it follows that the relative share of labor income has increased in comparison with that of capital.

Under the assumed conditions of unit homogeneous technology, with x_1 being labor-intensive relative to x_2, this is the necessary outcome. The capital-labor ratio in both industries must have increased as the economy moved from A to B. It follows that the relative price (or wage) of capital must have fallen. Consequently, $I_a > I_b$.

Actually, if both products are produced subject to constant returns to scale, we also know that income of capital has declined, whether measured in terms of the other factor or in terms of either commodity. Because the capital-labor ratio has increased in both industries, the marginal productivity of capital has necessarily declined in both industries. As we shall see later in greater detail (Chap. 14, Sec. 7), this also leads to the conclusion that real income, or the satisfaction of those supplying capital, has fallen. However, the relative incomes of capital and labor are always obtainable by using the analysis presented in this section, provided that competitive conditions prevail in the factor markets.

Thus, with constant returns to scale, it may be concluded that if trade increases the output of one commodity, the relative and absolute income share of the factor that is employed with relatively greater intensity in this commodity will increase. If the conditions of the factor-proportions theory of international trade are fulfilled, trade will benefit the relatively abundant factor and hurt the relatively scarce factor of production.

Those who enjoy a three-dimensional analysis will find it easy to expand our present argument to include three, rather than only two, factors of production. As a final remark we should stress again the importance of the assumption of unit homogeneous production functions. Note that only in the case of unit homogeneous technologies is the product exactly distributed among factors of production. If either of the two commodities were subject to increasing costs, O_1a or O_1b would no longer represent national income; in this case national income would be greater, including also some producers' or entrepreneurial return or rent of land.

12.8 Factor Prices and Commodity Prices in International Trade

In this section we shall show an important relation between commodity and factor prices. So far we have shown how conditions of production may be translated through the box diagram into the production possibility locus of the economy. We also know the relation between the slope of this latter locus and the commodity prices and the relation of relative factor prices to each level of output. However, we do not have any simple way of relating factor and commodity prices directly.

To do so, consider the box diagram in Figure 12.8.1. Both commodities are produced subject to constant costs. Assume that output takes place at point A on the contract curve. As usual, relative factor prices are given by the common tangency passing through A. The only new thing in the box diagram is the illustration of the unit isoquants of the two products.

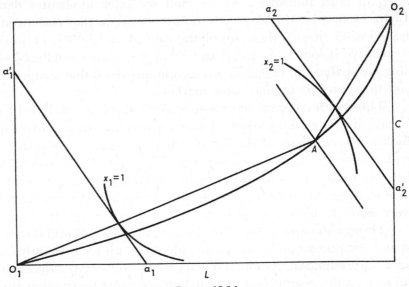

FIGURE 12.8.1

Consider a line tangential to the unit isoquant of x_1, with intercepts a_1 and a_1'. It may be stated algebraically as

$$k = L + \frac{w_C}{w_L} C \tag{8.1}$$

where k is a constant representing the cost, measured in terms of labor, of any combination of labor and capital along the line, hired at factor prices w_L and w_C. Observe that, for $C = 0$, $k = L$; thus the segment O_1a_1 measures k. Rational producers will produce one unit of x_1, given factor prices w_L and w_C, using the combination of inputs indicated by the point of tangency of the unit isoquant and the constant-cost line. Thus k is the cost of producing one unit of x_1. It is also the unit (or average) cost and marginal cost measured in terms of labor for any level of output produced from capital and labor hired at the same factor prices, i.e., w_C and w_L. This follows from the assumption of constant cost or unit homogeneous technology. But, under competitive conditions, price (also expressed in terms of labor) is equal to marginal cost, and consequently

$$k = \frac{p_1}{w_L} = O_1a_1 \tag{8.2}$$

must hold for any level of output produced along the line O_1A, and in particular for the level of output produced with optimal allocation of national resources between the two products at A. An analogous argument yields

$$\frac{p_2}{w_L} = O_2a_2 \tag{8.3}$$

Combining relations 8.2 and 8.3, we obtain the relative prices of x_1 and x_2 for an economy producing under assumed conditions at point A on the contract curve. Noting that the entire derivation may be carried out by using capital rather than labor as numéraire, we may now summarize all the results obtained so far, namely,

$$\frac{p_1}{p_2} = \frac{MC_1}{MC_2} = \frac{O_1a_1}{O_2a_2} = \frac{O_1a_1'}{O_2a_2'} = -\frac{dx_2}{dx_1} \tag{8.4}$$

where the last fraction expresses the negative inverse of the slope of the transformation curve and MC is marginal cost.

Again this analysis is applicable to situations with any number of commodities and factors of production. Of course, in such cases it is impossible to construct a box diagram. However, the translation from factor prices into commodity prices is possible. Once all relative factor prices are known, it is possible to derive a hyperplane, tangent to the unit equal product surface. Its intercepts with the different factors' axes reflect the prices of the product in terms of each particular factor of production, assuming again, of course, unit homogeneous technology.

12.9   The Factor-Price Equalization Theorem

It follows from most of our discussion in this chapter that if free international trade is permitted, i.e., if commodity prices are equalized internationally, the relative prices of productive factors will tend toward equalization. This will happen because, loosely speaking, the relative scarcity of some factors in different countries will be alleviated through trade: products produced primarily from scarce factors will tend to be imported, and thus some of the pressure on such resources will be taken off.

It is possible to show that, under some conditions, equalization of factor prices will be complete. The simplest case arises when only two countries are trading, using two (identical) factors of production, and each producing only two goods. Let us again assume unit homogeneous technologies, identical for each product in the two countries. One product is always labor-intensive relative to the other. Also it is assumed that both products are produced in both countries, that is, that international trade does not lead to a complete specialization in either country. It follows immediately from the discussion of the preceding section that equality of relative factor prices implies equality of commodity prices. With equal relative factor prices and identical technologies in both countries, the important segment $O_1 a_1$ will be the same for each country; so will $O_2 a_2$. Consequently, the *absolute* prices of x_1 and x_2, respectively, expressed in terms of either factor, will be equal in both countries. In turn, equality of commodity prices must imply equality of factor prices, under the assumed conditions, because to any point on the transformation curve corresponds uniquely only one commodity-price ratio and only one point on the contract curve, and to that latter point corresponds only one factor-price ratio. It may be useful at this point to realize that if the dimensions of the production box in Figure 12.8.1 were changed, i.e., if factor endowments were altered, *ceteris paribus*, the lines $O_1 A$ and $O_2 A$ would now intersect at a new point, such as A. This point would again be a point on the contract curve, now expressing a new allocation of resources and a new combination of outputs. However, the factor and product prices corresponding to A would remain unchanged.

If the assumption of uniform factor intensity of the two products is relaxed, the theorem of factor-price equalization will not necessarily hold. The lack of uniformity will arise if, for some relative factor prices, one commodity will appear as, say, capital-intensive compared with the other commodity and for some other set of relative factor prices as labor-intensive. Effectively, in such a case, if factor endowments of one country are such that x_1 is capital-intensive and x_2 labor-intensive, while endowments of the other yield the reverse relation between x_1 and x_2, equal relative factor prices, *per definitionem*, could never arise. Yet commodity prices will still be equalized, and both countries may produce both products. This case is mentioned here only as an intellectual curiosity; it has very little relevance for any real situations. Actually, the entire factor-price equalization theorem is based on much too restrictive assumptions to apply fully to the situation of the real world.

Scores of instances may be mentioned in which the assumptions are not met in actual trading. The reader may undertake such an enumeration. The real merit of the theorem seems to be that it indicates the tendency of factor prices toward equalization under international trading rather than complete equalization itself.

Using algebra, it is possible to relax the assumption of two commodities and two factors and prove the following: If there are n commodities internationally traded and produced in both countries and m factors of production used, then relative and absolute factor prices will be equalized if

$$n \geq m \tag{9.1}$$

Using the geometrical concepts shown in this and the preceding sections, some readers may find it interesting to prove for the case where $n = 2$ and $m = 3$ that factor-price equalization is impossible. Note that in this case the contract curve becomes a curve in a three-dimensional box. As a general rule, equality of all three factor prices in the two countries, anywhere along such a locus, will be impossible.

DEMAND CONDITIONS IN INTERNATIONAL TRADE

13.1 Individual Preferences and Trade

In Chapter 5 we used the concepts of supply and demand for exports and imports, each referring to a relation between quantities and *money* prices. Strictly speaking, the use of relations expressing demand as a function of a single money price is justifiable only if it is possible to assume that all other prices in the economy are invariant. If other prices are changing, they should also be introduced into the demand schedule explicitly. Of course, at least in theory, we might think of a hypothetical demand relation that is derived under the assumption that all other prices and real income are invariant. But such a demand curve would be of very little analytical value, for instance, in examining the conditions of the foreign-exchange market. Here, in the process of adjustment, prices both of exports and of imports are changing. For every given export price, there will be one given demand curve for imports. For a whole range of possible export prices there will be an infinity of import demand curves. Clearly, if we had introduced such a complication into our discussion of the foreign-exchange market, hardly any meaningful theorem could have been derived in Chapter 5.

The great advantage of the approach of pure theory is that it enables us to study the simultaneous adjustment of the entire economy, that is, of all the relevant variables, to changing conditions of one type or another. Only in the following chapter shall we be able to show such a general equilibrium operation of the model of international trade. Before we can do it, however, we have to complete our survey of the different building blocks of the complete equilibrium model.

Our first task is to relate a country's demand for imports or supply of exports to individual preferences or individual demand conditions. This disaggregation may appear as surprising at first. We did not consider each individual's labor or capital supply or each individual's technique of production in the preceding chapter; why then should we disaggregate here? The explanation is simple. It is possible to assume that the states of the arts are quite comparable in a given country in a given period. Also, no great mistake is made by assuming that in the short run the total supply of productive resources of each individual is fixed and consequently that the total national stocks of such resources are given. The single additional assumption of full employment makes it possible to express the production possibilities of an economy as a single transformation function.

Demand conditions, on the other hand, may and most often will be different for different individuals and at different levels of income. Preferences of the ith individual in the economy may be expressed as an ordinal function

$$U_i - U_i(x_1 \ldots , x_n) \tag{1.1}$$

where the x's represent quantities of commodities consumed and U is an ordinal index of utility increasing with any x. By "ordinal" we understand a measure allowing only of comparisons "equal," "greater than," and "smaller than," since it is impossible to measure utility in terms of numbers that would indicate exactly by how much one situation is preferred to another. The ordinal utility index permits us, however, to order any number of different combinations of commodities such as $x_1^0, \ldots , x_n^0$ according to their desirability.

The usual way of expressing the utility relation 1.1 in a simple two-commodity case is to draw a set of equal satisfaction or indifference curves expressing all possible combinations of commodities x_1 and x_2 yielding the same level of satisfaction. Of course, the equation of such a contour (or surface) can be obtained as

$$U = \text{constant} \tag{1.2}$$

We define as the marginal rate of substitution between commodities j and k, the inverse of the slope dx_j/dx_k of the indifference curve or surface in the $x_j - x_k$ plane defined by a constant level of all other commodities. Of course, in the simple case where only x_1 and x_2 enter the utility function, there is only one such plane and hence, for any given level of consumption of the two commodities, only one marginal rate of substitution, $MRS_{1/2}$. The usual assumption about the behavior of a rational consumer is that the marginal rate of substitution $MRS_{j/k}$ is negative, continuously diminishing (or, on the limit, constant) as more of commodity x_k is consumed. In other words, with all levels of consumption but two constant, it is possible to keep an individual equally well off—if reducing his consumption of one product by *equal* amounts—only at the cost of *increasing* increments of consumption of the other product.

One important theorem of the demand theory may now be stated: If the consumer is able, in one way or another, to transform one commodity into another according to a prescribed continuous function, $f(x_1, \ldots, x_n) = 0$ linear or concave toward the origin, he will find himself at a maximum of satisfaction if he consumes at a point where

$$MRT_{j/k} = MRS_{j/k} \qquad (1.3)$$

for all j and k. Here MRT, the marginal rate of transformation, is derived from the f function as MRS is derived from the U function. The slope of the production possibility curve constructed in the preceding chapter is a special case of a marginal rate of transformation. The proof of the theorem is very simple. If it did not hold, a movement along f from the point defined by relation 1.3 could improve the satisfaction of the individual. But this is impossible because the f function and the equal satisfaction surface do not intersect at the optimum point and are not convex in the same direction.[1]

This conclusion is immediately apparent from Figure 13.1.1 for the two-commodity case. The consumer, who is left free to consume anywhere along the contour f, will maximize his utility at point E, where the f contour is tangent to the indifference curve.

Now, under conditions of perfect competition, the f function for every individual will become a linear surface (plane), simply

---

[1] This proposition may also be shown using the so-called Lagrangian multiplier. The function U will be maximized subject to a constraint f, provided that $d(U - A \cdot f) = 0$, where A is an arbitrary constant. This yields, subscripts representing partial derivatives

$$\sum_n (U_{x_i} - A \cdot f_{x_i})dx_j = 0$$

This expression will be zero if each term in the parentheses is zero, and consequently, for any j, k,

$$\frac{U_{x_j}}{U_{x_k}} = \frac{f_{x_j}}{f_{x_k}}$$

But this expression is equivalent to relation 1.3 above.

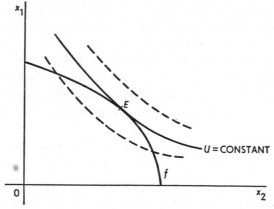

FIGURE 13.1.1

expressing the fact that every individual in a competitive market is able to transform any given bill of goods in his possession at fixed prices into any other bill of goods consistent with his initial endowment (or real income). Assuming that the initial collection of goods represents his current production, the real income of every individual may be expressed in terms of the first commodity as

$$Y^0 = x_1^0 + \frac{p_2}{p_1}x_2^0 + \cdots + \frac{p_n}{p_1}x_n^0 \tag{1.4}$$

where the x^0's represent the different levels of output, and the p's corresponding prices. Assuming that the individual either does not save at all or, if he saves, he does so in order to purchase durable products, his entire real income Y^0 will be allocated among the different products x_1, i.e.,

$$Y^0 = x_1 + \frac{p_2}{p_1}x_2 + \cdots + \frac{p_n}{p_1}x_n \tag{1.5}$$

in such a way that all relations 1.3 are fulfilled. Because the f function now is expressed by relation 1.5, all the marginal rates of transformation, such as $MRT_{k/1}$, will now be equal to minus the ratio of prices of the two commodities considered, such as $-(p_k/p_1)$. It will be observed that there are $n - 1$ independent relations such as relation 1.3, functions of the n x's; for example,

$$-\frac{p_k}{p_1} = MRS_{k/1} \qquad k = 2, \ldots, n \tag{1.6}$$

where $MRS_{k/1}$ will generally be a function of all the x's; specifically, it is minus the partial derivative of U with respect to x_k, divided by the partial derivative of U with respect to x_1. These relations, together with relation 1.5, are sufficient to determine the level of consumption of all commodities, $x_1^c, \ldots, x_n^c$.

We may now give three important definitions:

i) Let us call an *income consumption line* a locus of all consumption points in the n-dimensional commodity space, corresponding to all possible levels of real income and a *given* set of commodity prices.

ii) Let us call a *price consumption line* a locus of all consumption points in the n-dimensional commodity space, corresponding to an initial level of real income expressed by the levels of output $x_1^0, \ldots, x_n^0$ and to all possible levels of relative prices of any pair of commodities, say p_j/p_k, all prices but p_j being constant. We may call all such points C, and the corresponding levels of consumption X_i, where $i = 1, \ldots, n$.

iii) From (ii) it follows that every X_i for a given level of outputs $x_1^0, \ldots, x_n^0$ will be a function of relative prices. Consequently, the difference between consumption and output of any given commodity will also be a function of relative prices. Thus we may write

$$x_i = X_i - x_i^0 = F_i\left(\frac{p_j}{p_k}\right) \qquad i = 1, \ldots, n \qquad (1.7)$$

where x_i expresses the offer of commodity i if negative and the demand for commodity i if positive. In particular, the offer or demand for commodity j may be expressed as a function of relative prices p_j/p_k, namely,

$$x_j = F_j\left(\frac{p_j}{p_k}\right) \qquad (1.8)^2$$

Using the commodity k as numéraire, that is, the commodity used as a means of exchange, relation 1.8 determines the quantities of commodity k payable or receivable in exchange for prescribed quantities of product j. Let us call a relation between all possible quantities of commodity j offered and corresponding (subjective) valuations of such an offer in terms of commodity k the *offer curve* of commodity

---

[2] More generally, it is possible to derive from relations 1.4, 1.5, and 1.6 consumption points X_i corresponding to any set of all $n-1$ relative prices p_k/p_1; thence, through a relation such as 1.7, the general offer and demand functions of the form

$$x_j = F_j\left(\frac{p_L}{p_1}, \ldots, \frac{p_n}{p_1}\right)$$

may be constructed.

j. It is clear that, with the price of all other commodities in terms of commodity *k* unchanged, the offer curve may be expressed in terms of any commodity assumed as numéraire, simply by relabeling the numéraire axis and adjusting its scale proportionately to the price of the two commodities used as numéraire.

In the simple situation where only two commodities are pro-

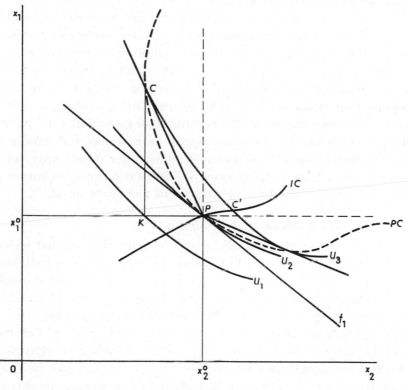

FIGURE 13.1.2

duced, consumed, and traded, all these propositions may easily be illustrated by means of a graph. In Figure 13.1.2 we find an indifference map represented by three contours corresponding to increasing levels of utility U_1, U_2, and U_3 and the production (or real-income) point P. Corresponding to relative prices expressed by the slope of f_1, we have traced the income consumption line IC; and, corresponding to the levels of output x_1^0 and x_2^0 and to relative prices varying between zero and infinity, we have the price consumption line PC. The algebraic difference between the coordinates of all points such as C on PC and the coordinates of P expresses a sale if negative and a purchase if positive. Point C on PC, for example, determines a triangle CPK indicating a sale of KP of commodity x_2 in exchange for CK of commodity x_1. The slope of its hypotenuse reflects the exchange ratio, or, as we shall later refer to it, the "terms of trade." If transferred into the first and third quadrants, the sales and purchases of the two commodities corresponding to different relative prices determine the offer curve.

It will be observed from the diagram that the individual will be more satisfied whenever he trades, that is, whenever the exchange ratio is other than that indicated by the slope of f_1. If relative prices are such that he wants to consume at, say, point C, he will definitely be better off. Often it is useful to decompose the movement of his consumption point from P to C (caused by a change in relative prices) into two stages or effects. One may be called the "income effect," measuring the increase in real satisfaction and producing the movement from P to C' along IC. The other stage, expressed by the movement from C' to C along U_2, indicates the substitution effect produced by the relative decline in the price of x_1.

13.2 The Problem of Aggregation

As we saw in the preceding section, once the original endowment (or output) and the set of ordinal preferences for an individual are known, his offer of, as well as demand for, any given commodity in terms of any other commodity may be found, showing his willingness to exchange one commodity for another, depending on the terms of trade or relative prices. There is no difficulty in obtaining a similar offer curve for two, three, or any number of individuals from the individual offer curves. For any given exchange ratio, the quantities of one commodity offered and the other commodity demanded by a number of people may be added. In Figure 13.2.1, for example, we show such an addition of offer curves OA and OB, to form a single offer curve $O(A + B)$. Because the same price ratio always applies to both individuals, the construction may simply be effected as a radial addition along the trading line, such as Ot. Note that Oc, measured along Ot, is equal to Oa plus Ob.

Such aggregate offer curves may then be used in determining the international equilibrium terms of trade, exports, and imports. Although this approach is more precise and lends itself well to disaggregation and thus to the study of the impact of trade on each particular individual, it has rarely been followed by international

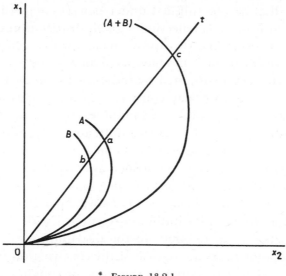

* FIGURE 13.2.1

economists. The usual approch is to deal with an entire nation as if it were a single individual. As we have already pointed out in the preceding section, a similar approach does not present great difficulties when it comes to the representation of real output; the economy as a whole may be represented by a single production possibility function. To assume that the preferences of an entire population may be represented by a single map of social indifference curves, on the other hand, is quite difficult. In the following section we shall show alternative sets of special assumptions justifying the use of a social indifference map, having the usual properties. In the rest of this section we want to show (1) how social indifference curves may be derived and (2) the difficulties connected with using such preference maps in deriving the offer curve of a community.

Suppose that two individuals, a and b, form a community. Consider further a point in a two-commodity space, say A, in Figure 13.2.2. Its coordinates, x_1^0 and x_2^0, represent a given level of output available for consumption to the community. Placing the origin of individual a's consumption at O and that of individual b at A, turning the axes applicable to each individual in opposite directions, we may construct a locus OA of optimum satisfaction of the two individuals (comparable to the contract curve or efficiency locus in the production box diagram). At every point of this locus, the marginal rates of substitution of x_1 and x_2 are equal for both individuals; this condition will always be fulfilled under perfect competition. Let us choose a point L on OA, reflecting a given distribution of resources (or income) between the two individuals. Two tangential indifference curves pass through L and have a common slope S. If we now let the level of satisfaction attained by individual a be measured by U_a and that of b by U_b, we may construct a contour passing through point A, reflecting all possible minimum levels of joint consumption of commodities x_1 and x_2 by the two individuals, permitting both to be equally as well off as they were at L. Such a contour, $U_{(a+b)}$ in the diagram, may be traced by a point such as A by sliding U_b along U_a in such a way that the two indifference curves are always tangential and the two sets of coordinate axes always parallel. We may call this contour a "community indifference curve," with the important qualification that it corresponds to the distribution of real income indicated by point L. As the nature of the construction indicates, its slope at point A will be equal to the slope of common tangency at L, namely, S.

Assume now that the distribution of resources between the two individuals, with the same total consumable resources of the community as those determined by point A, is such as to yield point M

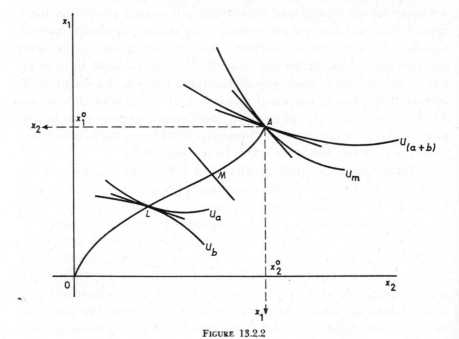

FIGURE 13.2.2

on the efficiency locus. The common tangency at M will generally have a slope different from S, and our construction will generally yield a community indifference curve different from $U_{(a+b)}$, say U_m. Of course, both community indifference curves pass through point A. Thus we may generalize and conclude that through any point in the $x_1 - x_2$ plane will pass an infinity of social indifference contours, each determined by the distribution of income between the two individuals or, to be more precise, by the specific fixed levels of individual satisfaction.

Returning now to the aggregate offer curve derived above, we may ascertain that at each of its points the offer curve will intersect a social indifference curve, having a slope given by the relative prices determining that point of the offer curve and consistent with the levels of satisfaction of the different individuals. But such community indifference curves cannot be constructed unless we know exactly the levels of utility of all individuals engaging in trade, consistent with that exchange ratio, and their individual indifference maps. What is more important, as we move along the offer curve, different social indifference curves will be reached that (1) may intersect and (2) do not reflect any single utility index that would allow us to conclude, as we did in the case of a single individual, that the community is better or worse off. Also, because there is generally no single nonintersecting indifference map of the community, it is impossible to derive the aggregate offer curve through a simple equalization of the marginal rate of transformation (here relative prices) and of the marginal rate of substitutions. At any point there will actually be an infinite number of different marginal rates of substitution of the community, depending again on the distribution of resources.

13.3 Justification of Community Indifference Curves

In order to be able to use community indifference curves in deriving the supply and demand conditions of a country in the same way as we usually do for a single individual, one of a number of different sets of alternative assumptions must be selected:

i) The community has only one inhabitant.

ii) The community, either by voting (this may present some difficulties) or through decision of a central authority, defines a single set of preferences.

iii) If ordinal preferences of every individual are identical and the level of income of all individuals is the same, whatever the level of the total income of the community, then our construction of the preceding section will yield a *single nonintersecting* map of community indifference curves. Such a map may be used both for purposes of offer-curve derivation and in deriving welfare propositions in exactly the same way as an indifference map of one individual.

iv) If all individuals have identical and homogeneous preferences (i.e., all income consumption lines are straight lines through the origin), the efficiency locus OA in Figure 13.2.2 becomes a straight line, and the marginal rates of substitution at any of its points are the same. As the reader may verify through a simple construction, this situation also yields a single nonintersecting map of community indifference curves actually identical with any of the individual sets of preferences. It is legitimate to use such a community map in deriving the offer curve of the community, but it cannot be used in discussing welfare effects of trade, except when special assumptions are made about the income distribution within the community.

v) Finally, as Professor Samuelson shows,[3] it is possible to assume a single nonintersecting social indifference map, if a welfare function of the community is known and if income is always reallocated among individuals in such a way as to equalize the marginal social utility of the last dollar received by, or withdrawn from, every individual. For a rigorous proof of this proposition, the reader is advised to turn to Professor Samuelson's work.

[3] P. A. Samuelson, "Social Indifference Curves," *Quarterly Journal of Economics,* February, 1956, pp. 1–22.

Chapter 14   GENERAL EQUILIBRIUM IN INTERNATIONAL TRADE

14.1   General Equilibrium with a Large Number of Products, Individuals, and Factors of Production

We have already stated in Chapter 4 our preference for the traditional approach of international economists, dealing with relatively simple theories and using only small numbers of variables. Not only is such an approach easier to comprehend, but often it permits derivation of, or leads to, theorems that otherwise would be out of reach. This is also the method used in the later sections of this chapter. In this section, however, for the sake of completeness and greater realism, we shall show briefly a case of general equilibrium with many variables, applied to international trade. This will be accomplished in two steps: first we shall show a general equilibrium system for a closed economy; in the second step we shall reduce it to a smaller number of relations and express the general equilibrium conditions of external trade between two countries.

There are innumerable ways of stating the general equilibrium conditions for a competitive closed economy. Because the number of equations and variables to be included is usually very large, it may appear difficult at first to comprehend the interdependence of all the relations. Consequently, it is convenient to break the general equilibrium down into a number of component parts that eventually may be put together in a single pattern. The approach we have chosen here is exactly the same as that used in Chapters 12 and 13, making the distinction between the conditions of supply, on the one hand, and of demand, on the other. Thus our first task is to derive a generalized production possibility function for the economy as a whole, showing for all inputs and outputs but one the minimum input or maximum output of one factor or commodity.

Suppose that there are n products x_j, produced by the productive sector of the economy from m factors v_k. Using superscripts to indicate the employment of each factor, we may state each production function as

$$x_j = x_j(v_1^j, \ldots, v_m^j) \qquad j = 1, \ldots, n \qquad (1.1)$$

there will be n such relations, one for each product. They are all assumed to be homogeneous of order 1.

In addition, we know that the marginal rate of substitution (MRS) of any pair of factors in any activity must be equal to minus the ratio of prices of the factors. Thus, using w_k as the price of the kth factor of production and w_1 for the first factor, we may write

$$\frac{w_k}{w_1} = -MRS_{k/1}^j \qquad k = 2, \ldots, m \qquad (1.2)$$

We recall that the marginal rates of substitution $MRS_{k/1}^j$ of the kth and first factor in the production of the jth product are functions of the v_k^j's and are derivable from relations 1.1 as minus the ratio of partial derivatives of x with respect to the relevant factors of production. There will be $m - 1$ such independent relations for each product, and consequently $n(m - 1)$ such relations for the economy as a whole.

Finally, we also have to state the simple fact that inputs of a given factor in all activities will be equal to the total supply of that factor, namely,

$$v_k = v_k^1 + v_k^2 + \cdots + v_k^n \qquad k = 1, \ldots, m \qquad (1.3)$$

There will be as many such relations as there are productive factors, i.e., m altogether.

Sets of relations 1.1, 1.2, and 1.3 contain $n + n(m - 1) + m$, i.e., $mn + m$ relations. As for the variables, there are mn factor inputs v_k^j to be determined, n products x_j, m total factor inputs v_k, and, finally, $m - 1$ relative factor prices—altogether, $mn + 2m + n - 1$ variables. Generally it will be possible to reduce the number of equations and variables by the same number and obtain one equation in any $m + n$ variables, such as

$$P(x_1, \ldots, x_n, v_1, \ldots, v_m) = 0 \qquad (1.4)$$

This is nothing else but a generalized form of the production possibility function, used in Chapter 12 in a simple two-commodity case. To make the analysis sufficiently simple, let us assume, as we did in Chapter 12, that all productive resources are given quantities. When dealing with a static situation, this assumption is quite realistic, except perhaps for the supply of labor. However, there would be no difficulty in dealing with one or more factors of production as variables. In this case, as was shown in Chapter 12, it is possible to treat a factor, say v_1, as one of the products x, provided that it is included with a negative sign, i.e., $-v_1 = x_j$.

The production possibility function may now be stated as

$$P(x_1, \ldots, x_n) = 0 \tag{1.5}$$

Under competitive conditions, we know that relative prices of any two products will be equal to minus their marginal rate of transformation. This may be stated as

$$\frac{p_j}{p_1} = -MRT_{j/1} \qquad j = 2, \ldots, n \tag{1.6}$$

where the $MRT_{j/1}$ is defined as minus the partial derivative of P with respect to x_j divided by the partial derivative of P with respect to x_1. Relations 1.5 and 1.6, n in number, may be solved for the n products, in terms of the $n - 1$ relative prices, namely,

$$x_j = x_j \left(\frac{p_2}{p_1}, \ldots, \frac{p_n}{p_1} \right) \qquad j = 1, \ldots, n \tag{1.7}$$

Relations 1.7 represent the n supply functions of the economy, showing for any given set of $n - 1$ relative product prices the n optimum outputs x_j.

To derive the demand equations, let us first state the budget equations of p different individuals in the economy, expressing the equality between income and expenditure for each individual. Using capital letters for quantities of products demanded, we have

$$\sum_j \frac{p_j}{p_1} X_j^i = \sum_k \frac{w_k}{p_1} v_k^i \qquad i = 1, \ldots, p \tag{1.8}$$

The v_k^i's are constant supplies of primary productive resources, such as labor, capital, or land, that the ith individual is supplying, and the sum of all such terms over i is equal to the total factor supply v_k appearing in relation 1.4. For any given set of relative product prices, all outputs are known from relations 1.7, and so is the optimal allocation of productive resources among different products, from relations 1.1 through 1.3. Consequently, the relative factor prices are also known. Thus it is possible to express each relative factor price appearing on the right-hand side of relation 1.8 as a function of the $n - 1$ relative product prices; or, if we prefer, the entire expression may be stated as real income Y^i of the ith individual, measured in terms of the first commodity and expressed as a function of the $n - 1$ relative product prices.

Given income, optimum consumption will be attained by each consumer if his marginal rate of substitution of any two products is equal to minus the ratio of prices of such two products, i.e.,

$$-\frac{p_j}{p_1} = MRS^i_{j/1} \qquad \begin{aligned} i &= 1, \ldots, p \\ j &= 2, \ldots, n \end{aligned} \qquad (1.9)$$

where each MRS^i is a function of the quantities of products X^i_j consumed by the ith individual. Finally, we have to state the condition that total demand for a commodity is equal to the sum of individual demands, namely,

$$X_j = \sum_i X^i_j \qquad j = 1, \ldots, n \qquad (1.10)$$

It will be observed that relations 1.8 through 1.10 are $pn + n$ in number. Recalling that the right-hand sides of relations 1.8 are the real incomes of each individual depending solely on relative product prices, we find that the three sets of relations contain the following variables: pn, individual consumptions X^i_j; n, total consumers' demands X_j; and $n - 1$, relative product prices. Altogether, there are $pn + 2n - 1$ variables. By solving, it will generally be possible to reduce the system to n equations in $2n - 1$ variables,

$$X_j = X_j \left(\frac{p_2}{p_1}, \ldots, \frac{p_n}{p_1} \right) \qquad j = 1, \ldots, n \qquad (1.11)$$

These are the n demand relations for the n products, each depending, as do the supply functions, on $n - 1$ relative prices. Because we assume competition and all technologies to be unit homogeneous, the total value of output must be equal to total factor income. But total factor income, by definition, equals total consumers' expenditure. From this it follows that *one* of the $2n$ relations 1.7 and 1.11 is dependent on, or derivable from, all the others. Consequently, the sets of equations 1.7 and 1.11 contain only $2n - 1$ independent relations. Adding to these relations n market equilibrium conditions

$$x_j = X_j \qquad j = 1, \ldots, n \qquad (1.12)$$

we have $3n - 1$ independent relations in $3n - 1$ unknowns. The system is consistent with an equilibrium solution of the general equilibrium of a closed economy.

If we are dealing with an open economy, that we may refer to as economy a, it is convenient to define a new set of variables, namely, the national excess demands for each commodity,

$$ED_j^a = X_j^a - x_j^a \qquad j = 2, \ldots, n \tag{1.13}$$

A general equilibrium representation of the economy of country b leads to a similar set of equations,

$$ED_j^b = X_j^b - x_j^b \qquad j = 2, \ldots, n \tag{1.14}$$

In each case we have stated the excess demands only for $n - 1$ products. As a consequence of the equality between domestic real product and real expenditure, the remaining one excess demand is dependent on and can always be derived from all the others, for any given set of relative product prices. The simple corollary of this statement is that, under the ideal conditions here assumed, the balance of autonomous payments can never get out of equilibrium.

If international trade is permitted, relative prices will be equalized between countries. We may now write a new set of equilibrium equations requiring that the excess demand of one country (in algebraic value, i.e., positive or negative) must be equal to minus that of the other country; that is,

$$ED_j^a = -ED_j^b \qquad j = 2, \ldots, n \tag{1.15}$$

These $n - 1$ equations will be sufficient to determine the $n - 1$ relative prices and consequently the $2n$ different levels of output and the $2n$ levels of consumption.

It should be observed that the equality of exports and imports of each country does not have to be used as an equation in determining the relative prices. It may be written as

$$ED_1 + \frac{p_2}{p_1} ED_2 + \ldots + \frac{p_n}{p_1} ED_n = 0 \tag{1.16}$$

for either country. But it must always hold, as we have already observed, because of the internal equality of income produced and income expended in each country. Note that throughout this exposition we have never mentioned absolute prices. These, in the context of the present analysis, will depend solely on the total money supply in each of the two countries. A single additional equation for each country, stating either income earned or spent or produced or distributed to productive factors, in terms of money will be sufficient to determine the absolute money prices of all commodities. Similarly, the exchange rate is a monetary variable and may be determined from any single money price in the two countries, as $r = p^a/p^b$.

Before concluding this section, we should point out that the general equilibrium approach is nothing more than a process of setting up structural equations in a general form, counting such equations and unknowns, and, wherever possible, checking whether equations are independent or not. Equality of the number of independent equations and unknowns guarantees neither the existence, the uniqueness, nor the stability of equilibria; the only true statement we are able to make is that in this case the system is consistent with an equilibrium solution. In Section 7 of this chapter we shall study a simple concrete case of general equilibrium of the type discussed in this section. With only two individuals in a country and only two products and two factors of production, it will become apparent how easily it is possible to obtain any large number of equilibrium solutions. It may be somewhat distressing to some and comforting to others to know how little we are able to learn from economic parameters about the outcome of an actual economic equilibrium.

14.2 The Two-Country, Two-Commodity Case of General Equilibrium; Summary of Professor Meade's Analysis

In this section we want to combine the analysis presented in the two preceding chapters and study the general equilibrium solution of two trading economies from given conditions of supply and demand. The demand conditions are assumed to be expressed in terms of single nonintersecting social indifference maps, as discussed in Chapter 13. The factor endowments and technologies of the two countries are embodied in the respective production possibility loci. Given the technologies and factor endowments of each economy, the conditions in the factor markets, resource allocation, and product composition will be known, once the terms of trade are determined. The case of variable factor supplies discussed in Section 5 of Chapter 12 is also compatible with the analysis of the present section, provided that a single production possibility function or production indifference curve can be assumed for each country.

Consider a plane divided into four quadrants through two rectangular coordinate axes x_1 and x_2, where x_1 and x_2 represent two different products. As indicated in Figure 14.2.1, the first quadrant describes conditions of trade; along its horizontal axis x_2 we measure exports of country 2 to country 1, along the vertical axis x_1 we measure exports of country 1 to country 2. The second quadrant describes the consumption of country 2; the amounts of x_1 and x_2 consumed are measured along the corresponding axes from origin O. Similarly, in the fourth quadrant we measure the consumption of x_1 and x_2 by country 1. The third quadrant may be used for measuring trade in opposite direction from that measured in the first quadrant, namely, exports of x_1 by country 2 and vice-versa. For the purpose of a static examination of an equilibrium solution, the first quadrant will be sufficient. However, should the structure of the two economies change considerably, passing from the first into the third quadrant, that is, a reversal of trade, could be envisaged.

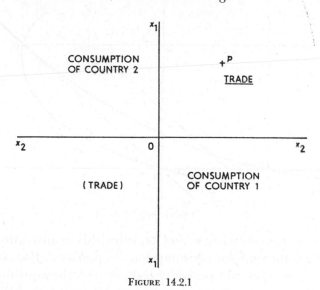

FIGURE 14.2.1

Now consider the production block of country 2 and place its origin at point p in the diagram in such a way as to keep corresponding axes parallel and with the curved side of the production block pointing westward. If there is a point on the production possibility curve falling into the second quadrant and the community produces at such a point, that point measures in the second quadrant the quantities of x_1 and x_2 consumed by the community. The essential point of Professor Meade's analysis is that there will be some terms-of-trade ratio and some positive or negative subsidy or transfer in terms of one product or the other or both that will move the production block of country 2 through competitive trading to the position described above, where the origin of the production block is at p. Let us now see in detail how such a transfer and such terms of trade can be determined.

In Figure 14.2.2 we show the production block of country 2 placed at point p. Point c_2 in the second quadrant, where the mar-

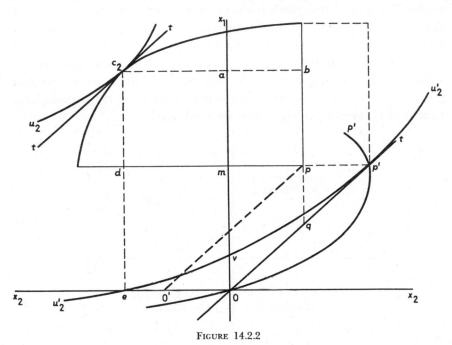

FIGURE 14.2.2

ginal rates of transformation and of substitution in country 2 are equal, reflects the optimal consumption of country 2. If such a point exists and all markets are perfectly competitive, the equilibrium exchange ratio can only be that indicated by the slope of common tangency at point c_2. But if this is the domestic price ratio in country 2 and free international trade prevails, the international terms of trade can only be equal to that slope. Because trade is measured in the first quadrant, let us draw a terms-of-trade line through point O having that slope (i.e., Ot). If the production block were as large as the extended block (*dotted line*) with origin at p', p' would represent a trading point, Ot would effectively be the terms of trade, and p' would also be a point on the offer curve of country 2. Although the true production block (production possibility locus) is smaller, it may be extended to the required dimension by giving a fixed subsidy in terms of x_2 to the private sector of country 2, equal to the length of the segment pp', or $O'O$. Thus we obtain the very important answer to our problem: Given the preferences of country 2 and its production possibility, the production block of the country will be located at point p, provided that (1) a subsidy in terms of the export commodity (x_2) is paid to the private sector equal to pp' and (2) the international terms of trade are equal to the slope of the line Op' or Ot.

Actually, there is an infinite number of possible subsidies that will produce the same result. The subsidy may be paid not in terms of commodity x_2 but in terms of x_1 or any combination of the two products, provided that its total value is constant and equal to that of pp' of x_2, valued at relative prices indicated by the terms of trade. Any such combined subsidy may be indicated by a point on Ot, within the segment qp'. For example, a subsidy pq paid in terms of x_1 would also place the origin of the production block at p, the terms of trade necessarily remaining unchanged. The only important difference in this case is that point q rather than p' would be a point on the offer curve of country 2, receiving as subsidy pq of x_1. International trade would now be reduced to the quantities of the two products indicated by the coordinates of q in the first quadrant. Generally, there will be as many trading points along $p'q$ and as many corresponding offer curves as there are conceivable combinations of physical subsidies in terms of x_1 and x_2, all combinations having the same money value.

If the production block's origin is at p and country 2 receives the required subsidy, it will consume Oa of product x_1 and Oe of product x_2. Its trade will vary, depending on the form of subsidy received. In particular, if the private sector of country 2 receives pp' of x_2 (its export commodity), it will export mp' of that same commodity and import Om of product x_1.

We have noticed that, in order for the origin of the production possibility block to be located at p and international trade to take place at p', two requirements are necessary; that of a given positive transfer pp' in terms of x_2, and that of a given terms-of-trade ratio equal to the marginal rates of substitution and transformation consistent with p. Two types of important loci may now be derived if only one requirement is made, the two being a generalized form of the price-consumption and income-consumption lines defined in the preceding chapter. Specifically, if a subsidy is fixed at a given level, say pp', and the terms of trade are allowed to assume all possible levels, an entire locus of points such as p' will be generated in the first and third quadrants. This is the offer curve of country 2, derived from given conditions of demand (indifference map in the second quadrant), given conditions of supply (production possibility) assuming that the community is receiving a given subsidy pp' of x_2. The income-consumption locus derived from the alternative conditions will be discussed in the next section.

The different points of the offer curve (with transfer pp') may easily be derived if the slope of Ot is changed and the enlarged block is moved along Ot until a tangency of that block with an indifference curve in the second quadrant is reached whose slope is exactly equal to the new slope of Ot. Such a position of the production block will define a new trading point (p') and a new consumption (c_2) of the community. We have drawn such an offer curve OP' in the diagram.

Perhaps the most important within the family of such offer curves is that corresponding to a zero transfer, i.e., the customary free-trade offer curve of country 2. This or any other offer curve corresponding to positive or negative transfer may be derived easily by using the so-called *trade indifference curves*. These may be derived, say, for the case of transfer pp' by sliding the enlarged production block along all the indifference contours in the second quadrant, in such a way as to preserve the axes of the block parallel to the x_1 and x_2 axes, and tracing all the positions of p', i.e., the origin of the enlarged block. Thus, for example, a trade indifference curve corresponding to a transfer pp' and to the level of satisfaction u_2 passes through p' and at each point has the slope of the corresponding common tangency of the production block and u_2. We have drawn this trade indifference curve u_2' in the diagram. It is now easy to see that the offer curve OP' may be derived from such a trade indifference map in the same way as any price-consumption line is derived from customary indifference curves—i.e., by finding for each terms-of-trade ratio a point on the trading line where the marginal rate of substitution is equal to that ratio. For example, p' is on the offer curve OP' corresponding to transfer pp' because Ot at that point is tangential to u_2'. It may be interesting to observe that the segment Ov measures an additional subsidy in terms of x_1 that the community would have to receive without trade in order to be as well off as when trading at p'.

Now it should be noted that the general equilibrium representation of trade and consumption may be derived for country 1 in the first and fourth quadrants in exactly the same way. In the simple case of free trade with zero subsidy, we obtain the equilibrium solution of trade, consumption, and production in both countries, illustrated in Figure 14.2.3. Note that total world output and consumption are now measured by the dimensions of the rectangle

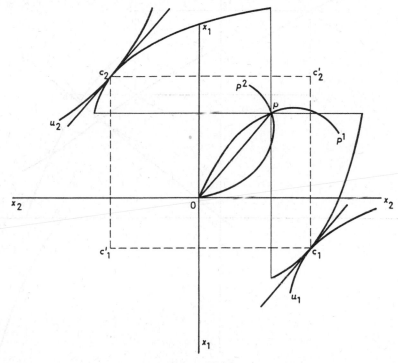

FIGURE 14.2.3

$c_1 c_1' c_2 c_2'$; the consumption of the two countries is measured by the coordinates of c_2 and c_1 in the second and fourth quadrants with reference to O, while output is measured by the coordinates of the same points in the same quadrants as consumption, but with reference to (or starting from) point p. Note also that the marginal rates of substitution and transformation in both countries are equal to the international terms of trade and domestic exchange ratios.

14.3 Other Important Concepts and Relations; the Income-Consumption Locus and the Efficiency Locus

In the preceding section we derived the offer curves of an economy corresponding to a given level of transfer. If the assumptions underlying the offer curve (fixed transfer and variable prices) are reversed—i.e., if the terms of trade are assumed invariant and the amount of transfer variable—a new locus Y_t^2 (see Fig. 14.3.1) can be derived in the first (or third) quadrant, showing the positions of the origin of the production block (such as point p in Fig. 14.2.2) that

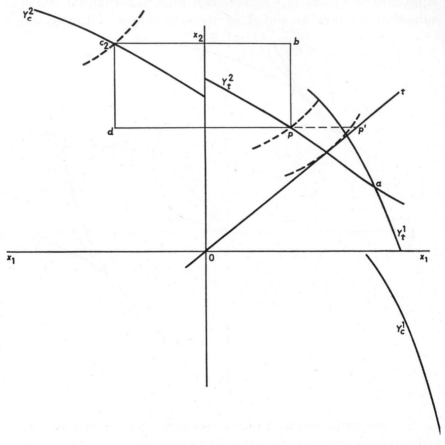

FIGURE 14.3.1

would be attained through optimal trading with different levels of subsidy (such as pp') and fixed international exchange ratio (such as the slope of Ot).

With reference to Figure 14.2.2, the income-consumption locus may be derived by letting the length of pp' vary and sliding the enlarged block along Ot to a point where the marginal rates of substitution and transformation (such as at c_2) are equal to the slope of Ot, the international terms of trade. Point p will now describe the desired locus Y_c^2. As the reader may easily observe, this locus is nothing else but a parallel translation of the income-consumption line Y_c^2 in the second quadrant, where the translation is performed through the rectangle defined by c_2, b, p, and d, i.e., by the outputs of x_1 and x_2 in country 2. One position of such a rectangle and the Y_t^2 and Y_c^2 loci are shown in Figure 14.3.1 corresponding to a given terms-of-trade ratio Ot. It should be noted that Y_t may also be derived as a simple income-consumption line from the trade indifference map explained in the preceding section, corresponding to a zero transfer. For each country, there will be a Y_t curve for every given trading ratio, some in the first quadrant, some in the third. The important fact to be noticed about each of these curves is that, as we move along any single one of them in one direction or the other, the social satisfaction (or real income) of the community is uniformly increasing or diminishing.

Similar loci may be constructed for country 1, namely, Y_t^1 and Y_c^1. Both Y_t^1 and Y_t^2 will intersect the trading line Ot defining them at the points of free-trade offer (where p coincides with p') . Only if the balance of payments is in equilibrium at the given exchange ratio will such intersections be in one place on Ot. In all other cases, such as that in the diagram, the two trade-income-consumption lines will intersect (in one or more points) off Ot. Point a in Figure 14.3.1 illustrates this situation. The economic significance of such points is that they show precisely the amount of transfer from one country to the other that would be needed to attain, through free international trade, corresponding levels of consumption in each of the two countries, given a prescribed terms-of-trade ratio. We shall discuss in greater detail this case of "pure transfer" in Section 5 of this chapter.

The case of a free-trade equilibrium without transfer is shown in Figure 14.3.2. The two trade-income-consumption lines intersect at e on Ot; e is the equilibrium trading point, its coordinates showing the exports and imports of the two countries. Through that point passes a third locus, E. It is a generalized efficiency locus, comparable to the Paretian contract curve; only it is more general because it reflects optimum conditions with respect to both production and consumption. It is defined as a locus of all equilibrium positions of the origins (p) of *both* production blocks attainable through trading and transfer of different sums of purchasing power (of product x_1 or x_2 or both) from one country to the other. Point e is the free-trade solution on that curve corresponding to zero transfer. There will be only

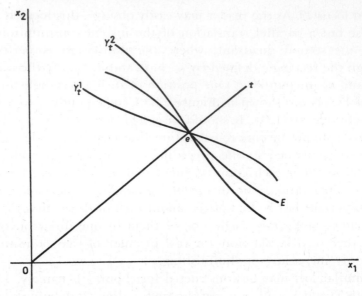

FIGURE 14.3.2

one such locus in the $x_1 - x_2$ plane. It can be derived as the locus of common tangencies of the two trade indifference maps. Because every pair of trade-income-consumption lines is defined by and consistent with one terms-of-trade ratio, every such pair must intersect on the efficiency locus E. Consequently, E may also be defined as the locus of all points of intersection of Y_t^1 and Y_t^2. Points e in Figure 14.3.2 and a in 14.3.1 are such intersections on the efficiency locus. It should be observed, however, that the points on E are not the trading points except in the case of free trade with zero transfer (such as e in Fig. 14.3.2); the trading points are, however, easily derivable from the terms of trade corresponding to each point on the efficiency locus and the amount of transfer necessary to produce such a solution. This case of transfer will be further explained in Section 5.

14.4 Barter Elasticities of Supply and Demand; Stability of Foreign-Trade Equilibrium

Elasticities of supply and demand relations in international barter exchange are as important in studying the stability of markets as they are in the usual partial analysis where prices are expressed in terms of money. In this section we shall first explain the meaning of the elasticity of a barter offer curve and show a simple derivation of such elasticity indexes. Later we shall express the sta-

bility conditions of a general equilibrium solution of international
trade in terms of these elasticities.

In partial and general equilibrium analysis the definitions of
elasticity of supply and of demand are the same. Using S and D to
express the supply and demand, respectively, of a given commodity
and s' and d' the corresponding elasticities, we may write

$$s' = \frac{dS}{dp} \cdot \frac{p}{S} \tag{4.1}$$

and

$$d' = \frac{dD}{dp} \cdot \frac{p}{D} \tag{4.2}$$

where p represents price and d indicates differentiation and may be
interpreted as a "small change in."

In a market where two commodities are traded (i.e., bartered)
for each other, the price of one product will always be expressed in
terms of the other. Thus, for example, in Figure 14.4.1 the price of
product x_2 will be equal to Oa/ac if trade takes place at point c.
Wherever trade takes place, the price of x_2 will always be measured

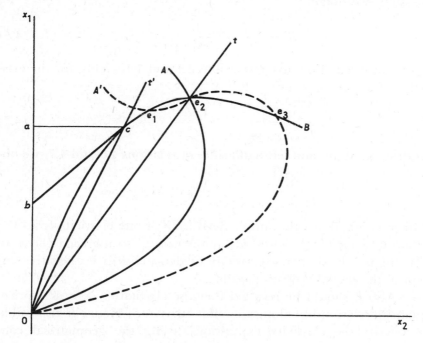

FIGURE 14.4.1

as the ratio of the quantities of x_1 and x_2 traded at that particular point, i.e.,

$$p_2 = \frac{x_1}{x_2} \qquad (4.3)$$

Similarly,

$$p_1 = \frac{x_2}{x_1} \qquad (4.4)$$

Let us now observe that in Figure 14.4.1 country B demands product x_2 in the international market and supplies or, what is the same thing, pays in terms of x_1. Its willingness to trade is expressed by the offer curve OB. The elasticity of demand of country B for product x_2 will be obtained if relation 4.3 is introduced into 4.2, and we observe that the quantity demanded is x_2. We have

$$d_B' = \frac{dx_2}{d(x_1/x_2)} \cdot \frac{(x_1/x_2)}{x_2} \qquad (4.5)$$

Carrying out the differentiation in the denominator of the first fraction of the right-hand side of the equation and simplifying the expression, we obtain

$$d_B' = \frac{1}{(dx_1 \cdot x_2/dx_2 \cdot x_1) - 1} \qquad (4.6)$$

A similar calculation, using relations 4.1 and 4.4, yields, for the elasticity of supply of country B,

$$s_B' = \frac{1}{(dx_2 \cdot x_1/dx_1 \cdot x_2) - 1} \qquad (4.7)$$

Adding the right- and left-hand sides of relations 4.6 and 4.7, we obtain

$$d_B' + s_B' = -1 \qquad (4.8)$$

This relation allows the simple derivation of one elasticity from the other. Of course, we should always be careful to use each elasticity with its proper sign; the elasticity of demand will be negative except in the case of Giffen's paradox.

Also it should be recalled that the elasticities express a price-quantity relationship along the offer curve OB. Hence it is possible to rewrite the elasticity expressions, using the geometrical concepts, as

$$d'_B = \frac{1}{m \cdot t - 1} \tag{4.9}$$

and

$$s'_B = \frac{1}{(1/m \cdot t) - 1} \tag{4.10}$$

where m is the slope of the offer curve OB and t the net barter terms of trade of country B. These relations lead to a very simple geometrical derivation of the value of the two elasticities. Considering point c on OB in Figure 14.4.1, we observe that m may be expressed as a ratio of two segments, i.e.,

$$m = \frac{ab}{ac} \tag{4.11}$$

and

$$t = \frac{ac}{Oa}. \tag{4.12}$$

Substituting relations 4.11 and 4.12 in 4.9 and observing that

$$Oa = Ob + ba,$$

we obtain

$$d'_B = -\frac{Oa}{Ob} \tag{4.13}$$

where Oa and Ob are two positive numbers measuring the lengths of two segments on the vertical axis. The elasticity of supply may then easily be derived from relation 4.8. The reader may find it interesting to derive such an elasticity directly as

$$s'_B = \frac{ba}{Ob} \tag{4.14}$$

However, here it is necessary to assign signs to the two geometrical segments; for instance, it may be assumed that measuring in the upward direction represents a positive number. Note that, in this case, ba will be positive or negative, depending on whether Ob is larger or smaller than Oa.

As usual, a market will be stable if, for prices lower than equilibrium, there is excess demand for a given commodity and if, for prices higher than equilibrium, there is excess supply. Thus, for example, the equilibrium at e_2 determined by OB and OA in Figure 14.4.1 is stable. However, the equilibrium determined by offer curves

OB and *OA'* at the same point will not be stable. Any small displacement from e_2 will make the terms of trade move until either equilibrium e_1 or e_3 is attained. Both e_1 and e_3 are stable equilibria.

A mere inspection of the shape of the offer curves indicates that, for an equilibrium to be unstable, the absolute values of the demand elasticities of the two offer curves must be quite low in the

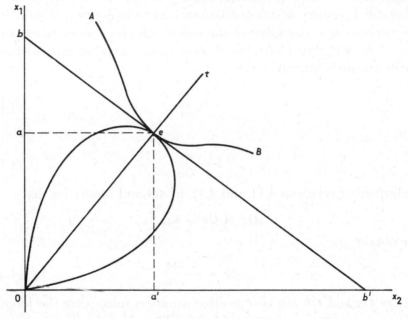

FIGURE 14.4.2

neighborhood of equilibrium. The answer as to how low exactly they have to be is provided if we consider Figure 14.4.2. The limiting case of instability is found when the two offer curves have the same slope at the point of equilibrium. For any absolute values of the elasticities of demand smaller than those producing this situation, the market equilibrium at point *e* will be unstable.

Using relation 4.13 and a similar one for country *A* and observing the common tangency to the two offer curves at *e,* we may write

$$d_A' + d_B' = -\left(\frac{Oa}{Ob} + \frac{Oa'}{Ob'}\right) = -\frac{Oa \cdot Ob' + Oa' \cdot Ob}{Ob \cdot Ob'} \quad (4.15)$$

But it will be noticed that the denominator of the right-hand side of the above expression measures the area of the rectangle defined by O, b, and b'. A simple consideration of equal triangles within this rectangle will convince the reader that the numerator of the right-hand fraction is equal to its denominator and, consequently,

$$d'_A + d'_B = -1 \qquad (4.16)$$

Thus, whenever the sum of absolute values of the two demand elasticities is smaller than 1, an equilibrium at the point where such elasticities were observed will be unstable; it will be stable when the sum of absolute values of the elasticities of demand is greater than 1. Using relation 4.8 we may also obtain from relation 4.16 the critical values for the elasticities of supply, namely,

$$s'_A + s'_B = s'_A + d'_A + s'_B + d'_B - (d'_A + d'_B)$$
$$= -2 + 1 = -1 \qquad (4.17)$$

For sums of elasticities of supply smaller than -1 the market will be unstable; it will be stable whenever the sum of supply elasticities is greater than that critical value.

14.5 International Transfer in Pure Theory

In Chapters 5, 7, and 8 we discussed the problem of transfer. In the first case, transfer was studied in the context of a competitive foreign-exchange market; in the second, with reference to income changes in a fully, as well as less than fully, employed economy; and in the last instance the relation between the exchange rate (or the terms of trade) and the level of income was established under conditions of free exchanges. In this section we shall study the effect of a transfer in a general equilibrium setting.

Most of the analysis whereon the solution of this problem is based has already been presented in Sections 3 and 4 of this chapter. Consequently, we may only summarize the essential points. The problem really may be reduced to the question of what happens to the terms of trade if a transfer of real purchasing power is effected from one country to the other. Once this question is answered, all other solutions of the simplified general equilibrium here considered follow immediately, either directly or with reference to the production possibility function analyzed in Chapter 12. The extent of controversy on this particular question that has appeared in the past hundred years or so only emphasizes the point that there is no unique answer to the problem. The terms of trade may deteriorate or improve as a result of transfer. Some simple conditions may be shown, indicating whether one or the other outcome should follow; however, neither condition can be deemed the more likely outcome.

We have already observed in Section 3 of this chapter that the position of the production origin p corresponding to all possible transfers of real resources from one country to the other will be found on the efficiency locus E, in Figure 14.3.2. Now consider Figure 14.5.1, showing the same situation as in Figure 14.3.2. A transfer of a given quantity of commodity x_1 from country 1 to country 2 will make the point p move from the free-trade position p_0 to a new point

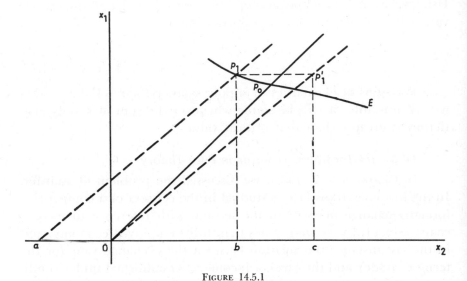

FIGURE 14.5.1

on E, p_1. Its precise location may be found through the construction of the two offer curves corresponding to the given amount of transfer, say Oa, measured along the horizontal axis. Alternatively, if the efficiency locus and all the common tangencies along it are known, a line may be found by trial and error, such as ap_1, fulfilling the conditions of transfer and optimal trading. The actual trading line will be parallel to it, to the right of it by the distance Oa; p_1' now is the new trading point. In the situation shown in the diagram the terms of trade have turned against the receiving country.

To establish whether the terms of trade will turn in one direction or the other, it is possible to use the trade-income-consumption lines Y_t discussed in Section 3.[1] We showed in that section that all

---

[1] See P. A. Samuelson, "The Transfer Problem and Transport Costs," *Economic Journal*, June, 1952, and June, 1954.

pairs of such lines must intersect on the efficiency locus E. Moreover, it is easy to see that, for any given exchange ratio, the corresponding loci Y_t^1 and Y_t^2 must be located on opposite sides of the efficiency locus. Note that, while the efficiency locus is generated by common tangencies of the trade indifference curves, the trade-income lines are loci of a constant marginal rate of substitution along the trade indifference curves. On the limit, if the two income lines coincide along a given stretch, they must, by definition, also represent the efficiency locus.

Through the original equilibrium trading point p_0 will pass two trade-income lines Y_t^1 and Y_t^2, as in Figure 14.3.2, and generally will intersect at that point. If transfer from country 1 to country 2 moves the point p to the left of the free-trade position, the terms of trade will improve for the receiving country if Y_t^1, to the left of p_0, is above the efficiency locus and Y_t^2 below it. If the opposite relation between Y_t^1 and Y_t^2 prevails, the terms of trade of country 2 will deteriorate. To the left of p_0, slopes along the efficiency locus must indicate better terms of trade for country 2 (steeper slopes) than those at p_0 if Y_t^1 is above E, because the slopes of trade indifference curves of country 1 are increasing below Y_t^1. These solutions pertain equally to the case of transfer from country 2 to country 1. If, to the right of p_0, Y_t^1 is above E, then such a transfer will improve the terms of trade of country 2, and vice-versa. Of course, if the two trade-income lines intersect again in at least one other place to the right or to the left of p_0 on the efficiency locus, the conditions are no longer sufficient to determine whether the terms of trade will improve or deteriorate because, in one region, Y_t^1 and, in another, Y_t^2 are above the efficiency locus. Only a complete general equilibrium reconstruction of each particular case can give the answer.

So far we have dealt with the situation wherein a transfer from country 1 to country 2 shifts the production origin p to the left and the opposite transfer to the right of p_0. Is this necessarily so? In other words, must a transfer always move the receiver to a preferable position if international trading is permitted? The answer is affirmative, if the system does not permit of any unstable solutions. Suppose that a transfer from country 1 to country 2 led to the situation illustrated in Figure 14.5.2. Here transfer would have produced a movement of point p to the right of p_0; in other words, the position of the receiver would have deteriorated as a result of transfer.

Observe that at point p_0 two free-trade offer curves intersect

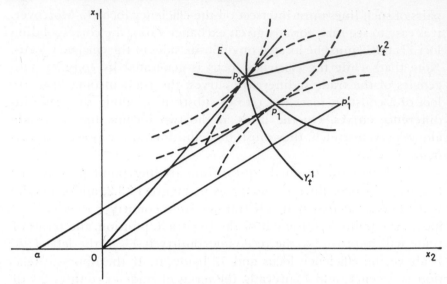

FIGURE 14.5.2

(without transfer) and that through point p_1' two offer curves would have to pass corresponding to a transfer of aO from country 1 to country 2. Following from the geometry of transfer here presented, two other offer curves would have to intersect at point p_1, originating at point a (rather than at O) and perfectly parallel to the offer curves passing through p_1'. The offer curves intersecting at p_1 would be derivable from the trade indifference maps without transfer—that is, maps generating the offer curves passing through p_0. Because a is to the left of O and p_1 to the right of p_0, either the two offer curves of country 1—one originating at O, the other at a—would have to intersect, or those of country 2 would have to intersect, if only one trade solution is permitted with or without transfer. But such intersection is impossible, because to any point in the first quadrant there corresponds only one marginal rate of transformation for each country; that is, through any point there passes only one trade indifference curve of one country, corresponding to zero transfer.

If the structure of the general equilibrium situation is such as to permit of a number of equilibrium solutions, some stable, some unstable, the situation illustrated in Figure 14.5.2 is conceivable. However, there will always be some solution in this case yielding the "normal" result, where the position of the receiving country is improved.

The criteria relating the effect of transfer on the terms of trade to the position of the income lines Y_t^1 and Y_t^2 make it possible to reconcile the results obtained in this section with the conditions shown in Chapter 7, relating the effects of transfer to the marginal propensities to import. Note that, for each country,

$$Y = p_1 x_1 + p_2 x_2 \tag{5.1}$$

where p_1 and p_2 are fixed prices consistent with the terms-of-trade ratio defining Y_t^1 and Y_t^2, and Y represents money income. Recalling that the marginal propensity to import in country 1 is $p_2 \cdot dx_2 / dY$ and, in country 2 $p_1 \cdot dx_1 / dY$, we obtain, by differentiating with respect to the import commodity relation 5.1 for each country, and rearranging somewhat,

$$\frac{p_2}{p_1} \cdot \left(\frac{1}{m_2'} - 1 \right) = A_2 \tag{5.2}$$

and

$$\frac{p_1}{p_2} \cdot \left(\frac{1}{m_1'} - 1 \right) = \frac{1}{A_1} \tag{5.3}$$

where m_1' and m_2' represent the marginal propensities to import by country 1 and country 2, respectively, and A_1 and A_2 are the slopes of the income-comsumption lines of country 1 and country 2. Note that these slopes must be identical, whether measured in the trade (first) quadrant or in the second or fourth quadrants showing consumption. Now let us recall that the critical condition for the two slopes is

$$A_1 = A_2 \tag{5.4}$$

If this is the case, the two trade-income lines coincide with the efficiency locus in the neighborhood of equilibrium, and there will be no change in the terms of trade within such a range if transfer is effected from one country to the other. Using relation 5.4 and multiplying the corresponding sides of relations 5.2 and 5.3, we obtain

$$1 = \left(\frac{1}{m_2'} - 1 \right) \left(\frac{1}{m_2'} - 1 \right) \tag{5.5}$$

and, after further simplification,

$$1 = m_1' + m_2' \tag{5.6}$$

This is precisely the important critical value of the two marginal propensities necessary for transfer to be exactly effected, without any need of price adjustment, i.e., change in the terms of trade. If

$$A_1 < A_2 \tag{5.7}$$

the left-hand side of a relation obtained in the same way as 5.5 would be greater than unity, and the sum of the two propensities would have to be smaller than 1. We recognize in this case the situation wherein transfer is not fully effected, and where, for the balance of payments to remain in equilibrium (as is always assumed in the present barter situation), the terms of trade of the receiving country have to improve. In terms of the geometrical conditions, indeed, the terms of trade of the receiver, country 2, will improve if the algebraic slope of $Y_?^2$ is greater than that of $Y_?^1$. If the opposite inequality holds, the terms of trade of the paying country will improve, the sum of the marginal propensities being greater than 1.

14.6 Balance and Imbalance of Foreign-Trade Accounts in Pure Theory

In Section 1 of the present chapter we discussed a "pure" case of international general equilibrium and came to the conclusion that the balance of payment on current account must be in balance. This result crucially depends on the assumption of equality between income and expenditure on the part of each individual and hence on the part of the entire economy. If everybody spends at any time exactly what he earns, the balance of payments can never get out of balance.

As we have shown in the accounting identities in Chapter 3 and in our discussion of the classical model in Chapter 6, it is only when savings and investment are introduced into the theory as new aggregates of national income and expenditure that exports and imports may differ. This assumption, at least implicitly, was made in our discussion of transfer in the preceding section. In Figure 14.5.1, the amount of real transfer aO, measured in terms of product x_2, also measures the deficit on current account of country 2 and surplus of country 1. The coordinates of point p_1 may be interpreted as exports and imports of, say, country 2; but it has to be observed that, given the equilibrium exchange ratio, the value of country 2's imports in terms of x_2 is measured by ab, while that of exports is only Ob.

Thus any case of surplus or deficit on current account in the context of pure theory may be interpreted as a transfer. The analysis and derivation of equilibrium conditions will always proceed along the lines presented in the preceding section. However, to decide whether such an inequality of exports and imports corresponds to an equilibrium of autonomous payments or not calls for some additional discussion. A number of cases should be considered.

The first and perhaps most normal situation is that in which the real transfer explained in our preceding discussion is financed through a long-term loan from country 1 to country 2. In this case, the deficit on current account of country 2 would have been accompanied by a flow of securities, representing the corresponding amount, toward country 1. The autonomous credits and debits of both countries would have remained equal. A disparity between savings and investment matching that of exports and imports would now have arisen in both countries. If the loan considered was a pure consumption loan—an assumption that is not strictly necessary—investment would have been zero in both countries, but positive saving would have taken place in country 1 and dissaving in country 2.

A similar analysis pertains to the case in which the real transfer was generated by a donation from country 1 to country 2. The balance of goods and services is now equilibrated through a grant. National incomes and expenditures differ by the corresponding amounts; only the balances of indebtedness of the two countries now remain unchanged.

Let us assume that investment takes place and is performed by individuals in the two countries in the form of accumulated (or decumulated) inventories of the two products. The demand for such investment depends on individual preferences as much as does demand for consumption. A difference between exports and imports on current account will always be matched by an excess of savings over investment—assuming, of course, that no donations are made. Starting from a situation where exports equal imports, let us consider the case where an autonomous increase in the propensity to save takes place in country 1, all other structural parameters remaining unchanged, including the supply of money in the two countries. This will tend to produce a surplus on current account in country 1 and a corresponding deficit on the part of country 2. A real transfer from country 1 to country 2 will be performed. The important question now arises as to the financial mechanism that will effect this adjustment.

One possible interpretation is that, with an increase in the propensity to save in country 1, the rate of interest will have a tendency to decline; capital markets being assumed competitive, capital will flow from country 1 to country 2, sufficient to finance the deficit on current account of the latter country. Savings in country 2 will fall short of investment by the amount of the current payments deficit of that country and by the amount of surplus of savings over investment in country 1. Total savings and total investment of both countries combined will be in balance. Again in this situation, the balance of autonomous transactions is preserved.

In the absence of competitive international capital markets, an increased propensity to save in country 1 would tend to increase the money balances on the part of nationals of country 1, thereby reducing the velocity of circulation in both countries taken together. The demand for imports and for domestic products would tend to decline in country 1. With perfect price and wage flexibility and continuing full employment of all resources in both countries, the general price level would tend to decline in both countries, while monetary reserves would flow into country 1. Such a flow, however, would continue only until a new equilibrium distribution of monetary reserves was reached concurrently with new equilibrium levels of savings, investment, exports, and imports in the two countries.

The case may be better understood if we interpret it as a reduction of money in circulation caused by increased hoarding on the part of nationals of country 2. The adjustment of the trade balance, savings, and investment will proceed along the same lines as in the case where in one country the supply of money is autonomously increased, with unchanged velocity of circulation. Suppose that country 2 prints new money and injects it into circulation through additional spending in domestic and foreign markets. This will increase the general price level in both countries. But, assuming that all individuals desire to hold real balances proportional to the level of real transactions, some monetary reserves now have to flow from country 2 to country 1. This will be effected through an excess of sales over spending abroad on the part of country 1. The difference will be paid for through a transfer of international reserves into the transactions balances of nationals of country 1. As long as the reserves transferred are perfectly acceptable to the nationals of country 1, the process will continue and will be stopped only when country 2 ceases expanding its money supply.

The important difference between the case of international investment or donation and the last two situations is that the latter give rise to an imbalance rather than a balance of autonomous credits and debits in the foreign-trade accounts.

Not of least importance is the case of devaluation in the context of the ideal conditions assumed in this section. In some sense it may contradict the entire elasticity approach to the question of devaluation. Already in the last section of Chapter 5 we have observed that, under the classical assumptions, nothing will happen to the general equilibrium solution of trade in *real* terms if one country changes the value of its currency with respect to the other currency and with respect to gold, while preserving a given gold-currency ratio, that is, while increasing money in circulation in proportion to devaluation. Only prices, expressed in terms of the currency of the devaluating country, will now increase *pari passu* with the rate of exchange and with the price of gold. Now what we usually understand by devaluation, when discussing it in the context of the adjustment theory, is a change of the value of currency without a proportional inflation of money supply in the devaluating country. This is exactly equivalent to a devaluation with proportional inflation of money (where nothing changes in the real solution of the system), followed by a reduction of money in circulation without a change of gold or foreign-exchange parity. But this will necessarily make currency relatively scarce in the devaluating country, and produce a real transfer towards the country whose currency has relatively appreciated, and a corresponding transfer of reserves in the opposite direction; here we recognize the effects of a change in the reserves ratio discussed earlier in this section.

Finally, a temporary imbalance can arise in international trade from a given change in the production possibility function of either country, or a permanent imbalance from continuous changing of the real productive capacity, provided that total money supply of the two countries taken together remains constant. Structural changes are discussed in greater detail in the last section of this chapter; but only the final barter equilibria are shown there, of course, without any transfer or imbalance. In the context of our present discussion, however, it will be apparent that before such a new equilibrium is reached, an imbalance, that is, a transfer, may arise. For example, an increased (real) productive capacity of country 2, with unchanged money supply in that country, will depress the general price level throughout the world. Real income of the growing country increasing in general more than that of the other, there can be expected a relative scarcity of currency in that country. Thus a real transfer may take place from country 2 to country 1, and a corresponding transfer of reserves from country 1 to country 2, re-establishing the desired equilibrium between real balances and real transactions in both countries.

14.7 General Equilibrium and Individual Preferences; Goods Prices, Factor Prices, Income Distribution, and Trade

Throughout this chapter we have assumed that the community's preferences may be expressed by a single and invariant indifference map. In the last section of the preceding chapter we pointed out the limitations that such an assumption imposes upon the general equilibrium analysis of foreign trade. Perhaps the most important limitation is that the use of social indifference curves generally does not permit of disproportionate variation in the incomes of different individuals; this is quite contradictory both to the normal state of affairs in the real world and to a large portion of pure theory of international trade dealing precisely with problems of income distribution.

Although the analysis that is required in handling the situation where relative income shares are permitted to vary is somewhat more complicated—at least at first—it is by no means unmanageable. We shall deal with this problem in the present section. Specifically, we want to examine the relations between the variables of a general equilibrium in the case where changing trade conditions redistribute real income among different individuals. Two situations may be considered. The first, by far the more realistic, is to consider two income groups—say, capital owners and laborers—separately as two component parts of the community. Each group may be assumed to have different preferences and incomes from the other; however, it is homogeneous within. The second alternative is to consider a community composed of two producers, both owning labor and capital, whose incomes are affected differently by international trade. The latter case is perfectly comparable to a situation wherein two countries form a single trading unit and trade with a third country, i.e., the rest of the world. Because, in the context of our present analysis, this situation is much easier to handle, does not correspond well with the conditions of the real world, and is technically treated in Chapters 15 and 18, we shall omit it from our discussion here. Instead, we shall concentrate more closely on the first case, in which income groups are determined by factor ownership.

First, we shall show the static equilibrium solution for an

economy engaging in international trade, whose population is divided into two distinct groups—laborers and capital owners. Our second task is to compare such a general equilibrium solution with another, generated by an alternative set of world prices. Finally, we shall show the bearing of this generalized analysis on a number of problems of foreign-trade equilibrium.

Consider Figure 14.7.1. Its apparent complexity is to be imputed to the fact that two general equilibrium solutions are compared in it. For the moment the reader may completely disregard all the geometrical relations drawn in dotted lines. The rectangle defined by points o and o_2 within the L (labor) and C (capital) axes is the usual box diagram expressing the supplies of labor and capital available to the economy. In it we find two unit isoquants, one for product x_1, measured from origin o_2, and another for x_2, measured from origin o. Both the dimensions of the box and the technology are invariant data. Moreover, both production functions are homogeneous of order 1. Suppose that the economy produces different amounts of x_1 and x_2, indicated by point b in the box. Relative factor prices at this point are equal to the marginal rates of substitution between labor and capital in both industries and are indicated by the slopes of the lines tangent to the unit isoquants at the point where factors are employed in proportions given by the position of point b. The same slope will also be found with two other lines, one passing through point b, i.e., bf, and the other through point o_2, i.e., o_2a.

Noticing that the horizontal axis passing through o measures labor input (*below*) and output of product x_2 (*above*), we may define units of measurement of x_2 in such a way that one unit of x_2 (on the upper side of the horizontal axis) is exactly equal to the total cost of producing one unit of x_2, expressed in terms of labor, at the prevailing relative factor prices. Geometrically, this requires that the intercept of the tangency to $x_2 = 1$ (*solid line*) with the horizontal axis be used as the unit of measurement in the northeast quadrant. We have marked such a scale on ox_2 and ox_1, i.e., on the axes defining this quadrant.

It is now immediately apparent that point f on the horizontal axis measures total output of product x_2, segment og measures total labor income expressed in terms of commodity x_2, and segment oa measures total national income at factor cost expressed in terms of the same commodity used as a numéraire. As we have shown in

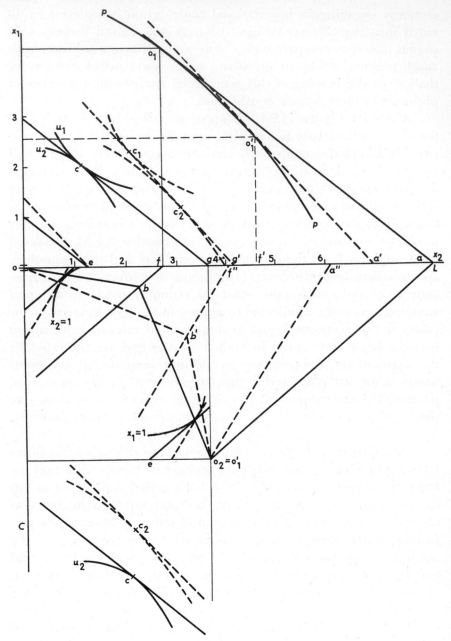

FIGURE 14.7.1

Chapter 12, relative prices p_1/p_2 will be indicated by the ratio of total unit costs of x_1 and x_2 expressed in terms of one factor of production or the other. Using labor as the measure of value, we find, from the box diagram, that

$$\frac{p_1}{p_2} = \frac{eo_2}{o1} = eo_2$$

The slope indicating this price ratio is constructed in the northeast quadrant as a straight line between point 1 on the vertical axis and point e on the horizontal axis. Note that oe is exactly equal to eo_2, on the lower horizontal axis, the total cost of producing one unit of x_1 expressed in terms of labor. Any line in the northeast quadrant having this slope reflects all combinations of products x_1 and x_2 purchasable with a given constant sum of money. One such locus, the budget line of the labor force, passes through point g, and another, expressing all combinations of the two products purchasable by the nation as a whole at current prices, passes through point a. Actually, the latter locus is the trading line of the country along which it can consume, provided that the world terms of trade are constant and expressed by the slope of that line.

Now it should be observed that only (of) of product x_2 is produced by the community. The output of x_1 will be found as the coordinate of point o_1, consistent with the established national income and relative product prices. It is also given by the isoquant of x_1 corresponding to point b in the production box diagram. The rectangle defined by o, f, and o_1 is now the consumption box diagram of the community, expressing total outputs of the two commodities. Point o_1, as we have indicated in the diagram, is one point of the production possibility curve (pp) of the economy; the slope of that locus at o_1 expresses relative commodity prices, found in the production box below the horizontal axis, and also indicated by the slope of the international trading line aO_1. If the economy is in isolation, this product mix and the entire analysis represent a feasible solution only if the corresponding product prices and income distribution leads to a national consumption also expressed by point o_1.

As we have drawn the indifference curves of the labor force and the capital owners, our solution is feasible. Observe that the social indifference curves of the capitalist group are measured in the southwest direction from point o_1 and also transposed into the southwest quadrant with respect to point o_2. Point c, where both factor groups have attained maximum satisfaction, reflects a consumption pattern exactly exhausting national output.

If the points of highest satisfaction did not coincide at c but were differently located on gc, the solution would be feasible only if international exchange were possible at terms of trade reflected by the slope of gc or ao_1. The differences of abscissae and of ordinates of such two points would then measure the exports and imports of the community. The reader should observe the wide range of trade patterns compatible with the solution. Depending on the preferences of capitalists and laborers, the country may be an exporter or an importer of large amounts of x_1 or x_2.

Using the same factor endowments and technological data, we have constructed in the diagram another solution, corresponding to a new product mix and to another set of world prices. The relevant loci are described as dotted lines, and the key points are generally marked in the same way as in the preceding solution, with "primes" attached. One technical difficulty in this construction should be pointed out. As factor prices change, the unit cost of x_2 expressed in terms of labor will no longer be equal to 1. Observe that the intercept of the line tangent to $x_2 = 1$ with the horizontal axis no longer is at $x_2 = 1$. Consequently, all data expressed on the lower side of the horizontal axis have to be adjusted by a correction factor to express the original scale on the upper side of the same axis. This yields pairs of points such as a' and a'', f' and f'', and so forth.

Because the consumption point of the laborers c_1 now is above the consumption point of the capital owners c_2, the community will have a shortage of product x_1 and hence will import it at terms of trade indicated by the slope of $g'c_1$ or $a'o_1'$. On the other hand, it will not use all its output of x_2; this surplus will be exported in payment for imports of product x_1. This is consistent with the "normal" expectation that x_2 will be exported when it becomes relatively more expensive and as relatively more of it is produced compared with the original situation of autarky.

However, this outcome is by no means necessary. This is our first important result, different from the usual situation wherein a single set of social indifference curves is assumed. It will be observed from the diagram that the new equilibrium levels of satisfaction of the two income groups may have been in such a position as to yield another point of autarky, or even exports of x_1 rather than x_2. As may be easily checked, such results are perfectly consistent with the position of the original indifference contours u_1 and u_2; in other words, exports or imports of x_1 are now possible, even though the indifference curves of each income group are not permitted to intersect.

These observations have an important bearing on the reciprocal demand of the community. Any number of *no-trade* exchange ratios, i.e., any number of autarky solutions, now are possible. In other words, the offer curve of the community may now start out from the origin and return to it, and it may do so any number of times. The only requirement that we may now impose on the form of an offer curve of a country is that it be single-valued with respect to a ray through the origin, i.e., single-valued with respect to the terms-of-trade line. Note that in the simpler situations discussed earlier in this chapter the offer curve could only start out from the origin but never return to it.

Thus a typical offer curve of our generalized general equilibrium solution may be the contour illustrated in Figure 14.7.2. This simply reflects the fact that there are three different sets of terms of trade leading to no international trade whatsoever. If a usual offer curve of the rest of the world were superimposed on the offer curve *aa*, a number of different configurations and a number of possible trading equilibria could arise. The reader may enjoy studying such alternative solutions.

One important fact should be noticed. If the offer curve inter-

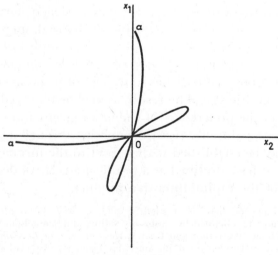

FIGURE 14.7.2

sects the origin more than once, it has to do so three, five, seven, or any odd number of times. This is because, for extreme values of terms of trade, where the economy specializes in one product or the other, both the laborers and the capital owners will gain from further trading; real income expressed in terms of the export commodity is now fixed, and so is distribution of income. The community offer curve will approach one of the two axes either in the first quadrant or in the third quadrant. In the diagram, for example, there are three terms-of-trade ratios leading to no trade, and the offer curve is asymptotic to the x_1 axis when the price of x_2 becomes very large compared with that of x_1, and asymptotic to the x_2 axis when the reverse price pattern prevails. Also it should be observed that, whatever the number of equilibria generated by the offer curve aa and an offer curve of the rest of the world, the number of stable solutions will always be odd and the number of unstable solutions even. While moving along aa in any direction, stable and unstable solutions will be encountered.

The analysis of the present section also makes it very easy to study the relation between the conditions of international trade and the real incomes of capital and labor.[2] We observe that, as factors of production are reallocated in the box diagram in Figure 14.7.1 from point b to point b', the marginal productivity of labor increases in both industries. This is expressed by the fact that the intercepts of the dotted tangencies to the unit isoquants with the labor axis have both moved closer to the origins o and o_2, respectively. In other words, total unit cost of both products expressed in terms of labor has dropped. The supply of labor being unchanged, income of labor expressed in terms either of commodity x_1 or x_2 must have increased. In the northeast quadrant this is reflected by the fact that the budget line of labor (*dotted*) has moved at all its points to the right of its original position gc. The result, as may be observed, is entirely independent of the preferences of the labor group and of the direction of international trade. Just the opposite, through a symmetrical argument, may be established with respect to the income of capital; namely, it must have declined as a result of a relative decline in the world price of the capital-intensive product.

[2] We are showing here in a slightly different way the results discussed in Section 7 of Chapter 12, obtained by Professors Stolper and Samuelson. See W. Stolper and P. A. Samuelson, "Protection and Real Wages," *Review of Economic Studies*, IX, No. 1 (November, 1941); reprinted in American Economic Association, *Readings in the Theory of International Trade* (Philadelphia, 1949).

Also it is possible to study the effects of a transfer to or from one or both income groups. Assuming that the world terms of trade are unchanged, any such transfer will affect only the position of the budget lines (*gc*) of the two income groups. This, of course, may move the offer curve of the community drastically in one direction or the other or even reverse the direction of trade. The result is relevant for the study of the effect of tariffs on international terms of trade in the case where tariff revenue is paid as a subsidy to the private sector of the economy. As may easily be observed from our construction, any small transfer to either income group may displace the offer curve of the economy to such an extent as to worsen the terms of trade of a country if import duty is levied, provided that the offer curve of the foreign trading partner is less than infinitely elastic. We will return to this problem in Chapter 16 in greater detail.

14.8 Structural Change, Economic Growth, and the Terms of Trade

In the context of the theoretical general equilibrium model discussed here, we understand by structural change any autonomous or induced change in one or more of the underlying parameters that we have classified as exogenous at the outset of our discussion. These are the preferences of the community, the technology, and the factor endowments in the different countries. The analysis of the preceding two chapters and of this chapter makes it possible to trace any given change in any of the three factors through the general equilibrium mechanism and establish the impact of any such change on the dependent variables—i.e., on the terms of trade, factor prices, outputs, and employments in the different trading countries.

It is consequently unnecessary to study in any detail each particular situation that might arise. It is up to the reader to accommodate the analysis in the desired direction. A number of volumes could not exhaust all the different possibilities. We may merely make a few remarks here concerning the essentials of the problem.

The conditions of supply of productive factors and of technology will be reflected in the form of the production possibility, i.e., of the transformation function of each particular community. How will this locus (or surface) be affected by a given increase in a given factor of production? In other words, what effect will growth of resources have on the productive potentiality of the economy? To obtain the precise answer, nothing can suffice short of a precise geometrical construction or calculation. One important general statement can be made, however, if constant returns to scale are present in all industries. If the different products entering the production possibility function use factors of production in different proportions, then the expansion of the production possibility locus, measured in terms of percentages, will be greater, the more intensive the use that the product in question makes of the expanding resource. To show this is particularly simple in the case of two products and two factors, where both production functions are unit homogeneous. Consider the box diagram, from which we derive the optimal levels of production of products x_1 and x_2, say, from capital and labor. If x_1 is relatively labor-intensive and x_2 capital-intensive, then it will be easily observed that the marginal rate of substitution of capital for labor (as measured under competitive conditions by the equilibrium price of capital relative to labor) will be greater if all resources are devoted to the production of the capital-intensive commodity x_2 and smaller if to the labor-intensive product x_1. In other words, the slopes of the isoquants at the two origins of the box diagram will be different. Let us now assume that the stock of capital available to the economy increases; the capital dimension of the box diagram will expand. As this happens, the output of the product x_2 (with relatively higher marginal productivity of capital if all resources are applied to its production) will benefit more percentagewise from the expansion of capital stock than x_1 would benefit if only x_1 were produced. The relative outward movement of the intercept of the production possibility curve with the x_2 axis will be greater than that of the other intercept. A similar proof may be designed for any point of the production possibility curve.

To find what effect technological change will have on the transformation function is even simpler. For example, neutral innovation in the technology of x_1, the production function remaining unit homogeneous, will make us renumber the isoquants of x_1 in the box diagram, without changing the equal product map at all. The production function of x_2 remaining unchanged, the production possibility curve will expand in the direction of the x_1 axis, while the intercept with the other axis will remain unchanged.

The empirical and more policy-oriented literature of international economics has been devoting a great deal of attention to problems closely connected with the subject matter of this section. Comparative rates of inflation in developed and underdeveloped countries, secular changes of terms of trade between these two world regions, impact of technological progress, capital accumulation, and population growth are all relevant examples. The analysis of the preceding two chapters and the present chapter, together with the remarks of this section, are well suited for dealing with all such problems and, within given assumptions, arriving at the desired answers. Moreover, it often enables us to avoid unnecessary complications or even mistakes resulting from the introduction of unnecessary or irrelevant elements of analysis. Thus, for example, it is possible to disregard monetary factors in considering long-range structural changes—to the extent, of course, that such monetary factors do not affect the real structure of the trading economies.

Perhaps the most often encountered problem is the secular movement of the terms of trade of developing and undeveloped countries. Deterioration of the terms of trade of the latter group has often been criticized and a number of explanations brought forth. Our general equilibrium analysis itself suggests a number of possible theories explaining the phenomenon; actually, all the correct theories may be, in one way or another, shown through a more or less complicated general equilibrium model.

Closely related to the problem of secular changes of the terms of trade is the theory of immiserizing growth, stating that a growing country may have its real income decline through a negative terms-of-trade effect. In other words, the gains in physical growth are more than offset by an adverse terms-of-trade or price effect.[3] Although this proposition may not be intuitively obvious, it was known to economists, perhaps in another context, even in the nineteenth century. We may think, for example, of the notion that a good harvest may make the farmers worse off than they would have been if crops had been less abundant. This also brings to our mind the important factor that may cause such a phenomenon—namely, a low elasticity of demand for the product that grows in supply.

To give at least one application of the general equilibrium analysis to problems of structural change, let us show rigorously that the growth of a country may lower its social welfare. We show it in a special case; consideration of such a special case, however, does not

[3] Jagdish Bhagwati, "International Trade and Economic Expansion," *American Economic Review*, December, 1958.

diminish the generality of the conclusion, because it will be immediately apparent that a range of similar results is possible for alternative assumptions. In Figure 14.8.1 we have reproduced an initial trading situation of a country, defined by the terms of trade line Op, the trading point p, and the consumption point c on the production possibility curve, falling in the second quadrant. The slope of the trading line Op equals that at the common tangency of a social indifference curve u_0 and of the production possibility

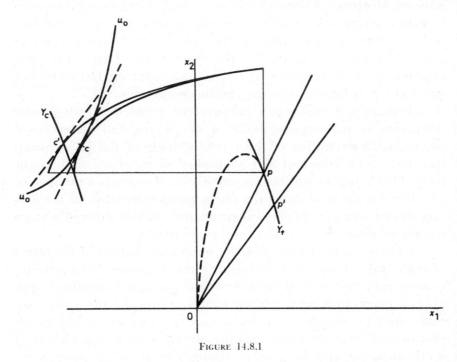

FIGURE 14.8.1

curve, reflecting the marginal rates of substitution and transformation at that equilibrium point. Suppose, now, that the technology of producing x_1 improves and the production block of the country expands in the horizontal direction to the dimensions indicated in the diagram by the contour containing c', where c' is the point of tangency of the expanded production block with a consumption indifference curve. Because the marginal rate of transformation and substitution at c' (indicated by the slope of the dotted tangency) are not equal to the slope of the international trading line Op, the position of the production block defined by point c' is not a feasible solution of competitive trading.

Through c', however, passes an income-consumption line Y_c defined by the marginal rate of substitution at c', and through p passes a trade-income-consumption line Y_t parallel to Y_c (i.e., parallel with respect to a translation defined by a rectangle defined by p and c'). Point p' on Y_t, defined by a trading line of equal slope to the marginal rate of transformation at c', must be a point of the offer curve of the country considered, after technological improvement, i.e., after growth took place. Now it is perfectly possible that the elasticity of foreign reciprocal demand for exports of the growing country is so low as to coincide with Y_t, within the range pp'. But if this is so, point p' is the equilibrium trading point of the growing country with the rest of the world, whose offer curve is given by the contour Opp' (*partially dotted*). Thus in the new equilibrium the origin of the enlarged production block will slide along Y_t toward p' and the equilibrium consumption point in the second quadrant along Y_c, down to a position well below u_0, the social indifference curve corresponding to the initial equilibrium. Consequently, the growth of the production possibility of the country considered has led to an over-all deterioration in its social welfare. This would similarly have been the case for a number of relatively inelastic foreign offer curves (in the relevant region), passing through the original equilibrium p.

We observe, as has been indicated at the outset of our discussion, that the terms of trade of the growing country have deteriorated a good deal. Whether the phenomenon here illustrated does reflect what has been happening to the terms of trade in the world over the past hundred years or so is a difficult question to answer. Different empirical investigations have produced various results, not independent of the specific periods considered. It is another proposition, however, to say that it may be less desirable for underdeveloped countries to develop traditional export industries, whenever foreign demand for such products is very inelastic. Under such conditions, policies aimed at the growth of the import-competing sector may yield greater improvement of real income.

Chapter

15

INTERNATIONAL TRADE
AND ECONOMIC WELFARE

15.1 Single Indifference Map; the Traditional Approach

The preoccupation of welfare economics is to evaluate, in a very broad sense of the word, the social efficiency of economic systems. In its application to international trade it is concerned primarily with the evaluation of social and individual gains (or losses) from different trading situations. In later chapters we shall study the impact of different forms of policy, such as tariffs, other trade restrictions, and customs unions, on the welfare of different countries. In this chapter we want to restrict our discussion to the evaluation of gains from free trade. More specifically, we shall study the impact of free trade on social and individual welfare in a country by comparing it with a situation of an economy in isolation or with another situation of free trade.

What we may term the "traditional" approach to the problem requires only a very simple and straightforward analysis. Actually, it is the same problem as the evaluation of the effect of exchange on individual welfare. The fundamental assumption used here is that the social satisfaction of a community may be described through a single nonintersecting indifference map, i.e., through a single ordinal utility function of the conventional form.

In Chapter 13 we discussed the different assumptions that are required to have such a single indifference map for the purpose of the theory of demand. All such sets of alternative assumptions will also be appropriate for the examination of the relation between exchange and social welfare, except one. In Chapter 13 (Sec. 3) the important postulate was to have a *single* indifference map, irrespective of whether in different trading situations each of its contours

262

(indifference curves) expressed the same or different levels of satisfaction. Here we have to make sure that a movement to a higher social indifference contour corresponds to a higher level of satisfaction. The one case that fulfills the first set of conditions and not the second is that corresponding to the assumption that all individuals have *identical* and *homogeneous* tastes. This yields a single indifference map, for all possible distributions of income. Such a map may be used in deriving the price- and income-consumption loci of

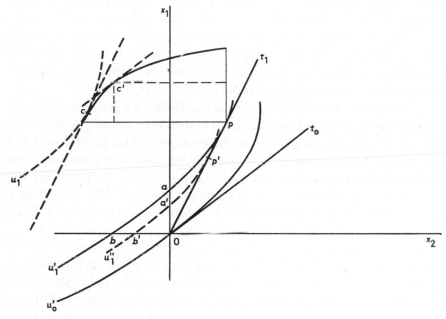

FIGURE 15.1.1

the community, but *not* in studying social welfare. Consumption at a higher indifference contour may and usually will mean a loss for some and a gain for some others.

With these remarks, remembering that all assumptions except assumption (iv) in Section 3 of Chapter 13 may be used in constructing single ordinal indifference maps applicable to welfare evaluation, we may now show the relation between international exchange and social satisfaction. The groundwork for this analysis was laid in the preceding chapter. Consider Figure 15.1.1. We find two trade indifference curves u_0' and u_1'. The first passes through the origin and the other to the left of it and above. Each was derived from a consumption indifference curve in the second quadrant by the process of sliding the production block as described in the preceding chapter. The consumption indifference line u_1 corresponding to the trade indifference line u_1' was drawn in the diagram. A trade indifference contour to the left and above another such locus expresses a higher level of satisfaction. Each trade indifference contour reflects the same level of social satisfaction as the corresponding consumption indifference curve provided that the supply of factors does not involve any disutility. If the production block represents a production indifference curve, i.e., corresponds to a given fixed level of disutility (in the sense of the analysis presented in Sec. 5 of Chap. 12), and the disutility of factor supply is independent of the utility of consumption, the trade indifference curves still are meaningful, each corresponding to a given utility index. A higher trade indifference contour still corresponds to greater satisfaction.

It should be remembered that the slope of a trade indifference curve expresses the marginal rates of transformation and substitution prevalent, under competition, in the economy. With no international trade, i.e., under conditions of autarky, the two marginal rates and the equilibrium domestic exchange ratio will be indicated by the slope of u_0 at the origin O, i.e., by the slope of Ot_0. The degree of social satisfaction under such conditions is measured by an index that we may denote, for simplicity, as u_0'.

If international exchange is now permitted at the terms of trade indicated by the slope of Ot_1, trade will take place at the point p, where the trading line is tangent to u_1' and where the highest level of satisfaction consistent with that exchange ratio is reached. From the properties of the trade indifference curves discussed and under the assumptions made, it follows that the country will attain a higher degree of social satisfaction with trade, as compared with the situation of no trade. A summary examination of the diagram immediately leads to another important conclusion; namely, the greater the difference between the terms-of-trade ratios with and without trade, the greater the increase in social satisfaction with the opening of trade.

While it is impossible to measure cardinally the gain from trade by comparing the two utility indexes u_1' and u_0', it is very easy to find the transfers of one product or the other, or both, that would make the community as well off without trade as it is with trade. For example, if with no trade the community were given gratis Oa of product x_1, or Ob of x_2, it would be indifferent between such an arrangement and trade without transfer at p.

It is often convenient to make the theoretical distinction between gains from trading and gains from productive specialization (under trade). To do this, we may consider a situation wherein the same preferences as above prevail, but where, for one reason or another, productive substitution (transformation) of one product for another is not feasible. The no-trade point of production being c' on the production block (as defined by the no-trade exchange ratio Ot_0), the production possibility block now is the rectangle defined by p and c'. Of course, such a production block would generate a different map of trade indifference curves. In particular, the contour u_1'' of such a map would be tangent to the terms-of-trade line Ot_1 at a point below p, i.e., at p'. This would be the trading point of the country if amounts of output were rigidly fixed by the position of c' on the production block, that is, if no productive specialization could take place. Necessarily, the gain from trade would now be smaller than in the former situation. In terms of product x_1, it is measured by the segment Oa' and in terms of the other product by the segment Ob'. This is what we may call the "gain from exchange." The residual, measured either by the segment $a'a$ or by $b'b$, may be referred to as "gain from productive specialization."

Let us now assume that a free-trading equilibrium is actually realized at point p; that is, the foreign offer curve passes through that point. Both countries are now gaining from international exchange, maximizing their respective levels of satisfaction consistent with the exchange ratio given by Ot_1. The income of the two taken together is maximized, in the sense that no movement of the two production blocks, both originating at one point (p in the free-trade situation), can ever improve satisfaction of one country without lowering that of the other. As we saw in the preceding chapter, an efficiency locus, i.e., a locus of all points having that property, passes through point p.

15.2 *International Trade and Individual Welfare*

On several occasions we have pointed out that the assumptions involved in representing collective satisfaction through a single indifference map are highly unrealistic. In Section 7 of the preceding chapter we rejected such assumptions and studied the case of international trade where incomes and satisfactions of different income groups (or individuals) are considered separately. Emphasis in that discussion was given to positive questions of economics rather than to the evaluation of welfare; however, the discussion is perfectly applicable to questions of individual utility.

If there is any trade among different individuals within a country prior to international trade, free international exchange, without redistribution of resources among individuals, will necessarily lead to reduced satisfaction on the part of some individuals and gains on the part of others. This proposition is completely self-evident and hardly requires any detailed proof. If there is international trade, the exchange ratios before and after trade must be different. Sellers of products whose relative prices decline as a result of trade necessarily lose, while others gain, satisfaction and real income. This will be observed in a rigorous fashion in the next section. It is precisely this redistribution of income resulting from international trading, already observed in the next to last section of the preceding chapter, that makes it almost impossible to use meaningfully unchanging social indifference maps when studying either trade equilibria or questions of welfare.

15.3 Potential and Actual Gains from Trade; Problem of Redistribution

International trade will almost always lead to income redistribution, with losses of satisfaction and real income by some and gains by others; thus any general statements concerning the impact of trade on social welfare are rendered empty and meaningless. It is generally agreed that it is impossible to add positive and negative changes, or absolute levels of satisfaction of different individuals to form a single aggregate index. And even if such an index were possible—if the losers were those who were experiencing a lesser degree of satisfaction before international trade—it might well happen that international trading would lead to a loss of social well-being.

To circumvent this difficulty, some economists choose to employ a criterion based on redistribution of income. Specifically, a given situation is judged preferable to another if a redistribution of income is (1) conceivable or (2) feasible within a given institutional setting or (3) actually performed, that would lead to a situation not worse than before for any, and better for some. It is a question of moral conviction whether condition 1, 2, or 3 is chosen, and requires personal responsibility rather than economic judgment. Leaving

such choices to the reader, we may now turn to the technical aspects
of the question.

Consider a nation composed of two individuals (or two groups
of individuals), each producing or being able to produce two
products, x_1 and x_2. Each of the two produces along a production
possibility curve, similar to that used for the nation as a whole in

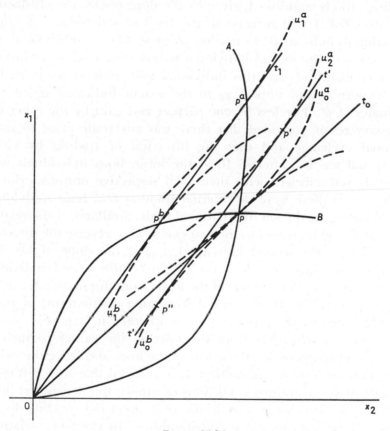

FIGURE 15.3.1

our previous discussion. For simplicity, let us assume that no
disutility or irksomeness is involved in such production. Both
individuals having ordinal indifference maps, the internal equilibrium of the two-man community may be obtained and studied in
precisely the same way as was the two-country equilibrium in the
preceding chapter. Figure 15.3.1 illustrates this situation. Offer
curves OA and OB determine a free-trade equilibrium at point
p and a corresponding exchange ratio given by the slope of Ot_0. Be-

cause, so far, no external trade is assumed, the market has to be cleared, under competitive conditions, at point p. The levels of satisfaction of individuals A and B are given by two ordinal utility indexes u_0^a and u_0^b, corresponding to the trade indifference loci tangent at p.

If international trade is now permitted and a new equilibrium trading ratio is established, given by the slope of Ot_1, the satisfaction of individual A will increase to the level of satisfaction u_1^a, corresponding to individual A's trading point p^a. On the other hand, the satisfaction of the second individual will decline to a lower ordinal index of utility u_1^b, and this individual will trade at point p^b, i.e., will export x_1 and import x_2 to the extent indicated by the co-ordinates of p^b. The loss by one partner and gain by the other is a necessary result, provided that there was any trade prior to international exchange and that the direction of trading by either individual was not altered. If, at the limit, both individuals were perfectly self-sufficient with their own respective outputs prior to trade, i.e., if there were no internal trade at Ot_0, both individuals would have gained from international trade. Similarly, if the relative price of x_2 had increased to such an extent as to reverse the direction of trading of the second individual, i.e., if the slope of Ot_1 had exceeded the slope of OB at the origin O, the second individual would have recuperated some of the losses from international trading inflicted upon him by the initial worsening of his terms of trade.

The important question now is whether it is possible to re-distribute real resources from the loser to the gainer to such an extent as to compensate all the loss of the loser and leave the gainer with some increase in satisfaction. It is assumed that such a transfer is made under prevailing conditions of supply and demand at home and abroad and under conditions of competitive trading by all parties. Two cases should be distinguished. In the first—relatively simple to handle—we assume that the foreign offer curve that has led to the terms of trade given by Ot_1 is infinitely elastic, i.e., coincides with Ot_1. In the second and more complicated situation we assume that such an offer curve has an elasticity lower than infinity.

If either A or B is permitted to buy or sell x_1 in exchange for x_2, always in the same proportions, given by the slope of Ot_1, it is very simple to consider a transfer from individual A to individual B, coupled with utility-optimizing trading. It may be assumed that the transfer is effected in terms of commodity x_2. A given quantity of

x_2 taken from A and given to B will simply establish a new trading line for both, parallel to Ot_1 and to the right of it. Along such a line, both A and B may reach any point through trading. As soon as transfer becomes sufficient to permit B to be at p'', the transfer may be arrested because B is now as well off as he was in the initial situation without international trading. Note that $t't'$ is tangent to u_0^b at p''. Moving along $t't'$ upward, we now observe that individual A is still in a position preferable to the original condition, u_2^a being a higher index of utility than u_0^a. A similar construction may be used in proving conclusively that if terms of trade are altered from one level to another, with international trade in both situations, a gain or loss will be realized by the community as a whole *with compensation,* depending on whether the terms of trade have moved farther away from a no-trade exchange ratio or nearer to it. In other words, the greater the difference between the autarkic terms of trade and the equilibrium terms of trade with international trading, the greater will be the potential gain. It may be useful to observe that, in the simple case considered so far, both individuals are permitted through transfer to move along their respective trade-income-consumption lines, of the type used in the preceding chapter. These were not drawn in the diagram.

The actual and potential gains from international trade proved here may conveniently be shown in the utility plane (or space) of Figure 15.3.2. Note that it is possible to deal with such a space, even though we are assuming ordinal utility; only we should remember that there is no other meaning of a north-south or east-west distance but that of sign. A point or locus farther up from another represents a higher level of satisfaction for individual A; similarly, a point or locus farther east corresponds to a greater satisfaction of individual B. A point of contact of two loci represents equal combinations of utilities. The original equilibrium with no international trade, defined by point p in Figure 15.3.1, corresponds to a given total output of the two products and a given distribution of utility between A and B. Suppose that such a distribution is illustrated by point e in Figure 15.3.2. If, with unchanged total availability of x_1 and x_2, the community were to redistribute income in one direction or the other, new points in the utility plane would be attained. All such points are illustrated by the locus f, expressing utilities corresponding to all possible *efficient* reallocations of x_1 and x_2 between A and B. Now if the terms of trade are permitted to vary between zero

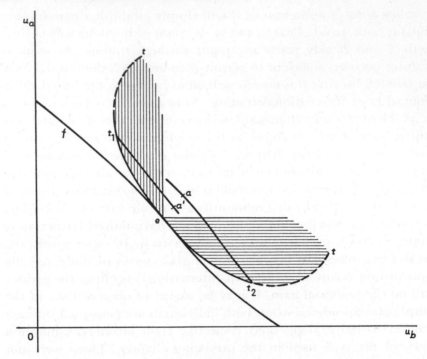

FIGURE 15.3.2

and infinity and *A* and *B* are permitted to trade accordingly, a new locus will be generated, reflecting the efficient levels of satisfaction attainable by the two individuals, given their production possibilities. Nowhere can such locus *t* be below the locus *f*, and only at one point will *t* be tangent to *f*, i.e., in the situation of autarky, determined by the trading line Ot_0 in Figure 15.3.1.

As international trade is permitted, the community will move from point *e*, say, to point t_1 on *t*, corresponding to the levels of satisfaction u_1^a and u_1^b. As we have shown in our preceding discussion, the utility of *B* has declined, while that of *A* has increased. The process of compensatory redistribution of resources explained above may now be illustrated by a movement along t_1a', in Figure 15.3.2, through the shaded area to a position in the northeast of *e*, where both individuals are better off than they were before international trade. Further, it may be shown that if the international terms of trade are invariant during the process of redistribution, no loci such as t_ia', starting from different points on *t*, above *e*, can intersect. This is simply the reflection of the fact that greater divergence of international terms of trade from the no-trade situation corresponds to a greater potential social gain.

We may now turn to the more intricate problem of redistribution after trade in the case where the foreign offer curve is less than infinitely elastic. The first thing to realize is that, with any foreign offer curve, the equilibrium terms of trade may not change, and consequently the previous conclusions will hold if redistribution does not generate any net additional demand for either commodity by the community of two individuals or groups. Of course, this is the situation (studied in the previous chapter) wherein the two trade-income-consumption lines, corresponding to the terms of trade with international trade but before redistribution, are parallel with respect to the slope of Ot_1 in Figure 15.3.1. This is the situation if the distance between the two income loci measured along a moving line of constant slope such as $t't'$ in Figure 15.3.1 is constant.

If redistribution from A to B were to generate additional net demand of the two-man community for x_1 with unchanged terms of trade (as in Figure 15.3.1), world terms of trade effectively must turn in favor of x_1, and vice-versa. Of course, we must assume stability in the international market. Improvement in the terms of trade for x_1 represents a movement of the trading line back toward the original equilibrium (without foreign trade) at point p in Figure 15.3.1. But this reduces in itself the necessity of further transfer, because the terms of trade are now more advantageous for B and because such terms of trade are less likely to call for further net purchases of x_1 by the community. The compensating process of transfer must stop short of the situation wherein the equilibrium terms of trade reach the slope of Ot_0, the autarkic terms of trade. This is easily realized if we observe that a trading equilibrium with terms of trade given by the slope of Ot_0, and transfer from A to B, would necessarily involve an over-compensation (that is, moving in Fig. 15.3.2 from the second into the fourth quadrant with respect to e) and would be likely to produce a net demand for x_2 rather than x_1 by the community. Consequently, the process of transfer must be arrested before the autarkic terms of trade are reached, at a level of compensation rendering B as well off as at autarky and A better off. Actually, the situation may now be illustrated in the same way as that of Figure 15.3.1, except for the fact that the terms of trade given by Ot_1 no longer represent the trading ratio with international trading and without transfer, but rather the terms of trade attained after the compensating transfer was effected. Of course, given our assumptions, the terms of trade before transfer will now be more advantageous for A than those after transfer. Also, in this reinterpretation of Figure 15.3.1, the segment $p'p''$ on $t't'$ now measures the equilibrium reciprocal demand of the foreign country at the terms of trade indicated by $t't'$ or Ot_1.

If transfer of resources from A to B were to generate net additional demand for x_2 with unchanged international terms of trade given by Ot_1, the terms of trade should, in actuality, turn in favor of x_2, i.e., move farther away from the no-foreign-trade position. But it follows from our previous discussion of the simple case of invariant terms of trade that the farther the terms of trade from such an original exchange ratio (given by Ot_0 in Fig. 15.3.1), the easier it is to effect compensation of B while preserving some gain for A. In addition, we know that if such a process of further improvement of the terms of trade for individual A were to continue far enough, the pattern of trade of B would be reversed and he too would eventually attain some gains.

Thus we come to the important conclusion of this section: free international trade will always lead to a situation from which it is possible to attain, through redistribution of resources, a greater satisfaction for both individuals of a community as compared with the situation wherein only domestic exchange was possible. Moreover, a greater divergence between the autarkic terms of trade and the equilibrium terms of trade with international trading will always indicate a greater potential gain for all members of the community. The representation of Figure 15.3.2 pertains, whatever the elasticity of foreign reciprocal demand.

These results may easily be generalized for a case with two products and an unlimited number of individuals if the foreign offer curve is infinitely elastic. Domestic traders may be considered in pairs, and the same analysis as before may be applied to each pair. The same can be done, with a little additional difficulty, for a less than infinitely elastic foreign offer curve. If there is a large number of commodities traded, the analysis becomes a good deal more complicated. For any pair of products, all others being held fixed, and two individuals, the preceding analysis again pertains; and social gains from trade with redistribution may generally be proved for any number of individuals and products.

PART IV

PART IV

Chapter 16 THEORY OF DIRECT TRADE POLICY

16.1 Tariffs and the Terms of Trade

When we examine the impact of an over-all import or export duty on the general conditions of an economy, it is profitable to use the general equilibrium approach discussed in the preceding five chapters. This permits us to examine directly the impact of a tariff on the principal variables concerning us, such as the terms of trade, income distribution, factor prices, output, consumption, and so forth. In this section we shall concentrate on the first relation, namely, that between a tariff and the terms of trade.

Let us assume that an economy produces two commodities and exports one in exchange for the other. The offer curve of the rest of the world is assumed given and invariant. Under such conditions it is possible to ascertain the impact of a tariff on the terms of trade, once the effect of the tariff on the offer curve of the country imposing the restriction is known. The traditional approach to the problem is extremely simple. We shall discuss it briefly at first. Later in this section we shall relax some of the assumptions that the traditional approach involves and show a number of more general cases.

Consider Figure 16.1.1. A free-trade offer curve OA of the community, as explained and derived in Chapters 13 and 14, is plotted in an $x_1 - x_2$ plane. Here x_1 is the commodity that the country in question is offering, and x_2 is the product it is demanding in the world market. One way of deriving an offer curve reflecting both the free-trade conditions of the private sector and, say, a 25 per cent ad valorem tariff is to measure to the left of OA one fifth of the horizontal distance between the vertical axis (OX_2) and OA. A dotted line OA' represents such a construction. Were the equilibrium *world* terms of trade indicated by the slope of Ot, the country

275

imposing the tariff would import Oa of commodity x_2 in exchange for Ob of x_1. Domestic producers, however, would be paying Ob' of x_1, while the government would receive as customs revenue bb' of the same commodity. The domestic, or what we may call "internal," exchange ratio is now given by the slope of Oc.

Now it should be observed that the position of the offer curve OA' depends not only on the rate of duty but also on the choice of

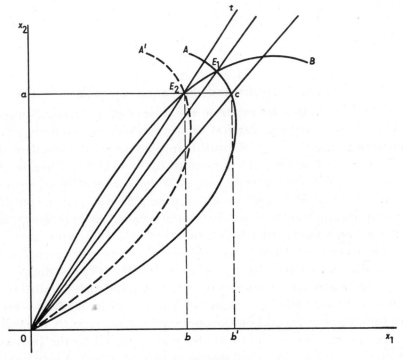

FIGURE 16.1.1

numéraire in which the government chooses to be paid. In our case it is commodity x_1. If the government required payment in terms of the other commodity, the offer curve expressing imposition of a tariff would be different. In effect, it could be constructed, for a 25 per cent duty, by measuring vertically one fourth of the distance between the horizontal axis (x_1) and any point on OA and adding this amount of commodity x_2 on top of the quantity of that commodity effectively demanded by the private sector. Such an offer curve (not drawn in the diagram) would then intersect the original free-trade offer curve at some point where there is less than unit elasticity of demand for x_2.

The effect of a tariff on the terms of trade is now easily found. Of course, if the foreign offer curve is infinitely elastic (i.e., a straight line through the origin), the terms of trade cannot be affected by a tariff imposed by the country exporting x_1. In all other cases, such as that illustrated by the foreign offer curve OB, the impact of a tariff on the terms of trade will depend on the position of the offer curve OA'. If it is to the left of the free-trade offer curve, the terms of trade of the country imposing the tariff will improve; if it is to the right, as it may be if the tariff is levied in terms of the import commodity and the elasticity of demand of the free-trade offer curve at the pretariff equilibrium is less than unity, the terms of trade will deteriorate. Clearly, the latter situation is less likely to occur.

In all our discussion so far, we have made an implicit assumption about the use of tariff revenue by the government; namely, the government is assumed to consume its revenue in one way or another. And it has to consume it in kind. If it were to trade the tariff proceeds in either the domestic or the foreign market or if it distributed the revenues to the private sector, the solution would generally be altered. The case where revenue is redistributed has a good deal of relevance in the discussion of the welfare impact of tariffs. We shall examine it in greater detail in the following section and use the results in Section 7 of this chapter.

The assumption that the government would levy its import duty in terms of only one commodity and either consume it entirely or store it is extremely unrealistic. Rather, it will trade such a commodity in the market in order to attain a more desirable distribution of its real resources. Alternatively, it might impose the duty directly payable in terms of both commodities and, by doing so, reach the desired pattern of its own consumption. It is possible to derive an offer curve of a country imposing a tariff, once the preferences of the government are defined. Such a set of preferences might, for example, be derived from the preferences of government employees or might be assumed as given through a decision of the head of the government.

Suppose that the government levies a 25 per cent import duty in terms of one commodity but is now permitted to trade that commodity in the international market, i.e., at world prices, in such a way as to maximize its own satisfaction. In other words, the government now levies a given per cent duty in money terms and spends this money in the world market by purchasing both commodities.

In Figure 16.1.2 we find two offer curves, OA and OA'', defined and constructed as in our preceding analysis. OA'' is the offer curve of the country imposing a given ad valorem tariff in terms of the export commodity. Consider a situation wherein the domestic exchange ratio is given by the slope of OC and the government levies a duty $E'c$, where E' indicates the equilibrium offer of the country with world prices given by OE' and a duty $E'c$ consumed or stored

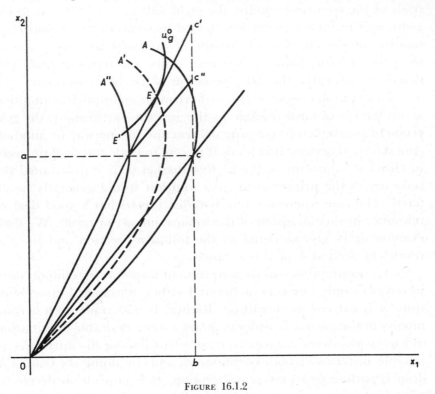

FIGURE 16.1.2

by the government. The fact that the government is permitted to trade its proceeds in the foreign market is now to be translated by saying that it is permitted to choose any point along $E'c'$. The slope of this hypotenuse is equal to the slope of Oc', i.e., the international terms of trade. The government will now maximize its satisfaction by choosing point E, where relative world prices are equal to the marginal rate of substitution of the two commodities, as given by the preferences of the government. Point E is a point on the offer curve of a country imposing an ad valorem tariff of $(E'c/aE') \cdot 100$ per cent whose government spends its tax receipts optimally in the world market. Note that exactly the same result would have been obtained if we had assumed that initially the government received its tariff revenue in terms of commodity x_2. Because Obc' and $E'cc'$ are similar triangles, the money value of cc' must be exactly the same as that of $E'c$, and the per cent rate of ad valorem duty $(E'c/aE') \cdot 100$ must also be equal to $(cc'/bc) \cdot 100$. Thus the government is in a position to attain the same point E through competitive trading in the world market, whether it initially levies its duty in terms of the export or the import commodity. A locus of all points such as E, constructed in precisely the same way, for all possible values of domestic relative prices, will yield the offer curve with tariff and optimum spending by the government. In the diagram such a locus is represented by the dotted line OA'.

While it is important to keep in mind the effect of such government policy on the position of the offer curve, the general conclusions as to the impact of a tariff on the terms of trade remain very much the same. Only in extreme cases where the government has a strong preference for the import commodity and where the elasticity of demand for imports is less than unity could the terms of trade deteriorate as the result of a tariff. Domestic prices, on the other hand, will generally turn against the export commodity. However, they might turn in its favor, if the foreign offer curve was very inelastic. The reader will easily be able to verify this proposition.

An alternative assumption, namely, that the government maximized its satisfaction by trading its tariff revenue in the domestic market, may be made about the purchasing policy of the government. It will be observed that in this case the same result must be reached as if the government were trading directly in the world market. Domestic prices are now given by the slope of Oc, and the government may choose any point along $E'c''$. But, because the domestic price ratio is assumed to be fixed, all additional supplies of x_2 must come from abroad, thus giving the government additional tariff revenue, measured by the horizontal distance between $E'c''$ and $E'c'$. Consequently, even if the government sells commodity x_1 in the domestic market, it will be receiving in exchange for it the domestic price, indicated by the slope of $E'c''$, plus the ad valorem rate of tariff. Thus the choices open to it again are reflected by the budget line $E'c'$, and point E, as before, is a point on the offer curve of the exporter of x_1.

One important remark should be made before concluding this

section. Our discussion so far has dealt with an import duty. However, as the barter character of exchange considered here suggests, all our conclusions pertain also to an equivalent ad valorem export tax, provided that the spending of the government is independent of one form of tax or the other. This hardly requires an elaborate explanation. Let us only observe that the tariff revenue measured by the segment $E'c$ in Figure 16.1.2 may be thought of either as an import duty of a given ad valorem rate, paid by importers on bc of the import product, or as an ad valorem export tax of the same rate paid by the exporters from exports of aE' of the export commodity. A similar statement can be made for an export or import duty levied in terms of the import commodity. In our diagram, the point E and the entire locus OA' will be obtained, irrespective of whether a given ad valorem duty is levied on exports or imports, provided that the preferences of the government are the same in both situations.

16.2 Tariffs and Distribution of Tariff Revenue

In the preceding section we assumed that the government used up in one way or another its tariff proceeds. When we study the effect of a new policy—namely, a tariff—on the general equilibrium variables, it seems more plausible to assume that certain other government policies are already established; e.g., that it has a given budget financed by other means. Consequently, it appears more realistic that the government either reduce its taxes by the corresponding amount, once the tariff is imposed, or, what comes to the same thing, that it redistribute among the private consumers the revenue it has earned from a customs duty.

The problem now becomes considerably more complicated, because the distribution of proceeds along consumers will generally affect the income- and price-consumption lines of different consumers and consequently also the free-trade offer curve of the whole economy. Thus the problem is now twofold. We have to derive not only the offer curve with tariff—as in the preceding section—from a free-trade offer curve but also the free-trade offer curve itself, corresponding to a given transfer of proceeds from the government to the consumers.

Professor Meade's geometrical approach is extremely valuable in tackling this problem. The reader may find it useful to return at this stage of our discussion to Chapter 14, where this analysis is studied. Let us examine the concrete problem where the government imposes a given ad valorem import duty payable in terms of the export commodity (x_1), of, say, $k \cdot 100$ per cent. At first, let us assume that the community has a single set of social indifference curves, everybody's income being always the same, with or without transfer, and everybody having the same preferences. In Chapter 14 we have shown that a community will have a single offer curve for any given set of consumers' preferences, given the production possibility locus and a *fixed* transfer of one or both commodities. We may simply

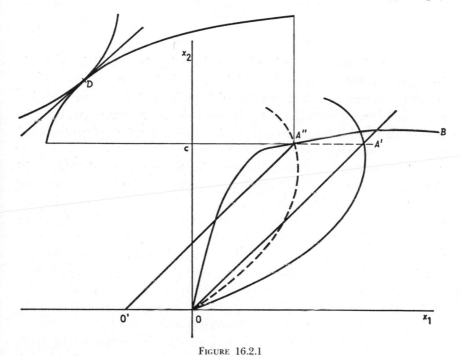

FIGURE 16.2.1

recall that such an offer curve may be derived in the usual way from preferences and a given production possibility function, if the latter is augmented (or diminished) by the amount of transfer.

In Figure 16.2.1 we show the diagram used in constructing such an offer curve. Point A'' is the position of the origin of the production block of the tariff-imposing country that would be attained if the private sector were permitted to trade and produce freely, while being paid a subsidy $O'O$, or $A''A'$. Here A' is a point on the free-trade offer curve of an economy operating under such conditions. Note that the slope of the terms-of-trade line OA' is equal to the marginal rate of substitution and the marginal rate of transformation in the x_1-exporting country, i.e., to the slope of common tangency at D.

Were the government to levy an import duty of exactly $A''A'$, while the domestic price ratio was exactly that given by OA', and a subsidy of $A''A'$ were given by the government to the private sector, point A'' would be a point on the offer curve of the economy imposing a tariff and disbursing its revenue to the private sector. The ad valorem rate of such duty is given again as

$$k = \frac{A''A'}{cA''} \tag{2.1}$$

For a given rate of ad valorem duty k_0, there will be a single infinity of points such as A'' and a single infinity of points such as A', determining the offer curves with tariff and the corresponding relation between internal supplies and demands, respectively. The reader may find it interesting to find one of a number of geometrical ways of constructing such loci.

A very important question remains to be answered: How will the general equilibrium solution be affected by this process of simultaneous taxation and proceeds distribution? Let us compare the outcomes thus obtained with the free-trade situation. We may imagine a third offer curve, say OA, expressing the free-trade supply conditions of the economy, i.e., conditions in which neither a subsidy is paid nor a tariff levied. A useful point of departure is to realize that such an offer curve would be perfectly identical with OA', if the income elasticity of product x_2 were zero. In this case the income-consumption lines of the economy, corresponding to different levels of transfer of x_1, would be straight lines, parallel to the horizontal axis. All offer relations, such as OA', would now be independent of the amount of transfer, and consequently all would be represented by a single contour. Also the free-trade offer curve would assume the same position, it being only a special case corresponding to zero transfer.

From this limiting case it follows that if, in a given region, commodity x_2 is an inferior good, i.e., its consumption declines with increasing income and unchanged prices, the hypothetical free-trade offer curve OA will lie to the right of OA' in the diagram. The domestic exchange ratio in this case will be more favorable to the export commodity under transfer than it would have been in the simple case, without transfer of proceeds to the private sector.

The normal case is one in which the income elasticity of product x_2 is positive. Here the free-trade offer curve would be to the left of OA'. The domestic price ratio will be less favorable to the export commodity under transfer than if an equal tariff without transfer were imposed in terms of commodity x_1. The terms of trade of the country imposing the tariff also will be less advantageous with transfer than they would have been without.

The important question is whether the terms of trade could now ever deteriorate as a result of a tariff (with transfer of proceeds) from the situation of free trade determined by OA. The answer may be given by showing that not even the same terms of trade could be obtained under assumed conditions. If the terms of trade under free trade and under tariff with transfer were to be equal, a free-trade offer curve would have to pass through A'' in the diagram. But this is impossible because we know that the marginal rate of substitution corresponding to A'' is given by the slope of $O'A''$, and no other marginal rate of substitution can correspond to that point if the community has a single nonintersecting trade indifference map, corresponding to zero transfer.

On the other hand, it is immediately apparent, and hardly requires proof, that if the preferences of different individuals are different and/or different sums of money are distributed to different individuals, this situation may arise. In this case the social trade indifference curves with and without redistribution may intersect. Actually, an infinity of marginal rates of substitution will now correspond to point A'', each determined by the distribution of income effected by the transfer of tariff proceeds. For greater detail on this point we refer the reader to Section 2 of Chapter 13. The conclusion is that if the government levies an import duty and distributes tariff proceeds equally or unequally to individuals who do not have identical and homogeneous tastes, the terms of trade of the country may or may not improve as a result of the tariff. It should be emphasized, however, that the more likely outcome still is that the terms of trade will improve, provided that the offer curve of the rest of the world is not infinitely elastic.

But even if the terms of trade of the tariff-imposing country were to worsen, this would have no special bearing on the gains from trade of that country. Rather, it is a result of some strong redistributive effect within the economy. We shall re-examine this problem more thoroughly in Section 8 of this chapter.

Before concluding this section, it should be pointed out that the construction of complete offer schedules such as OA' and OA'' in our diagram is by no means necessary in analyzing a particular case of foreign-trade equilibrium. Suppose that an offer curve of the rest of the world, such as OB, passes through A'' in Figure 16.2.1. To the equilibrium at this point on OB there uniquely corresponds a level of ad valorem tariff levied in terms of x_1 by the country exporting x_1. This tariff rate k is determined as in relation 2.1. In a similar way, to any point on OB we may make correspond a number k expressing the tariff rate that would yield that point as equilibrium, given the conditions of supply and demand of the country exporting x_1. To find the equilibrium solution of international trade corresponding to any given rate of tariff k_0, we now only have to find that rate (if any) on OB. The tariff rate, together with the position of that particular point, will immediately determine the internal exchange ratio and the point of domestic supply and demand such as A' in the diagram. It may easily be proved under the assumptions made here that the rates of tariff k generating equilibria along OB are a uniformly decreasing function of the arc of OB, measured from O.

16.3 Partial Analysis of Trade Restrictions

Often we are not so much interested in the effect of tariffs or quotas on the conditions of the economy as a whole as in the effect of a particular tariff on a given market. The examination of this case by means of the partial supply and demand relations is straight forward, and often quite illuminating. A number of different effects of a tariff on a particular market may now be distinguished; such effects are illustrated in Figure 16.3.1.

Here we find a market demand curve D for commodity x and a supply relation, derived by adding the domestic and foreign supply functions S_1 and S_2. Imposition of an ad valorem tariff of $t \cdot 100$ per cent, where t is defined as E_1E_2/cE_2, will raise the domestic price by dP_1 and lower the world or foreign prices by dP_2. In the initial equilibrium, P_1 and P_2, the domestic and foreign price, respectively, are equal and indicated by the equilibrium solution of the market without tariff, at E_3. Let us designate this initial price level by $P\ (= P_1 = P_2)$. We may now survey briefly the different effects of tariff.

    i) The first is the effect on the domestic price of commodity x,

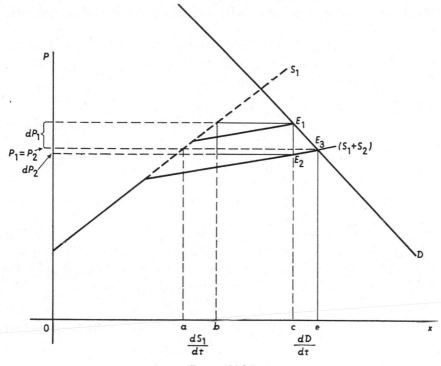

FIGURE 16.3.1

i.e., dP_1. It will depend on the rate of tariff t, on the initial price P, on the elasticities of supply and demand, and, finally, on the quantities of the commodity imported and produced domestically in the initial equilibrium. Once these factors are known, this effect may be approximated, for a given rate of tariff t, by[1]

$$dP_1 = P \cdot t \cdot A \qquad (3.1)$$

where

$$A = \frac{-s_2 S_2}{S_1(d - s_1) + S_2(d - s_2)} \qquad (3.2)$$

where S_1 and S_2 represent the initial values, or the quantities produced domestically and imported, respectively; s_1 and s_2 are the corresponding elasticities of supply in the vicinity of the initial equilibrium, while d is the elasticity of demand. This effect is indicated in

[1] This result will easily be obtained by differentiating the equilibrium condition $D(P_1) - S(P_1) - S(P_2) = 0$ with respect to t, and observing that $P_1 = P_2(1 + t)$, with $t = 0$ in the initial equilibrium.

the diagram on the vertical axis by dP_1. Note that it will be positive, unless d is infinite.

ii) The change in the foreign price, dP_2, will be equal to the difference between the change in the domestic price dP_1 and the tariff, i.e., tP. It will be approximated as

$$dP_2 = P \cdot t(A - 1) \qquad (3.3)$$

where A is the same as in relation 3.1, defined by 3.2. Observe that A will be equal to $+1$ if the elasticity of foreign supply is infinite, and, consequently, foreign price cannot change if a tariff is imposed. On the other hand, with the elasticity of domestic supply infinite, A is zero, and the entire adjustment to the tariff takes place through a reduction in foreign prices.

iii) The effect on demand, measured by the segment ce in the diagram, may now simply be calculated from the change in domestic price dP_1, the elasticity of demand d, and the total demand D in the initial situation, before tariff was imposed. We have

$$dD = d \cdot t \cdot D \cdot A \qquad (3.4)$$

iv) Similarly, the effect on domestic supply will be found as

$$dS_1 = s_1 \cdot t \cdot S_1 \cdot A \qquad (3.5)$$

v) The impact of tariff on foreign supply, or what we may call the "import effect" of the tariff, is

$$dS_2 = s_2 \cdot t \cdot S_2(A - 1) \qquad (3.6)$$

This change is equal to minus the algebraic sum of the demand and domestic supply effects, i.e.,

$$dS_2 = dD - dS_1 \qquad (3.7)$$

In terms of the diagram, this simply indicates that imports are reduced from the amount measured by the segment ae to that measured by bc.

vi) Next, imposition of a tariff will have an effect on government revenue. This is measured graphically by the rectangle with base bc and height E_2E_1. Such a change in tax revenue dR may now be expressed as

$$dR = t \cdot (P - dP_2)(S_2 - dS_2) \qquad (3.8)$$

where P is the initial foreign (and domestic) price and dP_2 and dS_2 are given by relations 3.3 and 3.7, respectively.

vii) Finally, the tariff will affect not only the level of domestic output of the industry but also its profit. Recalling that the supply curve of the industry is the sum of marginal cost curves of its individual members, we observe that the profit of the industry will be increased approximately by

$$dPr. = dP_1 \left(S_1 + \frac{1}{2} dS_1 \right) \tag{3.9}$$

Another way of looking at this magnitude is to consider it as a protective quasi-rent accruing to domestic producers. It may be referred to as the "protective effect" of a tariff. In effect, the government, by imposing a tariff, penalizes foreign producers and domestic consumers in favor of itself and of domestic producers. The exact importance of such transfers may be ascertained from the preceding nine equations, provided that the required parameters are known.

Before concluding this section, three additional facts should be pointed out. A specific, rather than an ad valorem, tariff may be analyzed in very much the same way; however, the portion of the supply curve imputable to imports will now be shifted in a parallel fashion upward. If the price changes that take place are not too important or if the foreign elasticity of supply is very high, relations 3.1 through 3.9 may again be used to approximate the different effects of a tariff. Otherwise they may easily be recalculated for the case of a specific tariff.

Second, it should be remembered that such an analysis may easily be applied without modification, if specific (or ad valorem) transportation costs enter the picture and if the foreign supply conditions reflect the condition in some other market of the same product. Finally, we should remember that the present approach may equally well be used in examining the different effects of an elimination of tariffs. Only the direction of the effects will be reversed. The reader may enjoy studying in a rigorous fashion the slightly more complicated case of tariff alteration rather than imposition or elimination.

16.4 Tariffs, Quantitative Restrictions, and Exchange Controls

For one reason or another, the government may desire to control directly the quantities of different commodities imported into the country. It may do so in at least two ways.

i) It may decree that only a given quantity of a product may be imported within a given period of time and issue import licenses, or arrest in time all imports that would exceed the stipulated quota.

ii) It may provide the importers with only a limited amount of foreign currency to be used in purchasing the particular commodity in question. Of course, in the latter case the government must have at its disposition sufficient tools of control to insure that other sources of foreign currency would not be used.

Because the technique through which such direct restriction is achieved does not have to concern us here, we may examine the two situations as a single case. We may consider again Figure 16.3.1. Suppose that at a given rate of exchange the equilibrium level of imports is indicated by the segment ae and the market equilibrium is established at E_3. A quota or restriction reducing physical imports to the amount indicated by bc will necessarily raise domestic price to a competitive level indicated by E_1. If the government hands out the import licenses free of charge and there is no monopolistic collusion on the part of foreign suppliers, the entire revenue that under tariff accrued to the government will now be acquired by the importers. All the other effects of the quota will be exactly the same as those of a tariff, inducing the market to move to point E_1.

Were the government to auction off the import licenses through a process of competitive bidding, all the economic effects of the quota would be indistinguishable from those of a tariff. In particular, the quota revenue of the government would be exactly the same as the tariff revenue. If, on the other hand, the exporters could collude and the importers could not, the revenue defined by relation 3.8 would go to the exporters, and neither the government nor the importers would make any extra gain. Finally, if both the exporters and the importers had a monopolistic control of their respective sides of the market, the situation would become one of bilateral monopoly, and no determinate solution could generally be found.

Of course, these conclusions are generally valid, whether a partial or a general equilibrium analysis is used. A quantitative restriction of imports to the amount indicated by Oa in Figure 16.1.1 will always affect the terms of trade of the country in exactly the same way as a tariff producing such an alteration of imports. As to the segment E_2c, representing the restrictive revenue (or rent), it will accrue to one commercial agent or another, depending on the conditions just explained in relation to partial equilibrium.

16.5 Tariffs and Multiple Exchange Rates

Although the motivation for multiple exchange rates may be different from that usually leading to tariff protection, multiple exchange rates and export or import duties may produce the same—or very similar—economic results. If the government of a country is able to split the foreign-exchange market into different segments, corresponding to different commodities traded, then it may effectively sell domestic or foreign currency to exporters or importers at different rates of exchange. Of course, the *conditio sine qua non* is that the central authority is able to enforce the allocation of currencies to a given product and no other.

Because, by definition, multiple exchange rates presuppose separate export and import markets for different commodities, the partial analysis appears better suited to this particular problem. A general equilibrium approach, however, is by no means impossible. We shall employ the partial approach in most of this section. As it resembles technically the approach used in Chapter 5, the reader may find it useful to return to that chapter and refresh his memory on the relationship between export and import markets, on the one hand, and the foreign-exchange market, on the other.

Consider, first, a country using a unique rate of exchange r_0 (price of foreign currency in terms of domestic currency) and consider the export market *in foreign currency* of a given commodity x. For simplicity, we assume that the foreign country does not produce that product; this assumption does not affect the generality of the results. Such a market, in terms of foreign prices P_f, is illustrated in Figure 16.5.1. While the demand curve D is assumed to be fixed in terms of foreign prices, the position of the supply function is determined, besides other factors, also by the level of the exchange rate r_0; accordingly, we have designated the supply function as $S_0(r_0)$. Under such conditions x_0 of the commodity will be exported at a foreign price P_f'', and at a domestic price $P_d = r_0 \cdot P_f$.

Suppose, now, that the government of the exporting country imposes an ad valorem export duty t, thereby moving the supply curve of exports in the foreign market to position S_1. The price in that market will rise to P_f^1, and exports will be reduced to x_1. The export duty revenue A expressed in foreign currency will equal the area of a rectangle formed by the segments Ox_1 and bE_1, i.e., $A = Ox_1 \cdot bE_1$. Duty revenue in terms of domestic currency will equal $r_0 \cdot A$.

Now the government of the exporting country could have affected the export market in precisely the same way by buying foreign currency directed toward the purchases of commodity x at a rate r_1 sufficiently low to move the supply curve in the foreign market to

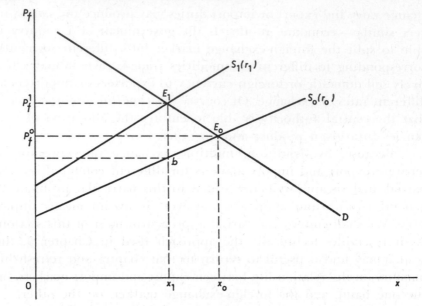

FIGURE 16.5.1

intersect D at E_1. Given the rate of duty t that has produced the equilibrium at E_1, r_1 is defined by the requirement that

$$\frac{r_0}{r_1} = 1 + t \tag{5.1}$$

Note also that in the diagram t is defined as $(x_1 E_1 / x_1 b) - 1$. If the government now proceeded to sell foreign currency (purchased at rate r_1) at the general rate r_0 in the foreign-exchange market, it would realize a profit of $x_1 \cdot P_f^1 (r_0 - r_1)$. But, using relation 5.1, it is easily found that this revenue of the government R is exactly equal to the revenue of an export duty t; i.e.,

$$R = t \cdot x_1 \cdot P_f^1 \cdot r_1 \tag{5.2}$$

Note that $P_f^1 \cdot r_1$ is the domestic export price.

The effect of a differential exchange rate may also be easily established if we consider the supply of foreign exchange generated by the export market of commodity x. Such a supply function, derived as in Chapter 5, is illustrated in Figure 16.5.2. At a unique rate of exchange r_0, Oe_0 of foreign currency would be supplied by importers of commodity x. By reducing r for this particular market to r_1, the government will acquire Oe_1 of foreign exchange. Its net revenue from the transaction, in terms of foreign currency, is measured by the

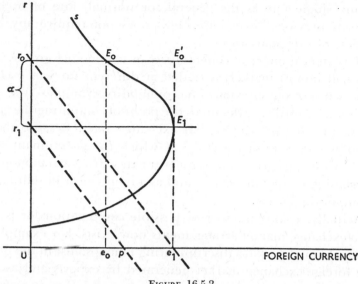

FIGURE 16.5.2

segment pe_1. The position of p will express the degree of proportionality between r_0 and r_1 and may be found, as indicated, by drawing a straight line through points r_0 and e_1 and a parallel line through point r_1 on the vertical axis. The net revenue of the government in terms of domestic currency is now measured as the area of the rectangle defined by segments pe_1 and $e_1E'_0$. As we have shown above, this is precisely the government revenue from an export duty having an identical restrictive effect.

An exactly symmetrical analysis may be applied to the import market. An ad valorem import duty of $t \cdot 100$ per cent is equivalent to a controlled increase of the price of foreign currency sold to importers by the government of the importing country by $t \cdot 100$ per cent. The proceeds of such a transaction, where foreign currency is assumed to be acquired by the government at the general rate of exchange, will again equal the revenue of a corresponding import duty.

So far we have discussed the situation wherein only one relatively unimportant commodity market is subject to a differential exchange rate, while the rest of trade is conducted under competitive conditions with a single rate of exchange. In the real world, wherever differential exchange rates are used, either a large number of exchange rates are used for a large number of different commodities, or export and import markets of only a few products represent a sufficient portion of foreign transactions that it is impossible to consider any single rate as the general, or normal, rate of exchange (r_0 in our previous discussion). This does not require any major alteration of our analysis.

If a larger number of commodities or commodity groups in the export and import markets is traded at different rates of exchange (in the sense of our previous one-commodity example), the above analysis satisfactorily applies up to the point of computing the gain of the government from differential exchange rates. Because there is now no general rate of exchange at which the government would sell or buy foreign currency, the government will act as a monopsonist in purchasing foreign currencies and as a monopolist in selling them to domestic importers.

Actually, a large number of possible combinations or possible foreign-exchange market arrangements now exists. For example, the government might act as a discriminating monopsonist in the portion of the foreign-exchange market generated by exports and as a discriminating monopolist in selling foreign currency to importers of different commodities. Thereby it would secure the maximum possible revenue (in terms of domestic currency), approximating a solution of optimum tariff. Or the government might fulfill only the first of these functions and sell foreign currency to domestic importers at a single competitive rate of exchange. Also, it might pursue a development policy by giving preferential rates for imports of investment goods and penalizing imports of luxuries or nonessential products through sales at high rates. Finally, the government might set its differential rates in buying foreign currencies in such a way as to maximize the return in terms of foreign currency or, if hard and soft currencies exist, to maximize earnings of the former. Clearly, in this case the government would attempt to shift the supply curves in all export markets, such as that illustrated in Figure 16.5.1, to the point of unit elasticity of the foreign demand function. Domestic currency would now be sold to foreign importers at high rates (here, of course, the price of domestic currency is defined as $1/r$) wherever the elasticity of demand for a particular product was low, and at lower rates where the elasticity was high.

It seems that in the real world, the use of multiple exchange rates most often is made with some of the latter alternatives just discussed in mind. A chronic scarcity of foreign exchange or of hard currencies may induce the government of some less developed countries to maximize their earnings of such currencies, provided that they are major producers of one or more products and consequently face relatively inelastic demand curves. Use of differential rates in resource allocation or as a tool of development policy will also frequently be encountered. Of course, in the latter case, rationing of foreign exchange might achieve similar results. In general, the use of discriminatory practices in a controlled foreign-exchange market may be an efficient solution—and may find partial justification—in cases where the internal fiscal and monetary controls of a country are not sufficiently well established. In the final analysis, however, these remarks should not lead us to the conclusion that multiple exchange-rate systems are efficient or desirable. Much like export and import duties, on the whole they lead to an over-all reduction in total world welfare. More will be said about the welfare implications of direct commercial restrictions later in this chapter and in Chapter 18.

16.6 Tariffs, Income Distribution, Factor Prices, Resource Allocation, and Output

In the first two sections of this chapter we examined the impact of a tariff on the terms of trade. In the first section the assumption was made that the government consumes in kind the tariff proceeds, while in the second we considered the case in which tariff proceeds are redistributed to the private sector. Changes in factor prices, income distribution, and other related variables that we propose to discuss in this section are closely related to the changes in terms of trade. We have only to realize that the relative price ratio that is relevant for the internal market of a country is the *internal* and not the *external* terms of trade. It is the former magnitude that will equal the marginal rate of transformation and the marginal rate of substitution within the country.

In the context of a simplified general equilibrium model used here, the relation between the commodity exchange ratio (i.e., the internal terms of trade), on the one hand, and factor prices, income distribution, factor allocation, and output, on the other, was shown rigorously in Section 7 of Chapter 12. Consequently, once the impact of a tariff on the domestic exchange ratio is established, the other effects can also be uniquely determined. We shall not reiterate the analysis of the relevant parts of our study at present; let us only summarize the principal conclusions and make a few important remarks leading toward a greater generality of the answers to the problem.

As we have shown, by far the most likely effect of a tariff on the domestic price of the export commodity will be negative. Only if the elasticity of reciprocal demand of the other country is very low or if an important redistribution of income between different consumers takes place, will the domestic price of the exported product improve relative to the domestic price of the imported commodity. Thus, if the internal terms of trade of the tariff-imposing country deteriorate, less of the export commodity will be produced. Productive resources will move from the production of the export product into the production of the import product, whose output will improve. If the export commodity is uniformly, say, capital-intensive with respect to the import commodity, the price of capital will decline relative to that of labor. The income share of labor will increase relative to the income share of capital. In other words, a tariff protecting a domestic labor-intensive industry will, as a general rule, benefit labor relative to capital.

The labor force will also realize an absolute gain in income, provided that all technologies are homogeneous of order 1, even in the case where the government levies an import duty without redistributing it. If the government redistributes tariff proceeds to the private sector, say to the losing factor, the real income of that factor may now increase, the loss in relative share being more than offset by the total gains from trade of the country as a whole. More will be said about this aspect of the problem later in Section 8.

16.7 Welfare Effects of Tariffs and Other Forms of Trade Restriction

The preceding section dealt with one aspect of social welfare, namely, income distribution. The purpose of the present section is to examine the global impact of a tariff on the social welfare of a country. We shall first present the traditional analysis of the problem. Later in this section and in the following one we shall consider the problem in the light of such further assumptions as income distribution within the country and redistribution of tariff proceeds.

If it is possible to assume that a country has a single and unchanging set of preferences and that the free-trade offer curve of the private sector is affected neither by a change of factor income shares

nor by redistribution of tariff proceeds to the private sector, the welfare effects of a tariff can be shown very easily. Actually, the situation
is no different from the case of an individual monopolist facing a
competitive reciprocal demand curve for his product. Suppose that
two trading economies engage in unrestricted trade in products x_1
and x_2. As shown in Figure 16.7.1, their trading position will be

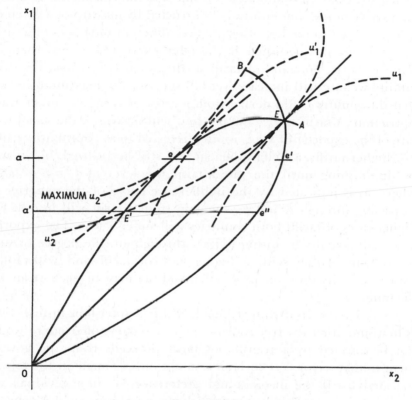

FIGURE 16.7.1

found at point E, where the market is cleared and where the terms
of trade or relative prices are indicated by the slope of OE. Because
both traders must equalize the marginal rate of substitution and the
relative price ratio at each point of the offer curve, this must also
hold for point E.

The indifference curve of the exporter of x_1 will be tangent to
the terms-of-trade line at E and also to the indifference curve of the
country exporting commodity x_2. The most efficient allocation of
consumption and production, given the factor endowments, pref-

erences, and technology of the two countries, is attained at point E. In other words, the satisfaction of one country cannot be increased without that of the other country being reduced.

However, the satisfaction of one country—say the exporter of x_2 —may be improved if it imposes a tax on its imports or exports and distributes tariff proceeds to the private sector. Such a tariff, if levied in terms of commodity x_2, can now be considered if a new offer curve of the community is constructed by measuring a given ad valorem rate t to the left of OB. Three different outcomes of a tariff may now be distinguished if the offer curve OA is less than infinitely elastic. For rates of tariff smaller than $t_0 = ee'/ae$, the community welfare will increase, yet fall short of the maximum benefit that the country could derive from a tariff or from any other trade restriction. A tariff of $t_0 \cdot 100$ per cent will maximize the social welfare of the exporter of x_2; t_0 is often referred to as "optimum tariff." For higher tariffs, a welfare benefit will still be realized, but it will be diminishing until the rate attains the level of $t_1 = E'o''/a'E'$, where, as is indicated by the indifference curve of the exporter of x_2 passing through E and E', the gain from a tariff will be nil. For higher rates of tariff, both countries will suffer a loss. The exporter of x_1 will actually be losing welfare throughout, the degree of such losses being larger with a higher rate of tariff and with lower elasticity of its own reciprocal demand, as may be seen from the diagram.

We have indicated in Section 2 of this chapter how unrealistic it is to assume that the free-trade or private sector's offer curve would not be affected by a transfer of tariff proceeds from the government to that sector. Yet such an assumption was made in the foregoing analysis. If the incomes and preferences of all individuals are identical, it is possible to consider the case wherein tariff revenue is redistributed to the private sector without assuming that the free-trade offer curve remains unchanged. This was shown in detail in Section 2 of this chapter.

At this point let us recall how a tariff rate t may be derived, producing an equilibrium at a given point of foreign offer curve OA, such as c, in Figure 16.7.2. In that diagram we find the usual production block. The slope of its common tangency with an indifference curve of country 2 (exporter of x_2) ,u_2, is the marginal rate of substitution and the marginal rate of transformation within that country. With an internal exchange ratio equal to that slope, the

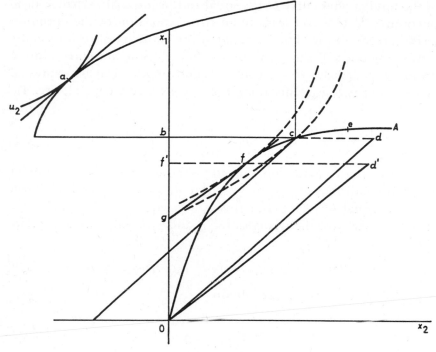

FIGURE 16.7.2

private sector will be induced under competition to trade up to point *d*, provided that it receives a subsidy equal to *cd*, in terms of its export commodity. If the tariff is exactly equal in absolute terms to that quantity (i.e., *cd*), *c* is a point on the offer curve of country 2 imposing a tariff of $cd/bc \cdot 100$ per cent ad valorem, and redistributing tariff proceeds in toto to the private sector. Of course, the usual assumption of equality of incomes within country 2 has to hold throughout.

Thus we obtain the answer to our question. Given the offer curve *OA* of country 1 and the supply and demand conditions of country 2, an equilibrium of international trading will be attained at point *c* (on *OA*) if the government of country 2 imposes an ad valorem tariff $t = cd/bc$. To any point such as *c* will correspond a given rate of tariff t_i yielding an equilibrium at that point. Point *e* corresponds to a zero tariff, i.e., to free trade. Point *f*, where a trade indifference curve of country 2 is tangent to *OA*, corresponds to the optimum tariff t_0.

It will be observed that at the point of optimum tariff the slope of the foreign offer curve OA is equal to the internal exchange ratio in country 2. This fact leads to an easy expression of the optimum tariff in terms of the absolute value of the elasticity of reciprocal demand of country 1, d_1. Let us recall that $|d_1|$, the absolute value of elasticity of demand of the country exporting x_1, can be expressed as a ratio of two segments along the x_1 axis (see Chap. 14, Sec. 4), i.e.,

$$|d_1| = \frac{Of'}{Og} \qquad (7.1)$$

Using our construction, the offer of x_2 and demand for x_1 under assumed conditions are given by point d', and the optimum tariff rate t_0 is equal to $fd'/f'f$. But this is also equal to Og/gf', because of the similarity of the triangles $Od'f'$ and gff'. Thus we may write

$$t_0 = \frac{Og}{gf'} = \frac{Og}{Of' - Og} = \frac{1}{(Of'/Og) - 1} \qquad (7.2)$$

And, using relation 7.1, we obtain

$$t_0 = \frac{1}{|d_1| - 1} \qquad (7.3)$$

or, what is equivalent,

$$t_0 = \frac{1}{s_1} \qquad (7.4)$$

where s_1 is the elasticity of supply of exports of country 1.

It is immediately apparent that if the absolute value of the elasticity of demand is smaller than 1 in a given region of OA, an optimum tariff cannot lead to an equilibrium within that region. Also we observe that if the elasticity of reciprocal demand of the partner country is infinite, the optimum solution is a zero tariff. This is only another way of saying that if the foreign offer curve is infinitely elastic, the country imposing a tariff cannot improve its welfare through such a policy.

The results concerning the welfare effects of a tariff will be similar to those found in the simple case where the free-trade offer curve always remains unchanged, whatever the tariff revenue redistributed to the private sector. Because the position of equilibrium on OA is moving in one direction with increasing rate of tariff imposed by the exporter of x_1, the same conclusions as before may be drawn. At first, social welfare will be increasing with higher rates of tariff up to the point of optimum tariff t_0, yielding point f on OA. Beyond that point, further tariff increases will lead to situations preferable to the free-trade solution but inferior to the optimum tariff solution. For some rate of restriction high enough, no benefit will be realized from tariff imposition, and any further raising of tariff will be detrimental to social welfare.

So far we have examined only the case wherein one country imposes a tariff while the other country's offer curve is given. The more realistic situation is where both countries try to reap gains from trade restriction. As examination of the market conditions will

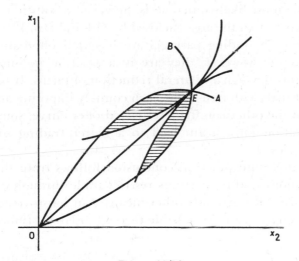

FIGURE 16.7.3

indicate, such a mutual retaliation will usually be detrimental to both countries. In Figure 16.7.3 we show again a free-trade solution at point F determined by two free-trade offer curves OA and OB. Because a restriction by country 2 can but yield trade solutions to the left of OB and restriction by country 1 solutions to the right of OA, the region of retaliatory action is restricted to the inner region defined by OA and OB, between O and E. As the two trade indifference curves drawn through E indicate, both countries can never gain from a tariff, and one country will gain while the other will lose only if the new equilibrium falls within one of the two shaded areas. Clearly, this is quite unlikely to happen, and the likelihood diminishes, the higher the elasticities of reciprocal demand. Whenever it is possible to assert that retaliatory tariffs leave international relative prices approximately unchanged, i.e., whenever the new equilibrium lies somewhere near *OE,* we may be almost sure that the reciprocal tariff has reduced social welfare in both countries.

If both countries always proceed to improve their welfare position whenever this is possible, given a restricted offer curve of the trading partner, an equilibrium can be reached only at a point where both traders have reached the optimum tariff consistent with the partner's restricted offer curve. Such a point must always exist within the area defined by *OA* and *OB.* As the reader may verify through a simple construction, it may fall within the shaded areas in Figure 16.7.3, or down to the origin, thus eliminating all international exchange. The most likely outcome is, however, a solution within the unshaded portion of the area enclosed by *OA* and *OB.* Whenever this is the case, both trading partners are less well off than they were with free trade; however, they are in a position to improve their respective lots through a bilateral reduction of tariffs. If one country is better off than with free trade, each country imposing an optimum tariff, given the other country's restricted offer curve, some bilateral tariff relaxation must again lead to a better trading solution for both countries.

One important practical conclusion follows from this analysis. Whenever both trading partners restrict trade through a tariff (or, for that matter, through any other means), an improvement in each country's welfare is always possible through bilateral trade liberalization.

16.8 Tariffs, Optimum Tariff, Individual Welfare, and Redistribution

We have pointed out earlier how unrealistic it is to assume incomes of all individuals equal when the impact of a tariff on either the terms of trade or social welfare is considered. As internal and external prices change with a changing rate of tariff, the incomes of some individuals will generally be reduced, while the incomes of others will increase. Both when we consider a general equilibrium situation wherein each individual is a producer and when different individuals are suppliers of different productive factors, incomes will not change *pari passu.* Consequently, save in the special cases pointed out in Chapters 13 and 15, it is not permissible to use a single social indifference map in analyzing the terms-of-trade and welfare effects of tariffs.

There is no other way to solve this difficulty but to consider the different producers or different owners of productive factors separately. To reduce the problem to manageable dimensions, let us consider that the economy is composed of only two individuals or two groups of individuals; within each group income and preferences always remain equal for all individuals. No special assumption has to be made about the relation of preferences of the two individuals or groups. Henceforth we may refer to one group or individual as A and to the other as B.

A and B may either be suppliers of capital and labor, respectively, or producers of commodities x_1 and x_2. Fixed total supplies of factors of production are assumed for the economy as a whole. Productive factors are perfectly free to move from one employment to the other if A and B are considered as suppliers of different productive factors. If A and B represent two different producers, each producer is assumed to have his own productive resources that he uses in producing x_1 and x_2 but does not rent out to the other individual. Of course, as long as factor prices are equalized through trade, the solution will be exactly the same, whether or not mobility of capital and labor between A and B is permitted.

Let us now consider a situation wherein no international trade takes place but A and B are permitted to supply factors of production or produce the two commodities under competitive conditions and trade with each other. Each individual consumes optimally, given his real income. Those conditions generally will yield an equilibrium point of production and consumption for the economy and for A and B separately. Let us designate the total outputs of the two products by x_1^0 and x_2^0. Corresponding to this solution of a general equilibrium for a closed economy, there will be two ordinal utility indexes u_A^0 and u_B^0, expressing the level of satisfaction of each individual. These levels of satisfaction define point a in a $u_A - u_B$ plane, shown in Figure 16.8.1.[2]

If different transfers are now effected between A and B, the factor endowments of the two individuals remaining unchanged, a whole locus of efficient points such as a can be derived, one for each given distribution of income. With Professor Samuelson, we may refer to such a locus as the "utility possibility curve" (U_p), corresponding to the factor endowments of the economy.

If the community now is permitted to trade internationally,

---

[2] We have used this representation and explained it in greater detail in Chapter 15.

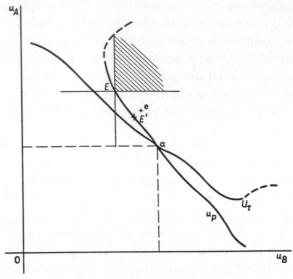

FIGURE 16.8.1

any given set of world prices will lead to a new set of levels of satisfaction of *A* and *B;* the locus of all such points may be called a "trade utility possibility curve" and is illustrated by U_t in the diagram. It passes through point *a* and is tangential there to $U_p;$ at all other points it shows preferable combinations of individual utility. This is because, in the situation of autarky, total output and consumption of the two products were fixed, while, with trade, all prices and output are permitted to adjust to conditions in the world market. As long as there is trade between *A* and *B* or as long as the community does not specialize in producing only one product, the locus (U_t) will be downward-sloping, because changing world terms of trade will make one individual lose and the other gain. As soon as one of the two conditions is not fulfilled, both individuals will gain from foreign trade, and U_t will have a positive slope. This is indicated by the dotted segments of the locus.

Now suppose that a free-trade equilibrium of international exchange is such as to produce a distribution of individual satisfactions indicated by point *E* on U_t. If the government imposes a tariff, without redistributing the proceeds to the private sector, this will generally produce a movement along U_t from *E* in the direction of *a*. Assume that the economy under such conditions settles at an equilibrium yielding a distribution of satisfaction indicated by *E'*. We know from Chapter 15 that such a solution is inferior to *E,* in the sense that no redistribution of income between A and B, combined with trading at the terms of trade leading to E, could ever make both individuals as well off as they were at point E.

The next step is to assume that the government distributes the tariff revenue to the private sector. It may do so in such a way as to compensate the individual whose satisfaction has declined as a result of the tariff; in other words, in our particular case it gives all the revenue to individual A. The economy now being permitted to adjust optimally to such a transfer, a new point in the $u_A - u_B$ plane, such as e, will be attained. It must be to the right of and above U_t and is likely to show a greater benefit for the individual who has received compensation.[3]

We now come to the key question. Is it possible to redistribute income within the community of A and B in such a way as to move the solution point into the shaded area northeast of E? In other words, is it possible to redistribute income in such a way as to improve the lot of both individuals, as compared with the free-trade solution at E?

Before we are able to try to give an answer, some assumptions have to be made about the conditions of the transfer. At least two alternatives can be found: (i) the government freezes the consumable resources available to the economy at the levels consistent with point e, or (ii) the government lets both individuals trade in the domestic and foreign market, levying and redistributing tariff on all imports.

As the second assumption is the more realistic of the two, let us proceed with our discussion with that assumption. First of all, it should be perfectly clear that there is always a tariff that will, after redistribution, lead to a position inferior for both individuals to the free-trade solution at point E in Figure 16.8.1. A prohibitive tariff is an extreme case leading to such conditions: it would bring the community of two individuals to the autarky solution at a. As a

---

[3] Observe that the latter situation is not necessary. An increment of resources on the part of one individual does not necessarily lead to a situation preferred by that individual, if trade is permitted. The terms-of-trade effect may be such that an inferior solution is reached. This case is referred to in the literature of international trade as "immiserizing" growth, and was discussed in Section 8, Chapter 14. However, even in such an extreme situation, point e must be above U_t. Actually, the terms-of-trade effect that has worsened the position of A will now improve the position of B to such an extent that he will be better off than he would have been on U_t, given the satisfaction of A that has resulted from transfer. The reader may enjoy using the analysis of Chapter 15, Section 8, in establishing this point rigorously.

prohibitive tariff does not yield any revenue, the solution would remain at *a,* prior to a transfer from individual *B* to individual *A.* Once such a transfer was effected, the solution point would move northwest from *a* along u_p. A solution within the shaded area northeast of *E* could never be attained.

It follows that the question we should ask is whether there is *some* rate of tariff that must always lead to a preferable situation for both individuals, given (1) redistribution of all tariff proceeds, (2) reallocation of resources among individuals, and (3) competitive trading in all markets. Let us examine, first, the limiting situation where the foreign offer curve is infinitely elastic. If this is the case, the world terms of trade cannot be affected, nor can the internal terms of trade after the tariff is imposed. Suppose that the tariff makes the community's distribution of utility move from *E* to *E'*. A subsequent transfer of tariff revenue to individual *A* yields point *e.* Through a geometrical proof similar to those used in Chapter 15, it may be shown that a transfer of purchasing power from individual *B* to individual *A,* with competitive trading and redistribution of the entire tariff revenue, can never improve the lot of both individuals, compared with the free-trade situation. In other words, under the assumed conditions, redistribution can never lead to a solution within the shaded area in Figure 16.8.1. Any redistributive path corresponding to any point such as *e* must intersect U_t to the right and below point *E* in Figure 16.8.1 and pass southwest of that point.

When the foreign offer curve is less than infinitely elastic, the situation becomes a good deal more complicated. It should be discussed at greater length, not only on its own merits, but also because it brings up the question of optimum tariff in the case of a larger number of individuals with different sets of preferences. To make the problem more manageable, let us assume that *A* and *B* no longer have an open choice of production possibilities but rather that each individual's output is fixed. Both individuals may produce both products. Consequently, the output of the tariff-imposing country is also fixed. This assumption does not diminish the generality of our results. The reader may enjoy proving for himself the propositions put forth below in the case where both individuals are permitted to choose a point of production on a concave production possibility curve.

In Figure 16.8.2 the production point of the economy is indicated by point O_B. Measuring the outputs of individual *A* from O_A

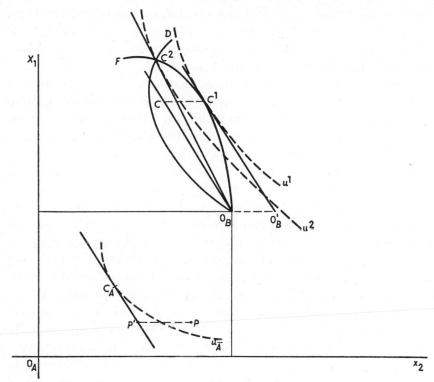

FIGURE 16.8.2

and that of B from O_B (in opposite directions), we assume that the original distribution of outputs among the two individuals is given by point P. Let us further consider a fixed level of satisfaction on the part of A, corresponding to the indifference contour marked $u_{\overline{A}}$ in the diagram. Now, for any given level of relative prices, it is possible to find an appropriate transfer of purchasing power from A to B or from B to A that will make the individual A consume at a point on $u_{\overline{A}}$. For example, if the relative prices of x_1 and x_2 were those indicated by the slope of $C_A P'$ and trade were permitted at such prices, the consumption of A at C_A could be induced through a transfer of $P'P$ of product x_2 from individual A to individual B.

As we have shown in Section 2 of Chapter 13, for a given level of satisfaction of A corresponding to $u_{\overline{A}}$, it is possible to derive from the indifference map of individual B a non-intersecting indifference map of the two individuals combined. Two contours of such a map, u^1 and u^2, were drawn in the diagram. Here $O_B D$ is the offer curve of the country imposing a tariff, based on the assumption that the government of that country always distributes purchasing power in such a way as to keep individual A at $u_{\bar{A}}$. On the other hand, $O_B F$ is the foreign offer curve. The free-trade equilibrium, under the assumed conditions, will be attained at C^2.

Suppose now that the government wants to impose an optimum tariff, corresponding to the constant level of satisfaction of individual A, that is, $u_{\bar{A}}$. It may do so by levying a customs duty amounting to CC^1 in terms of the export commodity x_2, thereby attaining an international trading point at C^1, with international terms of trade given by the slope of a line passing through that point and O_B. If the customs revenue is now transferred to individual B and any necessary interpersonal transfers are made between the two individuals to keep A at $u_{\bar{A}}$, the community of A and B will be able to trade up to the point C^1 at the domestic exchange ratio given by the slope of O_BC or O'_BC^1. The satisfaction of B has necessarily improved as compared with the initial free-trade situation, while, by definition, that of individual A has remained unchanged.

It should now be noticed that, for any other given level of satisfaction of A (such as $u_{\bar{A}}$), there will generally be another "optimum" social indifference curve (such as u^1) and corresponding to it another degree of optimum tariff. For any level of satisfaction of individual A, this important conclusion holds: The other individual will be made better off through an optimum tariff and redistribution of tariff revenue than he was under conditions of free trade. Moreover, this same conclusion holds for any positive rate of tariff smaller than the optimum tariff and for some range of tariffs exceeding the optimum.

We may now summarize these conclusions using the utility possibility curves, as we did earlier in this section. For a given foreign offer curve, there will be a utility possibility curve in an ordinal utility plane of u_A and u_B, corresponding to competitive free trading and different levels of income of individuals A and B. Such a curve is illustrated in Figure 16.8.3 by U_p. Corresponding to the optimum tariff, a less than infinitely elastic foreign offer curve, and all conceivable allocations of income between A and B, there will be another utility possibility curve, U_0, everywhere to the right and above U_p.

Now to answer our original question, namely, whether there is some degree of tariff and some redistribution of purchasing power that may make both individuals better off than with free trade, we

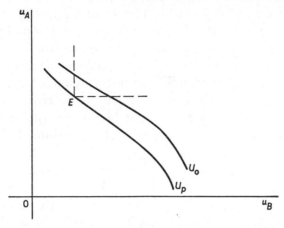

FIGURE 16.8.3

have only to realize that point E on U_t in Figure 16.8.1, corresponding to free trade, is also on a utility possibility curve such as U_p in Figure 16.8.3. Consequently, there must be some tariff—actually a whole range of tariffs—that with redistribution of income will improve the lot of both individuals. In the limiting situation of a perfectly elastic foreign offer curve, the optimum tariff is a zero tariff, and U_0 will coincide with U_p in Figure 16.8.3.

16.9 Tariffs, the Balance of Payments, and National Income

Throughout this chapter we have either used a general equilibrium approach based on the assumption of full employment or discussed tariffs in the setting of partial analysis, where no explicit mention is made of the relation between factor employment and the tariff. Such assumptions often do not describe most ideally the conditions prevailing in the real world. For one reason or another employment of productive resources may not be full at all times, and the balance of payments may not always adjust immediately, or at all, to changing economic conditions.

Very often tariffs were used by different countries as a tool of affecting either the balance of payments or national income or both. It is the purpose of this section to study in theory the relation between an import tariff, level of income in an under fully employed economy, and the balance of payments.

Under the assumed conditions, three important effects of a tariff may be distinguished. On the one hand, a tariff will raise the price and thereby reduce the volume of imports; this will affect employment in the rest of the world. The second effect is that domestic products are now relatively less expensive and consequently some domestic output will substitute for imports. Finally, if we assume that the government's budget is balanced, tariff revenue will constitute an additional income of the government; if the budget is to remain in balance, such a revenue has to be redistributed to the private sector. This will most often take the form of reduction in other taxes. Whatever the form of redistribution, the effective demand of the tariff-imposing economy will increase, and this will further affect the position of a new equilibrium.

An income and foreign-trade equilibrium of two countries, both operating at less than full employment, may easily be described, and the different effects of a tariff may be studied. Let us first show the equilibrium conditions. To make our analysis resemble the discussions of foreign-trade equilibria in Chapters 7 and 8, let us define the rate of tariff t as

$$t = r - 1 \tag{9.1}$$

where r is the price of imports including a tariff, while the c.i.f. price, without tariff, is equal to 1. The physical units of measurement of real income are defined in such a way as to make all domestic and export prices equal to 1. The rate of exchange also is equal to unity and is invariant. Of course, in the vicinity of the equilibrium, all supply elasticities are infinite. Consequently, a price may be different from 1 only because a tariff is imposed on a particular aggregate of commodities.

The propensity to consume and invest domestic products by country 1 (the country imposing a tariff), m_{11}, may now be expressed as

$$m_{11} = m_{11}(Y_1, r) \tag{9.2}$$

where Y_1 is real income of country 1, as defined and explained in Chapter 8. In effect, the propensity to spend on domestic products will depend on the real income of country 1 and on r, i.e., the price of imports. With a higher r, i.e., a higher tariff, it is very likely that expenditure on domestic products will increase, while that on imports wll be reduced.

The propensity to import by country 1, for reasons just indicated, will also depend on r; moreover, it is expected that imports will also vary with real income of the importing country. Thus we have

$$m_{21} = m_{21}(Y_1, r) \tag{9.3}$$

Note that, as in our previous discussions, the first subscript refers to the country of origin, where income is generated, while the second refers to the country of destination, on whose income the propensity depends.

The propensity to import and to consume domestic produce for country 2 may be written as functions of the real income of that country only, because domestic prices and import prices are invariant, equal to unity. Consequently,

$$m_{22} = m_{22}(Y_2) \tag{9.4}$$

and

$$m_{12} = m_{12}(Y_2) \tag{9.5}$$

These four propensities express the relation between real income (or employment), on the one hand, and the level of spending, on the other, for a given level of tariff imposed by country 1, provided that the tariff revenue is not returned to the private sector of country 1. If such a redistribution takes place, relations 9.2 and 9.3 have to be altered.

The tariff revenue A may be expressed for any given level of tariff t as

$$A = (r - 1) \cdot m_{21} \tag{9.6}$$

If such a revenue is returned to the private sector of country 1 in full, the propensity both to import and to consume domestic products of country 1 will increase. In the former case we may express such an increase as $a \cdot A$, and in the latter as $b \cdot A$, remembering that

$$a + b + MPS_1 = 1 \tag{9.7}$$

This equation simply asserts that a dollar subsidy to the private sector must either be saved or be expended on imports or on domestic products. Actually, a and b may generally be assumed to equal the marginal propensity to import (MPM) and the marginal propensity to consume domestic products plus investment in domestic products ($MPC_d + MPI_d$), respectively.

The two propensities of country 1 now may be restated as

$$M_{11} = m_{11}(Y_1, r) + b \cdot (r - 1) \cdot m_{21}(Y_1, r) \tag{9.8}$$

and

$$M_{21} = m_{21}(Y_1, r) \cdot [1 + a(r - 1)] \tag{9.9}$$

Introducing relations 9.4, 9.5, 9.8, and 9.9 into the usual equilibrium income relations,

$$Y_1 = M_{11} + m_{12} \tag{9.10}$$

and

$$Y_2 = M_{21} + m_{22} \tag{9.11}$$

we are in a position to determine the equilibrium levels of income of the two countries, and find their balance of payments for any given level of tariff t. It should be observed that if t is zero, we have nothing else but the equilibrium conditions used in deriving the simple foreign-trade multiplier with foreign repercussion.

If t is considered as a variable parameter, differential analysis will show the changes in incomes and the balance of payments resulting from any prescribed change in the rate of tariff. The reader may compute for himself such results. We shall restrict ourselves here to the simpler case wherein a tariff is imposed, starting from an initial situation of free trade. Differentiating the equilibrium conditions with respect to r and remembering that the initial value of r is 1 (see relation 9.1), we obtain

$$\begin{vmatrix} (1 - m'_{11}) & -m'_{12} \\ \\ -m'_{21} & (1 - m'_{22}) \end{vmatrix} \begin{Vmatrix} \dfrac{dY_1}{dr} \\ \\ \dfrac{dY_2}{dr} \end{Vmatrix} = \begin{vmatrix} (m_{21}b + d_{11}^+ m_{11}) \\ \\ m_{21}(a + d_{21}) \end{vmatrix} \tag{9.12}$$

where d_{21} is the price elasticity of imports of country 1 and d_{11}^+ is the cross-elasticity of demand for domestic products of that same country. Primes are used to indicate partial derivatives with respect to real income, i.e., the marginal propensities.

Writing t_0 to express dr, i.e., the rate of tariff imposed, we now easily obtain the three important results, namely, the impact of tariff by country 1 on its own real income, on the income of its trading partner, and the change in the balance of payments. We have

$$dY_1 = t_0 \cdot \frac{1}{D} \cdot [(m_{21}b + m_{11}d_{11}^+)(1 - m'_{22}) + m_{21}m'_{12}(a + d_{21})] \tag{9.13}$$

$$dY_2 = t_0 \cdot \frac{1}{D} \cdot [(1 - m'_{11})m_{21}(a + d_{21}) + m'_{21}(m_{21}b + m_{11}d_{11}^+)] \tag{9.14}$$

and

$$dB_1 = m'_{12}dY_2 - m'_{21}dY_1 - t_0 \cdot (a + d_{21})m_{21} \tag{9.15}$$

where

$$D = (1 - m'_{11})(1 - m'_{22}) - m'_{12}m'_{21} \qquad (9.16)$$

To illustrate these somewhat cumbersome expressions through a numerical example, let us assume a 10 per cent tariff imposed by country 1, say, the United States, using the same numerical values of the parameters as in the examples of Chapter 8. There we considered a symmetrical world with respect to all parameters and the size of the economies, assuming for both countries

$$m_{ii} = 480 \qquad m_{ij} = 20 \qquad m'_{ii} = 0.85$$
$$m'_{ij} = 0.05 \qquad d^+_{ii} = 0.05$$

with two alternative assumptions for the value of elasticity of demand for imports, namely, (i) $d_{ij} = -1$, and (ii) $d_{ij} = -2$. Moreover, we take $a = 0.1$ and $b = 0.8$. The results are reproduced below

Change in	Y_1	Y_2	B_1
Assuming $t_0 = 0.1$ and			
$d_{ij} = -1$........+25.5	-3.5	+0.35
$d_{ij} = -2$........+20.5	-18.5	+1.85

A summary examination of the numerical results and of the algebraic solutions indicate a number of interesting results. Perhaps the most significant is that a tariff, under conditions here assumed, will not necessarily improve the balance of payments. If the elasticity of demand for imports in the tariff-imposing country is high, the balance of payments is very likely to improve. If only a little or no improvement of the balance of payments takes place, the income of the free-trade country may not be seriously affected. The income of the tariff-imposing country is likely to increase, such an increase being the greater, the higher the cross-elasticity of demand for domestic products and the lower the elasticity of demand for imports. The conditions for the incomes of the two countries to increase or to be reduced may easily be obtained if the terms in square brackets on the right-hand side of relations 9.12 and 9.13 are put equal to zero. Thereby the borderline case of no change in real income and employment is established, permitting the study of requirements to be imposed on the different parameters, leading to one type of outcome of the other.

Finally, it should be noted that, although we have assumed in our analysis that tariff revenue is redistributed to the private sector, the above results may also be used in examining the effects of tariff without such an assumption. In that case, a and b in relations 9.12, 9.13, and 9.14 have to be put equal to zero. Of course, this renders the solutions much simpler and more manageable.

It is also of interest to observe that the analysis presented here pertains—with minor modifications—to the case of quantitative restrictions. For any given level of imports, imposed by the restriction, there will be some level of tariff, say t_q, having the same impact on the volume of imports. It is possible to compute t_q from relations 9.9 and 9.13 and a condition $M_{21} = M_{21}^0$, where M_{21}^0 expresses the volume of imports permitted to enter country 1. Under competitive trading, domestic prices will be as high with a quantitative restriction as they would have been with a tariff t_q.

If the government auctions import licenses to domestic importers or to foreign exporters, government revenue will be affected in the same way as with tariff. If licenses are given to domestic importers, the parameters a and b may be altered, depending on the spending habits of those who earn the rent arising from restriction. If foreign exporters are granted the export permits, such a rent will be earned by the foreign country, a and b will be zero, and similar parameters will have to be introduced into the income equations of the foreign country.

Chapter 17

ECONOMIC POLICY AND THE EXTERNAL AND INTERNAL BALANCE

17.1 Introduction

Implementation of economic policy, or what is often referred to simply as economic policy itself, is a set of actions deliberately undertaken by the government in order to attain certain economic aims. It stems from and finds its justification in the general consensus that the course of an economy, if left entirely to itself, would not be the most desirable. Economic policy is as old a phenomenon as the state itself; it is only its aims, methods, and intensities that have varied in time. The problem of economic policy occupies an important place in the entirety of economic doctrine. Some economists would go so far as to argue that there is no other justification of economic theory except through and for the sake of economic policy.

Perhaps more than any other problem, the balance of payments and its relation to domestic economic conditions have always constituted an important preoccupation of economic policy makers. In the first three parts of our study, problems of economic policy have occupied only a secondary role. Nevertheless, the theory of international trade presented in these chapters is, with very few exceptions, designed with consideration of its applicability to problems of policy. As we have already pointed out in Chapter 1, it is primarily this quest for a workable theory of international trade that justifies the neglect of a more general theory, dealing with unlimited numbers of variables and unlimited numbers of functions and parameters. In dealing with both the adjustment mechanism and the pure theory of trade, we have adopted a simple, generally accepted analytical framework, using relations and parameters (such as elas-

313

ticities and marginal propensities) that may be ascertained empirically from observed data.

In this chapter we want to (i) state the problems and the theory of economic policy in a summary fashion, (ii) relate such a theory to the theory of international trade proper, and (iii) examine some of the most important issues of policy in relation to external and internal balance.

Whenever the government takes an active role in influencing the operation of the economy, we may speak of "economic policy." There are innumerable ways in which the central authority may pursue economic policies, just as there are innumerable purposes or aims of such policies. The spectrum between the most and least comprehensive economic policies is as wide as that between a tariff on a single commodity and complete governmental control of the type encountered at present in the centrally planned Communist economies. The more extreme types of economic control of the latter order present special problems of their own and have very little relevance for our discussion. The framework we want to adopt is that typified by the Western free economies, where most of the production, pricing, and investment decisions are taken by either private individuals or groups. Government activity is restricted primarily to direct and indirect taxation, public spending, debt management, monetary policy, and, on a somewhat different plane, moral suasion.

Of course, the aims of government policy may be as numerous as are the economic variables in the system. The important difference between the Western type of economic policy and the centrally planned type is that in the former case the government is permitted to use only a few policy tools in exercising indirect influence upon certain markets, whereas the centrally planned systems have virtually unlimited power to interfere directly through order or decree.

It is precisely the scarcity of policy tools available to the governments of free economies that causes what we may call the "problem of economic policy" and calls for a systematic exposition. It is self-evident that, with only a few tools of policy, it may be difficult to regulate a large number of markets. It is also apparent without any detailed investigation that if not all policy aims can be attained, conflicts may arise, calling for the ordering of policy aims according to their respective merits. Such problems are the subject matter of the theory of economic policy.

17.2 Theory of Economic Policy

Perhaps the simplest way of introducing the theory of economic policy is to consider first the situation in which no deliberate interference is exercised by the government on the economy. Under such conditions the equilibrium solution of the economy at each point in time may be thought of as determined by a number of independent structural relations among the variables of the system. Let us assume that there are n such relations. These will generally suffice to determine equilibrium values of n variables x_k, such as prices, incomes, levels of output of different products, and so on. Further, we assume that the form of the n structural relations is perfectly described by a number of parameters, independent of the equilibrium solution of the period. These, m in number, may conveniently be designated as A_i $(i = 1, \ldots, m)$. The parameters A_i will reflect such factors as preferences, factor endowments, population size, state of technology, union power, degree of monopoly, etc. In some cases foreign prices and demand conditions may also be included in the group of structural parameters A_i.

While the structural parameters are independent of the solution of the economic system, they need not remain constant over time. Effectively, it is the change in these parameters that causes the economic conditions, i.e., the solutions x_k, to assume different values in different periods. Two types of structural parameters should be distinguished. Some are perfectly autonomous, and consequently their value for our purposes depends only on time, namely,

$$A = A(t) \tag{2.1}$$

Population growth in an advanced economy or technological change may illustrate this case. On the other hand, some structural parameters, although independent of the current equilibrium of the economy, may depend on past values of the solutions x_k. Of course, these parameters may also depend on time directly; thus they may be expressed as

$$A = A(t, x_{1,t-1}; \ldots, x_{n,t-j}) \tag{2.2}$$

Perhaps the most typical example of this case is the stock of capital. At each period it may be computed as the sum of all past net investments.

We may now state mathematically the set of n structural relations determining the equilibrium of the economy as

$$f_i(x_1, \ldots, x_n; A_1, \ldots, A_m) = 0$$
$$i = 1, \ldots, n \quad (2.3)$$

Because we have assumed that the structure of the economy at each period in time is fully described by the structural parameters, the f_i's are independent of time. For any period t there will be in the n-dimensional solution space a point Z_t, determined through relations 2.3 and, to the extent that some of the structural parameters assume the form of relation 2.2, determined by the history of the system.

Let us now assume that at some or all periods t, the general consensus of the society postulates that there is some other point in the solution space, say z_t, that is socially preferable to Z_t. For example, Z_t may contain a 10 per cent unemployment, while z_t only 3 per cent. The government may now undertake measures to induce the economy to settle at z_t rather than Z_t. To do this, it has to alter the structure of the economy, i.e., some or all of the parameters A_i. Usually not all the parameters can be altered; those that may be are usually referred to as policy *tools* or policy *instruments*. We shall henceforth refer to such tools by the symbol B_g, while keeping the A_i's to express the autonomous parameters out of the reach of the government's direct interference. All parameters B must be independent of each other. If a given value of one always implied a value of another, such a functional relation would have to be introduced into relation 2.3 (or 2.4), thus reducing the number of policy instruments.

Let us now leave aside for a while the dynamic aspects of the problem of policy and consider a static situation, as described by, say z_0 and Z_0. Some of the coordinates of Z_0 may either always remain the same as corresponding coordinates of z_0 or be deemed socially unimportant or irrelevant. With Professor Tinbergen, let us refer to such variables as *irrelevant* variables, assume that they are f in number, and use for them the notation y_f. The remaining variables x_k are the *target variables* with which the government is exclusively concerned and that it wants to bring to the desired position z_0. There are k such variables, and, of course, $k + f$ must be equal to the original number of variables n. The existence of irrelevant variables may be expressed by saying that there are two points z_0 and

Z_0' in a k-dimensional subspace of the solution space, this subspace being all that the government is interested in. We may refer to it as the "policy space."

Using the concepts and notations explained in the above paragraphs, we may now rewrite relations 2.3 to include the target variables, irrelevant variables, autonomous parameters, and policy tools. We have

$$f_i(x_1, \ldots, x_k; y_1, \ldots, y_f; A_1, \ldots, A_j; B_1, \ldots, B_g) = 0 \quad (2.4)$$
$$i = 1, \ldots, n$$

For given values of all parameters A and B but one, say B_1, there will generally be an infinity of solutions such as Z. All points Z corresponding to all admissible values of B_1 will trace out a contour in the n-dimensional solution space and a contour in the k-dimensional policy space; let us designate such a contour in the policy space by b_1. Now let us assume that there is only one target variable; in other words, the policy space has only one dimension. The target value of such a variable, say x_1, is $x_1 = x_1^0$. Unless b happens to be parallel to, and not coincident with, the hyperplane defined by $x_1 = x_1^0$ in the vicinity of the original equilibrium Z_0, established before any government interference took place, there will generally be some value of B_1 yielding $x_1 = x_1^0$. In other words, b_1 will somewhere intersect the hyperplane defined by $x_1 = x_1^0$. An additional qualification has to be made: the arc covered by Z moving away from its original position Z^0 defined by B_1^0 must be a monotonic function of B_1. If it were not so, the policy could become ineffective for some values of B_1; in other words, the contour b_1, even if not parallel to the plane $x_1 = x_1^0$, might never reach it.

In summary we may state that when one policy tool is used and only one target is sought, the policy space will generally coincide[1] with the solution contour (such as b_1) in that space, and consequently the target may be attained for some value of the policy parameter.

This conclusion may easily be extended to situations of a larger number of targets and tools. If one policy tool is available and two targets are aimed at, it will generally be impossible to attain both targets by using a single policy parameter B. Here the policy space has two dimensions, while the solution contour b in that space does not coincide with it; it is only a one-dimensional contour in that space. Assuming that the target variables are x_1 and x_2, this may be

---

[1] I.e., there is no point in the policy space that would not also be in b_1.

observed from Figure 17.2.1. Variation of B_1 traces out b_1; but it would be only by accident that b_1 would attain z', the target point defined by x_1^0 and x_2^0. On the other hand, if two policy parameters or tools may be used, the locus of feasible solutions in the policy space coincides with the policy space itself, in this particular case with the $x_1 - x_2$ plane. Consequently, z' can be attained.

Similar reasoning may be extended to any number of policy tools and target variables. The important conclusion is that, to attain a given number of targets, it is generally necessary to have the same number of policy tools. There may be exceptions to this rule. For

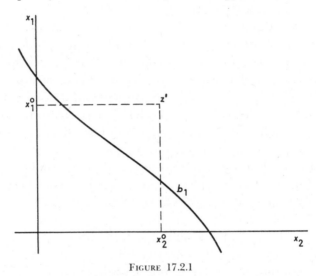

Figure 17.2.1

example, if b_1 in Figure 17.2.1 happened to pass through z', only one tool of policy would be needed in reaching two aims. On the other hand, if the solution locus $b_{1,2}$ generated by different values of B_1 and B_2 were parallel to the intersection of two hyperplanes given by $x_1 = x_1^0$ and $x_2 = x_2^0$, the two policy tools would not be sufficient, and a third tool would have to be utilized in attaining z'. Also it would be possible to use any other pair of policy parameters besides B_1 nd B_2. Moreover, there is the possibility that two policy parameters influence only one structural relation and leave unaffected all other relations. In this situation the pair should be considered, for the purposes of our present analysis, as a single parameter. This case has a good deal of relevance for concrete problems of policy. If, for example, deficit spending and monetary policy acted on only one structural relation, say f_1, the economy would still be constrained to a single infinity (a contour) of solution points defined by the intersection of all the remaining structural relations $f_2, \ldots, f_n$.

We may now return briefly to the dynamic situation wherein both the actual solutions of the economy and the targets in the policy space are continuously changing in time. At any moment there is an actual solution point Z'_t and a target point z'_t. Only with given policies, i.e., given values of the parameters B, such that $z'_t = Z'_t$ for any time period t, will it be unnecessary to alter policy. In all other situations means have to be sought to produce such an equality. The static problem is sufficiently complex in itself; the dynamic problem of policy is much more so. If there is any time lag between the time a policy is conceived and the time it becomes effective, a mere observation of the solutions Z' at time t will not suffice. It will be necessary to predict at any point in time the solutions Z' for future periods, in order to design policies producing the target solution z' in the future.

The mention of this dynamic problem of economic policy seems to be justified because it is relevant to practical policy making. In the real world the time lags involved in policy implementation are very important; often, particularly with regard to countercyclical policy, they frustrate the very purpose of economic policy. The situation is comparable to one wherein a moving object is aimed at; it could be attained only by a projectile moving at infinite speed, or if its future position could be predicted, or by accident.

17.3 A Simple Illustration

It seems desirable to supplement our theoretical discussion of the preceding section by a simple illustration of the problem of economic policy. Suppose that there are only two target variables x_1 and x_2, no irrelevant variables, and two structural relations f_1 and f_2. We may think of x_1 as the balance of payments and x_2 as the per cent rate of unemployment. The two structural relations assume the form

$$f_1 \equiv A_1 x_1 + A_2 x_2 - B_1 = 0 \qquad (3.1)$$

and

$$f_2 \equiv A_3 x_1 - B_2 x_2 = 0 \qquad (3.2)$$

where A_1, A_2, and A_3 are three autonomous parameters, while B_1 and B_2 are parameters that may be controlled by the government. The policy space and the solution space are identical. In Figure

17.3.1 we show graphically the structural relations f_1 and f_2, corresponding to given values of the A's and the B's, in the $x_1 - x_2$ plane. Here Z is the observed solution of the economy, reflecting 5 per cent unemployment and a deficit of two billion dollars.

All the propositions put forth in the static case of the preceding section may now be easily illustrated. Here z is the target point, corresponding to a balanced foreign-trade account and a 3 per cent rate of unemployment. Variation of a single policy parameter cannot attain z, but it can fulfill either one or the other target requirement.

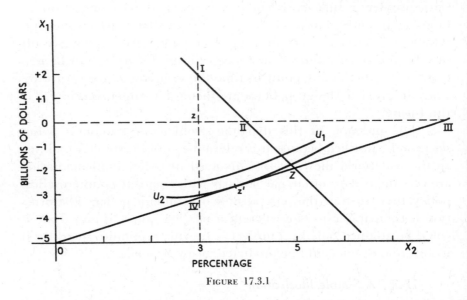

FIGURE 17.3.1

For example, B_1, if increased sufficiently, may move f_1 to pass through point *III*, where the balance of payments is in equilibrium; unemployment, however, has increased. A reduction in B_1, on the other hand, may bring employment to the desired level with a balance-of-payments deficit of over three billion. If only the other policy instrument B_2 is used, the slope of f_2 will be altered and either point *I* or point *II* will be attained, thus fulfilling either one or the other policy aim. Only alteration of both B_1 and B_2 will bring about the desired levels of both x_1 and x_2 simultaneously.

If f_1 were redefined to include B_2 also, say

$$f_1 \equiv A_1 x_1 + A_2 x_2 - B_1 - B_2 = 0 \qquad (3.3)$$

and f_2 remained unchanged, it would again be possible to attain z, through a policy using both B_1 and B_2. However, if B_2 did not appear in f_2 at all, variation of both policy parameters in relation 3.3 would not suffice to attain both targets, and $(B_1 + B_2)$ should be considered as a single policy instrument.

In practice, it quite frequently happens that the desirability of a certain solution or target increases or decreases with the variable itself. Thus it may happen that beyond a certain value, usually that indicated by z, all values of a target variable are acceptable. In our example, any solution producing at least zero balance of payments and, at the most, 3 per cent unemployment may be considered as desirable. In other words, for $x_1 > 0$, x_1 becomes an irrelevant variable, and, for $x_2 < 3$, x_2 becomes an irrelevant variable. If this is the case, the target is no longer a point such as z but an area to the left and above z. Whenever its frontier is attained, the aim of economic policy may be deemed fulfilled. A solution such as that indicated by point I, reached through the alteration of a single policy variable B_2, may illustrate such a case.

It seems that the greatest practical difficulty that most Western governments are facing with respect to economic policy is the scarcity of efficient tools of policy. The social, political, and economic costs of acquiring additional tools of policy or of pushing a given policy beyond certain limits may be considerable. Therefore, in many practical cases, where a number of target variables are sought, it is impossible to fulfill all targets. Suppose that in our simple example only the first tool of policy B_1 were available, B_2 now being classified as an autonomous structural parameter. Only solutions along f_2 are now feasible. The government would have to decide how much it was willing to give up of each target value (i.e., coordinates of z).

In theory, if the government did have a consistent set of preferences with respect to balance-of-payments deficits and the rate of unemployment, expressed in terms of social indifference curves (such as u_1 and u_2 in the diagram), it would choose point z'. This point is most desirable, given the restriction that only points on f_2 are attainable. In practice, decisions of this type have to be made by every government; however, no well-defined sets of preferences are used or defined for the purpose. Usually, rough qualitative weights have to be employed by the practical policy maker in evaluating the importance of different targets. Such weights are more often based on ignorance or often-irrelevant political tradition than on a sound evaluation. A good deal of the difference in the economic platforms of political parties in the United States can be reduced to differences in weights assigned to unemployment, on the one hand, and to the rate of inflation, on the other. We shall return to these questions later in this chapter.

17.4 Short-Run Policy Aiming at External and Internal Balance

Any economic policy will generally have two types of effects. On the one hand, it will influence the equilibrium of the economy in the short run; on the other, by doing this, it will also affect the structural parameters of the economy in the future. We observed in Section 2 of this chapter that some of the structural parameters A_i will depend on the history of the economy. A policy designed at present to increase investment will both increase employment in the short run and productivity in the long run. A government-sponsored program to stimulate basic research, besides employing some resources in the short run, will improve technology in the long run.

Consequently, it is not perfectly legitimate to make a distinction between short- and long-run policies; almost all policy actions have both effects. Nevertheless, it is useful to introduce the distinction for the purpose of our analysis. What really distinguishes short- from long-run policies is the primary purpose or intent in the minds of the policy makers. Policies that are intended to correct the long-run path or trend of the economy should be referred to as "long-run policies"; policies aiming at cyclical maladjustments let us call "short-run policies." Operationally, the tools of long-run policy are more abundant than those of short-run policy. While in the latter case only the policy tools proper (as defined in Sec. 2), are available, long-run policies may also affect the structural parameters to the extent that those depend on past values of some of the endogenous variables.

In practice, there may be a very large number of minor policy targets and tools, all related in one way or another to the balance of payments. We shall not be able to examine all such cases; rather, we shall restrict ourselves to the discussion of the few principal policies. To do this, let us use the framework of aggregative analysis presented in Chapter 6 and elaborated in other chapters of Part II. The reader may find it useful at this point to refresh his memory by returning to Chapter 6, primarily to its second section.

In Figure 17.4.1 we have reproduced the income-determining

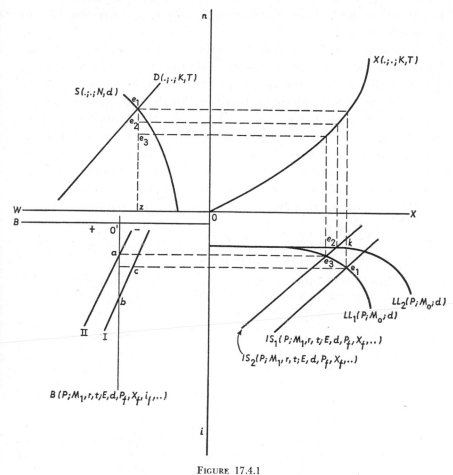

FIGURE 17.4.1

graph used in Chapter 6, slightly altered to show explicitly the balance-of-payments position; the latter is shown in the third quadrant. Just to summarize the concepts used, let us point out that the first quadrant reflects the production conditions of the economy, the second describes the labor market, the third the balance of payments, and the fourth—actually most important for short-run considerations—the equilibrium between effective demand and the monetary conditions of the economy. Each of the functions shown is designated in the usual way, such as *LL, IS, X, S,* or *D.* Variables shown on the axes are not stated explicitly in the functions because their impact is reflected by the shape and position of the function itself; these are target and irrelevant variables. On the other hand, each function depends on three groups of factors, corresponding to the definitions given in Section 2.

The first group contains the target variables (in our case only P, the domestic price level) that do not appear on one of the axes. Clearly, a change in domestic prices will alter the position and the shape of some of the functional relations. In the second group, separated by a semicolon, we find the tools of policy, or instruments, while in the third group we have stated the most important autonomous parameters, as defined in Section 2 of this chapter. In other words, the first group contains the x's or y's not appearing on the axes, the second group the B's, and the third group the A's.

We may survey briefly all these variables and parameters:

i) *Target Variables*

n short-run level of employment.

X level of output or *NNP* (of course, in the short run this will be determined uniquely by the level of employment, i.e., once n is known, X is also known).

B the balance of autonomous payments; to be further explained presently.

P general level of domestic prices.

W real wage.

ii) *Irrelevant Variables*

i the rate of interest; in more refined problems of policy, this may be assumed to represent a vector of two or more interest rates, such as short- and long-run rates, to the extent that they may be affected independently through operation in short- and long-term capital markets.

w money wage; this variable may be considered as irrelevant because it is uniquely determined by the level of prices and the real wage; of course, the policy problem could be reformulated to include money wage and the price level as targets; or we could consider this variable as a policy instrument.

iii) *Tools of Policy*

M_0, M_1 usually these two parameters should be considered as identical, reflecting the money supply, as controlled by open-market operations, rediscount-rate policies, and the reserve ratio. To include the possibility of buying and selling securities in markets of securities of different maturity, we may think of two policy parameters M, one acting primarily on short-term rates, the other on long-term rates. Many policy makers consider such a diversification of security-market operations as a powerful tool of policy. Others, including the present writer, are doubtful about the possibility of splitting the capital market effectively into a number of fairly independent parts.

r price of foreign currency in terms of domestic currency, i.e., the rate of exchange.

t this policy tool should always be considered as a vector containing a large number of forms of fiscal policy and government spending, including direct and indirect taxation of all forms, tariffs, quantitative restrictions, selective changes in tax rates and government spending aimed at redistributive effects, and so forth.

iv) *Autonomous Factors, Assumed Invariant in the Short Run*

N available labor force.

K capital stock.

T technology.

d demand conditions; this factor will be found in a number of relations, expressing, alternatively, the impact of people's preferences on supply of labor, demand for imports or domestic consumption, the liquidity preference, and so forth.

P_f foreign level of prices.

i_f average rate of interest abroad.

X_f real output and income of foreign countries.

d_f foreign demand conditions.

E general business expectations, to the extent that they are not based on any of the autonomous variables listed.

This list by no means exhausts the different possible variables or parameters to be included in the discussion of problems of short-run economic policy. The reader may, however, employ the analytical framework of this and following sections in expanding or adjusting the model to include any additional aspect of the problem. One set of variables omitted here from explicit consideration ought to be mentioned: savings and investment. To a given point on a known *IS* schedule will correspond equilibrium values of these two variables. Their levels usually are not of direct concern to us when discussing short-run policy. They will, however, be relevant when dealing with problems of growth and long-range policy.

Before examining the concrete cases of economic policy, the balance-of-payments schedule (shown in the third quadrant of the diagram) should be explained in a little greater detail. It contains two of the four functions underlying the *IS* curve in the fourth quadrant, namely, the difference between exports and imports on current account. Moreover, it also includes autonomous capital movements. Consequently, the horizontal difference between the vertical axis originating at *O'* and the *B* schedule measures the outflow (inflow) of gold plus short-term accommodating capital inflow (outflow). As indicated by the signs on the *B* axis, there is a balance-of-payments deficit if the equilibrium point on the *B* schedule is to the right of *O'b* and a surplus if to the left of *O'b*. In summary, we define the *B* function (expressed in the diagram by two alternative schedules *I* and *II*) as

$$B = \text{Exports on current account}$$
$$- \text{ imports on current account}$$
$$- \text{ net autonomous capital outflow} \qquad (4.1)$$

There is a very large number of possible situations that may arise from the alternative use of different policy tools and from the different short- or long-run structural properties of the system. This fact calls for some type of organization of our discussion. Thus we propose to study first the individual impact of each of the three or four policy tools separately. Next, we shall discuss the most important situations wherein more than one tool of policy is used in achieving a given target. In the following section we shall examine the case in which the rate of exchange is permitted to adjust freely to conditions in the foreign-exchange market, while the remaining tools of policy are employed to attain internal stability. Throughout the discussion of this and the next section we shall depend heavily on the analysis of Part II.

i) *The Exchange Rate as a Tool of Policy.* Although the rate of exchange or the value of the currency will usually have an impact on the level of income and employment, economists almost without exception agree that it would be most unwise to use an administered exchange-rate adjustment in coping with short-run income fluctuations. This proposition hardly deserves elaborate explanation. We may only mention a few important facts. If the economy is depressed and its balance of payments is in long-run equilibrium, then it may be expected in the short run that its external balance will be positive if the rest of the world is prosperous and be somewhere near equilibrium if the rest of the world undergoes a similar recession. In the latter case a currency devaluation can only be considered as a beggar-my-neighbor policy by the rest of the world and lead to retaliation à la 1930's. But even if the rest of the world is less severely hit by declining activity, it seems preferable for the depressed country to employ other tools of policy in restoring internal equilibrium. Effectively, if it were to devalue, its balance of payments would most likely improve even further, and, unless devaluation were fully offset by domestic price inflation, the currency would become undervalued in the long run. In addition to these factors, foreign-exchange speculation and inefficient relocation of domestic productive resources make frequent controlled adjustment of the rate of exchange most unwarranted.

Thus, keeping in mind that the rate of exchange should generally be used as a tool of policy only in coping with longer-range structural maladjustments, we may examine the impact of this tool on the different target variables. Most of the quantitative theory underlying this problem is contained in the first three sections of Chapter 8. There we show that currency depreciation will necessarily increase income and employment of the depreciating country, provided that it has some unutilized labor force and capacity. The balance of payments, on the other hand, may either improve or deteriorate, depending on the specific nature of the problem. The important fact is that the Marshall-Lerner conditions, applicable to the full-employment situation and examined in Chapter 5, will no longer pertain in determining the direction of change in the balance of payments.

Now consider Figure 17.4.1 and assume that the equilibrium of the economy is determined by IS_2 and LL_2. The equilibrium in the fourth quadrant is indicated by e_2. All the autonomous parameters (A) are assumed given. In the third quadrant schedule I pertains, and consequently the external balance is in a substantial deficit. A small devaluation, not inducing IS_2 to move to the right of point k on LL_2, may be expected not to affect the position of LL_2, domestic prices remaining largely unchanged. Provided that the elasticity of demand for imports and the cross-elasticity of demand for domestic produce are sufficiently high, the schedule I in the third quadrant will move to the left, and the deficit will be reduced. With low values of these elasticities, on the other hand, the balance of payments may deteriorate or remain unchanged, while real income and employment increase. So far, there is no impact on the capital account in the balance of payments because the rate of exchange has remained unchanged.

A substantial devaluation of the currency that would push the IS_2 schedule far to the right of point k, say all the way to IS_1, if prices remained unchanged, will have more complex effects. First of all, as, in the process of adjustment, full employment is reached (defined by point e_1 in the second quadrant), prices will be bound to increase. But this will induce the LL_2 schedule to move to the left. Also the IS curve will now move to the left from its hypothetical position IS_1, because the resulting terms-of-trade effect will tend to offset partially the original impact of a higher price of foreign currency. Thus full employment will be reached, but prices will tend to rise. The equilibrium level of price and interest rate will be found for such values of these two variables as will make the LL and IS curves intersect at full employment, presumably somewhere between k and e_1 in the fourth quadrant.

On top of the impact on the current account of the balance of payments, as discussed above, two additional forces will now influence the external balance. On the one hand, domestic inflation will tend to push the balance-of-payments schedule to the right, thus reducing the gains on current account or increasing the losses. On the other hand, a higher rate of interest, as indicated by the slope of the B schedule, will tend to offset this effect through an improvement in the capital account of the foreign-trade balance. Ideally, if the negative terms-of-trade effect and the positive interest-rate effect were of equal intensity, only the primary effect of devaluation would prevail.

Although possibly less interesting in practice, the case of currency appreciation should be briefly examined because of a certain asymmetry of impact that it may involve. While prices usually move upward easily, they may be extremely inflexible in the downward direction. Suppose that, starting from an original equilibrium determined by point e_1 in the fourth quadrant and the schedule II in the third, the government proceeds to appreciate the currency to eliminate a balance-of-payments surplus and possibly reduce inflationary pressures. If prices are inflexible, the LL_1 curve will not be affected, and a new equilibrium may be reached at e_3 on IS_2. The IS curve has shifted to the left only because of the exchange-rate effect on the terms of trade. Assuming that the B schedule has moved to position I, the balance-of-payments surplus would have turned into a deficit, because of both the terms-of-trade effect on the current account and the impact of lower interest rates on the capital account. The real wage would most likely have remained unaffected in this case, but employment would have been reduced. The orthodox Keynesian theory would call for an increase in real wages and hence also in money wages. However, this is quite unlikely in the context of this particular situation.

Next let us assume that both prices and money wages are equally flexible in the downward direction. The real wage again is unlikely to be affected in this case; however, the leftward shift of IS resulting from a currency appreciation will now be accompanied by a rightward shift in the LL curve, say all the way to LL_2. But, as prices decline, part of the impact of appreciation will be offset by the impact of domestic prices on the terms of trade, and the IS curve will tend to return to the right from IS_2. In these and all other respects, this situation is perfectly symmetrical with that of currency devaluation discussed above.

Finally, the case is conceivable, often argued by Keynes, where prices are flexible in the downward direction while money wages are not. In this situation, the previous case largely obtains, except possibly for some income redistribution effects. Note that now real wage will not remain at the original level Oz but will rise to the abscissa of point e_2 on D in the second quadrant.

Let us now summarize the most important conclusions. The rate of exchange should generally not be used as a tool of policy in coping with short-run cyclical disequilibria. However, if more fundamental maladjustment arises, exchange-rate adjustment will generally have a powerful impact on employment, if such impact is possible with the given total labor force. If price elasticities of demand are high, the balance of payments is also likely to improve as a result of currency devaluation. The strength of such an effect will be proportional to unemployment, provided that the internal mobility of productive resources is satisfactory. If in the process of adjustment to devaluation a position near full employment is reached, prices will generally tend to rise, and so will the rate of interest. Monetary policy, to be discussed presently, may counteract such an in-flationary pressure at the cost of even higher interest rates. Such an action may have further beneficial impact on the balance of autonomous payments.

ii) *Taxation and Government Spending as a Tool of Policy.* We are now turning from the policy parameter r to the policy parameter t. We observe that this tool of policy appears in the *IS* function in the fourth quadrant and in the *B* schedule in the third. Let us assume again that all the autonomous parameters are fixed and so are the remaining policy parameters r, M_1, and M_2. Contrary to the usual impact of the rate of exchange, global fiscal policy, broadly defined to include government spending also, will act generally on the balance of payments in one direction and on the level of real income and employment in the other. Under simplified assumptions, these two effects were studied rigorously in Chapter 7; effectively, alteration of t may always be translated into an autonomous shift in effective demand.

Assuming a balanced budget, in the context of a longer-range policy, increased government spending will tend to shift the *IS* curve to the right and the balance-of-payments schedule also to the right. This will generally increase employment and worsen the balance of payments. Of course, the balance-of-payments effect may be reduced or eliminated altogether through selective taxation and spending. For example, the government might heavily tax groups with a high marginal propensity to import and spend on products with very little import content. The primary effects could now improve the balance of payments. Secondary multiplier effects, however, could hardly be ineffective.

Again it will be the proximity to full employment that will determine whether increased government spending will be translated primarily into higher prices or higher income. With respect to the balance of payments, however, the price and income effects resulting from increased government spending will be additive in worsening the current account. The capital account, on the other hand, may be improved, provided that the rate of interest increases.

In the case of an unbalanced budget, permissible in the case of countercyclical policy, the same conclusions pertain; however, the strength of the impact on employment and the balance of payments should be expected to be much higher than with a balanced budget. If the balance of payments is in long-run equilibrium, the impact of cyclical stabilization through deficit or surplus spending should not be feared. In fact, the autonomous forces producing the cycle are always likely to turn the balance of payments in such a way as to provide a cushion for the effects of government stabilization.

Nevertheless, the case should not be overlooked in which prices and wages are sticky downward and flexible upward. Here active combatting of recessions through taxation and government spending may affect the trend of prices in the upward direction. In this case, of course, such policies may lead to long-run maladjustment in the balance of payments and may be unwarranted even in the short run.

Selective indirect taxation or spending, such as tariffs or subsidies, may change income and the balance of payments in one way or the other. Such measures, generally undesirable in coping with the three target variables at hand, were discussed in Chapter 16.

iii) *Money Supply as a Tool of Policy.* Let us first make the usual assumption that there is only one rate of interest relevant for the determination of the Keynesian equilibrium, connected directly with only one tool of policy, M_0. Thus we may disregard M_1 in the *IS* function and the *B* schedule. Actually, it is not necessary to assume that there is only one rate of interest; short- and long-term rates of interest may still be different, as they actually are in the real world. But, in order to use only one policy parameter M_0, we have to assume that the short-run rate always remains in a given functional relation to the long-term rate.

With this assumption it is comparatively easy to examine the impact of monetary policy on the three important target variables, B, n, and P. In Section 7 of Chapter 7 we presented a rigorous analysis of precisely this case, under a set of simplified assumptions. Returning now to Figure 17.4.1, we observe that the only schedule that will be directly affected by a change in money supply is the *LL* curve. A reduction in money supply will tend to move the *LL* curve to the left, in much the same way as would an increase in prices.

An under-full-employment position at a rate of interest above minimum, such as at point e_3 in the fourth quadrant, is compatible only with downward inflexible prices and wages. If prices were flexible, the *LL* curve would always be moved to the right through reduced prices, and higher equilibrium income would be established at point e_2. Monetary ease may substitute for price flexibility and attain point e_2. Any further increase in money supply will not have any effect on either employment, prices, or the balance of payments, all additional injections of money increasing only monetary hoards rather than stimulating new transactions. The balance of payments, on the other hand, will always deteriorate as the equilibrium in the fourth quadrant moves from e_3 to e_2, as indicated by the slope of schedules I and II in the third quadrant. Note that, so far, no price changes have been assumed, and consequently there is no reason for either balance-of-payments schedule to shift to another position. The balance-of-payments deterioration results from both increased income and capital outflow on account of lower rates of interest.

It may be useful to point out at this stage of the argument the important difference between monetary and fiscal action with respect to the balance of autonomous payments. While the latter attains higher levels of income with zero or positive change in the interest rate, the former does so, if at all, through lower interest rates. Thus the monetary stimulus to the economy has two negative effects on the balance of payments; fiscal action or government spending will generally worsen the current account and improve the capital account. The net outcome in the latter case is difficult to ascertain. To do so, we would have to stipulate in greater detail the conditions prevalent in international capital markets and the marginal propensities to import. It is clear that either monetary or fiscal policy may cause an upward movement of prices; in this situation the terms-of-trade effect may further adversely affect the current account.

Let us now state briefly the significance of the case in which both M_1 and M_0 are taken as independent, or at least partially independent, tools of policy. If the monetary authorities are permitted to operate in two different securities markets—say, in that of long-term government securities and that of three-month bills—and if these two markets are fairly independent, it may be possible that the two corresponding rates of interest will also be independent, at least to a degree. Thus, for example, the central bank could borrow in the short-term capital market and lend by purchasing long-term securities. This could keep short-term rates high and long-term rates relatively low; of course, uncertainty and some degree of imperfection of the capital markets has to be assumed for this to happen. In the longer run especially, it can be assumed that the cross-elasticities connecting the two markets will be quite high.

In our structural relations represented in Figure 17.4.1 we

have introduced a parameter M_0 to reflect total money supply, a parameter essential in determining the position of the *LL* curve. On the other hand, M_1 is a policy parameter reflecting what may be described as the degree of activity bringing about inequality between short- and long-term rates. While the short-term rate of interest is still measured on the lower part of the vertical axis, the *IS* curve may now move to the right or to the left of its original position. This will depend on whether long-term rates are lower or higher than the long-term rate of interest, which, in our preceding analysis, was uniquely related to the level of the short-term rate.

Of course, for the same reasons, the parameter M_1 also has to appear in the balance-of-payments schedule of the third quadrant. A drop in the long-term rate with unchanged short-term rate not only may move the *IS* curve to the right because of increased investment spending but may also affect the balance-of-payments schedule either through reduced inflow of long-term funds or through increased imports, should substitution of imports for savings take place at lower rates of interest.

The important policy argument to be retained is that if short-term rates always had to decline together with long-term rates before business conditions could improve, an additional drain on monetary reserves would have to occur because of short-term capital outflow. In periods when international short-term capital markets are highly volatile and unstable for one reason or another, this argument has a good deal of validity. However, the question still remains whether it is possible to effect the desired gap between different rates of interest through open-market operations. Of course, legally set interest rates coupled with capital market controls could always produce the desired effect. But the social cost of such a policy tool might exceed the benefit derivable from it.

We may now survey the three principal tools of policy simultaneously and evaluate their combined impact on the three principal targets. Neither the rate of exchange, nor fiscal, nor monetary policy is capable of inducing all three target variables to move in the desired direction. If the economy is depressed, so that prices may be expected to remain stable even if real income and employment increase and the balance of payments is in a structural deficit, devaluation is highly commendable. It will raise employment and usually improve the balance of payments. Expansion through fiscal policy will be effective with respect to employment and may have a fairly neutral effect on the balance of payments, provided that international capital movements are sufficiently interest-elastic and prices do not rise too much with increasing effective demand. Monetary policy, effective in raising real income only if the rate of interest can be reduced, will generally have a strong negative impact on the balance of payments. Such balance-of-payments deterioration will be greater, the greater the income elasticity of imports and the interest elasticity of international capital movements.

The important question remains whether it is at all possible to attain a balance-of-payments equilibrium, full employment, and price stability simultaneously, if, in the initial situations, deficiency is realized in all three target variables. In theory, considering the number of policy tools, the number of target variables, and the form of the structural equations, there should be some appropriate "dose" of each of the three policies that would attain all three targets simultaneously. Effectively, as we are going to see, this is so. Two important cases have to be considered. In the first, prices are assumed to be flexible in both directions; in the second case we assume that they never can decline. In the first case the target may be formulated as "stable or lower prices"; in the latter case the only possible target is price stability.

Let us first consider the case of perfect price flexibility. As we have already seen, the only possibility of less than full employment in this case is that effective demand expressed by IS falls short of point k and intersects the LL curve at a point such as e_2. The monetary authorities may now restrict money supply at will, thus moving the LL curve to the left and upward, except, of course, for a portion of its horizontal segment. As this process continues, prices and money wages will continuously be bidden down, very much in the same way as in the classical theory. This will push the LL curve back to pass through point k. But, as prices decline, the terms-of-trade effect will keep shifting the IS curve to the right. Suppose that it attains point k, i.e., full employment, before the balance-of-payments equilibrium is reached. If the central bank now continues reducing the supply of money, the intersection of LL and IS will start creeping along ke_1 in the downward direction, while interest rates start increasing and prices keep falling. The rise in interest rates will provide an additional stimulus to balance-of-payments improvement. There will generally be some degree of scarcity of money that will produce a balance-of-payments equilibrium and full employment at a lower level of prices than that corresponding to the initial equilibrium. The use of only one tool of policy in this case should be explained by the fact that there was not a single target value but a whole range of values of permissible price levels; this has reduced the number of targets by one. Moreover, once full employment was attained, the employment target could remain at that level. Were the external balance reached through monetary policy and declining prices prior to full employment, further price deflation would have produced a surplus. If the equilibrium of the foreign trade were strictly required, the government could have appreciated the currency first by a sufficient amount and then proceeded to restrict the supply of money until both the external and the internal balance were attained simultaneously. Thus two tools would effectively have been used in attaining two targets.

It appears from the preceding discussion that the case of *target ranges* rather than point targets pointed out in Section 3 is extremely important in practice. It often simplifies the problem of policy by reducing effectively the number of targets without affecting the number of tools. Whenever the number of targets falls short of the number of policy parameters, an infinity of different combinations of policies and policy intensities may be used in achieving a given goal. In all such situations, the problem of finding the most efficient policy arises.

Let us now turn to the more intricate and more realistic situation in which prices are inflexible in the downward direction. Suppose that the initial situation is reflected by point e_3, i.e., the intersection of IS_2 and LL_1, and the balance-of-payments schedule I in the third quadrant of the diagram of Figure 17.4.1. The balance of payments is in deficit, part of the labor force is unemployed, and prices are at the level determining LL_1. Exchange devaluation being probably the most potent tool in coping with both unemployment and balance-of-payments difficulties, let us assume that the first step is taken along these lines. This will tend to shift the IS curve to the right of e_3 and the balance-of-payments schedule to the left of point b. As long as the IS curve remains to the left or at e_1, there will be little reason for prices to rise, the LL curve passing through e_1 thus remaining unchanged if the money supply is not changed. Suppose now that the IS curve reaches e_1 through devaluation before the balance of payments attains equilibrium. One of the further policies that the government now may pursue is to let the rate of exchange drop further, while offsetting the inflationary gap; i.e., the *IS* curve is always kept at e_1 through reduced taxation and government spending. Thus prices will remain unchanged, full employment will be preserved, and the balance-of-payments equilibrium will gradually be approached. Eventually, with some mix of the t and r policy parameters, with unchanged money supply and unchanged price level, all three targets will be attained.

The fact that the government did not have to use monetary policy at all indicates that in the particular problem at hand, again, there was one tool in excess of the minimum required. Consequently, numerous policy combinations of different intensities are available. Of course, if the government also considered the rate of interest as a target variable, there would generally have been only one way of attaining all four targets.

These conclusions again seem rather inconsistent with our theoretical proposition that the same number of policy tools will generally be needed in attaining a given number of targets. In the context of the theoretical model used here they are not. The only requirement for prices not to rise used so far was that there be no inflationary gap, in other words, that there be no intersection of the *IS* and *LL* curves to the right of the vertical line ke_1 in the fourth quadrant of the diagram. Thus it takes only one tool of policy to preserve full employment and price stability, once full employment is reached. The other tool—the rate of exchange in the case discussed above—may then be used in attaining the external balance. Actually, we are facing here the situation discussed in Section 3, where it is sufficient to keep one solution point on the frontier of a region (here it is the line ke_1) to fulfill one target of policy.

Some other target might be introduced into the problem at hand, thus equaling the number of tools and objectives and reducing the number of solutions to one. For example, the government might desire a minimum use of fiscal policy and government spending, i.e., a minimum balanced budget. Or it might desire to keep the rate of interest at a given level.

Actually, the problem of policy as discussed so far does not describe perfectly the conditions of the real world. It is not always realistic to assume that prices will start increasing only when full employment is attained and an inflationary gap occurs. Prices may start rising or inflationary pressure be felt well before full employment is reached. We may assume that such an inflationary tendency is an inverse function of the rate of unemployment, i.e., of $N - n$. If it is at all possible to use monetary restriction to counter such an inflationary strength—this countering force being an inverse function of the money supply—then to any prescribed level of unemployment deemed desirable there will correspond a single solution of our general problem of policy. Thus, if a 3 per cent unemployment were desired, together with external equilibrium and price stability, there would generally be only one set of the three principal policy parameters—r, t, and M—yielding the three targets simultaneously. It is precisely this aspect of the problem that makes the attainment of external and internal balance and of price stability extremely difficult in practice. Sometimes the three targets are even sought without altering the value of the currency. This may be impossible to accomplish.

Although the analytical apparatus presented in this section is quite adequate to examine any special situation of policy, under any assumed set of conditions, we may employ it here in handling specifically the "absorptionists'" case. Suppose that an economy is operating at full employment, while experiencing a balance-of-payments deficit. Translated in terms of the diagram in Figure 17.4.1, we are in the situation described by IS_1 and LL_1 in the fourth quadrant and I in the third. If the country were to devalue, IS_1 should initially move to the right, and I to the left in the direction of an improved balance of payments. However, with constant money supply an inflationary gap now has to arise; prices will go up and so will the rate of interest. But as prices rise, some of the effect of devaluation—but never all of it—will be eliminated and the IS_1 schedule will tend to return to its original position; also I in the third quadrant will travel part of the way back to where it started. Note, however, that in the case of the latter schedule some improvement of the autonomous balance will persist, not only on account of the fact that prices could not have risen as much as the value of the currency has declined, but also because now the rate of interest is somewhat higher.

If the monetary authorities were to peg the rate of interest at its predevaluation level by injecting new money, the beneficial impact of devaluation could be entirely offset by inflation and no improvement in the balance of payments would take place. On the other hand, if, simultaneously with devaluation, credit were further tightened—thus moving LL_1 to the left—the entire inflationary gap could be closed through an interest rate adjustment with very little inflation. In that case, devaluation could be at least as powerful a tool in restoring external balance as it would have been with unemployed labor and capacity.

Alternatively, together with devaluation, the government could employ fiscal measures in attaining the desired target. With selective fiscal policy, as we have argued already, this could even be accomplished without changing the value of domestic currency.

A wage-price policy—a case that we have not been concerned with so far in our discussion—aiming at lower prices through moral suasion or other devices could on its own, paradoxically, only create an inflationary gap. However, if coupled with drastic monetary restriction, price deflation would lead to a downward movement of both the *LL* and *IS* curves, and to a balance-of-payments improvement, both through a higher rate of interest and lower domestic prices. Of course, the question still remains to be answered whether it is at all possible to deflate prices and money wages at full employment without recurring to direct controls.

17.5 Internal Balance and Price Stability under Flexible Exchange Rates

Most of the groundwork for our present discussion was laid in the preceding section. Also, a rigorous treatment of income effects under flexible exchange rates was presented in the last two sections of Chapter 8. In terms of the policy problem defined in the preceding section, we are now dropping one policy parameter—namely, the rate of exchange r—and one target variable—namely, the balance of payments B. In Figure 17.4.1, the B schedule now becomes identical with $O'b$ in the third quadrant. The rate of exchange now becomes an internally determined variable and may be considered either as a target variable because of its relation to the terms of trade or as an irrelevant variable, depending on the nature of any particular problem of policy.

Let us consider the simpler case in which the rate of exchange is not a target variable. First we observe that, as the rate of exchange is freed and the balance-of-payments schedule collapses into axis $O'b$, the *IS* curve will also be affected. Can we say anything about the new position of a given *IS* curve, corresponding to a given set of autonomous parameters, given prices, and government spending and taxation? Suppose that with fixed exchange rates the balance-of-payments schedule *II* corresponds to *IS₂*. There is a point e_3 on *IS₂*, corresponding to the rate of interest indicated by point *a* in the third quadrant, that will also be on the new schedule IS_2' (not in the diagram) expressing conditions of effective demand under free exchange rates. This is so because at point *a* the external payments and receipts are in balance, at the rate consistent with IS_2. Consequently, the new curve IS' will attain its position through a rotation around point e_3. At points below e_3 (at higher rates of interest) it will be to the left of IS_2, and vice-versa for points above. Effectively, the IS_2 function did correspond to balance-of-payments deficits in the region above e_3. These deficits, eliminated now through an autonomous equilibration of the foreign-exchange market, will generally increase effective demand. Thus the IS_2' schedule will pass through e_3 on IS_2 and generally be flatter, i.e., have a lower slope.

From this observation it follows that monetary policy, with prices rigid in the downward direction, will generally be more effective under free exchange rates in affecting the level of real income than it would be with rigid exchange rates. For example, if the IS_2' curve passed through *k,* monetary ease (with rigid prices) would be sufficient in restoring full employment with free exchange rates, while it could raise real income only up to point e_2 if rates were fixed.

It is not immediately apparent how the impact of fiscal policy and government spending will compare under fixed and flexible exchange rates. An equal shift to the right of both IS_2 and IS_2' caused by altering the l parameter would, of course, indicate a greater gain in real output under fixed exchange rates. We do not know, however, whether an identical increase in government spending would produce an equal shift in the IS curve under fixed or flexible exchange rates. To examine this question, we have to use some of our findings of the last two sections of Chapter 8. There we showed, under somewhat simpler assumptions than those of the present discussion, that under normal conditions an increase in effective demand will benefit primarily the country generating such an increase, if the exchange rate is free. On the other hand, with fixed exchange rates, the greatest benefit will usually be derived by the country producing most of the supply for increased effective demand. On the limit, we noticed in Section 5 of Chapter 8 that if an increase in demand by nationals of country 2 takes the form of increased demand for imports only, the real income of country 1 will increase a good deal more than that of country 2. Just the opposite will happen under identical assumptions with flexible exchange rates. Moreover, the effect of an autonomous change in effective demand on the income of either country will depend on the magnitude of the price elasticities. If these are low, the country originating the increase in effective demand will benefit a lot, while the other will come out with a considerably lower level of real income. With higher elasticities of demand for imports and cross-elasticities of demand for domestic products, the gain in income of the demand-generating country will increase somewhat less, but the income of the other country may drop only very little or even increase somewhat. The rate of exchange will always turn against the country gaining more in income. The size of such currency depreciation will vary in proportion to the magnitude of the elasticities of demand for imports.

The over-all conclusion that we may draw from Chapter 8 for our present purpose is that (i) exchange-rate flexibility will generally reduce or eliminate altogether the leakage of increased demand to the rest of the world, thus usually letting the country itself benefit more from an autonomous increase of domestic demand than it would with rigid exchange rates; and (ii) provided that the elasticities of demand for imports are not too low, a country will be more protected from the effects of foreign changes of business conditions under fluctuating exchange rates than it would be with a fixed rate of exchange. The rationale of the important point (i) is that improved conditions of domestic demand will usually depreciate the currency somewhat; the country will thus benefit both from a terms-of-trade effect on employment and from the original increase in domestic spending. Under fixed exchange rates the former effect would generally be absent.

Thus we may state as a plausible hypothesis that an equal change in the policy parameter *t* will act as a stronger stimulus to the economy under free exchange rates than under a fixed exchange rate. What is the same thing, the *IS'* curve will tend to shift farther to the right than the *IS* curve would. This difference may be expected normally to be large enough to more than offset the opposite effect of the difference of the slopes of *IS* and of *IS'*.

Provided that the assumption is made that inflation can arise only from an inflationary gap at full employment, it is now possible again to attain full employment without inflation, through fiscal policy alone or through a combination of fiscal and monetary policies. Monetary policy alone will be sufficient if the rate of interest does not fall into the liquidity trap before full employment is attained. The problem of finding the most efficient combination of policies is again present. The policy of fluctuating exchange rates itself is definitely to be preferred, on account of the increased power it gives to monetary policy. The power of fiscal policy and government spending will usually, but not necessarily, be enhanced through fluctuating rates in coping with under-full employment.

17.6 Economic Policy, Long-Run Structural Changes, and the External Balance

In the preceding two sections we have completely disregarded the structural parameters, assuming that such factors as technology, capital stock, labor force, demand conditions, and foreign conditions are invariant. In the real world these factors change. Their change usually is slow and gradual; nevertheless, it is this change in structural parameters that produces the changing economic conditions and creates the need for economic policy. If these long-run factors were not in a state of continuous flux, there would be no such need. The policy parameters could be set at an appropriate level to guarantee a continuing satisfactory state of the economy, and the problem of policy would largely disappear.

We observed earlier in this chapter that some of the structural parameters may be assumed to be perfectly autonomous, not depending on the internal working of the economy, while some others are conditioned by the past performance of the economy. To the extent that the structure of the economy is determined by factors of the first variety, economic policy can only take it for granted and operate through the tools discussed in the preceding sections in influencing the target variables in the desired direction. In the second case, however, long-range policies may be designed, affecting present conditions of the economy in such a way as to influence some of the structural parameters in the future.

In relation to the foreign-trade balance, the important fact to be pointed out is that the structural parameters in different countries not only change in time but, what is more important, are different and change at different rates. Unless short-run policy is specifically designed to keep the external balance continuously in equilibrium, only by accident could the external balance remain unchanged over any long period of time. We often are puzzled by the occurrence of a fundamental disequilibrium of the balance of payments in a world where economic policy is primarily directed toward internal conditions and where rates of exchange are fixed over fairly long periods of time. In fact, a more surprising situation would arise if no balance-of-payments difficulties under such conditions ever occurred.

There are a large number of structural changes that may affect the external balance. Most, if not all, of them may be studied by means of the analysis presented in this study. In particular, the simple representation used in the preceding sections and represented in Figure 17.4.1 may be useful. Thus changes in technology or capital stock will be translated by a shift in the production function (first quadrant) and in the demand for labor, i.e., the marginal productivity of labor (second quadrant). Autonomous changes in demand will affect the *IS* curve, as well as the balance-of-payments schedule. Changes in the labor force (N), on the other hand, will influence the position of the supply curve of labor. But it is important to observe that such alterations of the labor supply will affect output and actual employment only to the extent that the economy operates under conditions consistent with full employment.

If money wages are fixed, an upward shift in the supply curve of labor (in Fig. 17.4.1) will tend to induce a drop in real wages if the marginal productivity of labor does not increase concurrently. This will necessarily induce prices to rise. The leftward shift of the *LL* curve that would result from higher prices may be offset through monetary expansion. However, the increase in effective demand resulting from an increased wage bill may be offset by an adverse terms-of-trade effect. Thus an increased labor force may both worsen the balance of payments and increase the problem of unemployment. Of course, as shown in the preceding sections, an adjustment of the rate of exchange or freely fluctuating exchange rates may neutralize the terms-of-trade effect on employment and on the trade balance.

An important factor tending toward a persistent disequilibrium of the balance of payments is different, more or less autonomous, rates of inflation in different countries. Our analysis shows that there may be a very large number of causes for such differences. Productivity changes in different countries, monetary and fiscal policy, union power, and product market imperfections may be mentioned as the most important factors. The *IS* curve in countries with comparatively stable prices will move to the right, while that of relatively inflationary economies will move to the left. The balance-of-payments schedules will be affected by the same forces and generally produce an improvement in the balance of payments of the former countries and a deterioration in the balance of the latter.

Another factor that doubtless influences the long-run trend of prices is the average level of unemployment. Depending on whether economic policy is aimed at, and results in, 5 or 2 per cent unemployment, the rate of inflation will be, say, zero or 3 per cent per annum. Professors Samuelson and Solow have produced fairly conclusive empirical evidence that in the United States price stability is consistent only with about 5 per cent unemployment and that, for any unemployment target lower than 5 per cent, prices are bound to rise. If such a hypothesis is correct, a mere difference in unemployment targets in different countries could produce a structural imbalance of external payments, even if the relation between unemployment and the rate of inflation were exactly the same everywhere. Moreover, because of the differences in structural parameters mentioned above, this relation (often referred to as the "Phillips curve") between inflation and unemployment in different countries may be—and, according to all evidence, actually is—different. Consequently, even if all governments aimed at equal rates of employment, divergent inflationary trends might occur and external imbalance result with rigidly set exchange rates.

Only a little has to be said about the impact of long-range economic policy on the trade balance. This, along with other variables, determines the balance of payments at any point in time, whether the structure of the economy is given by perfectly autonomous factors or by factors depending on past performance and past policies. The important long-range policy is that aimed at increase in the rate of growth. The two important avenues toward such an aim are a high rate of capital accumulation and a fast path of technological improvement. The short-run economic atmosphere conducive to both is a high level of economic activity, possibly combined with increased government spending on basic research, and moral suasion directed toward the producers and the unions.

On a priori grounds it is difficult to evaluate the net impact of such a policy on the trade balance. Both favorable and unfavorable effects will be present. High levels of employment and investment will most likely tend to worsen the trade balance. Prices may rise faster because of a greater strain on productive resources. However, inflationary pressure may also be reduced if the economy uses its capacity more fully and an increased rate of growth of productivity makes it possible to meet union demands for higher wages more easily, without passing such increases on to consumers. Faster growth and higher levels of real income will have an unfavorable impact on the current account. Increased productivity of capital and higher rates of interest will tend to attract foreign capital and thus improve the capital account.

Adding all these factors together, it seems that in the long run the effect on the trade balance of the policy here discussed will be nil or negative. However, with greater certainty, it may be argued that the immediate effect of the policy will be a considerable worsening of the trade balance; but later on, in five years or so when— and if—the desired targets of higher productivity and greater stock of productive resources are more closely attained, most of the beneficial effects are likely to become operative.

Chapter 18

THEORY OF CUSTOMS UNIONS

18.1 Introduction and Plan of Discussion

The theory of customs unions occupies a special and somewhat peculiar position in the theory of international trade. On the one hand, as a field, it is a special discipline within international trade, on the other hand, owing to the analytical framework within which it is discussed, the usual international trade analysis may appear as a special case of the analysis of economic integration.

The usual assumption of trade between two countries has to be relaxed when we discuss customs unions. At least three or more countries must be considered in speaking about economic integration; economic effects and repercussions have to be ascertained not only for the countries entering the union but also for the rest of the world. It is this peculiarity of the theory of customs unions that justifies a special treatment of the subject.

The aim of this chapter, therefore, is twofold. First, we shall try to answer the major problems connected with the creation and existence of customs unions or other forms of economic integration; and, second, in doing so, we shall construct a more complete and hence more realistic case of international trade, where a larger number of countries are considered simultaneously.

It is impossible—and fortunately unnecessary—to define precisely the case of economic integration. Depending on a virtually unlimited number of permutations of institutional arrangements, there is virtually an unlimited number of forms that a customs union may assume. The spectrum ranges from a partial mutual reduction of protection on a single product among a limited number of countries to complete trade liberalization and abolition of tariffs, combined with co-ordination of internal policies and possibly a common currency. Various terms are used to describe the different "intensities" of integration. However, because there is no clear dividing line between one form and another and because such terms are often used loosely and do not correspond to the same thing in the writings of different authors, we prefer not to adhere to such terminology. Rather, we shall speak about integration in general and in each given case specify the particular form we are discussing. For the purposes of our analysis, let us simply state that all the cases of integration, aside from any other arrangements, involve some discriminatory and mutual trade liberalization on the part of at least two countries. Henceforth, let us refer to any such situation as a "customs union."

The discussion of most of the preceding chapters has a direct relevance to our present discussion and suggests the organization of the present chapter. Actually, in most cases, exposition of the customs-unions case simply requires a generalization of our previous results. In the first of the following five sections of this chapter we shall discuss what we may call the "pure" theory of customs unions. The assumption of full employment will again be made; however, a larger number of countries have to be considered. In Section 3 we shall examine the balance-of-payments adjustment process in relation first to the creation of a customs union and then to its current operation. In Section 4 we shall examine some important long-run and institutional factors relevant for the discussion of economic integration, and in Section 5 we shall consider the criteria to be used in evaluating the welfare effect of customs unions. Finally, the last section will deal briefly with the interaction between economic integration and other internal and external economic policies of member countries.

We shall not try to exhaust the subject in considering all the different insitutional forms and arrangements of integration. Our task in this chapter is to consider the customs union in its general form and, wherever possible, to provide the reader with an analytical framework that may be used in dealing with any particular situation. The extensions of our analysis to special cases either will be directly apparent to the reader or will be pointed out explicitly in the course of our discussion.

18.2 The Pure Theory of Customs Unions

Let us begin by stating our assumptions. Again, we consider a simplified world; but a little less simplified than that we assumed in the earlier chapter dealing with the pure theory of trade. We assume that two countries enter into a customs union, while a third country, representing the outside world, is not included in the arrangement and consequently is discriminated against. At a later stage two countries of the outside world will be briefly considered. Only two factors of production—say, capital and labor—are used by each country and—for the moment—movement of factors of production from one country to another is impossible. At this point we refer the reader to Chapter 11, where we argue that such assumptions are not as restrictive for application to the conditions of the real world as they might at first appear.

Before deciding how many commodities we want to include in our analysis, we should pause and see to what extent the generality of our results will be affected by such a choice. So far we have generally assumed that only two commodities are produced and consumed by each country. There does not seem to be any more reason to deal with a larger number of commodities in discussing the case of customs unions than there is in discussing a simple two-country equilibrium of foreign trade.

Under the assumptions made so far, any single commodity may be traded in a number of different ways: (i) it may be exported from the two members of the union and imported by the rest of the world; (ii) it may be exported from the rest of the world and imported by the two union members; (iii) it may be exported from one union member and imported by the other member and imported by the third country (rest of the world); or (iv) it may be exported from one union member and imported by the other member and exported by the rest of the world. If only two commodities enter international trade and only two commodities are produced and consumed, cases (i) and (ii) become symmetrical, and thus treatment of only one of the two is required; similarly for cases (iii) and (iv). Moreover, cases (i) and (ii) are uninteresting from the point of view of customs-union analysis, because no discrimination is possible when both union members trade in the same direction. Consequently, if only two commodities enter our model of international trade, only two symmetrical cases, reducing to a single situation of trade, are interesting and should be examined. This is the situation wherein one of the union members competes in the other union member's market with the exports of the rest of the world, i.e., with the third country.

If more than two commodities are traded, each commodity may still be classified into one of the four groups mentioned above, unless, of course, the establishment of the customs union makes a given commodity pass from one classification into another. The likelihood of this happening is rather slim if the degree of discrimination created by the union is small—in either case we shall not consider such a situation. Trade in all commodities entering groups (i) and (ii) again is uninteresting, for the same reasons as above: no discrimination is possible. If we now identify the two countries entering the union as country A and country B, the cases classified so far under (iii) and (iv) now permit of four rather than only two situations: every commodity may be either imported by country A or imported by country B, while it is either exported or imported by the rest of the world.

If we now permit ourselves the same simplification that we often make in the two-country analysis, that is, if we aggregate all export and import commodities of the two union members into two commodity bundles, two situations are to be distinguished: calling the A exportables commodity A and the B exportables commodity B, the first situation arises if the rest of the world is a net importer of A and the second if it is a net exporter of A. Again these two situations are symmetrical and, for the purpose of our analysis, may be treated as a single situation. With three countries, however, an additional difficulty arises and may call for another interpretation. Some exportables of A will be imported by the third country, and some exported. A way around this difficulty would be to distinguish between commodity groups A_1 and A_2, as well as B_1 and B_2, where the subscripts 1 and 2 show whether either commodity group is exported or imported by the rest of the world; then, imposing the condition *ceteris paribus* on commodity groups 1, it would be possible to analyze the trade situation of commodity groups 2 and vice-versa. Either of the two interpretations is compatible with the analysis below.

To conclude our statement of assumptions, let us say that all markets are perfectly competitive, no external or internal economies or diseconomies are present, and consequently each industry produces under conditions of constant cost (i.e., all industry production functions are unit homogeneous). If transportation costs are present in international transactions, these may be counted as part of the tariff. Of course, in such a situation a customs union, from the point of view of our theoretical analysis, could never be complete.

Thus, keeping in mind the justification of the two-commodity case and the restrictiveness of such an assumption, we may now proceed to construct a simple model of a customs union. To do it, let us first define and explain a very simple and useful concept: the excess offer, or *excess reciprocal demand*. It is a relation between a number of terms-of-trade ratios and the quantities of two commodities that would be offered and demanded, jointly by two countries, to and

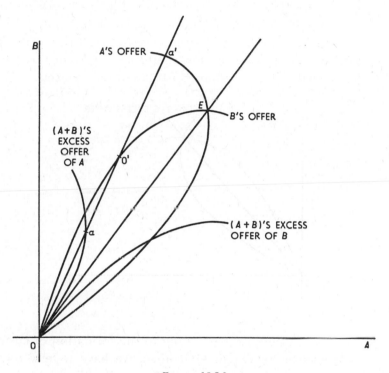

FIGURE 18.2.1

from a third country. An excess-offer curve of two countries, in our case two countries entering a customs union, can be constructed from the two offer curves of the two countries. Following from our assumption of mutual trade between the two countries, such two offer curves have to be concave toward each other, as shown in Figure 18.2.1. If the exchange ratio is that indicated by the slope of *OE* in Figure 18.2.1, the international trade of *A* and *B* will be exactly balanced, and consequently there will be no excess demand or offer for either product by *A* and *B* combined. We notice that the excess offer curve $O (A + B)$ passes through the origin at that price ratio. If

A becomes more expensive and the terms of trade move to the level indicated by the slope of *OO'*, the offer of *B* by country *B* will no longer be sufficient to match the demand for that product by country *A*. Such excess demand for *B* (or offer of *A*) is now indicated by the segment *O'a'* on *OO'*. The distance *O'a'* measured from the origin *O* now yields point *a*, a point of the excess-offer curve of countries *A* and *B*. Similar constructions will yield all points of the locus *O (A + B)*. It will be clear to the reader that a complete three-country trading equilibrium will be obtained if we plot the offer curve of the third country against the excess-offer curve of the two union countries combined. The terms-of-trade ratio, such as *OE* in Figure 18.2.2, will clear simultaneously all three markets.

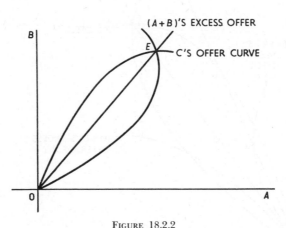

FIGURE 18.2.2

A number of questions pertaining to the formation of customs unions now may be answered. Of course, we have to rely on the analysis of the preceding chapters of the study. The most important effects of a customs union that we should like to examine are those (i) on the internal and external price ratios in the three countries, (ii) on the relative factor prices, and (iii) on relative income shares in each country.

To make the analysis more manageable, we assume, along with a number of older writers on the subject, that imposition of a tariff does not affect the conditions of reciprocal demand of the private sector of the economy. Where only the effects of tariffs on the terms of trade and other variables are considered, this assumption is not too restrictive. It is always possible to assume that the government consumes the tariff revenue. A prescribed pattern of such consumption determines the precise position of an offer curve with tariff. This was discussed in greater detail in Chapter 16.

If, however, we are concerned with the welfare evaluation of a customs union, the assumption of an invariant free-trade offer curve is more restrictive. In this case we have to consider the satisfaction of the different communities derived both from trade and from redistributed tariff revenues. But the latter will usually have an impact on conditions of reciprocal demand of the private sector. While we shall carry out the analysis using the assumption of an invariant offer curve of the private sector, it ought to be pointed out that all our results shown in this chapter might also be obtained in the more realistic situation where redistributive effects are explicitly included in the analysis.

Among the three major groups of problems outlined above, it would seem that the most important is the one concerning the different price or terms-of-trade ratios. All the other propositions, i.e., those concerning factor prices and income distribution, may then be

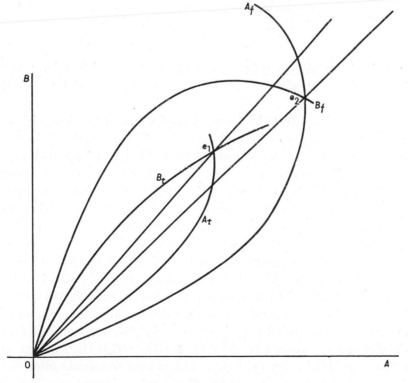

FIGURE 18.2.3

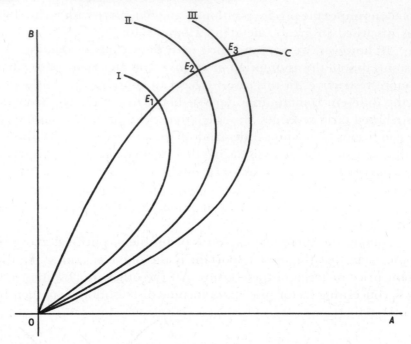

FIGURE 18.2.4.

derived fairly easily by using the analysis presented in Chapters 12, 13, and 14. They will be explained and summarized later in this section.

To see what effect the formation of a customs union will have on the different price ratios and on the volumes of trade of the three countries, let us consider simultaneously Figures 18.2.3 and 18.2.4. In the first diagram we show the free-trade offer curves of country A and country B, i.e., OA_f and OB_f, and the offer curves of the two countries imposing tariff on imports, OA_t and OB_t. To the latter situation of protection corresponds the excess-offer curve O, II in Figure 18.2.4. Free trade between the union countries, on the other hand, yields an excess-offer curve of the union O, III. The excess-offer curve of a free-trade union discriminating against the third country will now be obtained by measuring, as usual, to the left of O, III the ad valorem per cent rate of the import duty applied to commodities imported from the third country. In our second diagram such an excess-offer curve is represented by O, I. Here OC is the foreign offer curve of the third country. It may either be a free-trade offer curve or one derived from a free-trade offer curve to include a given rate of tariff. The two important equilibria in Figure 18.2.4 are E_1 and E_2, showing the trade of the two union countries with the third country. The first represents the situation in which the customs union is in operation, the second the *status quo ante*. The two world price ratios OE_1 and OE_2 clear all markets simultaneously under each of the two sets of conditions assumed. On the other hand, E_3 indicates the ideal equilibrium solution of free trade among all countries.

Before we continue our analysis of the situation just laid out, let us remark on the case of partial liberalization of trade between countries A and B. In such a case the entire analysis as for complete liberalization applies, except that we have to substitute for the offer curves OA_f and OB_f two other relations expressing the new level of reduced tariff.

Clearly, there is no unique answer to the question of what will happen to the terms of trade between the two countries entering the union as a result of such an agreement. This will depend on the levels of tariffs that were applied between the two union countries prior to liberalization, as well as on the elasticities of all the offer curves involved, including the offer curve of the rest of the world. The terms of trade of the third country will always be the terms of trade applied in the intra-union exchange corrected by the tariff levied on imports to the union from the third country.

Before being able to show what will happen to the terms of trade within the union, we have to pause a little and see how the all-important excess-offer curve of the union will be altered by an internal elimination of tariffs. As we have drawn the offer curves in Figure 18.2.3, the free-trade excess-offer curve O, III in Figure 18.2.4 came out to the right of O, II. But this is not a necessary result; the curve might have intersected OC at E_2 or to the left of this point. The discriminatory effect of a customs union, of course, will be stronger, the farther to the left the free-trade excess-offer curve falls, i.e., the more the trade of the third country is restricted. We should recall at this point that the actual excess-offer curve will be still further to the left than the free-trade excess offer, this divergence being determined by the level of tariff applied to imports from the nonunion country. Examining Figure 18.2.3, it becomes apparent that the discriminatory effect of a union will be stronger, the smaller the sum of elasticities of reciprocal demand in the neighborhood of e_2 and the larger in the neighborhood of e_1. Actually, to be exact, there are a number of possible configurations of the union countries' offer curves that the reader is advised to study in evaluating the terms-of-trade effects and the degree of discrimination of a customs union. It is not within the capacity of the author to express such criteria fully in any simple form.

Nevertheless, one of the special cases is quite interesting and deserves rigorous evidence. It is usually thought that a customs union will always involve some degree of discrimination against the third country; in other words, that the O, I excess-offer curve in Figure 18.2.4 should always intersect OC to the left of the equilibrium E_2. Indeed, this is by far the more likely outcome, but it is not a necessary one.

Suppose that the equilibrium world trading ratio prior to the establishment of a customs union between countries A and B is given by the slope of OE in Figure 18.2.5. The trading points of the two countries are given by E and F, respectively, and the corresponding excess offer of commodity A (A's exportable) is given by the segment EF. Suppose, further, that the rate of ad valorem tax,

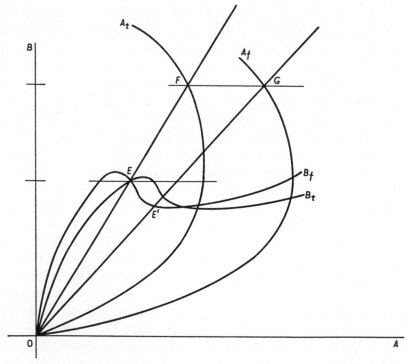

FIGURE 18.2.5

levied in terms of commodity A, is given by the difference of slopes of OE and OG. The free-trade and protective offer curves of country A have the usual shape, passing through points G and F, respectively. The free-trade and protective offer curves of country B are given by OB_f and OB_t, respectively.

Corresponding to this situation in the markets of the union countries, in Figure 18.2.6, we have constructed in the same way as in Figure 18.2.4 the three important offer curves $O, I; O, II;$ and

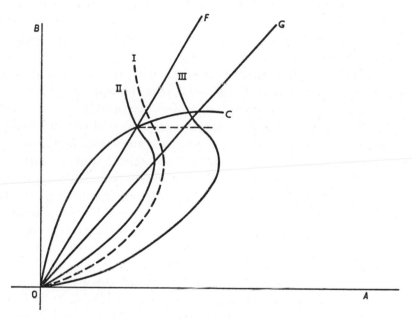

FIGURE 18.2.6

O, III. The excess-offer curve under conditions of free trade in the union and no tariffs imposed on imports from the third country (O, III) must be farther to the right of O, II (excess offer with tariff but without discrimination) in the vicinity of the pre-union equilibrium than the ad valorem import duty. This follows from the fact that the excess demand for B given by EF in Figure 18.2.5 falls short of that given by $E'G$. Hence O, I will be to the right of O, II. The third country will benefit in this case rather than suffer from discrimination.

We may now return briefly to the price ratios established within the customs union. Of course, precise results can be derived only when we consider the particular conditions of each case, using the analytical apparatus just set out. Nevertheless, we may make a few general statements. Assuming that the levels of tariff were about the same everywhere before the union was established and assuming fairly normal conditions of foreign demand in all countries, there is no reason for the free-trade excess offer of the union *O, III* in Figure 18.2.4 to assume too different a position from the excess offer *O, II*. However, because the tariff is still being imposed on imports from the third country, the excess offer with tariff (i.e., *O, I*) will almost always be to the left of *O, II* in Figure 18.2.4. Thus world prices, i.e., the terms of trade of the third country, will almost always turn against the third country, while for the intra-union price ratio the greatest likelihood is that it will turn somewhat in favor of country *B* (i.e., exporter of *B*) . Only in cases of extreme discriminatory effect will the terms of trade of the third country deteriorate to the point where the intra-union terms of trade turn in favor of *A*.

This, however, does not mean that the over-all trading position of country *A* should deteriorate. On the one hand, it will benefit from a large expansion of trade; on the other, it will reap tariff revenue from its trade with the third country. No such revenue will accrue directly to country *B*, which in our simple model imports only from *A*. However, country *B* will benefit from the trade expansion and possibly from somewhat improved intra-union terms of trade. We shall discuss some of these propositions in greater detail in Section 5 of this chapter.

The general equilibrium solution for all three countries may be easily shown by using Professor Meade's geometry. It would be too cumbersome to show both situations, that before and after the union is established; for purposes of comparative statics, the simple derivation by means of the excess-offer curve appears more convenient. In Figure 18.2.7 we show the general equilibrium solution of a customs union between two countries, with a third country that is not a member. It is an extension of the two-country solution presented and discussed in Chapter 14.

Along the vertical axis we measure consumption of commodity *B* and along the horizontal axis that of commodity *A*; P_A represents the consumption of country *A*, measured from origin *O*, and the production of that country, measured from *O''*. The segment *O''*, *O'''* that also contributes to consumption of country *A*, measures the tariff revenue of that country; P_B shows the consumption of commodities *A* and *B* by country *B* along the horizontal and vertical

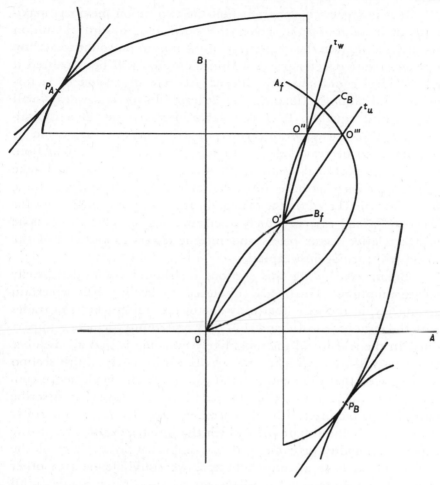

FIGURE 18.2.7

axes of the fourth quadrant, and the outputs of the two commodities, if measured on B's production block from the origin O'. The slope of Ot_u represents the intra-union terms of trade and also, of course, the marginal rate of transformation and of substitution within the two countries. On the other hand, $O't_w$ has the slope equal to the world terms of trade or relative world prices. If the third country does not impose any tax on either its imports or its exports, the domestic price ratio and hence the marginal rate of transformation in that country will equal the relative world prices. Finally, OA_f, OB_f, and $O'C$ are the free-trade offer curves of country A, of country B, and of country C, respectively.

It is immediately apparent that the two union members maximize their joint output, given the tariff rate toward nonunion countries and given the offer curve of the nonunion countries. Absolute and relative factor prices within the union will be equalized if all the ideal conditions are fulfilled (see the discussion of factor-price equalization in Chap. 12) or at least—in the real world—will tend toward equality. If A is a labor-intensive and B a capital-intensive product, wages in country A will tend to increase and in country B to decrease relative to the other factor of production. Changes proportional to those in relative factor prices will take place in the income shares of capital and labor, if supplies of these factors are unaffected by the change in trade and output. Except for the very special case in which discrimination benefits the outside world, relative factor prices and income shares in the rest of the world will turn against capital.

Before concluding this section, we should reconsider briefly our assumptions. The model discussed so far involves a certain asymmetry, in the sense that only one of the union countries trades with the rest of the world and thus only one country levies an import duty. In the real world the most likely outcome is that all member countries will trade with the rest of the world. Early in this section we suggested that the asymmetrical case might be made more consistent with the real conditions of trade if it was assumed to describe only half the picture. With reference to Figure 18.2.1, we have really discussed only the situation in which the union's excess offer of the export commodity of country A was imported by the rest of the world. As we have already indicated, we could define two other commodities or groups of products, say, D and E, that would fulfill just the opposite condition: for example, E, the export product of country B, would be in excess supply by the customs union within the relevant range of the terms of trade. All the preceding discussion would apply to this situation, except that the role of the two union countries would be reversed. If, as is the case in the real world, all types of products were traded simultaneously, we should have to assume that in the process of adjustment all the outputs and inputs of products A and B were unchanged.

We have also made the assumption that the rest of the world is composed of only one country. There is no difficulty, however, in letting the offer curve of the rest of the world represent an excess-offer curve of any number of countries. Such a relation would be derived in the same way as the excess offer of the union. The only point that should be stressed in this situation is that discrimination by the customs union would now hurt some of the outside countries and benefit others, depending on whether they were importers or exporters of the products supplied by the customs union to the world market. In the context of the real world, again, most countries will be both exporters and importers of the products supplied by the customs union. The most likely outcome is that most countries' losses from discrimination will not be fully compensated for by possible gains. By the same token, the union as a whole and each of its members will be likely to gain. The apparent asymmetry of effects on the two union members arising in the case of two commodities will generally disappear with a large number of products traded. Somewhat loosely, it may also be concluded that the union's gains will more than offset the losses of the rest of the world. We shall elaborate on this proposition in Section 5.

18.3 Customs Unions, the Balance of Payments, and Income Adjustment

In the preceding section we have been discussing the price, wage, and income distribution effects of a customs union within the framework of pure theory. Let us recall that this approach is based on the assumptions of perfect price and wage flexibility, full employment of all resources, and a balanced trade. In the real world, these assumptions are only rarely fulfilled. Price rigidity, fixed exchange rates, under-full employment, and trade imbalance are more frequently encountered in today's world than the ideal conditions of the classical world.

Along very much the same lines as in Chapters 7 and 8, we want to examine in this section the balance-of-payments adjustment process of a customs union. Income here is the principal adjustment variable; however, relative price effects have also to be considered, at least to the extent that discriminatory tariff adjustments affect prices and hence the demand for imports or domestic products. Although we assume fixed rates—in conformity with today's practice—the impact of a customs union on the foreign-exchange market, if it were free, may be easily ascertained by implication from the state of the balance of autonomous payments of each particular country.

As we saw in the preceding section, the formation of a customs union will generally have two effects. On the one hand, trade within the union will be expanded; on the other hand, trade with the outside world will usually be contracted. If the conditions of a Keynesian world prevail, this will in greatest likelihood affect the incomes and the balance of payments of the countries within and outside the union. Depending on such changes, the authorities of the different countries will have to resort to some measure in order to re-establish (1) the internal balance and (2) the external balance. These problems of policy were discussed in the preceding chapter and will be examined briefly in relation to the present topic in Section 6 of this chapter. At present, let us examine the direct effects of a customs union on income and the balance of payments and, by implication, on all the important propensities (i.e., to consume, to import, to save, and to invest).

We have set ourselves two tasks for this section. First, we should like to formalize a simple model reflecting the income and balance-of-payments adjustments to the formation of a customs union. Second, using such a model together with some qualitative reasoning, we shall analyze the most important aspects of such an adjustment. However simple, the model that we are going to present here is not simple enough to permit an easy evaluation of income and balance-of-payments effects of general validity. However, its use becomes extremely simple and straightforward whenever we are able to assign to its parameters some at least approximate actual values.

As in the preceding section, we assume that there are three countries altogether, of whom two form a customs union, while the third, representing the rest of the world, is discriminated against. Exchange rates are rigid, and factor costs in all countries are constant and equal to unity. Prices are equal to such factor costs except where tariffs are added onto such costs. In the latter case import prices will still be equal to unity, but domestic consumers will have to pay for such imports $p = 1 + t$, where t represents the rate of import duty. To simplify the analysis, we consider all domestic expenditures on domestically produced commodities, such as investment, consumption, or government spending, as a single aggregate represented by M_{ii}; this should be read as imports of the ith country from the ith country. The reader will find it easy to separate such a term into its component parts, should the analysis call for it. Similarly, we may use a symmetrical notation for all the trade aggregates M_{ij}—to be read as imports from country i to country j or, alternatively, exports of country i to country j. All the M's express volumes rather than values and are assumed to be a function of the real income Y of the country indicated by the second subscript. However, they may shift up or down, depending on relative prices. We shall return to this point presently. The increase or decrease in total effective demand in country i will be expressed in the same fashion as in our discussion of Chapter 7, namely, as $a \cdot k_i$. In the initial equilibrium, in our particular case before the union is created, a is equal to zero; it is only its small change da that is relevant for our analysis. The significance of k_i will emerge later from our discussion; at present let us merely state that it is to express the net impact of tariff changes or of any other policy on aggregate demand.

With these observations, a simple three-country model of simultaneous income determination may be defined as

$$Y_1 = M_{11} + M_{12} + M_{13} + a \cdot k_1 \tag{3.1}$$
$$Y_2 = M_{21} + M_{22} + M_{23} + a \cdot k_2 \tag{3.2}$$
$$Y_3 = M_{31} + M_{32} + M_{33} + a \cdot k_3 \tag{3.3}$$

These three equations are sufficient to determine the three unknowns Y_1, Y_2, and Y_3. Differentiating with respect to a, the changes in these three variables may be obtained for any given set of values k_1, k_2, and k_3. Thus we have

$$\frac{dY_1}{da} = \frac{1}{D} \cdot \begin{vmatrix} k_1 & -M'_{12} & -M'_{13} \\ k_2 & (1 - M'_{22}) & -M'_{23} \\ k_3 & -M'_{32} & (1 - M'_{33}) \end{vmatrix} \tag{3.4}$$

$$\frac{dY_2}{da} = \frac{1}{D} \cdot \begin{vmatrix} (1 - M'_{11}) & k_1 & -M'_{13} \\ -M'_{21} & k_2 & -M'_{23} \\ -M'_{31} & k_3 & (1 - M'_{33}) \end{vmatrix} \tag{3.5}$$

and, finally,

$$\frac{dY_3}{da} = \frac{1}{D} \cdot \begin{vmatrix} (1 - M'_{11}) & -M'_{12} & k_1 \\ -M'_{21} & (1 - M'_{22}) & k_2 \\ -M'_{31} & -M'_{32} & k_3 \end{vmatrix} \tag{3.6}$$

where D is the value of the determinant,

$$D = \begin{vmatrix} (1 - M'_{11}) & -M'_{12} & -M'_{13} \\ M'_{21} & (1 - M'_{22}) & -M'_{23} \\ -M'_{31} & -M'_{32} & (1 - M'_{33}) \end{vmatrix} \tag{3.7}$$

As stated so far, the above is a simple extension of the foreign-trade multiplier analysis, as presented in Chapter 7, to three countries. Equations 3.4 through 3.6 show the change in each of the three countries' incomes resulting from a given shift of effective demand by $da \cdot k_i$, for any prescribed values of the marginal propensities M'. Its applicability, within the assumptions made, is perfectly general; the model may be used in dealing with any case of income adjustment of three countries. In order to study the particular case of the customs union, where the first two countries are members and the third country remains on the outside, the parameters k_i have to be given a special interpretation. These parameters have to express the impact of discriminatory tariff reductions.

If country 1 and country 2 reduce tariffs vis-à-vis each other, some substitution of imports from the other union member for domestic commodities and for imports from the third country will undoubtedly take place, irrespective of the level of income. Depending on such price-elasticity effects, the terms k_1 and k_2 may be either positive or negative, while k_3 almost certainly will be negative.

We may resolve k_1 into its component parts,

$$k_1 = m_{11} + m_{12} + m_{13} \tag{3.8}$$

each m_{ij} expressing the shift of M_{ij} resulting from the formation of the customs union. Each of the nine propensities appearing in relations 3.1 through 3.3 may now be written as

$$M_{ij} = M_{ij}(Y_y) + a \cdot m_{ij} \tag{3.9}$$

Because factor costs everywhere are assumed to be constant and equal to unity and the difference between factor costs and prices may arise solely from tariffs, each m_{ij} can be a function only of the rate of tariff imposed by the jth country on its imports from (i) one foreign country and from (ii) the other foreign country. Note that domestic prices of domestic produce are always equal to 1. Thus, provided that we have sufficient knowledge of the elasticities and cross-elasticities of imports and of domestic demand, all m_{ij}'s may be calculated, once the tariff adjustments brought about by the union are known.

More precisely, the reader will find it easy to establish that, say, m_{12}, expressing the shift of the propensity to import of country 2 from country 1, for small changes in the tariff rates, may be found as

$$m_{12} = M_{12} \cdot \left(e_{12} \frac{dt_{12}}{1 + t_{12}} + e_{12}^{3} \frac{dt_{32}}{1 + t_{32}} \right) \cdot \frac{1}{da} \qquad (3.10)$$

where e_{12} represents the demand elasticity for imports from country 1 to country 2 with respect to the price of such imports, while e_{12}^{3} represents the cross-elasticity of imports from country 1 to country 2 with respect to the domestic price of imports of country 2 from country 3. The fractions within the parentheses multiplying the elasticities express the changes in tariff rates expressed in terms of the original price levels. Note, for example, that $1 + t_{32}$ is the domestic price of imports of country 2 from country 3. Of course, in the case where the customs union does not apply a common tariff on its imports and no country changes its tariffs toward the third country, the second term in the parentheses will be zero. In relation 3.10, M_{12} expresses the initial equilibrium level of imports from country 1 to country 2. The term $1/da$ will appear in all expressions m_{ij}. However, once the m_{ij}'s are substituted in the k_i's and these are introduced into the solution equations 3.4, 3.5, and 3.6, the term da will cancel on both sides of the equations. For example, equation 3.4 will now read

$$\frac{dY_1}{da} = \frac{1}{da} \cdot \frac{1}{D} \cdot A \qquad (3.11)$$

where A is a determinant whose value is calculable from the marginal propensities, the own and cross-elasticities entering the terms m_{ij}, and the original levels of imports and domestic consumption. Now da may be cancelled on both sides of relation 3.11; thus we obtain directly the change in the income of country 1 resulting from the formation of the customs union. The same applies to the other two countries.

The change in the balance of payments of country 1 and similarly of both other countries may now be obtained as

$$dBP_1 = M'_{12}dY_2 + M'_{13}dY_3 - M'_{21}dY_1 - M'_{31}dY_1 \\ + da(m_{12} - m_{21} - m_{31}) \qquad (3.12)$$

observing that m_{13} is zero. The change in the balance of payments of the customs union may be found either as the sum of the changes of the trade balances of the two union countries,

$$dBP_u = dBP_1 + dBP_2$$

or as the reverse of the balance of the third country, i.e., $-BP_3$.

Before turning our attention to the analysis of possible income and balance-of-payments effects of the customs union, let us return for a while to the model defined by relations 3.1 through 3.3. We have already observed that its applicability is much broader than a mere examination of the impact of a formation of a customs union. Subsequent adjustments in tariffs may equally well be analyzed by using the model. Moreover, any deliberate policy of any government affecting any of the nine propensities may be related to income changes and balance-of-payments changes through relations 3.4 through 3.6. In all cases it is necessary only to define and evaluate precisely the parameters k_i and a. If, for example, the government of country 1 decides to increase its spending on domestic products by one billion dollars without raising taxes, $k_1 = m_{11} = +1$, while $k_2 = k_3 = o$; da is equal to one billion.

We may begin our examination of balance-of-payments and income effects by considering the case where the two members of the union (countries 1 and 2) are perfectly comparable, in that they have the same marginal, average, and total propensities to spend on domestic products and to import from the partner country, on the one hand, and from the third country, on the other. Tariff rates of all three countries are the same prior to the establishment of the union. The elasticities and cross-elasticities also are symmetrical for the two member countries. Such a situation will yield the same change in the incomes of countries 1 and 2—their mutual balance of payments will remain unaffected—while, as a most likely outcome, the balance of payments of each and of the union as a whole will improve toward the third country. The third country, on the other hand, will usually see both its income and its balance of payments deteriorate. However, this is not a necessary result. The internal increase in income of the two member countries may be such as to offset the discriminatory effects on imports from the third country, so that this country's income will not suffer.

A symmetrical solution of the customs-union problem is most unlikely. The parameters of the three countries will generally not have the required symmetrical values. Thus the most likely outcome is that the incomes and the balances of payments of all three countries will be affected differently. The only general statement that may be made with a fair degree of certainty is that, on the whole, the union members' incomes will benefit, while the income position of the third country will deteriorate. As for the balance-of-payments effects, the results are less certain. In essence, the problem here considered is comparable to the simpler situation discussed in the last section of Chapter 16. All will depend on the magnitudes of the marginal propensities and the price elasticities. The balance of payments of the rest of the world may deteriorate—perhaps as a more likely outcome—but it might also happen that the income effects on imports into the protected area and into the rest of the world would be so strong as to reverse this expectation. In particular, the balance of payments and even income may be improved for primary-product-producing countries outside the union, who enjoy low price and high income elasticities of demand for their products. Only the complete solutions exhibited above will furnish precise answers in each particular case.

If a customs union were formed under conditions of flexible exchange rates, the direction of change of that variable could usually be ascertained from the changes in the balances of payments of the different countries under fixed rates. Thus the more normal outcome would be a relative appreciation of the currencies of the union countries. This in turn would tend to have a beneficial effect on the incomes of the non-member countries, who would now be able to sell their products within the integrated area at lower prices and substitute some of their domestic products for imports. On the other hand, it could be expected that the union incomes would be somewhat lower than with fixed exchange rates, on grounds of the factors of effective demand just stated. On the whole, it seems that flexibility of exchange rates would generally provide for a better and more equitable allocation of world output than would fixed rates.

Also, it ought not to be overlooked that the rigorous theory presented in the first part of this section is based on the assumption of stability of internal price levels. To the extent that the union members operate near full employment, the original increase in effective demand will certainly have an impact on the price levels in these countries, and vice-versa for the nonmember countries. If this happens, very much the same offsetting effects will take place as those likely to arise under flexible exchange rates: the rest of the world will now be better off than it would have been if prices had remained unchanged within the union.

Together with higher prices in the union countries and lower in others, rates of interest will be likely to undergo similar changes in the two parts of the world. The change in the balance of payments on capital account would in that case tend to reinforce the deterioration of the current account of the nonunion countries. If interest rates were to be held unchanged in the union countries, as a matter of policy, further price inflation in these countries should be expected, and an improvement, rather than a deterioration, in the over-all balance of the nonunion countries could ensue.

18.4 Long-Run Effects, Market Imperfections, and Other Factors Leading to a More Realistic Theory of Customs Unions

The preceding two sections provide the positive groundwork of the static and comparative static analysis of customs unions. To complete the survey of the theory, two important areas remain to be discussed. One pertains to the welfare effects of customs unions and will be discussed in Section 5. The other bears on the long-run aspects of economic integration and on some realistic deviations from the ideal conditions assumed so far. We shall devote to it this section.

In our preceding analysis we have assumed throughout that the structural parameters, such as preferences, technology, factor endowments, income elasticities, and so forth, are given and that the only effects of the customs union are those on the level of tariffs and possibly on other policy variables. The creation of a customs union and the adjustment of the world economies to it is a long-lasting process. During long periods of time the structure or structural parameters of the different countries may change substantially. To the extent that such changes are autonomous, they fall within the sphere of the general analysis of international trade. To the extent, however, that they are brought about by the existence and operation of the customs union, they should be examined within the theory of customs unions.

Another set of valid arguments, often brought up in the discussion of economic integration, is concerned with the so-called external and internal economies leading to a greater technical or economic efficiency of production within the union. So far we have assumed in our analysis that costs are independent of the scale of production; that is, the technologies of the different industries are assumed to be homogeneous of order 1.

If internal economies are present in a given productive activity, this assumption is no longer valid; the technology will now have to be approximated by a homogeneous function of order greater than 1, that is, one in which increasing returns to scale take place. But, if this is the case, the average cost will be declining and the marginal cost be below it, either indefinitely or at least up to a point of a quite substantial level of output in relation to the size of a national market. It is clear that perfectly competitive conditions are not compatible with such a case. Prices in such an industry cannot be set at marginal cost, and a monopolistic or oligopolistic structure will generally ensue.

Before the customs union is created, owing to the protection of national markets, output will generally be restricted and prices be high in each particular country. Elimination of internal tariffs, unless counteracted by new international cartelization, will generally lead to lower prices, a greater degree of specialization, and, what is most important, production at a more efficient scale. On the limit, with an important enlargement of markets, an oligopolistic industry may be transformed into one operating under perfectly competitive conditions.

External economies, on the other hand, will generally lead to a pattern of diminishing costs for the industry as a whole, while each particular firm may operate at or beyond its minimum-cost point. Such conditions are still consistent with perfect competition and hence, with appropriate adjustment, may be analyzed by using the usual tools of general equilibrium. The transformation function will now be less concave, or even convex, compared with what it would have been in the absence of external economies. The likelihood of complete specialization in each particular country will now increase, and the gain in physical output of the union countries taken together, resulting from integration, will be greater.

It is sometimes argued that the argument of external and internal economies, however convincing in theory, usually does not apply to cases of integration in the real world. It appears that those arguing in such a way depend too much in their analysis on the oversimplified general equilibrium models, where only two or a few products are produced by each country. Indeed, if the income of a nation with, say, ten million consumers were to be spent entirely on two or three products, hardly any industry or firm could operate at a point on the declining phase of its cost curve. If, however, thousands or millions of different and differentiated products are produced and consumed, as is the case in the real world, the assertion no longer holds. The experience of economic integration in western Europe or, for that matter, of a complete customs union in the United States provides convincing evidence. Actually, it may be argued that customs unions among countries in a comparable stage of economic advancement and fairly comparable natural-resource endowments may expect to derive their greatest benefit precisely from economies of large-scale production.

The agreement establishing a customs union will often provide explicitly for easier movement of labor, or at least of some types of labor, from one country to another. Moreover, the cultural, political, and economic rapprochement of the member countries may, in fact, provide for greater facility of such movements. This will, at least within the competitive framework, add to the factor price-equalizing effect of the union brought about by the commodity price equalization. Consequently, marginal physical products of labor will be more nearly equalized and thus the over-all efficiency of the free-trade region be improved. Of course, it may be argued that the enlargement of the labor market—as much as of any other market—is a two-edged sword that may both improve competitive conditions and hamper them. The latter alternative would arise if the width of the market had any influence on collusive practices of either workers or employers. In my opinion the forces tending toward greater competitiveness will prevail over those of collusion. The obvious reason is that, while the market is effectively enlarged through a mutual reduction or elimination of tariffs, antitrust legislation usually remains the same and most often is not more lenient toward international than toward national collusive practices.

The operation of long-term and short-term capital markets and consequently the allocation of reproducible resources will also generally, *de facto* or *de jure,* be improved. Often exchange controls are imposed and capital movements controlled among fairly disconnected economies. The formation of a customs union will most often require some degree of synchronization of internal and external economic policies on the part of member countries. If external balance is more nearly attained, the mobility of short- and long-term funds will also improve. On its own merits, the expansion of mutual trade will render the member economies more connected and consequently more nearly similar in cyclical fluctuations. This will call for similar monetary and fiscal policies. Consequently, short-term interest arbitrage and possibly exchange-rate arbitrage and speculation will be diminished, and there will be greater leeway in the balance of payments for long-term investment seeking higher marginal productivity of capital.

Both these factors—the enlargement of labor markets, on the one hand, and that of capital markets, on the other—and, in addition, the direct impact on efficiency through equalization of marginal productivities may yield other significant benefits. Besides altering the factor endowments of the different member countries, they may alter the technology itself. Better laborers' and entrepreneurial skills often accompany movements of labor and capital. Such intangible or less tangible benefits of customs unions may be very significant, particularly if it comes to integration of countries at different levels of economic, technical, and cultural advancement.

The infant-industry argument, although it is related to the different types of economies of scale discussed above, deserves special mention. It is often used for individual undeveloped countries in justifying their protection. As we saw quite clearly in Section 2 of this chapter, a customs union will almost always have some protective or discriminatory effects. Such protection within a union formed by a number of less advanced countries may supply precisely the desired difference between import prices and domestic marginal costs that will permit growth of an industry where it could not have taken place otherwise. After some years, when the industry improves its efficiency, the union may then proceed in reducing its barriers toward the outside world and thus further enhance world efficiency. The great advantage of the infant-industry-type union over the infant-industry tariff is obviously the fact that the former proceeds through liberalization, the latter through restriction.

Next to the benefits from the different types of internal and external economies, it may also be argued that even the absolute rate of capital accumulation and hence of economic growth will be increased. On grounds of the discriminatory effects of a customs union, the normal expectation is that real incomes within the union will reach a higher level, if this is possible. As we saw in the preceding section, how important this effect will be depends on the shifts in effective demand, k_i. These depend on the shifts of the individual propensity schedules, m_{ij}. The m_{ij}'s, finally, depend on the own and cross-elasticities of demand for domestic consumption, domestic investment, and imports from the different parts of the world. If the cross-elasticities are low and the own elasticities high, the most likely outcome is that the "short-run" level of income within the union will be a good deal higher after its creation. If this is the case, net investment and the rate of accumulation within the union are likely to increase, either on account of a positive marginal propensity to invest, or on account of improved expectations, or, finally, on account of a long-run acceleration principle.

Two arguments may be offered for the prevalence of the desired levels of the own and cross-elasticities. On purely theoretical grounds, a tariff reduction within the union will reduce the general price level; this, as the most likely hypothesis, will increase real expenditure in the union countries and reduce real savings at any given level of income. The other argument is not new, but only a variant of the so-called "new-goods" factor of demand. Many of the commodities affected by the internal elimination of tariffs will have a special attractiveness of their own from being new in a part of the customs union where tariffs formerly rendered their purchase uneconomical. The price and income elasticity of demand for such products will usually be higher than those relating to domestic "old" products.

Of course, to the extent that all, or some, of these factors do influence favorably either the absolute level of income at each period of time or the rate of growth of the union, the outside world must also necessarily benefit from it. Such gains must be used as an offsetting factor to the losses that almost unavoidably the customs union will inflict on the rest of the world, through its immediate terms-of-trade and income effects. It is possible to refer to such an effect as long-run external trade creation, as opposed to short-run external trade diversion and internal trade creation. These benefits may be very important if we assume a sufficiently long view of the customs-union problem.

But there is, or at least may be, another beneficial effect of a customs union on the outside world. Even with full employment, an assumption made in Section 2, the demand for imports of some products from third countries is bound to increase, provided that these same products are not also produced within the protected area. This may pertain to any commodities but primarily has relevance for trade in raw materials.

As we have shown in Section 2, after the union is created, prices and hence marginal rates of transformation in the union countries will be equalized. This will lead to a more efficient allocation of resources and to an increase in physical output of most products. This is illustrated in Figure 18.4.1. Prior to the customs union, one country produced at P_1 and the other (whose production possibility is superimposed on that of the first country at P_1) at P_2. With respect to the origin O, P_2 represents total output of A and B prior to the union. Note that the marginal rates of transformation in the two countries are different, this difference being imputable to tariff. With union trade liberalization, marginal rates of transformation are equalized, and the union production point moved to P_2', where more of both A and B is being produced.

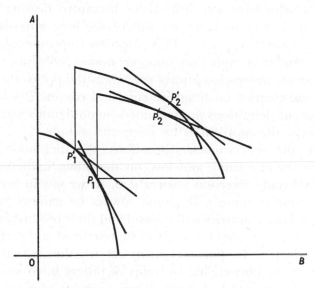

FIGURE 18.4.1

Demand for all factors of production employed at least approximately in proportion to output must increase. Typically, industrial materials, whether used directly or indirectly in production, fall within this category of productive factors. If the sole or principal supplier of such materials is the rest of the world, imports from and the balance of payments and income of these areas will all benefit.

Finally, we should make reference to the locational aspects of a customs union. It would be necessary to explain the theory of location before we could relate it rigorously to our special problem of integration. We cannot do so here. However, let us point out that internal reduction or elimination of tariffs and the resulting enlargement of markets may make possible a more efficient locational pattern within the union. Note, for example, that, prior to the union's entering into effect, a location of a producer on or near the national border was uneconomical, even though it might have been most efficient according to a more objective locational criterion. Also, it ought to be observed that such locational benefits could not be attained unless at least some union members shared a common border.

18.5   Customs Unions and Economic Welfare

Those who have scrutinized the literature dealing with the subject matter of customs unions will realize how important a role the welfare aspect has played. This emphasis is quite explainable in view of the fact that, more than other economic problems, the discussion of customs unions has always verged on the political. Although international treaties, tariff agreements, and conferences have often given clear-cut definitions and assumed unambiguous attitudes, for an economist the problem is by no means simple.

From the very earliest discussions, the dichotomy between benefit, on the one hand, and loss, on the other, or between trade creation and trade diversion was realized. As we saw in Section 2, in the static context there will almost always be gainers and losers; the trade of some countries will expand and their production become more efficient, the trade of others will be restricted and their terms of trade deteriorate. To pass judgment on whether actual losses of some people are outweighed by gains of others is, to say the least, an extremely grave task. Yet all those countries who have entered into a customs union have made such a judgment.

In evaluating the welfare effects of a customs union, there are at least two broad avenues of approach. One may be termed "cardinalist," the other "ordinalist." The former, under extremely tenuous assumptions, is capable of absolute conclusions; the latter, with somewhat less tenuous assumptions, may only state that a customs union is beneficial to the world as a whole *if.* . . . Now this *if* is usually followed by a statement of a required transfer that would have to be made in one way or another in order to improve the lot of every country. The practical question then arises whether it is a sufficient justification of a customs union if such a transfer is possible or whether a compensatory transfer is actually to be required.

Professor Meade, to whom a good portion of the theory of customs unions should be credited, uses the concept of cardinal utility coupled with the assumption of interpersonal comparability.[1] This implies that the utility of each individual is measurable in terms of a cardinal index permitting of precise numerical comparisons of different levels of satisfaction for one individual as well as of such comparisons among individuals. We shall first examine this approach. Later we shall employ the criterion of ordinal utility. Within its framework, we shall derive some important theorems establishing the relation between the structure of the different economies entering and not entering a union, the degree of tariff reduction, and the desirability of a customs union. Many of the results obtained through cardinal analysis may also be established by using the concept of ordinal utility. As the latter approach requires somewhat less unrealistic assumptions, we prefer to conduct most of our analysis in this way.

Using the cardinalist approach, for small reductions of tariffs on the part of the union countries, a simple index of utility gain or loss resulting from the arrangement for the whole world may be established, namely,

$$dU = I_U = \sum_{i=0}^{n} (p_i - c_i)dx_i \qquad (5.1)$$

where p_i and c_i represent the price and the unit cost of the ith commodity, respectively, while dx_i is the change in world output and consumption of the ith commodity resulting from a customs union, and U is a world cardinal utility index. Of course, a positive dU represents a gain in world satisfaction, and a negative dU a loss. Assuming, for simplicity, that all the tariffs to be reduced by the union are the same, say t, and assuming the structures of all economies given, U is a function of t. Thus the gain from a complete elimination of tariffs within the union would become

$$I_U = U(o) - U(t) \qquad (5.2)$$

The very important relation, however, remains relation 5.1. Its great merit is its simplicity and also the fact that both costs and prices are empirically ascertainable, while the size of the dx_i's may be calculated if we have some knowledge of the elasticities of supply and demand of the different products x_i. The reader should be aware, however, that if major changes in the structure of tariffs take

[1] See especially J. E. Meade, *The Theory of Customs Unions* (Amsterdam: North Holland Publishing Co., 1955).

place, the p's and c's will change also for most commodities, and this may introduce a bias into the estimator I_U. There are reasons to believe that such a bias would not affect the sign of the index.

To derive Professor Meade's index, let us assume that every individual j has a cardinal utility function,

$$u_j = u_j(x_j^i \ldots, v_j^k \ldots) \tag{5.3}$$

where x_j^i expresses the consumption of the ith commodity by the jth individual and v_j^k his supply of the kth factor of production. The world utility function will be written as

$$U = \sum_j u_j \tag{5.4}$$

and a small change in such utility,

$$dU = \sum_j du_j \tag{5.5}$$

Because

$$du_j = \sum_i u_{j,i} dx_j^i + \sum_k u_{j,k} dv_j^k \tag{5.6}$$

and

$$\frac{u_{j,i}}{p_i} = \frac{-u_{j,k}}{w_k} = A_j \tag{5.7}$$

where A_j represents the marginal utility of income of the jth individual, w_k the wage of the kth factor of production, and the u_j with a second subscript represents a partial derivative, we may write

$$du_j = A_j \left(\sum_i p_i dx_j^i - \sum_k w_k dv_j^k \right) \tag{5.8}$$

Assuming, now, with Professor Meade that the marginal utility of everybody's income is the same, we assign to it the value *one*, thus defining our utility scale, and obtain from relations 5.5 and 5.8

$$dU = \sum_i p_i \sum_j dx_j^i - \sum_k w_k \sum_j dv_j^k \tag{5.9}$$

Now we observe that the second summations in the two terms of the right-hand side of relation 5.9 are nothing else but the total changes of commodity i demanded and of factor v^k supplied in the world. Thus we may write

$$dU = \sum_i p_i dx^i - \sum_k w_k dv^k \tag{5.10}$$

But, assuming that all production functions are homogeneous of order 1, the second term of the right-hand side expresses the change in total factor cost of all commodities produced, and thus may be also written as

$$\sum_i c_i dx^i$$

where c_i represents the average cost of the ith commodity. Expressing thus relation 5.10, we obtain relation 5.1.

To believe that we should be closer to an ideal world if all marginal utilities of income were equalized does not yet mean that they are equal. Indeed, large differences of income per capita do exist between nations and within nations, and consequently the assumption of equality of marginal utilities, if such an assumption is at all admissible, is extremely tenuous. If we permit ourselves to deal with nations as single units, it is possible to adjust Professor Meade's index to account for possible differences in marginal utilities of income between different nations. Let us designate such an index for the nth nation as A_n, and the change of quantity of the product x^i produced in country n, x_n^i, and consumed x_N^i. Now the index of world utility gain or loss becomes

$$dU = \sum_n A_n \left(\sum_i p_n^i dx_N^i - \sum_i c_n^i dx_n^i \right) \tag{5.11}$$

The distinction must now be made between changes in commodities produced and consumed in each particular country; however, provided that the same information is available as that needed in computing the simple index in relation 5.1, this computation will be almost equally easy. Of course, every policy maker will have to use his own *subjective* values of A_n. The assumption of some inverse proportionality of A and per capita income might be agreed upon by many. This, of course, would make a customs union among undeveloped countries appear quite desirable. The same would hold for a union among industrialized nations such as the European Seven and Six, liable to be less discriminatory toward the poor than toward other industrialized countries.

It would be beyond the scope of the present study to elaborate on concrete cases and applications of this approach. For this we refer to Professor Meade's original work. Let us only point out the utility of Professor Meade's index in handling concrete cases of individual commodities or groups of commodities where we have some a priori or statistical knowledge about the magnitudes of elasticities and cross-elasticities of supply and demand. Such economic indexes, coupled with data reflecting outputs, trade, and consumption (always observable), may rapidly lead to approximate results, sufficient in dealing with concrete questions of policy.

Let us now turn our attention to the other possible approach, namely, that of ordinal utility. We have used this concept extensively in Chapters 13, 14, 15, and 16. Let us just recall that, in essence, because cardinal interpersonal and personal comparisons are excluded, it uses the criterion of potential or actual gains with compensation. In other words, whenever a policy change takes place or the economic structure changes, we pose the question whether, if all losers were compensated to the point of indifference between the *status quo ante* and the *status quo post,* there would still be a gain on the part of some other individuals. If such a compensation is possible, we say that the change that has brought about the reallocation of resources is potentially beneficial, and vice-versa. The nuance between *actual* and *potential* benefit is very important and often overlooked.

There is another distinction to be made with respect to the ordinalist approach to welfare evaluation. The compensating transfers may be made either within the framework of the general equilibrium system or independently of it. In the first case we let the general equilibrium adjust to the process of transfer. In the latter we let the system find its equilibrium corresponding to the change in policy or structural parameters and then effect a real transfer in the desired direction, without considering how the new levels of real income may affect the general equilibrium solution. Of course, the desirability of a given policy—here, of a customs union— will be proved more strongly if the proof is based on the first type of transfer. In this case we may speak of a feasible solution, in contrast to a proof based on the other type of transfer that, in practice, may not be feasible.

We may begin our discussion with a set of simple but nevertheless quite important remarks. They pertain to the simplest situation, wherein two countries enter into a customs union and are facing an infinitely elastic offer curve of the rest of the world. Throughout the rest of this section we assume a single nonintersecting indifference map of the community. For a more detailed discussion of this assumption we refer the reader to Chapter 13.

Let us assume that there was no discrimination of one kind or another prior to the union and that the two union members were imposing tariffs of equal rate on all imports. The infinitely elastic world offer curve is given by the line OP_w in Figures 18.5.1 and 18.5.2. The rate of tariff is indicated by the difference of slopes of

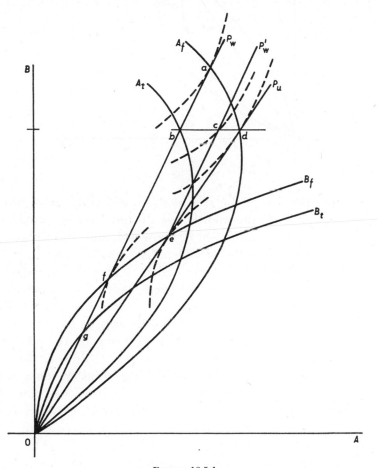

FIGURE 18.5.1

OP_w and OP_u in Figure 18.5.1. The trade of the union countries with the rest of the world before the union is indicated by the segment gb, corresponding to OE in Figure 18.5.2. When the union is established, country B will trade with A along OP_u up to point e, and the excess supply of country A will be sold at world prices, up to point c. The segment cd represents the tariff revenue of country A.

Because the world offer curve is infinitely elastic, we may

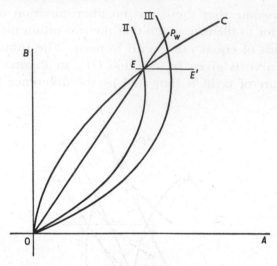

FIGURE 18.5.2

conclude that the loss of the rest of the world from discrimination is nil or negligible. Consequently, we do not have to consider any compensating transfer to the rest of the world, and the only criterion to be used in evaluating the welfare effects of the union is whether the union itself has gained or whether it would have gained if appropriate transfers within it had been made. As we observe from the position of the indifference curves[2] (*dotted lines*) in Figure 18.5.1, country B has gained a good deal by moving from the trading point g to e. Country A's movement from b to c, on the other hand, corresponds to a loss of social satisfaction. However, the union members might agree on a compensating transfer. One way of effecting this would be to transfer physical quantities of commodity A from the exporter of B to the exporter of A, letting both countries exchange their consumable resources at world prices in such a way as to maximize their utility. This, of course, would permit both countries to settle at their respective points of maximum efficiency, consistent with world prices, that is, country A would attain the point a and country B point f. Both points are preferable, each from the point of view of the corresponding country, to the situation before union. However, it is important to note that they could have been attained in a more direct way (without a union combined with internal transfer) through a complete liberalization of trade.

[2] These may be interpreted either as regular indifference curves or, with more generality, as trade indifference curves, explained in Chapter 14.

It would be more realistic to assume that, while real resources are transferred from one union member to the other, the two are permitted to trade at the intra-union exchange ratio, tariff being levied on imports from the rest of the world. Under such conditions the free-trade (most efficient) solution points f and a could not be attained. However, it is possible to show that both union countries may be made better off than they were prior to integration. It follows from our discussion of Section 4 (see Fig. 18.4.1) that, for any given world terms of trade and any given rate of import duty, the elimination of tariffs within the union countries will lead to a greater real output within the union. With fixed world prices, given by the slope of OP_w in Figure 18.5.1, and with continuous trading under the assumed conditions, it will always be possible to redistribute the product and tariff revenue of the union in such a way as to make both members better off than they were prior to integration.

Thus we may formulate our *first conclusion:* If the union faces an infinitely elastic offer curve, i.e., fixed prices in world markets, it will benefit from a mutual tariff reduction combined with mutual compensation. But it could have gained at least as much if it had freed its trade entirely. Because there cannot be any loss on the part of the outside world from discrimination, the effect on world welfare will also be beneficial. In practice, this case corresponds to small customs unions, who do not supply a major share of any commodity in the world market.

The *second* important *conclusion* derives from the first: There cannot be any special gain from a customs union, as opposed to complete trade liberalization, unless the offer curve of the rest of the world is less than infinitely elastic. Whether there is a potential advantage to discriminatory trade liberalization with a less than infinitely elastic world offer curve remains to be seen.

To study this situation, let us consider the case in which the union, once established, always compensates the rest of the world to the point where it would be as well off as it was before the union was created. Such a compensation is extremely simple, because the customs union may reduce or increase its external tariff to the point where the terms of trade of the world would remain unchanged. In other words, if, for instance, the free-trade excess-offer curve of the union were in the position of O, III in Figure 18.5.2, the union could always adjust its external tariff to the level indicated by EE'. Now the excess-offer curve *with tariff* O, I (not drawn in the diagram) would intersect the less than infinitely elastic offer curve of the world OC, at point E, and the world terms of trade would remain unchanged. Also, the welfare position of the outside world would remain unaffected. Of course, if the free-trade excess offer were to the left of O, II, this type of compensation would require a subsidy rather than a partial reduction of tariff. Such a subsidy, however, would not have to be considered on grounds of inefficiency; in this case the criterion for evaluating whether the union is desirable or not would be reduced to the question whether complete liberalization of trade by the union countries is beneficial or not to themselves.

Let us consider again Figure 18.5.1 and study a special "central" case that will be useful to us throughout the following discussion. Suppose that segments gb and fa, both measured along OP_w, have equal length. This would imply that O, II and O, III intersect or coincide at point E on OC in Figure 18.5.2. In words, this indicates that if the customs union first reduced its mutual tariffs to zero and then proceeded in compensating the rest of the world through tariff reduction to the point of complete elimination of tariff, the world terms of trade would not be altered. Also, the welfare position of the rest of the world would not be affected; yet, because both union members would now be at their efficient points a and f, respectively, the welfare position of the world as a whole as well as of the union would be augmented.

This establishes our *third conclusion:* If complete trade liberalization on the part of union countries does not affect the world terms of trade, even though the world offer curve is less than infinitely elastic, then the union is potentially desirable; that is, it is possible to improve the position of every country. Starting from this situation, two cases present themselves: (i) the free-trade excess-offer curve O, III lies to the left of O, II, and (ii) it lies to the right. In the latter case, only a partial compensatory reduction of tariffs is necessary in order to keep the rest of the world as happy as it was prior to the union. In case (i), as we have indicated, no subsidy beyond complete elimination of tariffs is necessary. It would be inefficient because, even if the offer curve of the rest of the world represented free trade, such a subsidy would move the world as a whole away from its most efficient resource allocation.

Let us first consider case (i). If the free-trade excess-offer curve O, III intersects OC to the left of point E, the union, while compensating the outside world to the point of complete elimination of tariffs, will now face more favorable terms of trade. This situation is illustrated in Figure 18.5.3. The slope of OP_1 represents the free-trade terms of trade, and that of OP_2 the terms of trade prevailing in the world markets before the union was established. Note that the segment aa' indicates a greater amount of trade than bb'; both are to be found on OP_1. Country A now has moved from point a' to point

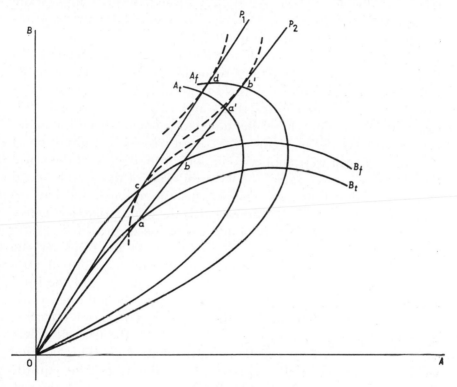

FIGURE 18.5.3

d and country B from a to c. Without internal transfer, the welfare position of country A has improved considerably, while that of country B may or may not have improved. However, as a simple construction (left to the reader) will indicate, a physical transfer of, say, commodity A from country A to country B will render the position of the latter country as desirable as before, while country A still will remain considerably better off than it was before the union. Indeed, as we have shown in Chapter 15, the free-trade position with terms of trade given by OP_1 is potentially preferable to free trade along OP_2. But the latter situation, as will easily be observed, is preferable to trade between the two union countries, with the same terms of trade (given by OP_2) and mutual discrimination.

Our *fourth conclusion* follows: If a complete trade liberalization on the part of union countries leads to an improvement in the union's terms of trade with the rest of the world, the union is potentially desirable. Actually, on grounds of equity, the union countries could be advised to free trade entirely; through appropriate internal transfers, both could improve their lots substantially without being blamed for discrimination.

The last situation corresponds to case (ii) of our foregoing distinction. Here only a partial tariff reduction, or even a tariff increase, is needed in order to preserve world terms of trade. To examine this case, let us return to Figures 18.5.1 and 18.5.2. It is precisely this case that is illustrated here. Because the segment *gb* indicates less trade than *fa*, *O, III* in Figure 18.5.2 must pass to the right of point *E*. If the old tariff were applied to imports from the rest of the world after the union was created, the terms of trade of the outside world would deteriorate. Thus, to compensate, the union would have to reduce its outside tariff. To find what is the appropriate compensatory tariff level and the corresponding solution of the three-country general equilibrium, let us turn to Figure 18.5.1. Consider the triangle *edc*. It may be transformed by altering the slope of OP_w, holding one angle *d* always on A_f, another, *e*, on B_f, and the third such as *c* being defined by the intersection of a horizontal line passing through *d* and a line having the slope of OP_w always passing through point *e*. There will be one position of the triangle where the length of *ec* will be exactly equal to that of *gb*. This position yields the solution of the system. Necessarily at such an equilibrium level the position of country *B* will be improved, while the welfare of country *A* may either improve or deteriorate. Again, a simple construction that we have omitted in order not to make the diagram too cumbersome will show the possibility of internal compensating transfer, yielding gain to both union members.

We come to the *fifth* and last welfare *conclusion:* If a customs union's complete trade liberalization improved the terms of trade of the world, the union might impose such a tariff as would leave the position of the outside world unaffected and still realize a global gain over and above its initial position. To sum up our lengthy discussion in one sentence: The customs union, under all conditions, will be beneficial to all the union members who agree on internal redistribution, even if it compensates the outside world for its losses, if necessary, up to the point of complete trade liberalization. On grounds of equity and economic efficiency, in all cases but one (case 5) , it is advisable for the union to free its trade entirely.

One remark remains to be made. In practice, internal compensation within the union will usually be unnecessary. With many commodities traded, the most likely outcome is that gains from trade realized on some products will be outweighed by relative losses on others, and thus the transfer will take care of itself automatically.

It is possible to establish a number of criteria of desirability of a customs union, depending on the structure of the different world economies and on the levels of tariffs and tariff reductions. Both Professor Meade's approach and the ordinal analysis presented in this chapter may be used in deriving such rules. Of course, it would be preferable, and only satisfactory, to examine each particular case separately on its own merits. Nevertheless, if we are willing to accept a certain degree of flexibility in arguing, so often useful in concrete policy making, such an approach is possible.

If we consider Figure 18.5.1, it is easily observed that if the two free-trade offer curves had about the same slopes near the origin O, there would be hardly any scope for trade and consequently for trade liberalization. Thus, all other things being equal, there will be the greater benefit to be expected from a customs union, the more different such slopes at O—in other words, the greater difference between the marginal rates of transformation in the two countries at autarky. Now such a difference may be brought about by a number of causes. The two countries, with comparable preferences, may have widely different production possibility loci. This in turn may be caused by a difference in technical skills or in factor endowments in the two countries. On the other hand, tastes may be widely different in the two economies, even with identical production possibilities. The two effects—difference in tastes and in production possibilities —may be either reinforcing or offsetting in their impact on the slopes of the free-trade offer curves.

Another factor already observed is the elasticity and slope of the offer curve of the rest of the world. Infinite elasticity will make it preferable for the union to free trade entirely. The slope of the offer curve again is an indication of the degree of complementarity between the rest of the world and the union.

Clearly, the degree of tariff reduction is also an important factor; the gains from a complete elimination of an internal tariff will be—*ceteris paribus*—greater the higher the initial tariff. On the other hand, a union through a partial elimination of internal tariffs may cause greater gain of total welfare than would a complete elimination of such a tariff. This interesting observation is due to Professor Meade. With fixed world terms of trade, gradual elimination of tariffs may be seen in Figure 18.5.1 as a movement of points *b* and *g* toward the corresponding free-trade points *a* and *f*. From the diminishing density of indifference curves encountered during such a movement, it may be concluded that there is a diminishing marginal gain from equal small tariff reductions. By a similar, somewhat loose, argument with reference to Figure 18.5.2, it may be claimed that there will be increasing marginal losses from trade liberalization within the union, on the part of the rest of the world. Adding up two such effects, at least in the context of cardinal analysis, it may be concluded that there is some optimum degree of tariff reduction, falling short of zero tariffs, within the customs union.

We have already indicated that a very small union will not be likely to benefit from a discriminatory tariff reduction over and above what it could gain through complete trade liberalization. Considering the other end of the spectrum, customs unions representing a large proportion of world trade are more likely to benefit as a result of mutual reduction of tariffs. Finally, the gains from a customs union will also depend on the degree of realization of economies of scale. But we have already discussed this problem in the preceding section.

18.6 Economic Policy and the Internal and External Balance of a Customs Union

The problem of economic policy in relation to the external and internal balance of an economy is not new to us. We devoted Chapter 17 to it. In most respects, our discussion of that chapter has a direct relevance to the problems of individual members of the customs union and thus to those of the customs union as a whole. Nevertheless, it may be useful to summarize at this point the most important problems of policy that a customs union may face and the possible alternative ways of solving such problems.

As we indicated in Section 3 of this chapter, the internal and external equilibrium of all countries entering a union, as well as the outside world, will almost without exception be disturbed by the formation of a union. In the long run, each country will have to re-establish its external balance and its internal balance.

To simplify the problem, let us assume again that only two countries form a union, while all the rest of the world is represented by a single country. There are two important targets that each of the two union members wants to achieve: (i) an over-all balance of autonomous payments and (ii) a satisfactory level of employment. A subsidiary constraint arises if some world currencies are convertible and some are not. In this case each member, or at least the union as a whole, has to aim at a balance of autonomous payments with the hard-currency countries, on the one hand, and the rest of the world, on the other. Thus the number of targets is increased by two, or at least by one. In addition, the two union members may want to minimize the rate of inflation of prices.

To cope with at least four policy targets, the two countries need at least four independent policy tools. In general, there are two broad avenues of approach. Either each country attempts to attain its targets independently of the other, or the two may reach their goals simultaneously, in harmony, through a common decision on policies to be taken. The disadvantage of the first approach is that the policies of the two countries may operate at cross-purpose and thus offset each other's effects. The situation may be compared to a case of "naïve" duopoly where each partner acts upon the assumption that the state of the other partner will not change. Clearly, the collective, or what is sometimes called the "union," method is preferable. It will generally reach the desired effects in a more efficient way.

To outline the different policy tools that the union members may use, let us start by considering the case of an extreme economic integration wherein both union countries adopt a common currency. Presumably, in such a case there will be a single central bank with a single monetary policy; the balance between the two countries will have to be established through fiscal policy and factor mobility, and, for all purposes of our analysis, the union may be treated as a single economy. The rules of action discussed in the preceding chapter apply in this case.

If the union members preserve their national identity with regard to currency and monetary policy, two cases have to be considered. On the one hand, both countries may free or adjust frequently their exchange rates toward each other and toward the rest of the world. On the other hand, they may keep their exchange rates fixed.

The first approach simplifies the matter substantially. Only the internal balance now has to be sought, external balance being preserved automatically. With unchanged exchange rates, the "normal" expected outcome following creation of a union is that the union members will both improve their balance of payments with the rest of the world and also employ more fully their productive resources. Now if the currencies of the union are permitted to float with respect to other currencies, the external balance of all union countries will be re-established with slightly appreciated currencies. Such an appreciation will restrain exports from the union to the rest of the world. Internal effective demand will be reduced, possibly to a level generating an income at, or slightly above, its pre-union level. The terms of trade of the union, as indicated by the pure theory, will generally tend to improve. A possible secondary loss of effective demand within the union may take place, resulting from an exchange liberalization. This would tend to counteract the initial loss of income and employment on the part of the rest of the world.

If the exchange rates are not freed and thus all four policy targets have to be met, most of the adjustment will have to be effected through price variation. With downward inflexible prices and wages, the surplus countries, presumably those within the union, will have to inflate roughly in proportion to their respective payments surplus. Such an adjustment may not be so harmful or so difficult, because the surplus countries here also happen to be those that experience greater pressure or pull of effective demand. If they were near full employment prior to the formation of the union, prices in such countries would be more likely to rise than prices in the rest of the world.

CONCEPTS AND TOOLS OF ANALYSIS

1 General Introduction

To a mathematician, the analytical tools used in this study may appear naïvely simple. To a nonmathematical economist, on the other hand, the frequent use of equations, mathematical symbols, and graphical representations may, at first sight, appear prohibitive or at least distasteful. It is to this latter reader that this discussion is addressed. A few hours spent on the following pages not only will enable the nonmathematician to comprehend without any difficulty all that is shown, derived, or explained in this study but also may familiarize him with an extremely useful set of tools, applicable to almost all fields of economic analysis.

In this book we do not make any claim of mathematical elegance, originality, or completeness. This is not a study in the field of applied mathematics but rather one in which mathematics is used minimally as a useful tool. It is the normal and usually rather simple situations that concern us here. Exceptions, borderline cases, and abnormal deformations of economic equilibria, which might be more interesting for a mathematician, only seldom occupy our attention.

In Sections 2 and 3 of this appendix we make an attempt to provide the reader with a sufficient knowledge of geometrical and mathematical tools to enable him to follow 99 per cent of the analysis in this study. In the 1 per cent of cases where we transgress these limits of mathematical sophistication, we either state simple results in the text, referring the reader for proof to a footnote, or explain the analysis needed for the proof along with the particular economic proposition considered.

2 Geometry

Geometrical representation has long been a useful tool of economic analysis. It has the great advantages of simplicity and clarity that make it accessible to virtually everyone in the field of economics. Its drawback as against algebraic analysis is its inability to handle situations with larger numbers of variables. Actually, geometrical representation is usually employed to describe two-variable situations and, at the maximum, by implication, cases with three variables. This disadvantage, however, is not so serious as would appear at first, because of the natural limitation of our minds to think in terms of simultaneous relations of large numbers of variables. Moreover, it is often possible to fix a number of relevant variables and study the interdependence of only two or three variables at a time. Relaxing the assumption of *ceteris paribus,* we are often able to obtain useful additional insights as to how the other factors affect the two or three variables originally considered.

In the present study we use geometrical analysis extensively—in particular, the exposition of the pure theory of international trade presented in Part III is heavily based on that tool. As opposed to the use of algebra, explanation of the geometrical tools of analysis most often constitutes the very essence of each particular proof or demonstration. Consequently, there is not much need here for any elaborate discussion of the use of geometry in economics. We assume understanding of a simple two-variable functional relation, expressed graphically. A demand or supply curve and a propensity schedule are good examples of such relations.

A few useful comments may be made concerning the graphical representation of three-variable relationships. They play an extremely important role in economic analysis and especially in the theory of international trade. Because simple geometry permits only of two-dimensional planes, the essence of the problem here is to reduce a relation from three to two dimensions, while preserving, for purposes of analysis, the three-dimensional characteristics of the function. This may be accomplished through vertical projection of some important contours of the three-dimensional surface onto a two-dimensional plane. The process is comparable to that used in cartography in mapping surfaces of different elevation.

The two important concepts of economic analysis that require such representation are the *production function* and the *utility function*. Consider a relation

$$x = f(a, b) \tag{2.1}$$

where x may represent either output or an index of satisfaction, and a and b either two inputs, or two products consumed. In the three-dimensional space, defined by three coordinate axes, x, a, and b, the relation may be visualized to describe a certain surface. To any given set of variables a_0 and b_0, using the above relation, we may make correspond one or a number of levels of x, i.e., x_0. If relation 2.1 describes a utility function or a production function, there will generally be only one level, x_0; in other words, to a given amount of inputs or consumptions a_0 and b_0 will correspond only one level of output or one level of satisfaction.

If we let x be equal to a constant, say $x = 1$, then

$$1 = f(a, b) \tag{2.2}$$

defines a contour traced on the surface defined by relation 2.1, having the important property of being in a plane that is parallel to the coordinate plane defined by axes a and b and at one unit of distance away from that coordinate plane. In other words, the minimum distance of the coordinate plane from the contour described by relation 2.2, at all its points, is equal to one. Relation 2.2 is then the vertical projection of the contour onto the coordinate plane and defines in the a-b plane the equal product locus (isoquant) or the equal satisfaction locus (indifference curve) corresponding to one unit of output or one unit of satisfaction. It is now possible to describe graphically relation 2.1 in three variables in a two-dimensional a-b plane by assigning different values to x and repeating the construction just outlined for all such values. This will yield a whole map of isoquants or indifference curves, one curve for each given level of x.

If it is possible to assume that utility may be measured in units of satisfaction, i.e., measured cardinally, in the same way as output is measured in physical units, it is possible to associate with each contour of the map a single number, expressing the corresponding level either of output or of satisfaction. This is always possible to do with respect to physical output. The cardinal measurability of satisfaction, however, is often disputed; in other words, the argument is put forth that a rational individual is unable to assign precise numerical indexes to his satisfaction. Rather, it seems more reasonable to assume that everyone is able to order all possible combinations of consumption according to whether they are preferable to, inferior to, or equally desirable as another collection of consumables. Such ordering no longer requires unique numerical indexes to be assigned to different levels of satisfaction. Instead, any set of indexes will be sufficient, under the sole condition that higher numbers are assigned to higher levels of satisfaction, lower to lower levels, and equal to equal satisfactions. This ordering is usually referred to as "ordinal," in contrast to the cardinal ordering. The contour of equal satisfaction is still perfectly well defined, because it corresponds to the same degree of satisfaction. Actually, if utility is measured through an ordinal set of indexes, it is conceptually easier to describe preferences through an indifference map than through a utility function.

Certain properties are usually assigned to the economically relevant parts of the production functions and the utility functions, understood as axioms of technology and rational consumer behavior. The first is that none of the equal product or equal satisfaction contours will ever be concave toward the origin of the *a-b* plane. The second postulates higher levels of output or satisfaction for points along a ray through the origin, farther away from the origin. A third postulate, derivable from the preceding one, is that the indifference or isoquant contours cannot intersect or touch each other.

Within the family of all functions fulfilling these requirements, there is one that plays a particularly important role in economic analysis. It is the group of *homogeneous functions*. A characteristic property of these functions is that the slopes of the equal product or equal satisfaction contours along a straight line through the origin are all equal, whatever the level of input or consumption. The economic interpretation of this property is that, under competitive conditions, with unchanged prices, an individual would always be consuming identical proportions of products *a* and *b,* whatever his income, and a producer would be employing factors or production in identical proportions, whatever his output.

In relation to production, where output is measurable in terms of a cardinal index, a further subgroup of *unit* homogeneous production functions should be defined. These functions have all the properties described so far and, in addition, fulfill the condition that an increase in all inputs by k per cent will increase the output also by k per cent. If this is the case, any single isoquant is sufficient in describing the entire production function, all other isoquants being derivable from that isoquant. For example, with the unit-output isoquant defined in the *a-b* plane, the two-unit isoquant can be derived by doubling the coordinates of each point on the unit isoquant and plotting such magnitudes in the *a-b* plane.

It will be observed that the unit homogeneous production function always describes the technology of an industry of identical firms, operating under competitive conditions, in the long run, whatever the technology of its representative or typical firm. The properties of unit homogeneous production functions are encountered here. Each firm operates at its minimum average-cost point. The supply curve of the industry is horizontal. With unchanged factor prices, the proportions of factors employed will be invariant and so will the proportion of each input to output of the industry. Expansion and contraction of output will be accomplished exclusively by the entry and exit of firms. It should also be observed that in this case no profit is realized by the entrepreneurs, and consequently the entire value of the product is distributed to the productive factors. This is another important property of unit homogeneous production functions: if a firm or an industry uses a unit homogeneous technology and sells its product and hires productive factors in a competitive market, no profit can be realized by the entrepreneur; the value of the product will be entirely distributed to productive factors, each earning the value of its marginal product.

3 Mathematical Tools

As we have pointed out in the introduction to this chapter, the mathematical technique used throughout this study may be summarized without any great difficulty.[1] It presupposes on the part of the reader, first, the ability to solve systems of no more than three linear equations in no more than three unknowns and, second, familiarity with total and partial differentiation.

We take the first aptitude for granted. Our only task here is to suggest an alternative method of solving linear equations, known as "Cramer's rule." It is by no means necessary; however, we often use

[1] For the original and more general exposition of the technique of comparative statics we refer the reader to P. A. Samuelson, *Foundations of Economic Analysis* (Cambridge: Harvard University Press, 1953), in particular chaps. II and III.

it in this study because of its simplicity, symmetry, and capacity to isolate certain elements of the solution relevant in studying the economic properties of particular situations.

Suppose that there are three linear equations in three unknowns, such as

$$
\begin{aligned}
a_{11}x_1 + a_{12}x_2 + a_{13}x_3 &= b_1 \\
a_{21}x_1 + a_{22}x_2 + a_{23}x_3 &= b_2 \\
a_{31}x_1 + a_{32}x_2 + a_{33}x_3 &= b_3
\end{aligned} \tag{3.1}
$$

where a's and b's are known constants and the x's are the unknowns. To solve the system by Cramer's rule, let us first write it in a different form, namely,

$$
\begin{bmatrix} a_{11} & a_{12} & a_{13} \\ a_{21} & a_{22} & a_{23} \\ a_{31} & a_{32} & a_{33} \end{bmatrix}
\begin{bmatrix} x_1 \\ x_2 \\ x_3 \end{bmatrix} =
\begin{bmatrix} b_1 \\ b_2 \\ b_3 \end{bmatrix} \tag{3.2}
$$

Relation 3.2 is nothing else but the system of equations 3.1 stated in terms of matrix rather than simple algebra. If we use a to represent the square matrix of nine coefficients, x the column matrix (vector) to represent the unknowns, and b the column vector of the constants, we may rewrite relation 3.2 as

$$
ax = b \tag{3.3}
$$

It is unnecessary to discuss here the rules of matrix algebra. The reader who wants to get acquainted with this field of mathematics will find many excellent sources on the subject.[2] For the present purpose, it is necessary only to keep in mind the equivalence of relations 3.1 and 3.2 and a similar equivalence of two equations in two unknowns with a matrix representation.

$$
\begin{bmatrix} a_{11} & a_{12} \\ a_{21} & a_{22} \end{bmatrix}
\begin{bmatrix} x_1 \\ x_2 \end{bmatrix} =
\begin{bmatrix} b_1 \\ b_2 \end{bmatrix} \tag{3.4}
$$

Let us now define the value of the determinant (or more simply, the determinant) of matrix a, i.e., $|a|$, as

$$
D = |a| = a_{11}a_{22}a_{33} + a_{21}a_{32}a_{13} + a_{31}a_{12}a_{23} - a_{13}a_{22}a_{31} \\
- a_{23}a_{32}a_{11} - a_{33}a_{12}a_{21} \tag{3.5}
$$

A simple rule for obtaining this expression from the coefficient matrix a is to transpose a's first two rows below the third row, so that a five-by-three matrix is obtained, and take products of terms

---

[2] E.g., R. G. D. Allen, *Mathematical Economics* (London: Macmillan & Co., Ltd., 1956), or R. Dorfman, P. A. Samuelson, and R. Solow, *Linear Programming and Economic Analysis* (New York: McGraw-Hill Book Co., Inc., 1958).

along the downward-sloping diagonals with a positive sign and those along the upward-sloping diagonals with a minus sign. Comparison of the right-hand side of relation 3.5 with the coefficient matrix in 3.2 will illustrate this point.

Similarly, if we call the coefficient matrix in relation 3.4 a', then D', or $|a'|$, the determinant of this matrix, will be found as

$$D' = |a'| = a_{11}a_{22} - a_{12}a_{21} \tag{3.6}$$

If D is different from zero, then the solutions of the three-variable case (relation 3.2) will be found as

$$x_j = \frac{D_j}{D} \qquad j = 1, 2, 3 \tag{3.7}$$

where D_j is the determinant of a matrix formed from D by substituting the column vector b (i.e., the right-hand side of relation 3.2) for its jth column.

Similarly, if D' is not equal to zero, then the solutions of the system in relation 3.4 become

$$x_j = \frac{D'_j}{D} \qquad j = 1, 2 \tag{3.8}$$

where D'_j, as in the three-variable case, is formed from D' by substituting the column vector b' for its jth column. Thus, for example, $D'_2 = a_{11}b_2 - a_{21}b_1$.

We may now give an example; consider

$$\begin{aligned} x + y \quad\quad &= \quad 1 \\ x - y + z &= \quad 0 \\ y + 2z &= -1 \end{aligned} \tag{3.9}$$

It becomes

$$\begin{bmatrix} 1 & 1 & 0 \\ 1 & -1 & 1 \\ 0 & 1 & 2 \end{bmatrix} \begin{bmatrix} x \\ y \\ z \end{bmatrix} = \begin{bmatrix} 1 \\ 0 \\ -1 \end{bmatrix} \tag{3.10}$$

and, consequently,

$$x = \frac{D_1}{D} = \frac{\begin{vmatrix} 1 & 1 & 0 \\ 0 & -1 & 1 \\ -1 & 1 & 2 \end{vmatrix}}{\begin{vmatrix} 1 & 1 & 0 \\ 1 & -1 & 1 \\ 0 & 1 & 2 \end{vmatrix}}$$

$$= \frac{1\cdot(-1)\cdot 2 + 0\cdot 1\cdot 0 + (-1)\cdot 1\cdot 1}{1\cdot(-1)\cdot 2 + 1\cdot 1\cdot 0 + 0\cdot 1\cdot 1} \frac{0\cdot(-1)\cdot(-1) - 1\cdot 1\cdot 1 - 2\cdot 1\cdot 0}{- 0\cdot(-1)\cdot 0 - 1\cdot 1\cdot 1 - 2\cdot 1\cdot 1}$$

$$= \frac{-2 + 0 - 1 - 0 - 1 - 0}{-2 + 0 + 0 - 0 - 1 - 2} = \frac{-4}{-5} = 0.8 \tag{3.11}$$

The remaining solutions may be obtained as an exercise.

We may now turn to the analytical method of comparative statics. Suppose that there are three variables, such as prices, incomes, outputs, or any other, to be determined. The equilibrium values of such three variables will generally be determined as a solution of a system of three equations in these three variables. One simple situation might be that described by relations 3.1. More generally, the three equilibrium relations may be nonlinear and may be written as

$$\begin{aligned} f_1(x_1, x_2, x_3) &= 0 \\ f_2(x_1, x_2, x_3) &= 0 \\ f_3(x_1, x_2, x_3) &= 0 \end{aligned} \tag{3.12}$$

Usually, but not necessarily, these three equations will permit of one set of values of the three variables, x_1^0, x_2^0, and x_3^0 satisfying simultaneously all three relations. Such values are then considered equilibrium solutions of the particular economic situation whose structure is described by relations 3.12. If no change in the three functions f_1, f_2, and f_3 took place over time, the economy would remain indefinitely in the state described by the x^0's.

The important problem to be answered by comparative statics is to determine the changes in the three equilibrium values x^0 resulting from a given change in the structural relations; such a change may be illustrated by a change in the demand function for imports, a shift in the consumption function, or many others. The fact that the three functions f may change may be expressed by introducing one or more parameters a, b, c, etc., into the functions f. The simplest situation, most relevant for our later discussion, is that in which there is only one such parameter. Thus let us write

$$f_i(x_1, x_2, x_3; a) = 0 \qquad i = 1, 2, 3 \tag{3.13}$$

It is now easy to see that for any given value of a, say $a = 1$, there will generally be a set of solutions such as x^0; we may refer to the solutions corresponding to $a = 1$, as x_1^1, x_2^1, and x_3^1. Assuming that the solutions x^0 correspond to $a = 0$, it would now be possible to consider the two corresponding sets of solutions x^0 and x^1. Comparison of the two would yield the desired result, namely, the change in the equilibrium values of the system resulting from an increase in a from zero to unity.

Nevertheless, it is often simpler to calculate the changes in the variables directly, using simple differential analysis. The former procedure requires complete knowledge of the different functions f, while the changes in equilibrium values may be calculated, at least approximately, from the partial derivatives of the functions in the vicinity of the original equilibrium, without knowing the functions themselves. It is precisely such partial derivatives (to be explained presently) or some simple functions thereof that are frequently used in economic analysis, both as abstract concepts and as empirical magnitudes. Elasticities of supply and demand, marginal propensities, and interest elasticities are some examples of such concepts.

To derive the changes in the variables x resulting from a small change in the parameter a, i.e., dx/da (here the letter d should be read as "small change in," and the entire fraction dx/da may be understood as the rate of change of x per unit of change in a), or what is often referred to as a multiplier coefficient, let us return to relations 3.13.

A small total change in the function f_i can be written as a sum of the products of changes of f_i, resulting from a small unit change in each variable or parameter, i.e., f_{i,x_j} or $f_{i,a}$, and the amounts of small change in these variables or the parameter. In symbols:

$$df_i = f_{i,x_1}dx_1 + f_{i,x_2}dx_2 + f_{i,x_3}dx_3 + f_{i,a}da = 0$$
$$i = 1, 2, 3 \tag{3.14}$$

Note that the sum, i.e., df_i, must be equal to zero, because f_i itself is zero for any values of the variables and of the parameter a. Terms such as f_{i,x_1} or $f_{i,a}$ represent the rates of change of the function f_i resulting from a small unit change in x_1 or a. In mathematical language they are usually referred to as the "partial derivatives" of the function f_i with respect to a given variable. Dividing all three relations in 3.14 by da and using the matrix representation of linear equations in three unknowns, relations 3.14 may be stated in the equivalent form

$$\begin{bmatrix} f_{1,x_1} & f_{1,x_2} & f_{1,x_3} \\ f_{2,x_1} & f_{2,x_2} & f_{2,x_3} \\ f_{3,x_1} & f_{3,x_2} & f_{3,x_3} \end{bmatrix} \begin{bmatrix} \dfrac{dx_1}{da} \\ \dfrac{dx_2}{da} \\ \dfrac{dx_3}{da} \end{bmatrix} = \begin{bmatrix} -f_{1,a} \\ -f_{2,a} \\ -f_{3,a} \end{bmatrix} \tag{3.15}$$

Using Cramer's rule or any other method of solving linear equations, it is now possible to obtain the desired solutions dx_i/da. The method for a two-function, two-variable case or a one-function, one-variable case is analogous to that just shown and will be derived by the reader. For example, a change in equilibrium price x resulting from a change in the parameter a in the demand function

$$D = D(x, a)$$

given a supply function,

$$S = S(x)$$

will be found from the equilibrium condition

$$S(x) - D(x, a) = f(x, a) = 0$$

as

$$\frac{dx}{da} = -\frac{f_a}{f_x}$$

We do not give any concrete examples to illustrate the technique; such examples will be found in abundance in our study. Let us only make a few general remarks here. The small changes in the functions f_i contained in the square coefficient matrix and in the column matrix on the right-hand side of relation 3.15 are parameters that have to be known either by assumption or through an empirical study. Often only the knowledge of their signs is sufficient to determine the direction of change of each particular x_i. In the context of our analysis, they are most frequently composed of terms such as the marginal propensities to import, consume, save, or invest, or elasticities of supply or demand. The terms $f_{i,a}$ often simply reduce to known numbers. This happens whenever the parameter a appears in the functions f_i as a linear term. In that case, of course, $f_{i,a} = K \cdot 1$, where K is a positive or a negative constant. We often refer to such a parameter that simply makes part of the entire function f_i shift in one direction or another as a "shift parameter."

In our later analysis it is often not the partial derivatives of the entire structural functions f that have an economic meaning but rather partial derivatives of their component parts. Consequently, something should be said about some of the rules of differentiation itself. We may state them briefly:

i) The partial derivative of a function not depending on the variable of change is zero, as, for example, with

$$f = f(x, y), \qquad f_z = 0$$

ii) The partial derivative of a sum of two or more functions is a sum of partial derivatives of those functions.

iii) The partial derivative of a product of two functions f_1 and f_2 is defined as follows:

$$(f_1 \cdot f_2)_z = f_{1,z}f_2 + f_1 f_{2,z}$$

where the second subscripts, as before, are used to indicate the variable that is changing. This rule can be extended by the reader to a product of any number of functions.

iv) The derivative of $f = A \cdot x$, where A is a constant, is

$$f_z = A$$

v) The derivative of $f = A\,(1/x)$, where A is a constant is

$$f_z = -A\,\frac{1}{x^2}$$

vi) A partial derivative of a function of a function, such a

$$f = f(y/x_1/, x_2, \ldots)$$

is

$$f_{x_1} = f_y \cdot y_{x_1}$$

All the other rules of differentiation and partial differentiation that are necessary in this study may be directly derived from these rules. Note, for example, that the derivative of $f = x^2$ may be obtained by combining rules (iii) and (iv), writing

$$f_z = (x \cdot x)_z = x \cdot 1 + 1 \cdot x = 2x$$

A few additional words should be said about partial differentiation leading to terms such as f_{1,x_1} and about its economic significance. As we have already pointed out, this process shows the change in f_i resulting from a change in one of the variables (or the parameter), all other variables and parameters contained in f being assumed constant. Perhaps an example will be useful at this point. Consider a demand curve, relating price, x_1, and quantity, x_2. Moreover, its position depends on the price of another commodity, a, assumed to be a parameter. For example, a may be the price of a product complementary to product x_2, controlled by the government. We may write the demand relation as

$$f \equiv x_1 - F(x_2, a) = 0 \tag{3.16}$$

For two given values of a—say $a = 1$ and $a = 2$—there will be two demand curves, i.e., two price-quantity relations. Note that the demand curve corresponding to $a = 2$ will be below the other, because we have assumed complementarity between the two products. The partial derivative of f with respect to the quantity of product x_2, i.e., f_{x_2}, now equals $-F_{x_2}$. The elasticity of demand, e, defined as the ratio of a small relative change in quantity to a small relative change in price, may now be expressed as

$$e = \frac{-x_1}{x_2} \frac{1}{f_{x_2}} = \frac{x_1}{x_2} \frac{1}{F_{x_2}} \tag{3.17}$$

Using the first of these relations, we may write

$$f_{x_2} = -\frac{x_1}{x_2} \frac{1}{e} \tag{3.18}$$

Thus, for any given values of x_1, x_2, and a, consistent with relation 3.18, the partial derivative of f with respect to x_2 is now expressed in terms of (1) the elasticity of demand, e, and (2) the particular price and quantity of the product demanded.

SELECTED BIBLIOGRAPHY

The purpose of this bibliography is to provide the reader with a convenient guide to the literature covering—at least approximately—the different aspects of international trade theory that were discussed in this study. We have attempted to organize the readings in accordance with the four substantive parts of the study, i.e., the balance-of-payments and national-income accounts, the balance-of-payments adjustment mechanism, pure theory, and theory and problems of economic policy. These four sections of the bibliography are preceded by a list of general treatises and works that could not have been included under any single heading. But even in the cases where a work is listed in a specific category, the correspondence between the field and the particular writing is often only approximate.

We do not pretend to have covered in the present study all the different aspects of the theory of international trade that will be found in the works listed here. We only hope that the present volume will be of assistance to the reader of international economics in approaching the literature. Because we were primarily concerned with the present state of international trade theory, this selection of readings places emphasis on recent works.

I. General Readings

ALLEN, R. G. D. *Mathematical Analysis for Economists*. London: Macmillan & Co., 1960.

———. *Mathematical Economics*. London: Macmillan & Co., 1959.

AMERICAN ECONOMIC ASSOCIATION. *Readings in the Theory of International Trade*. Homewood, Ill.: Richard D. Irwin, Inc., 1949.

ANGELL, JAMES W. *The Theory of International Prices: History, Criticism, and Restatement*. Cambridge, Mass.: Harvard University Press, 1926.

BAUMOL, WILLIAM. *Economic Dynamics*. New York: Macmillan Co., 1959.

CASSEL, GUSTAV. *Fundamental Thoughts in Economics*. New York: E. Benn, Ltd., 1929.

399

CASSEL, GUSTAV. *The Theory of Social Economy.* 1st ed. New York: Harcourt, Brace & Co., 1924.

CAVES, RICHARD. *Trade and Economic Structure.* Cambridge, Mass.: Harvard University Press, 1960.

CHALMERS, HENRY. *World Trade Policies.* Berkeley: University of California Press, 1953.

CONDLIFFE, JOHN B. *The Commerce of Nations.* New York: W. W. Norton & Co., 1950.

DORFMAN, ROBERT, SAMUELSON, PAUL A., and SOLOW, ROBERT M. *Linear Programming and Economic Analysis.* New York: McGraw-Hill Book Co., Inc., 1958.

ELLSWORTH, PAUL T. *International Economics.* New York: Macmillan Co., 1940.

————. *The International Economy: Its Structure and Operation.* New York: Macmillan Co., 1950.

ENKE, STEPHEN, and SALERA, VIRGIL. *International Economics.* Englewood Cliffs, N.J.: Prentice-Hall, Inc., 1957.

Explorations in Economics: Notes and Essays Contributed in Honor of F. W. Taussig. New York: McGraw-Hill Book Co., 1936.

GRAHAM, FRANK D. *The Theory of International Values.* Princeton, N.J.: Princeton University Press, 1948.

HABERLER, GOTTFRIED. *A Survey of International Trade Theory.* Princeton, N.J.: Princeton University Press, 1955.

————. *Theory of International Trade: With Its Applications to Commercial Policy.* London: William Hodge & Co., 1950.

HARRIS, SEYMOUR E. *International and Interregional Economics.* New York: McGraw-Hill Book Co., Inc., 1957.

HARROD, ROY. *International Economics.* Chicago: University of Chicago Press, 1958.

HEILPERIN, MICHAEL A. *The Trade of Nations.* New York: A. A. Knopf, 1957.

HICKS, JOHN R. *Essays in World Economics.* Oxford: Clarendon Press, 1959.

————. *Free Trade and Modern Economics.* Manchester: Norbury, Lockwood & Co., 1951.

JOHNSON, HARRY G. *International Trade and Economic Growth.* Cambridge, Mass.: Harvard University Press, 1958.

KILLOUGH, HUGH B., and KILLOUGH, LUCY W. *International Economics.* Princeton, N.J.: D. Van Nostrand Co., 1960.

KINDLEBERGER, CHARLES P. *International Economics.* Homewood, Ill.: Richard D. Irwin, Inc., 1958.

————. *The Terms of Trade: A European Case Study.* New York and Cambridge, Mass., 1956.

LERNER, ABBA P. *Essays in Economic Analysis.* London: Macmillan & Co., 1953.

MARSH, DONALD B. *World Trade and Investment: The Economics of Interdependence.* New York: Harcourt, Brace & Co., 1951.

MEADE, JAMES E. *An Introduction to Economic Analysis and Policy.* New York: Oxford University Press, 1938.

———. *Theory of International Economic Policy.* Vol. I: *The Balance of Payments.* New York: Oxford University Press, 1955.

———. *Theory of International Economic Policy,* Vol. II: *Trade and Welfare.* New York: Oxford University Press, 1955.

METZLER, LLOYD A. "The Theory of International Trade," *Survey of Contemporary Economics,* ed. HOWARD S. ELLIS. Homewood, Ill.: Richard D. Irwin, Inc., 1948.

OHLIN, BERTIL. *Interregional and International Trade.* Cambridge, Mass.: Harvard University Press, 1935.

SAMUELSON, PAUL A. *Foundations of Economic Analysis.* Cambridge, Mass.: Harvard University Press, 1958.

SCHELLING, THOMAS. *International Economics.* Boston: Allyn & Bacon, 1958.

SNIDER, DELBERT A. *Introduction to International Economics.* Homewood, Ill.: Richard D. Irwin, Inc., 1958.

TAUSSIG, FRANK W. *Free Trade, the Tariff, and Reciprocity.* New York: Macmillan Co., 1920.

———. *International Trade.* New York: Macmillan Co., 1927.

———. (ed.) *Selected Readings in International Trade and Tariff Problems.* Boston: Ginn & Co., 1921.

———. *Some Aspects of the Tariff Question.* Cambridge, Mass.: Harvard University Press, 1931.

VINER, JACOB. *International Economics: Studies.* Glencoe, Ill.: Free Press, 1951.

———. *International Trade and Economic Development.* Oxford: Clarendon Press, 1953.

———. "International Trade Theory," *Encyclopedia of the Social Sciences,* Vol. VIII. New York, 1932.

———. *Studies in the Theory of International Trade.* New York: Harper & Bros., 1937.

WHALE, BARRETT. *International Trade.* New York: Thornton Butterworth, 1932.

WILLIAMS, JOHN H. *Postwar Monetary Plans and Other Essays.* New York: A. A. Knopf, 1947.

WU, CHI-YUEN. *An Outline of International Price Theories.* London: Routledge, 1939.

II. Balance-of-Payments and National-Income Accounts

RUGGLES, RICHARD, and RUGGLES, NANCY D. *National Income Accounts and Income Analysis.* New York: McGraw-Hill Book Co., Inc., 1956.

SALANT, WILLIAM. "International Transactions in National Income Accounts," *Review of Economics and Statistics,* November, 1951.

UNITED NATIONS DEPARTMENT OF ECONOMIC AFFAIRS. *Studies in Methods,* No. 2: *STAT. SER.F/2 A System of National Accounts and Supporting Tables* (September, 1953).

UNITED STATES DEPARTMENT OF COMMERCE. *National Income: A Supplement to the Survey of Current Business.* Washington: U.S. Government Printing Office, 1954.

————. *United States Income and Output: A Supplement to the Survey of Current Business.* Washington: U.S. Government Printing Office, 1958.

III. The Balance-of-Payments Adjustment Mechanism

Books

BALOGH, THOMAS. *The Dollar Crisis: Causes and Cure: Report to the Fabian Society.* Oxford: Blackwell, 1949.

BLOOMFIELD, ARTHUR I. *Capital Imports and the American Balance of Payments, 1934–1939: A Study in Abnormal International Capital Transfers.* Chicago: University of Chicago Press, 1950.

FANNO, M. *Normal and Abnormal International Capital Transfers.* Minneapolis: University of Minnesota Press, 1939.

HEGELAND, HUGO. *The Multiplier Theory.* Lund Social Science Studies, Vol. IX. Lund: Gleerup, 1954.

HARRIS, SEYMOUR E. (ed.). *Foreign Economic Policy for the United States.* Cambridge, Mass.: Harvard University Press, 1948.

IVERSON, C. *Some Aspects of the Theory of International Capital Movements.* Copenhagen: Levin & Munksgaard, 1936.

KINDLEBERGER, CHARLES P. *International Short-Term Capital Movements.* New York: Columbia University Press, 1937.

————. *The Dollar Shortage.* Cambridge, Mass.: Technology Press, 1950.

MACHLUP, FRITZ. *International Trade and the National Income Multiplier.* Philadelphia: Blakiston Co., 1943.

POLAK, J. J. *An International Economic System.* Chicago: University of Chicago Press, 1954.

ROBINSON, JOAN. *Beggar-My-Neighbor Remedies for Unemployment: Essays on the Theory of Employment.* Oxford: Blackwell, 1947. Reprinted in AMERICAN ECONOMIC ASSOCIATION, *Readings in the Theory of International Trade.* Homewood, Ill.: Richard D. Irwin, Inc., 1949.

————. *The Foreign Exchanges: Essays on the Theory of Employment.* Oxford: Blackwell, 1947. Reprinted in AMERICAN ECONOMIC ASSOCIATION, *Readings in the Theory of International Trade.* Homewood, Ill.: Richard D. Irwin, Inc., 1949.

SCHLESINGER, EUGENE R. *Multiple Exchange Rates and Economic Development.* Princeton, N.J.: Princeton University Press, 1952.

SOHMEN, EGON. *Flexible Exchange Rates: Theory and Controversy.* Chicago: University of Chicago Press, 1961.

STUVEL, GERHARD. *The Exchange Stability Problem.* Leiden: H. E. Stenfert Kroese, 1950.

Articles

ALEXANDER, SIDNEY S. "Effects of a Devaluation: A Simplified Synthesis of Elasticities and Absorption Approaches," *American Economic Review,* March, 1959.

―――. "Effects of a Devaluation on a Trade Balance," *International Monetary Fund Staff Papers,* April, 1952.

BLACK, J. "A Savings and Investment Approach to Devaluation," *Economic Journal,* June, 1959.

BLOOMFIELD, ARTHUR I. "Foreign Exchange Rate Theory and Policy," *The New Economics: Keynes' Influence on Theory and Public Policy* (ed. SEYMOUR E. HARRIS). New York: A. A. Knopf, 1948.

BRESCIANI-TURRONI, C. "The Purchasing Power Parity Doctrine," *L'Egypte Contemporaine,* May, 1934. (Shorter version in the author's book, *The Economics of Inflation.* London: G. Allen & Unwin, 1937.)

BRISMAN, SVEN. "Some Reflections on the Theory of Foreign Exchange," *Economic Essays in Honor of Gustav Cassel.* London: G. Allen and Unwin, Ltd., 1933.

BRONFENBRENNER, M. "The Keynesian Equations and the Balance of Payments," *Review of Economic Studies,* Vol. VII, No. 3 (June, 1940).

BROWN, A. J. "Trade Balances and Exchange Stability," *Oxford Studies in the Price Mechanism* (ed. T. WILSON and P. W. S. ANDREWS). Oxford: Clarendon Press, 1951.

CASSEL, GUSTAV. "Abnormal Deviations in International Exchanges," *Economic Journal,* 1918.

―――. "International Trade, Capital Movements, and Exchanges," *Harris Foundation Lectures: Foreign Investments.* Chicago: University of Chicago Press, 1928.

―――. "The Present Situation of the Foreign Exchange," *Economic Journal,* Vols. I and II (1916).

ELLIOTT, G. A. "Transfer of Means-of-Payments and the Terms of International Trade," *Canadian Journal of Economics and Political Science,* November, 1936.

ELLIS, HOWARD S. "The Dollar Shortage in Theory and Fact," *Canadian Journal of Economics and Political Science,* August, 1948.

―――. "The Equilibrium Rate of Exchange," *Explorations in Economics: Notes and Essays Contributed in Honor of F. W. Taussig.* New York: McGraw-Hill Book Co., 1936.

―――. *German Monetary Theory,* Part III: *Price Levels and Foreign Exchange under Inflation.* Cambridge, Mass.: Harvard University Press, 1939.

ELLSWORTH, PAUL T. "Exchange Rates and Exchange Stability," *Review of Economics and Statistics,* February, 1950.

GIERSCH, HERBERT. "Akzelerationsprinzip und Importneigung," *Weltwirtschaftliches Archiv,* Vol. LXX (1953). English translation in *International Economic Papers,* No. 4, International Economic Association. New York: Macmillan Co., 1954.

GILIOLI CASELLI, MARILIA. "Gli Effetti del Multiplicatore del Commercio Estero sul Reddito Nazionale in Regime di Scambi Internazionali Vincolati," *Rivista di Politica Economica,* June, 1953.

HABERLER, GOTTFRIED. "The Choice of Exchange Rates after the War," *American Economic Review,* June, 1945.

———. "Currency Depreciation and the Terms of Trade," *Wirtschaftliche Entwicklung und soziale Ordnung* (ed. ERNST LAGLER and J. MESSNER). Vienna, 1952.

———. "The Market for Foreign Exchange and the Stability of the Balance of Payments: A Theoretical Analysis," *Kyklos,* Vol. III, No. 3 (1949).

———. "Transfer und Preisbewegung," *Zeitschrift für Nationalökonomie,* January and August, 1930.

HAHN, F. H. "The Balance of Payments in a Monetary Economy," *Review of Economic Studies,* February, 1959.

HANSEN, A. H. "A Note on Fundamental Disequilibrium," *Review of Economics and Statistics,* November, 1944. Reprinted in *America's Role in the World Economy.* New York: W. W. Norton & Co., 1945; and in *Foreign Economic Policy for the United States* (ed. SEYMOUR HARRIS). Cambridge, Mass.: Harvard University Press, 1948.

HARBERGER, ARNOLD C. "Currency Depreciation, Income, and the Balance of Trade," *Journal of Political Economy,* February, 1950.

———. "Pitfalls in Mathematical Model-Building," *American Economic Review,* December, 1952.

———. "A Structural Approach to the Problem of Import Demand," *American Economic Review, Papers and Proceedings,* May, 1953.

HICKS, JOHN R. "The Long Run Dollar Problem: An Inaugural Lecture," *Oxford Economic Papers,* New Series, No. 5 (1953). Reprinted in *Essays in World Economics.* Oxford: Clarendon Press, 1959.

HINSHAW, RANDALL. "Currency Appreciation as an Anti-Inflationary Device," *Quarterly Journal of Economics,* November, 1951, and February, 1952.

HOLZMAN, FRANKLIN D., and ZELLNER, ARNOLD. "The Foreign-Trade and Balanced Budget Multipliers," *American Economic Review,* March, 1958.

JOHNSON, HARRY G. "The Transfer Problem and Exchange Stability," *Journal of Political Economy,* June, 1956.

———. "The Transfer Problem: A Note on Criteria for Changes in the Terms of Trade," *Economica,* May, 1955.

JONES, RONALD E. "Depreciation and the Dampening Effects of Income Changes," *Review of Economics and Statistics,* February, 1960.

KENNEDY, CHARLES. "Devaluation and the Terms of Trade," *Review of Economic Studies,* Vol. XVIII (1) (1949/50).

KEYNES, JOHN M. "The German Transfer Problem," *Economic Journal,* March, 1929. Reprinted in AMERICAN ECONOMIC ASSOCIATION, *Readings in the Theory of International Trade.* Homewood, Ill.: Richard D. Irwin, Inc., 1949.

KRUSE, ALFRED. "Die Mechanismen des Zahlungsbilanzausgleichs," *Wirtschaftstheorie und Wirtschaftspolitik: Festgabe für Adolph Weber* (ed. ALFRED KRUSE). Berlin, 1951.

LAURSEN, SVEND, and METZLER, LLOYD A. "Flexible Exchange Rates and the Theory of Employment," *Review of Economics and Statistics,* November, 1950.

LEONTIEF, WASSILY. "Note on the Pure Theory of Capital Transfer," *Explorations in Economics: Notes and Essays Contributed in Honor of F. W. Taussig.* New York: McGraw-Hill Book Co., Inc., 1936.

MACHLUP, FRITZ. "Dollar Shortage and Disparities in the Growth of Industry," *Scottish Journal of Political Economy,* October, 1954.

———. "Elasticity Pessimism in International Trade," *Economia Internazionale,* February, 1950.

———. "Relative Prices and Aggregate Expenditure in the Analysis of Devaluation," *American Economic Review,* June, 1955.

———. "The Theory of Foreign Exchanges," *Economica,* November, 1939 and February, 1940. Reprinted in AMERICAN ECONOMIC ASSOCIATION, *Readings in the Theory of International Trade.* Homewood, Ill.: Richard D. Irwin, Inc., 1949.

———. "Three Concepts of the Balance of Payments and the So-Called Dollar Shortage," *Economic Journal,* March, 1950.

MAHR, ALEXANDER. "Die wesentliche Bedingung des Gleichgewichts der Zahlungsbilanz," *Economia Internazionale,* May, 1951.

METZLER, LLOYD A. Review of MACHLUP's *International Trade and the National Income Multiplier, Review of Economics and Statistics,* February, 1945.

———. "The Transfer Problem Reconsidered," *Journal of Political Economy,* June, 1942. Reprinted in AMERICAN ECONOMIC ASSOCIATION, *Readings in the Theory of International Trade.* Homewood, Ill.: Richard D. Irwin, Inc., 1949.

———. "Underemployment Equilibrium in International Trade," *Econometrica,* April, 1942.

MIYAZAWA, KENICHI. "Foreign Trade Multiplier, Input-Output Analysis and the Consumption Function," *Quarterly Journal of Economics,* February, 1960.

MORISHIMA, MICHIA. "Notes on the Theory of Stability of Multiple Exchange," *Review of Economic Studies,* June, 1957.

MUNDELL, ROBERT A. "The Monetary Dynamics of International Adjustment under Fixed and Flexible Exchange Rates," *Quarterly Journal of Economics,* May, 1960.

NURKSE, RAGNAR. "Domestic and International Equilibrium," *The New Economics: Keynes' Influence on Theory and Public Policy* (ed. SEYMOUR E. HARRIS). New York: A. A. Knopf, 1948.

OHLIN, BERTIL. "The Reparation Problem: A Discussion," *Economic Journal,* June, 1929. Reprinted in AMERICAN ECONOMIC ASSOCIATION, *Readings in the Theory of International Trade.* Homewood, Ill.: Richard D. Irwin, Inc., 1949.

ORCUTT, GUY H. "Exchange Rate Adjustment and Relative Size of the Depreciating Bloc," *Review of Economics and Statistics,* February, 1955.

———. "Measurement of Price Elasticities in International Trade," *Review of Economics and Statistics,* May, 1950.

PAISH, F. W. "Banking Policy and the Balance of International Payments," *Economica,* November, 1936. Reprinted in AMERICAN ECONOMIC ASSOCIATION, *Readings in the Theory of International Trade.* Homewood, Ill.: Richard D. Irwin, Inc., 1949.

PIGOU, A. C. "Disturbances of Equilibrium in International Trade," *Economic Journal,* September, 1929. Reprinted in A. C. PIGOU and D. H. ROBERTSON, *Economic Essays and Addresses.* London: King, 1931.

———. "The Foreign Exchanges," *Quarterly Journal of Economics,* November, 1922.

———. "Reparations and the Ratio of International Interchange," *Economic Journal,* December, 1932.

REES, G. L. "Price Effects and the Foreign Trade Multipliers," *Review of Economic Studies,* Vol. XX (3) (1952/53).

ROBERTSON, DENNIS H. "The Transfer Problem," *Essays in Monetary Theory.* London: Staples Press, 1946.

ROBINSON, ROMNEY. "A Graphical Analysis of the Foreign Trade Multiplier," *Economic Journal,* September, 1952.

SAMUELSON, PAUL A. "The Transfer Problem and Transport Costs," *Economic Journal,* June, 1952, and June, 1954.

SMITH, W. L. "Effects of Exchange Rate Adjustments on the Standard of Living," *American Economic Review,* December, 1954.

SPRAOS, JOHN. "Stability in a Closed Economy and in the Foreign Exchange Market, and the Redistributive Effect of Price Changes," *Review of Economic Studies,* June, 1957.

STOLPER, WOLFGANG. "Stand und ungelöste Probleme der Theorie des Aussenhandelsmultiplikators," *Zeitschrift für die gesamte Staatswissenschaft,* Vol. 108 (1952).

TERBORGH, GEORGE. "Purchasing Power Parity Theory," *Journal of Political Economy,* April, 1926.

TINBERGEN, JAN. "The Relation between Internal Inflation and the Balance of Payments," *Banco Nazionale del Lavoro Quarterly Review,* October–December, 1952.

IV. Pure Theory of International Trade

Books

MEADE, JAMES E. *A Geometry of International Trade.* London: George Allen & Unwin, 1952.

MOOKERJEE, SUBIMAL. *Factor Endowments and International Trade: A Study and Appraisal of the Heckscher-Ohlin Theory.* Bombay: Asia Publishing House, 1958.

MOSAK, JACOB L. *General Equilibrium Theory in International Trade.* Bloomington, Ind.: Principia Press, 1944.

RANGNEKAR, S. B. *Imperfect Competition in International Trade.* Bombay: Oxford University Press, 1947.

YNTEMA, THEODORE O. *A Mathematical Reformulation of the General Theory of International Trade.* Chicago: University of Chicago Press, 1932.

Articles

BALDWIN, ROBERT E. "Equilibrium in International Trade: A Diagrammatic Analysis," *Quarterly Journal of Economics,* November, 1948.
———. "The New Welfare Economics and Gains in International Trade," *ibid.,* February, 1952.
———. "Secular Movements in the Terms of Trade," *American Economic Review,* May, 1955.

BALOGH, THOMAS. "Static Models and Current Problems in International Economics," *Oxford Economic Papers,* June, 1949.

BALOGH, T., and STREETEN, P. P. "The Inappropriateness of Simple 'Elasticity' Concepts in the Analysis of International Trade," *Bulletin of the Oxford University Institute of Statistics,* March, 1951.

BEACH, WALTER E. "Some Aspects of International Trade under Monopolistic Competition," *Explorations in Economics: Notes and Essays Contributed in Honor of F. W. Taussig.* New York: McGraw-Hill Book Co., 1936.

BECKER, G. S. "A Note on Multi-Country Trade," *American Economic Review,* September, 1952.

BENHAM, FREDRIC. "The Terms of Trade," *Economica,* November, 1940.

BENSUSAM-BUTT, D. M. "A Model of Trade and Accumulation," *American Economic Review,* September, 1954.

BHAGWATI, JAGDISH. "Immiserizing Growth: A Geometrical Note," *Review of Economic Studies,* June, 1958.
———. "International Trade and Economic Expansion," *American Economic Review,* December, 1958.

BLACK, J. "Economic Expansion and International Trade: A Marshallian Approach," *Review of Economic Studies,* 1955–56.

BROWN, A. J. *Industrialization and Trade, the Changing World Pattern and the Position of Britain.* Oxford: Royal Institute of International Affairs, 1943.

CORDEN, W. M. "Economic Expansion and International Trade: A Geometrical Approach," *Oxford Economic Papers,* June, 1956.

DANIERE, ANDRÉ. "American Trade Structure and Comparative Cost Theory," *Economia Internazionale,* August, 1956.

DEVONS, ELY. "Statistics of United Kingdom Terms of Trade," *The Manchester School,* September, 1954.

DIAB, M. A. *The United States Capital Position and the Structure of Its Foreign Trade.* "Contributions to Economic Analysis," Vol. XI. Amsterdam: North Holland Publishing Co., 1956.

DORRANCE, G. S. "The Income Terms of Trade," *Review of Economic Studies,* Vol. XVI (1) (1948–49).

ELLIOTT, G. A. "The Theory of International Values," *Journal of*

Political Economy, February, 1950. [Review article of F. D. GRAHAM's *The Theory of International Values*.]

ELLSWORTH, P. T. "Comparative Costs, the Gains from Trade, and Other Matters Considered by Professor Viner," *Canadian Journal of Economics and Political Science*, May, 1939.

————. "A Comparison of International Trade Theories," *American Economic Review*, June, 1940.

————. "The Structure of American Foreign Trade: A New View Examined," *Review of Economics and Statistics*, August, 1954.

ENKE, S. "The Monopsony Case for Tariffs," *ibid.*, February, 1944.

————. "Monopolistic Output and International Trade," *Quarterly Journal of Economics*, February, 1946.

FINDLAY, R., and GRUBERT, H. "Factor Intensities, Technological Progress, and the Terms of Trade," *Oxford Economic Papers*, February, 1959.

GILBERT, J. C. "The Present Position of the Theory of International Trade," *Review of Economic Studies*, October, 1935.

GRAHAM, FRANK D. "The Theory of International Values Re-examined," *Quarterly Journal of Economics*, November, 1923.

HABERLER, GOTTFRIED. "Real Cost, Money Cost, and Comparative Advantage," *International Social Science Bulletin*, Spring, 1951.

————. "The Relevance of the Classical Theory under Modern Conditions," *American Economic Review Papers and Proceedings*, May, 1954.

————. "Some Problems in the Pure Theory of International Trade," *Economic Journal*, June, 1950. Reply: BALOGH, THOMAS. "Welfare and Freer Trade—A Reply," *Economic Journal*, March, 1951. Rejoinder: HABERLER, GOTTFRIED. "Welfare and Freer Trade—A Rejoinder," *Economic Journal*, December, 1951.

————. "The Theory of Comparative Costs Once More," *Quarterly Journal of Economics*, February, 1929.

HARROD, ROY F. "Factor-Price Relations under Free Trade," *Economic Journal*, June, 1958.

HECKSCHER, ELI F. "The Effect of Foreign Trade on the Distribution of Income," *Ekonomisk Tidskrift*, Vol. XXI (1919). Reprinted in AMERICAN ECONOMIC ASSOCIATION, *Readings in the Theory of International Trade*. Homewood, Ill.: Richard D. Irwin, Inc., 1949.

HOFFMEYER, E. "The Leontief Paradox Critically Examined," *Manchester School*, May, 1958.

IMLAH, ALBERT H. "Real Values in British Foreign Trade, 1798–1853," *Journal of Economic History*, November, 1948. Reprinted in *Economic Elements in the Pax Britannica*. Cambridge, Mass., 1958.

————. "The Terms of Trade of the United Kingdom," *Journal of Economic History*, November, 1950. Reprinted in *Economic Elements in the Pax Britannica*. Cambridge, Mass., 1958.

ISARD, WALTER, and PECK, MERTON D. "Location Theory and International and Interregional Trade Theory," *Quarterly Journal of Economics*, February, 1954.

JOHNSON, HARRY G. "Economic Expansion and International Trade," *Manchester School*, May, 1955. Reprinted in H. G. JOHNSON, *International Trade and Economic Growth; Studies in Pure Theory*. Cambridge, Mass., 1958.

―――. "Factor Endowments, International Trade, and Factor Prices," *Manchester School*, September, 1957. Reprinted in H. G. JOHNSON, *International Trade and Economic Growth: Studies in Pure Theory*. Cambridge, Mass., 1958.

JONES, RONALD W. "Factor Proportions and the Heckscher-Ohlin Model," *Review of Economic Studies*, 1956–57.

KAJIMA, K. "Equilibrium in International Trade: A Diagrammatic Analysis of the Case of Increasing Cost," *Annals of the Hitotsubashi Academy*, October, 1955.

KEMP, MURRAY. "The Relation between Changes in International Demand and the Terms of Trade," *Econometrica*, January, 1956.

KLEIMAN, E. "Comparative Advantage, Graham's Theory, and Activity Analysis," *Economica*, August, 1960.

LANCASTER, K. "The Heckscher-Ohlin Trade Model: A Geometric Treatment," *Economica*, February, 1957.

―――. "Protection and Real Wages: A Restatement," *Economic Journal*, June, 1957.

LAURSEN, SVEND. "Production Functions and the Theory of International Trade," *American Economic Review*, September, 1952.

LEONTIEF, WASSILY. "Domestic Production and Foreign Trade: The American Capital Position Re-examined," *Proceedings of the American Philosophical Society*, September, 1953. Reprinted in *Economia Internazionale*, February, 1954.

―――. "Factor Proportions and the Structure of American Trade: Further Theoretical and Empirical Analysis," *Review of Economics and Statistics*, November, 1956.

―――. "The Use of Indifference Curves in the Analysis of Foreign Trade," *Quarterly Journal of Economics*, May, 1933. Reprinted in AMERICAN ECONOMIC ASSOCIATION, *Readings in the Theory of International Trade*. Homewood, Ill.: Richard D. Irwin, Inc., 1949.

LERNER, ABBA P. "Diagrammatical Representation of Demand Conditions in International Trade" (1), *Economica*, August, 1932. Reprinted in *Essays in Economics Analysis*. New York, 1953.

―――. "Diagrammatical Representation of Demand Conditions in International Trade" (2), *Economica*, August, 1934. Reprinted in *Essays in Economic Analysis*. New York, 1953.

―――. "Factor Prices and International Trade," *Economica*, February, 1952. Reprinted in *Essays in Economic Analysis*. New York, 1953.

―――. "The Symmetry between Import and Export Taxes," *Economica*, August, 1936. Reprinted in *Essays in Economic Analysis*. New York, 1953.

LOVASY, GERTRUD. "International Trade under Imperfect Competition," *Quarterly Journal of Economics*, August, 1941.

MacDougall, G. D. A. "British and American Exports: A Study Suggested by the Theory of Comparative Costs, Part I," *Economic Journal,* December, 1951; Part II, *ibid.,* September, 1952.

McKenzie, L. W. "Equality of Factor Prices in World Trade," *Econometrica,* July, 1955.

———. "On Equilibrium in Graham's Model of World Trade and Other Competitive Systems," *ibid.,* April, 1954.

———. "Specialization and Efficiency in World Production," *Review of Economic Studies,* Vol. XXI (3) (1953–54).

Mason, Edward S. "The Doctrine of Comparative Cost," *Quarterly Journal of Economics,* November, 1926.

Matthews, R. C. O. "Reciprocal Demand and Increasing Returns," *Review of Economic Studies,* 1949–50.

Meade, J. E. "The Equalization of Factor Prices: The Two-Country Two-Factor Three-Product Case," *Metroeconomica,* December, 1950.

Meier, G. M. "The Theory of Comparative Costs Reconsidered," *Oxford Economic Papers,* June, 1949.

Metzler, Lloyd A. "Graham's Theory of International Values," *American Economic Review,* June, 1950.

Morgan, E. V., and Rees, G. L. "Non-Traded Goods and International Factor Price Equalization," *Economica,* November, 1954.

Mundell, R. A. "International Trade and Factor Mobility," *American Economic Review,* June, 1957.

———. "The Pure Theory of International Trade," *ibid.,* March, 1960.

Myint, H. "The 'Classical Theory' of International Trade and the Underdeveloped Countries," *Economic Journal,* June, 1958.

———. "The Gains from International Trade and the Backward Countries," *Review of Economic Studies,* 1954–55.

Pearce, I. F. "A Further Note on Factor-Commodity Price Relationships," *Economic Journal,* December, 1959.

Pearce, I. F., and James, S. F. "The Factor-Price Equalisation Myth," *Review of Economic Studies,* 1951–52.

Raj, K. N., and Sen, A. K. "Alternative Patterns of Growth under Conditions of Stagnant Export Earnings," *Oxford Economic Papers,* February, 1961.

Robertson, Dennis H. "The Terms of Trade," *International Social Science Bulletin,* Spring, 1951. Reprinted in *Utility and All That and Other Essays.* London: George Allen & Unwin, 1952.

Robinson, R. "Factor Proportions and Comparative Advantage: Part I," *Quarterly Journal of Economics,* May, 1956; Part II, *ibid.,* August, 1956.

Robinson, Joan. "The Pure Theory of International Trade," *Review of Economic Studies,* Vol. XIV (2) (1946–47). Reprinted in J. Robinson, *Collected Economic Papers.* Oxford, 1951.

Rybczynski, T. N. "Factor Endowment and Relative Commodity Prices," *Economica,* November, 1955.

SAMUELSON, PAUL A. "A Comment on Factor Price Equalisation," *Review of Economic Studies,* 1951–52.

———. "The Gains from International Trade," *Canadian Journal of Economics and Political Science,* May, 1939. Reprinted in AMERICAN ECONOMIC ASSOCIATION, *Readings in the Theory of International Trade.* Homewood, Ill.: Richard D. Irwin, Inc., 1949.

———. "International Factor-Price Equalization Once Again," *Economic Journal,* June, 1949.

———. "International Trade and the Equalization of Factor Prices," *ibid.,* June, 1948.

———. "Prices of Factors and Goods in General Equilibrium," *Review of Economic Studies,* 1953–54.

———. "Social Indifference Curves," *Quarterly Journal of Economics,* February, 1956.

———. "Welfare Economics and International Trade," *American Economic Review,* June, 1938.

SAVOSNICK, K. M. "The Box Diagram and the Production Possibility Curve," *Ekonomisk Tidskrift,* November, 1958.

STAEHLE, HANS. "Some Notes on the Terms of Trade," *International Social Science Bulletin,* Spring, 1951.

STEVENS, R. W. "New Ideas in the Theory of International Trade," *American Economic Review,* June, 1951.

STOLPER, WOLFGANG. "A Method of Constructing Community Indifference Curves," *Schweizerische Zeitschrift für Volkswirtschaft und Statistik,* April, 1950.

STOLPER, WOLFGANG, and SAMUELSON, PAUL A. "Protection and Real Wages," *Review of Economic Studies,* Vol. IX, No. 1 (November, 1941). Reprinted in AMERICAN ECONOMIC ASSOCIATION, *Readings in the Theory of International Trade.* Homewood, Ill.: Richard D. Irwin, Inc., 1949.

TINBERGEN, JAN. "The Equalization of Factor Prices between Free-Trade Areas," *Metroeconomica,* April, 1949.

VALAVANIS-VAIL, STEFAN. "Leontief's Scarce Factor Paradox," *Journal of Political Economy,* December, 1954.

VANEK, J. "An Afterthought on the 'Real Cost–Opportunity Cost' Dispute and Some Aspects of General Equilibrium under Conditions of Variable Factor Supplies," *Review of Economic Studies,* June, 1959.

———. "An Alternative Proof of the Factor Price Equalization Theorem," *Quarterly Journal of Economics,* November, 1960.

VINER, J. "Angell's *Theory of International Prices,*" *Journal of Political Economy,* October, 1926.

———. "The Doctrine of Comparative Costs," *Weltwirtschaftliches Archiv,* Vol. XXXVI (1932).

———. "International Trade Theory and Its Present Day Relevance," *Economics and Public Policy: Brookings Lectures, 1954* (6). Washington: Brookings Institution, 1955.

Vines, J. "Professor Taussig's Contribution to the Theory of International Trade," *Explorations in Economics: Notes and Essays Contributed in Honor of F. W. Taussig.* New York: McGraw-Hill Book Co., 1936.

Walsh, V. C. "Leisure and International Trade," *Economica*, August, 1956.

Whitin, T. M. "Classical Theory, Graham's Theory and Linear Programming in International Trade," *Quarterly Journal of Economics*, November, 1953.

Wijnholds, H. W. J. "The Theory of International Trade: A New Approach," *South African Journal of Economics*, September, 1953.

Williams, J. H. "International Trade Theory and Policy—Some Current Issues," *American Economic Review, Papers and Proceedings*, May, 1951.

———. "The Theory of International Trade Reconsidered," *Economic Journal*, June, 1929. Reprinted in AMERICAN ECONOMIC ASSOCIATION, *Readings in the Theory of International Trade.* Homewood, Ill.: Richard D. Irwin, Inc., 1949.

Wolfe, J. N. "Transport Costs and Comparative Advantage," *Journal of Political Economy*, August, 1959.

V. Theory and Problems of Economic Policy

Books

Balassa, Bela A. *The Theory of Economic Integration.* Homewood, Ill.: Richard D. Irwin, Inc., 1961.

Beveridge, William. *Tariffs: The Case Examined.* London: Longmans, Green & Co., 1932.

de Graaf, J. *Theoretical Welfare Economics.* Cambridge, England: Cambridge University Press, 1957.

Keynes, J. M. *(A Tract on) Monetary Reform.* New York: Harcourt, Brace & Co., 1924.

Meade, James E. *Problems of Economic Union.* Chicago: University of Chicago Press, 1953.

———. *The Theory of Customs Unions.* Amsterdam: North Holland Publishing Co., 1955.

———. *Trade and Welfare. (The Theory of International Economic Policy,* Vol. II.) New York: Oxford University Press, 1955.

Pigou, A. C. *Protective and Preferential Import Duties.* London: Macmillan & Co. , 1906.

Tinbergen, Jan. *On the Theory of Economic Policy.* Amsterdam: North Holland Publishing Co., 1952.

———. *International Economic Integration.* Amsterdam: Elsevier, 1954.

Viner, Jacob. *The Customs Union Issue.* New York: Carnegie Endowment for International Peace, 1950.

Articles

Alexander, Sidney S. "Devaluation versus Import Restrictions as an Instrument for Improving Foreign Trade Balance," *International Monetary Fund Staff Papers*, April, 1951.

ANDERSON, KARL L. "Tariff Protection and Increasing Returns," *Explorations in Economics: Notes and Essays Contributed in Honor of F. W. Taussig.* New York: McGraw-Hill Book Co., 1936.

BALDWIN, ROBERT E. "The Effect of Tariffs on International and Domestic Prices," *Quarterly Journal of Economics,* February, 1960.

BICKERDIKE, C. F. "The Theory of Incipient Taxes," *Economic Journal,* December, 1906.

BLACK, J. "Arguments for Tariffs," *Oxford Economic Papers,* June, 1959.

CORDEN, W. M. "Tariffs, Subsidies and the Terms of Trade," *Economica,* August, 1957.

ELLIOTT, G. A. "Protective Duties, Tributes and Terms of Trade," *Journal of Political Economy,* December, 1937.

――――. "The Relation of Protective Duties to Domestic Production," *Canadian Journal of Economics and Political Science,* May, 1940.

FLEMING, M. "The Optimal Tariff from an International Standpoint," *Review of Economics and Statistics,* February, 1946.

GEHRELS, FRANZ. "Customs Unions from a Single-Country Viewpoint," *Review of Economic Studies,* 1956–57.

GIERSCH, H. "The Trade Optimum: A Contribution to the Theory of Economic Policy," *International Economic Papers,* No. 7. London and New York, 1957.

GORMAN, W. M. "The Effect of Tariffs on the Level and Terms of Trade," *Journal of Political Economy,* June, 1959.

――――. "Tariffs, Retaliation, and the Elasticity of Demand for Imports," *Review of Economic Studies,* June, 1958.

DE GRAFF, J. "On Optimum Tariff Structures," *Review of Economic Studies,* Vol. XVII (1) (1949/50).

GRAHAM, F. D. "Some Aspects of Protection Further Considered," *Quarterly Journal of Economics,* February, 1923.

――――. "Some Fallacies in the Interpretation of Social Cost: A Reply," *ibid.,* February, 1925.

HAGEN, EVERETT E. "An Economic Justification of Protectionism," *Quarterly Journal of Economics,* November, 1958.

HARBERGER, A. C. "Some Evidence on the International Price Mechanism," *Journal of Political Economy,* December, 1957.

HEMMING, M. F. W., and CORDEN, W. M. "Import Restriction as an Instrument of Balance of Payments Policy," *Economic Journal,* September, 1958.

HENDERSON, A. "The Restriction of Foreign Trade," *Manchester School,* January, 1949.

HENDERSON, SIR HUBERT O. "The Functions of Exchange Rates," *Oxford Economic Papers,* January, 1949. Reprinted in *The Interwar Years and Other Papers.* Oxford: Clarendon Press, 1955.

JOHNSON, HARRY G. "The Cost of Protection and the Scientific Tariff," *Journal of Political Economy,* August, 1960.

――――. "Optimum Tariffs and Retaliation," *Review of Economic Studies,* 1953–54. Reprinted in *International Trade and Economic Growth:*

Studies in Pure Theory. Cambridge, Mass.: Harvard University Press, 1958.

KAHN, RICHARD F. "Tariffs and the Terms of Trade," *Review of Economic Studies*, Vol. XVI (1) (1947–48).

KALDOR, NICHOLAS. "A Note on Tariffs and the Terms of Trade," *Economica*, November, 1940.

LIESNER, H. H. "The European Common Market and British Industry," *Economic Journal*, June, 1958.

LITTLE, I. M. D. "Welfare and Tariffs," *Review of Economic Studies*, Vol. XV (2) (1949–50).

MEADE, JAMES E. "The Balance of Payments Problems of a European Free-Trade Area," *Economic Journal*, September, 1957.

METZLER, L. A. "Tariffs, International Demand, and Domestic Prices," *Journal of Political Economy*, August, 1949.

————. "Tariffs, the Terms of Trade, and the Distribution of National Income," *Journal of Political Economy*, February, 1949.

OHLIN, BERTIL. "Protection and Non-Competing Groups," *Weltwirtschaftliches Archiv*, Heft 1 (1935).

DE SCITOVSKY, TIBOR. "A Reconsideration of the Theory of Tariffs," *Review of Economic Studies*, Vol. IX (2) (Summer, 1942). Reprinted in AMERICAN ECONOMIC ASSOCIATION, *Readings in the Theory of International Trade*. Homewood, Ill.: Richard D. Irwin, Inc., 1949.

SMITHIES, ARTHUR. "Modern International Trade Theory and International Policy," *American Economic Review, Papers and Proceedings*, May, 1952.

INDEX

This book has been set on the Linotype in 11 point Baskerville, leaded 2 points, and 10 point Baskerville, leaded 1 point. Chapter titles and part and chapter numbers are in 18 point Spartan Medium. The size of the type page is 27 by 45 picas.